OXFORD POLITICAL THEORY

Series Editors: David Miller and Alan Ryan

REPUBLICANISM

OXFORD POLITICAL THEORY

Oxford Political Theory presents the best new work in contemporary political theory. It is intended to be broad in scope, including original contributions to political philosophy, and also work in applied political theory. The series will contain works of outstanding quality with no restriction as to approach or subject matter.

OTHER TITLES IN THIS SERIES

Justice as Impartiality
Brian Barry

Real Freedom for All: What (if Anything) Can Justify Capitalism?
Philippe Van Parijs

Justificatory Liberalism: An Essay on Metaphysics and Political Theory
Gerald Gaus

The Politics of Presence: Democracy and Group Representation
Anne Phillips

On Nationality
David Miller

Multicultural Citizenship: A Liberal Theory of Minority Rights
Will Kymlicka

REPUBLICANISM

A THEORY OF FREEDOM
AND GOVERNMENT

PHILIP PETTIT

CLARENDON PRESS · OXFORD
1997

Oxford University Press, Great Clarendon Street, Oxford OX2 6DP

Oxford New York

Athens Auckland Bangkok Bogota Bombay
Buenos Aires Calcutta Cape Town Dar es Salaam
Delhi Florence Hong Kong Istanbul Karachi
Kuala Lumpur Madras Madrid Melbourne
Mexico City Nairobi Paris Singapore
Taipei Tokyo Toronto
and associated companies in
Berlin Ibadan

Oxford is a trade mark of Oxford University Press

Published in the United States
by Oxford University Press Inc., New York

British Library Cataloguing in Publication Data
Data available

Library of Congress Cataloging in Publication Data
Data available
ISBN 0–19–829083–7

1 3 5 7 9 10 8 6 4 2

Typeset by Hope Services (Abingdon) Ltd.
Printed in Great Britain
on acid-free paper by
Biddles Ltd.,
Guildford & King's Lynn

For
Rory and Owen,
remembering Annecy

PREFACE

I argued in *The Common Mind* (1993, 1996) for a social philosophy that is at once anti-collectivist and anti-atomist. The philosophy is anti-collectivist in rejecting the idea that individuals are the playthings of aggregate social forces; they are not numbers in a game of historical chance, not pawns in a march to historical destiny. The philosophy is anti-atomist in insisting that nevertheless the notion of the solitary individual is essentially bogus: people depend on one another, and in more than a causal way, for the very ability to think; they are essentially social creatures. In the concluding part of the earlier book, I sketched some implications of this philosophy for political theory and I mentioned the attractions of republicanism for anyone who holds by such a view. I do not explicitly discuss those implications in the present book, but it should be clear that I consider it as a sequel to the earlier volume. Many commentators on *The Common Mind* looked for a fuller account of republicanism, and of the difference between republicanism and liberalism. I hope that this book will provide what they were seeking.

I discovered republicanism about ten years ago, when I was engaged in work with John Braithwaite on criminal justice and political ideals, in particular the ideal of liberty. Conscious of older, republican ways of thinking about political liberty, we wondered how it could be possible to see the ideal as inherently social in character—to see it as equivalent to citizenship in a republic—and at the same time to see it as a distinctively subjective value that enabled the person enjoying it to have a sense of psychological security and status. And then we realized that such a way of thinking about liberty became accessible once you made two things central. First, that there is a big difference between constrained interference that is designed for a common good—say, the interference of a law that no one contests—and arbitrary interference. And second, that there is a big difference between just happening to avoid such arbitrary interference—say, because the powers that be quite like you—and being more or less invulnerable to it. Make those things important and it is very natural to think of freedom as the social status of being relatively proof against arbitrary interference by others, and of being able to enjoy a sense of security and standing among them. The approach casts freedom as non-domination: as a condition under which a person is more or less immune, and more or less saliently immune, to interference on an arbitrary basis.

This idea of freedom immediately caught my imagination. Perhaps that was because it made sense of my experience when, intending to be a priest, I had spent years in establishments that I learned later to describe, in Erving Goffman's phrase, as total institutions. While such schools and seminaries offered wonderful opportunities for study and comradeship, they certainly did not teach us to look the authorities in the eye, confident of knowing where we stood and of not being subject to capricious judgement. On the contrary, they communicated a sense of systematic vulnerability and exposure to the governing will, sometimes even making a virtue of the practice. I had come to rail against the subordination inherent in such training, and the notion of freedom as non-domination offered a satisfying way of explaining what was wrong with it. Our formation had tried to cultivate unfreedom; it was designed to make students passive, unassertive, unsure of where they stood. Mary Wollstonecraft wrote in the 1790s of the way that women's subordination turned them into creatures who learned to bow and scrape, and to achieve their ends by ingratiation. She might have been writing of us.

Since the experience of subordination is so widespread, I hope that readers will share with me the sense that there has to be something attractive about the sort of liberty which requires that you are not dominated by another and which enables you, therefore, to look others in the eye. I am encouraged in that hope by the conviction that this is indeed how traditional republicans had conceived of liberty when they argued that its antonym was slavery or subjection, and when they depicted exposure to the arbitrary will of another as the great evil to be avoided. I am not a historian of ideas and it took a lot of time, and some considerable re-education, before I was in a position to see that a recurrent motif in republican thinking, down to and including the American and French Revolutions, was an emphasis on this notion of liberty as a status that could only be achieved when others were deprived of arbitrary powers. It was particularly intriguing to realize that that notion of liberty went out of fashion only as it became clear, towards the end of the eighteenth century, that with citizenship extended beyond the realm of propertied males, it was no longer possible to think of making all citizens free in the old sense: in particular it was not feasible, under received ideas, to think of conferring freedom as non-domination on women and servants. If freedom was to be cast as an ideal for all citizens, then freedom would have to be reconceived in less demanding terms; and reconceived, as I argue, it certainly was.

But this book is not just the presentation of an alternative notion of freedom, with some account of its historical rise and fall. If we take the goal of the state to be the promotion of freedom as non-domination—if we reappropriate the republican ideal—then we can begin to see the outlines of a commanding political philosophy. Freedom as non-domination has attractive institutional implications, and, so far as that is possible in advance of more detailed empirical work, the book tries to outline the main lessons. Some of the implications presented will have a familiar republican ring, such as the linkages with equality, community, and civic virtue, and the emphasis on constitutionalism and on the checking of government. Others will be more surprising, such as the argument about the policies that a republic ought to pursue and the sort of democracy that it ought to implement. Freedom as non-domination supports a rich, even a radical set of political policies, providing an ecumenical ground for what might otherwise seem like sectional demands on the state. And freedom as non-domination supports a conception of democracy under which contestability takes the place usually given to consent; what is of primary importance is not that government does what the people tells it but, on pain of arbitrariness, that people can always contest whatever it is that government does.

I am indebted to a large group of people for helping me in various ways to develop the ideas in the book and to get them on paper. Wittingly or unwittingly, Phillip Adams and Paul Finn prompted me to write a full-length book in defence of my views on republican liberty and government. Quentin Skinner helped to give me the courage of my convictions, directing me to the historical bodies of literature which bore them out, offering much-needed encouragement and providing very helpful comments on a first draft of the book. Geoffrey Brennan interrogated me at every point in the development of the argument, besides collaborating in work on the idea of regard-based regulation—this is important in the last two chapters—and made republicanism feel like a distinctive and significant commitment. But unquestionably John Braithwaite did more than anyone else to shape my thinking and writing on republican themes. He moulded my ideas on almost every topic covered in the book, helping to ensure that I did not lose touch, as I hope I have not lost touch, with empirical and practical issues.

The philosophers and political scientists at the University of Auckland provided me with sustained and incisive comments on the material of the first half of the book when, as a Foundation Visitor, I presented it in a set of lectures there in 1994. I benefited from the reactions of French and Swiss audiences when I was fortunate enough, in 1996, to hold visiting positions under the auspices of the Institut Universitaire de France (held at the Université de Caen) and the Université de Neuchâtel. And I learned significantly from the comments of a group of Dutch colleagues when I gave some presentations in May 1996 at Erasmus University, Rotterdam. I hope I will be forgiven if I do not try to name all of the individuals who provided me with useful comments among those and among other audiences.

I owe great debts to a small number of colleagues and students who have always been ready to discuss ideas related to the book: in particular to Frank Jackson and Michael Smith, from whom I continue to learn more than I shall ever be able to say, but also to Moira Gatens, Knud Haakonssen, Elisa Kaczynska-Nay, Christine Parker, Deborah Russell, Caroline West, and John Williams. I am indebted to many others for comments, in some cases lengthy written comments, on the emerging arguments of the book: David Braddon-Mitchell, Paul Bourke, Valerie Braithwaite, Andrew Brien, Tony Coady, Susan Dodds, John Ferejohn, Bob Goodin, Barry Hindess, Ian Hunt, Duncan Ivison, Chandran Kukathas, Douglas MacLean, David Miller, Kevin Mulligan, Tom Nagel, Pasquale Pasquino, Mark Philp, Ian Ravenscroft, Jean-Fabien Spitz, John Uhr, Catherine Valcke, David West, and Susan Wolf. I am very grateful for the unfailing assistance provided by Chris Treadwell in preparing the typescript and for the extraordinary level of encouragement and cooperation that I received from my editors, Tim Barton, Dominic Byatt, and Sophie Ahmad. The book is dedicated to my children, Rory and Owen, as much in their mother's name as in mine; for even if Eileen McNally can disclaim responsibility for what I have written, she cannot deny that she helped enough in the writing of it to co-own the dedication.

I said in the preface to *The Common Mind* that I could not have prepared the book in a more fitting and supportive setting than the Research School of Social Sciences at the Australian National University in Canberra. I can say the same of this book. The interdisciplinary intensiveness of the School, the presence and connection that it gives to the best Australian and international scholarship, and the intellectual generosity that is characteristic of its staff and students: these are precious assets that have sustained me throughout the course of my work on republican theory. I am lucky, and happy, to belong.

Canberra
May 1996

CONTENTS

Introduction   1

PART I. REPUBLICAN FREEDOM

1. Before Negative and Positive Liberty   17

2. Liberty as Non-domination   51

3. Non-domination as a Political Ideal   80

4. Liberty, Equality, Community   110

PART II. REPUBLICAN GOVERNMENT

5. Republican Aims: Causes and Policies   129

6. Republican Forms: Constitutionalism
   and Democracy   171

7. Checking the Republic   206

8. Civilizing the Republic   241

Republicanism: A Propositional Summary   271

Bibliography   282

Index   297

INTRODUCTION

Ideas and politics

It would be utopian to think that what happens in politics is a function of the normative ideas that circulate in and around the political world. The form that institutional policies assume, and the shape in which institutional patterns stabilize, are determined as much by the interests of the parties involved, and by their views on empirical questions—by their views, for example, on what is electorally and institutionally feasible—as it is by their ideas as to how things ought ideally to be.

Yet normative ideas are of the first importance in political life. For it is only possible for politicians and public officials to gain support for the policies they pursue to the extent that they can represent them as legitimate: to the extent that they can represent them as policies that are motivated by this or that agreed, or more or less agreed, commitment. Even the secret police of Eastern European societies couldn't keep communist regimes in place once it became a matter of common recognition that the ideals associated with those regimes were not well conceived, or at least not well targeted, and that few continued to believe in them.

The normative ideas that circulate in and around political life are rarely as coordinated, of course, as the ideas that permeated communist systems. In today's advanced democracies they come in different currents that whirl and eddy around the prominent policy-making issues. Sometimes these currents move together and create a momentum in support of one or another policy direction; sometimes they pull against one another and generate a chaotic and unpredictable pattern.

The main currents that wash around our policy-making rocks are easy to identify. One is the current of economic ideas about the importance of satisfying the preferences, whatever they are, that people bring to the social world and about the need to devise efficient disciplines—usually market-like disciplines—for ensuring maximal preference-satisfaction. Another is the current of ideas about people's universal rights, whether these rights be conceived in a thin or a rich fashion, and about the requirement that political institutions respect and foster the enjoyment of those rights. Yet another is the current of ideas that gives prominence to issues of welfare or fairness or equality—or that focuses on corresponding grievances like poverty or exploitation, subordination or oppression—and that argues for a system which delivers this or that set of valued outcomes. And another, of course, is the current of democratic ideas that associates legitimacy, more or less exclusively, with whatever policies and patterns derive from the will of the people, as majority opinion is described in this tradition, or at least from the will of the people's elected representatives.

These currents in the whirlpool of contemporary politics are often represented, usefully enough, as rival languages or discourses of legitimation. They are languages or discourses—and not, for example, theories or ideologies—because they allow those who speak them to disagree and debate with each another on matters of detailed policy. They consist in shared assumptions that are abstract enough to leave room for differences and germane enough to act as constraints on debate about those differences; they make conversation possible without predetermining its direction. While they share many common idioms—one, as we shall mention, is the idiom of freedom—they are sufficiently distinct to be cast as rival systems for the political criticism and legitimation of institutional arrangements.

Political philosophy

Granted that politics is inevitably conducted in normative language: in the language, now of this current of ideas, now of that. Granted, in other words, that politics always has the aspect—the partial aspect—of a conversation. What does this say about the role of the normative political theorist: or, if you prefer, the political philosopher?

It implies that whatever else the political philosopher may do, one obvious project is the examination of the languages of political discussion and legitimation, the critique of various of the assumptions from which those languages start, the exploration of how far the languages cohere with one another and with the languages of other times and places, and the search for new and broader terms in which to frame political debate.

This is both a humdrum and an exciting task. It is exciting to the extent that it challenges the philosopher to step back and examine matters that pass without notice in the hurly-burly of engaged debate. It holds out the possibility of making the language in which you choose to discuss political issues truly your own. You can become aware of the presuppositions it carries, and mould them to your own mind, rather than being carried along in a medium of debate and thought that commits you in ways that systematically escape notice. To the philosopher's eye the unexamined language, whether it be a language of politics, or ethics, or free will, or consciousness, is not worth speaking: it may introduce too many unwanted assumptions. The excitement of the task described here, like that of any philosophical task, is the excitement of mastering your medium, assuming a degree of control over thoughts that will otherwise control you.

But the task described here is also humdrum. For whatever the individual philosopher achieves in the way of insight and mastery, all that he or she can ever hope to represent is one contribution, at one specific time, in one specific forum, to a conversation that is destined to outrun any efforts they may make to direct it. The conversation of politics, such as it exists in today's advanced democracies, is constantly evolving and shifting, as now one language, now another, comes to the fore, and as the debate turns now in this direction, now in that. No one individual, and so no one philosopher, can expect to do more than play a very humdrum part. They can expect to make their voice heard only in a small circle, and if they reach other audiences that will almost always be because others happen to be saying related things: they are part of a conversational cascade.

It is very important that philosophers recognize this limitation on what they may hope to achieve. If a philosopher comes to the business of political conversation with the ambition of providing the political philosophy to end political philosophies—the philosophical voice to drown out all other voices—then they are bound to be disillusioned. And such disillusion can breed an attitude of despair and scepticism towards the possibilities of conversation in general. It can lead theorists to imagine, as so many contemporaries like to imagine, that there is no real conversation in politics, only the play of naked power: that political argument and exchange never amounts to anything more than the ceremonial waving of flags. Finding that they cannot bend the public conversation to the grain of their own reason, they conclude that there is no reason there at all: not even the sort of reason that is never quickly implemented, never perfectly implemented, never implemented under just its own impetus, and never implemented on all fronts at once.

Such theorists look at developments over the last two hundred years, for example, and refuse to see any signs of conversationally motivated agreement or influence. They fail to notice the long, broken, but still influential debates that took place in various countries on such issues as the abolition of slavery, the reform of pocket boroughs, the provision of compulsory education, the extension of the franchise, the admission of women to parliament, the provision of social security, the systematic organization of hospitals, and the development of public health schemes. They make it a badge of professional insight to find grounds for cynicism about the value of any such development or about its having occurred as the result, even in part, of reasoned demand or reasoned outrage.

But to say that no one individual philosopher can expect to do much alone is not to say that political philosophy as such does not achieve anything significant. The prospect of political conversation coming entirely adrift from the reflection of political philosophers is a bleak and chilling scenario. For it is mainly by virtue of the work of such theorists that the terms of political conversation are systematically interrogated and interrelated, and occasionally renewed or replaced. A conversation without any corner for sustained reflection of this kind would quickly run to ground in a babel of dogmatic assertion and counter-assertion. If political philosophers did not exist, we would have to invent them.

The republican turn

So much on the nature of politics—or at least on the conversational aspect of politics—and on the role of political philosophy. What, then, do I intend to achieve by my efforts in this book?

I want to remind my colleagues in political philosophy—and, ideally, in the more general audience that the discipline sometimes attracts—of a sort of grievance, and a sort of ideal, that has not been given enough attention in contemporary debates. I want to articulate the grievance in question as a complaint about being dominated and the ideal in question as a vision of being free. I want to show that this language of domination and freedom—this language of freedom as non-domination—connects with the long, republican tradition of thought that shaped many of the most important institutions and constitutions that we associate with democracy. And I want to argue that there is very good reason to find a place again for this language in contemporary political discussion. Thinking about politics in terms of the demands of freedom as non-domination gives us a very full and persuasive picture of what it is reasonable to expect of a decent state and a decent civil society.

The grievance I have in mind is that of having to live at the mercy of another, having to live in a manner that leaves you vulnerable to some ill that the other is in a position arbitrarily to impose; and this, in particular, when each of you is in a position to see that you are dominated by the other, in a position to see that you each see this, and so on. It is the grievance expressed by the wife who finds herself in a position where her husband can beat her at will, and without any possibility of redress; by the employee who dare not raise a complaint against an employer, and who is vulnerable to any of a range of abuses, some petty, some serious, that the employer may choose to perpetrate; by the debtor who has to depend on the grace of the moneylender, or the bank official, for avoiding utter destitution and ruin; and by the welfare dependant who finds that they are vulnerable to the caprice of a counter clerk for whether or not their children will receive meal vouchers.

Contemporary thought suggests that individuals in these positions retain their freedom to the extent that they are not actively coerced or obstructed. But whether or not they avoid interference, they certainly have a grievance. They live in the shadow of the other's presence, even if no arm is raised against them. They live in uncertainty about the other's reactions and in need of keeping a weather eye open for the other's moods. They find themselves in a position where they are demeaned by their vulnerability, being unable to look the other in the eye, and where they may even be forced to fawn or toady or flatter in the attempt to ingratiate themselves.

It turns out, so I argue here, that under an older, republican way of thinking about freedom, individuals in such a dominated position are straightforwardly unfree. No domination without unfreedom, even if the dominating agent stays their hand. Being unfree does not consist in being restrained; on the contrary, the restraint of a fair system of law—a non-arbitrary regime—does not make you unfree. Being unfree consists rather in being subject to arbitrary sway: being subject to the potentially capricious will or the potentially idiosyncratic judgement of another. Freedom involves emancipation from any such subordination, liberation from any such dependency. It requires the capacity to stand eye to eye with your fellow citizens, in a shared awareness that none of you has a power of arbitrary interference over another.

The older, republican tradition of which I speak is the tradition associated with Cicero at the time of the Roman Republic; with Machiavelli—'the divine Machiavel' of the *Discourses*—and various other writers of the Renaissance Italian republics; with James Harrington and a host of lesser figures in and after the period of the English Civil War and Commonwealth; and with the many theorists of republic or commonwealth in eighteenth-century England and

America and France. I focus most often on the 'commonwealthmen' who dominated English and American political thought in the late seventeenth and in the eighteenth century. The commonwealthmen were devoted to the ideal of freedom as non-domination—freedom as escape from the arbitrary—and they helped to shape habits of political reflex and thought that still survive today. Their distinctive refrain was that, while the cause of freedom as non-domination rests squarely with the state and its officials—it is mainly thanks to the state and the constitution, after all, that people enjoy such freedom—still those officials are also an inherent threat and people have to strive to 'keep the bastards honest'; the price of liberty is eternal vigilance.

When traditional commonwealthmen and republicans hailed the ideal of freedom as non-domination, they only ever imagined that it was an ideal for an élite of propertied, mainstream males; they were all men, after all, and men of their times. But there is every reason why we should reappropriate their ideal and reintroduce it as a universal ideal for the members of a contemporary society. That, at any rate, is my own conviction, as will become clear in the course of the book. I believe that the notion of freedom as non-domination fits with many of our agreed preconceptions, that it picks up important desiderata that are already inscribed in many of our institutions, and that it can serve to articulate a compelling account of what a decent state and a decent civil society should do for its members.

I said earlier that there are many languages of legitimation present in the world of democratic politics today. One of the striking features of those languages, however, is that all of them, at one point or another, invoke the notion of freedom; all of them share a common idiom of freedom or liberty. The language of economics directs us to the free market and to the freedom to make whatever contracts we will with one another; the language of rights focuses on rights of free thought, free expression, free movement, and the like; the language of welfare and fairness and equality, or of poverty and exploitation and subordination, claims to articulate the requirements necessary for enjoying freedom or for making freedom effective. And the language of democratic legitimation harps on the legitimacy of what a free people freely decide, and on the way in which individual persons share in that collective freedom.

This overlapping idiom of freedom gives an indication of the importance that all of us, or at least all of us who identify with western-style democracies, naturally assign to the notion of freedom. However we interpret it, the notion has mantric standing in our thought. The fact of this status means that my argument about the republican ideal of freedom has more than antiquarian or analytical interest. I maintain that the traditional, republican ideal of freedom supports and unifies a compelling manifesto of political demands, and that if a state and a society looks after the freedom as non-domination of its members, then most other desiderata will look after themselves. Whatever may be said of this claim, the centrality of the notion of freedom means that it should at least command attention. It may be mistaken but it surely isn't boring.

Neither, I should say, is the claim idiosyncratic. I am not alone in finding the republican tradition of thought a fruitful source of ideas and ideals. Historians like John Pocock (1975) and Quentin Skinner (1978; 1983; 1984) have not only made the tradition visible to us in the past couple of decades; they have also shown how it can give us a new perspective on contemporary politics. Skinner in particular has argued that it can give us a new understanding of freedom and my own argument builds on this, as I indicate in the first chapter. Legal thinkers like Cass Sunstein (1990*a*; 1993*a*; 1993*b*), on the other hand, have gone back to the republican tradition in its distinctively American incarnation in the late 1800s, and have made a strong case for the claim that the tradition suggests a distinctive way of interpreting the US Constitution and, more generally, that it gives us an insightful overview on the role of government. I make a variety of connections with Sunstein's work in the later part of the book. Criminologists and regulatory theorists like John Braithwaite, with whom I have actively collaborated, find in the republican tradition a set of compelling ideas for articulating both the demands that we should place on a regulatory system—say, the criminal justice system—and the expectations that we should hold out for how those demands can be best met (Ayres and Braithwaite 1992). And these are just a few thinkers among many commentators who have begun to chart republican connections, and sometimes to draw actively on republican ideas, in recent years.[1]

Republicanism, populism, liberalism

When thinkers like Skinner, Sunstein, and Braithwaite describe themselves as republican, and when indeed I describe myself in that way, I

---

[1] e.g., Nicolet (1982), Ferry and Renaut (1985), Michelman (1986), Elkin (1987), Pagden (1987), Weintraub (1988), Taylor (1989), Oldfield (1990), Bock *et al.* (1990), Rahe (1992), Fontana (1994), Hutton (1995), Blom (1995), Spitz (1995*a*), Viroli (1992; 1995). See too Pettit (1996*c*).

should mention that the tradition with which we identify is not the sort of tradition—ultimately, the populist tradition—that hails the democratic participation of the people as one of the highest forms of good and that often waxes lyrical, in communitarian vein, about the desirability of the close, homogeneous society that popular participation is often taken to presuppose (Philp 1996). The republican tradition that is characterized in this book is not inherently populist in this way and indeed, as we shall see later, not particularly communitarian. Republican freedom is a communitarian ideal, in a sense explicated in Chapter 4, but the ideal is compatible with modern pluralistic forms of society. And while the republican tradition finds value and importance in democratic participation, it does not treat it as a bedrock value. Democratic participation may be essential to the republic, but that is because it is necessary for promoting the enjoyment of freedom as non-domination, not because of its independent attractions: not because freedom, as a positive conception would suggest, is nothing more or less than the right of democratic participation.

This point is important to stress because the term 'republican' has come to be associated in many circles, probably under the influence of Hannah Arendt (1958, 1973), with a communitarian and populist approach (Viroli 1992: 286–7). Such an approach represents the people in their collective presence as master and the state as servant, and suggests that the people ought to rely on state representatives and officials only where absolutely necessary: direct democracy, whether by assembly or plebiscite, is the systematically preferred option. The commonwealth or republican position, by contrast, sees the people as trustor, both individually and collectively, and sees the state as trustee: in particular, it sees the people as trusting the state to ensure a dispensation of non-arbitrary rule. For this position direct democracy may often be a very bad thing, since it may ensure the ultimate form of arbitrariness: the tyranny of a majority. Democratic instruments of control will certainly be desirable and indispensable, but they are not the be-all and end-all of good government.

So much for the populist alternative to republicanism. What now of the relationship between the republican tradition, as I envisage it, and perhaps the more salient alternative that is represented by the liberal conception of politics?

The republican tradition, as I shall argue, shares with liberalism the presumption that it is possible to organize a viable state and a viable civil society on a basis that transcends many religious and related divides. To that extent many liberals will claim the tradition as their own. But liberalism has been associated over the two hundred years of its development, and in most of its influential varieties, with the negative conception of freedom as the absence of interference, and with the assumption that there is nothing inherently oppressive about some people having dominating power over others, provided they do not exercise that power and are not likely to exercise it. This relative indifference to power or domination has made liberalism tolerant of relationships in the home, in the workplace, in the electorate, and elsewhere, that the republican must denounce as paradigms of domination and unfreedom. And it has meant that if liberals are concerned with issues of poverty, ignorance, insecurity and the like, as many are, that is usually because of some commitment independent of their commitment to freedom as non-interference: say, a commitment to the satisfaction of basic needs, or to the realization of a certain equality between people.

Liberalism, as I construct it here, is a broad church (Ryan 1993). I think of liberals as those who embrace freedom as non-interference. I distinguish between left-of-centre liberals, who stress the need to make non-interference an effective value, not just a formal one, or who embrace values like equality or the elimination of poverty in addition to the value of non-interference, and right-of-centre liberals—classic liberals or libertarians (Machan and Rasmussen 1995)—who think that it is enough to establish non-interference as a formal, legal reality. But I should mention that many left-of-centre liberals will be unhappy with this way of casting things (Larmore 1993: ch. 7; Holmes 1995). They will see their liberalism as having more in common with the republican position than with the libertarian (Ackerman 1991: 29–30) and they would probably want to give up the taxonomy of populism, republicanism, and liberalism in favour of an alternative like populism, republicanism/liberalism, and libertarianism.

There is something to be said for this alternative. I mentioned that, where the populist image of government represents the people as master and the state as servant, the republican or commonwealth image depicts the people as trustor, the state as trustee. Left-of-centre liberals would almost certainly endorse this trustor–trustee image also, and one attraction in the proposed taxonomy is that libertarianism can be linked to a third and different image of the relationship between people and state. Self-described libertarians tend to think of the people as an aggregate of atomized individuals—an aggregate without a collective identity—and they represent the state as ideally nothing more than an apparatus for accommodating individuals in the pursuit of their atomized concerns. The model is not that of master and servant, nor that of trustor and trustee, but rather that of an aggregate of individuals and an apparatus for ensuring their individual satisfaction. For those who like taxonomies that go deep on a number of dimensions, the best available may be: populist, republican/liberal, and libertarian.

But this consideration notwithstanding, I intend to stick with my presentation of liberalism as a broad church that encompasses both left-of-centre liberals and libertarians. The reason is that my primary focus is on how different theorists think of freedom, and I believe that most of those who describe themselves as liberals—most, not all (see Gaus 1983; Raz 1986)—think of freedom in the negative way as non-interference; certainly they do not think of it in the republican fashion as non-domination. Left-of-centre liberals will find the republican line advanced in this book attractive in its institutional implications. But I think that most of them should be ready to admit that the line is supported here from a distinctive base. It may be a base that was familiar to those in the commonwealth tradition that they admire—it may have been familiar to the likes of Harrington and Locke, Montesquieu and Madison—but it is not a base that is generally recognized in self-consciously liberal writing.

Some historians of thought will baulk at the breezy way in which I speak here and later of the republican as distinct from the liberal or populist traditions, and a word of qualification is required. While this book starts from a notion of freedom with a distinctive historical provenance, and while I have emphasized that aspect of things in this introduction, the book is not essentially tied to many controversial theses in the history of ideas. Perhaps republicanism is not deserving of the name of a tradition, for example, not being sufficiently coherent or connected to be treated in that way. Perhaps there is such a break in the new seventeenth-century concern about the power of the state—the power of the state as distinct from that of the powerful—that we cannot see a single tradition spanning that rupture (Pasquino, forthcoming; see also Michelman 1986; Manent 1987). Or perhaps there are other grounds for subdividing what I present as one tradition into different periods or strands. I do not have to commit myself on these detailed sorts of question.

All that I strictly need to claim is that the representation of freedom as immunity to arbitrary control is found in many historical authors, that it is a distinctive and challenging conception of the ideal, and that it is worthy of consideration in contemporary political philosophy. I go further than that, of course, in the story that I tell about republican thought. I treat the belief in freedom as non-domination as a unifying theme which binds together thinkers of very different periods and very different background philosophies. And I suggest that the commitment to this theme generates shared institutional concerns among such thinkers: concerns about the character of law and government, about the checks and controls on public authorities, and about the cultivation of virtue and the avoidance of corruption. But this historical aspect of the book is secondary. If historians of ideas find it misleading, then they should regard the more substantive historical suggestions as simplifications that are justified only by the colour that they give to my philosophical claims.

The case for republicanism

Why should I expect populists and liberals, whether liberals of a rightist or a leftist bent, to give a hearing to the republican approach? Every grand approach to politics gives us an axiom or set of axioms from which judgements on more particular institutional matters are meant to flow; the axioms need not represent a unique base of justification, as in a foundationalist scheme, but they do claim to be a good starting-point for organizing intuitions. Any such approach is bound to be judged, then, on two fronts: one, for the attractions of the axiom or axioms, both in themselves and in the organizational role that they are allotted; and two, for the plausibility and adequacy of the theorems that are derived from those axioms. The picture fits with John Rawls's (1971) method of reflective equilibrium, as described later in this book.

Republican theory should recommend itself to all competitors, I believe, in the axiom from which it starts. The republican conception of liberty should appeal to liberals, in so far as it focuses on people's individual power of choice and thus has much in common with the negative notion of freedom as non-interference. And it should appeal to populists in so far as it requires, as I argue, that non-dominating government has to track the interests and ideas of ordinary people; this is the idea that lies behind the positive, populist notion of freedom as democratic self-mastery. The central axiom of republican thought is not a newfangled notion, and is not even a notion, like justice or equality, that depends for its attraction on the acceptance of a controverted vision. It is traditional and modest enough, in itself, to make a claim on the attention of all comers.

But though republican theory is organized around a modest and traditional starting-point, it is extremely fruitful and challenging in the theorems about government institutions which it enables us to derive. It does not leave us with the sparse and heartless sort of government with which rightist liberals pretend to be satisfied. And it does not support the interventionist, majoritarian rule—the potentially tyrannical sort of rule—which populists have to countenance. It points us in a direction that is closest to that embraced by left-of-centre liberals, as the book exemplifies, offering a rival axiomization of many of their intuitions. But the rival axiomization has two advantages. First, it starts from a base that is less contentious than the base which leftist liberals generally espouse; it offers a common ground on which to argue, for example, with their rightist opponents. And second, the republican axiomatization develops even shared intuitions in a highly distinctive and yet compelling way. As will become clear, for example, it offers an attractive way of justifying egalitarian and even communitarian intuitions. And it supports an exciting way of rethinking democratic institutions, in which the notion of consent is displaced by that of contestability.

The plan of the book

And so finally to the plan of the book. Chapter 1 tells the story of how the republican notion of freedom emerged and stabilized, and of how it was eclipsed at the very moment of its most conspicuous success in the debates surrounding the American Revolution. It was at this time that the notion of freedom as non-interference took over from that of freedom as non-domination, so I suggest, and that liberalism replaced republicanism as the dominant political philosophy. Chapter 2 gives a philosophical articulation of the notion of freedom as non-domination, regimenting the idea formally and displaying its points of contrast with freedom as non-interference. Chapter 3 argues for the capacity of freedom as non-domination to serve as a guiding ideal for the state. And then Chapter 4 charts the connections between freedom as non-domination and the values linked with it in the French trio of *liberté, égalité, fraternité*; this chapter is designed to display the egalitarian and communitarian character of freedom as non-domination, and to show the appeal that it should have as a political ideal.

Those first four chapters are followed by four that look at the institutional ramifications of organizing a state and a civil society so that the cause of freedom as non-domination is served as well as possible. Chapter 5 looks at what is going to be required of a modern state if it is to guard against the arbitrary sort of interference that individuals and groups may practise against one another in virtue of having different levels of resources, different levels of *dominium*. And then Chapter 6 looks at what is necessary if such a republican state is to promote non-domination successfully, and is not itself to represent a form of domination associated, in a twin term, with *imperium* (Kriegel 1995). Where Chapter 5 describes the aims of the republican state in controlling *dominium*—the causes with which it should identify, the policies which it should sponsor—Chapter 6 describes the forms that the state must assume if it is to control *imperium*: in particular, it describes the sort of constitutionalism and democracy required to guard against this danger. Chapter 7 looks at what can be done to make the realization of such republican aims and forms resilient or stable, providing regulatory checks against shortfalls and abuses. And Chapter 8 rounds off the discussion by arguing that if the republican state is to achieve its ends in relation to *dominium* and *imperium*, it must connect with a form of civil society in which republican values are firmly entrenched: it cannot expect to work such wonders on its own. Although this connection with civil society is left until last, it is of the utmost importance. Someone who reads just the first seven chapters of the book will miss one of the most significant aspects of the republicanism it defends.

PART I

REPUBLICAN FREEDOM

CHAPTER 1

Before Negative and Positive Liberty

I. Negative and positive liberty

Contemporary discussions of social and political organization are dominated by a distinction which Isaiah Berlin (1958) made famous. This is the distinction between what he, following a late-eighteenth-century tradition (Lind 1776), describes as negative and positive liberty.

Negative liberty, as Berlin conceives of it, involves the absence of interference, where interference is a more or less intentional intervention of the sort exemplified, not just by the physical coercion of kidnap or imprisonment, but also by the coercion of the credible threat ('Your money or your life'; 'Your money or the bailiff'). I am negatively free 'to the degree to which no human being interferes with my activity' (Berlin 1958: 7): to the extent that I enjoy unimpeded and uncoerced choice.

Positive liberty, according to Berlin, requires more than the absence of interference, more than just being let alone by others. It requires the agent to take an active part in gaining control or mastery of themselves: the self with which they identify must take charge of the lesser or more partial selves that lurk within every individual. I am positively free to the extent that I achieve 'self-mastery, with its suggestion of a man divided against himself' (Berlin 1958: 19).

Berlin shaped the allegiances of contemporary theorists in marking out negative liberty as a sensible ideal and in raising serious doubts about the credentials of positive. The self-mastery ideal of positive liberty may seem attractive, he argued, but it easily gets interpreted in an ominous fashion: say, as the ideal of becoming able, perhaps with the help of state discipline, to master one's lower self; as the ideal of transcending the divided, atomistic self by assimilation to the greater whole of the national spirit; or as the ideal of suppressing decentralized, individual will by becoming part of a self-determining polity which reveals and realizes what is in the common interest.

Berlin did more than make negative liberty look attractive, positive liberty ominous. He also managed to insinuate that, while most modern, down-to-earth thinkers have taken liberty in the negative sense, the positive construal of liberty was associated with earlier, more suspect sources. He finds the negative conception in 'the classical English political philosophers', like Hobbes, Bentham, and Mill, in luminaries of French enlightenment like Montesquieu, Constant, and de Tocqueville, and in American heroes like Jefferson and Paine: in short, in the pantheon of modern liberalism. He associates the positive conception, on the other hand, with continental romantics like Herder, Rousseau, Kant, Fichte, Hegel, and Marx; with religious and quasi-religious groupings of Buddhists, Christians, and Stoics; and with radical, even totalitarian, political thinkers like Jacobins and communists.

In advancing this scenario of heroes and anti-heroes, Berlin made contact with the tradition of distinguishing ancient from modern liberty (Spitz 1995*a*). The clear suggestion is that, whereas positive liberty is something of the past—the liberty of the ancients—negative liberty is a truly modern ideal. While negative liberty is an enlightenment value with which we can all now identify, so it is suggested, positive liberty is the sort of ideal that appeals only to such celebrants of pre-modern times as the romantic afficionados of counter-Enlightenment. The ancient–modern distinction had been brought to prominence early in the last century by Benjamin Constant (1988) in a famous essay on 'The Liberty of the Ancients and the Liberty of the Moderns'. Constant's modern liberty is Berlin's negative liberty, and his ancient liberty—the liberty of belonging to a democratically self-governing community—is the most prominent variety of Berlin's positive conception. Modern liberty is being left to the rule of your own private will, ancient liberty is sharing in the rule of a public, democratically determined will. The modern ideal is characteristically liberal, the ancient characteristically populist (Riker 1982).

I believe that the negative–positive distinction has served us ill in political thought. It has sustained the philosophical illusion that, details aside, there are just two ways of understanding liberty: in one, freedom consists in the absence of external obstacles to individual choice; in the other, it involves the presence, and usually the exercise (Taylor 1985: essay 8; Baldwin 1984) of the facilities that foster self-mastery and self-fulfilment: in particular, the presence and exercise of those participatory and voting facilities whereby the individual can unite with others in the formation of a common, popular will.

The negative–positive distinction has sustained a historical narrative to go along with this philosophical dichotomy of private and populist liberty. Under that story, the concerns of those who speak of liberty in premodern times are almost always concerns with democratic membership and participation and the fulfilment that such belonging allegedly brings; they are concerns of the kind that would have been perfectly fulfilled for the citizens of classical Athens, for example, at least as Athens appears in the soft, nostalgic focus of the counter-Enlightenment (Arendt 1973; MacIntyre 1987; contrast Finley 1973; Fustel de Coulanges 1920). The concerns of moderns, on the other hand, are seen as the product of a changing, more individualistic society that spurns the ideal of public participation in favour of the ideal of a private sphere of activity in which each individual can get their own way. If democratic participation is supported within this philosophy of liberty, that is not because it is a good in itself, but rather because it serves a useful purpose in the protection of the individual.

I believe that these philosophical and historical oppositions are misconceived and misleading and, in particular, that they conceal from view the philosophical validity and historical reality of a third, radically different way of understanding freedom and the institutional requirements of freedom. I describe this third approach as republican, and my aim in the present chapter is to inscribe republicanism on the map—the historical and philosophical map—of available alternatives (see Spitz 1995*b*).

In speaking of republicanism, I refer to the long republican tradition—and, indeed, the broad republican tradition—that has become the focus of interest for a recent school of historical scholarship (Fink 1962; Raab 1965; Baron 1966; Pocock 1975; Skinner 1978; Pagden 1987; Oldfield 1990; Bock *et al.* 1990; Fontana 1994). This tradition had its origins in classical Rome, being associated in particular with the name of Cicero. It was resurrected in the Renaissance, featuring powerfully in the constitutional thinking of Machiavelli, and it played an important role in the self-conception of the northern Italian republics: the first modern European polities. It provided a language which dominated the politics of the modern West and had a particular salience in the Dutch Republic, during the English Civil War, and in the period leading up to the American and French Revolutions.

The big names of this more modern republican tradition include Harrington, Montesquieu, and perhaps de Tocqueville; they also include Rousseau, of course, though they should only do so, by my lights, if his work is interpreted in a non-populist way (as in Spitz 1995*a*). The tradition often received its most trenchant applications, however, not in the works of well-known writers, but in texts like *Cato's Letters* (Trenchard and Gordon 1971) and the *Federalist Papers* (Madison *et al.* 1987). The first of these texts was associated with the so-called commonwealthman tradition that survived in England from the period of the English Revolution through until the late eighteenth century (Robbins 1959; Fink 1962; Raab 1965). The second of the two texts, and of course the one better known, was an outstanding formulation of the associated transatlantic ideology: the ideology that lay behind the American Revolution (Bailyn 1967).

The republican tradition was unified across time, partly by a deference to the same textual authorities, partly by a shared enthusiasm for the ideals and the lessons of republican Rome, partly by an emphasis on the importance of having certain institutions in place: for example, an empire of law, as it was often put, not an empire of men; a mixed constitution, in which different powers serve to check and balance each other; and a regime of civic virtue, under which people are disposed to serve, and serve honestly, in public office. The most important unifier of the tradition, in the end, may be the habit of conceptualizing liberty in a distinctive fashion. But that is something which should emerge here, not something that I want to take for granted at the beginning.

Anti-monarchism was often a feature of the republican tradition, particularly during the English Civil War and again after the American and French Revolutions. But republicans were anti-monarchists only so far as they considered that a monarch would inevitably seek absolute power and would offend against the sort of liberty they prized. Thus they were happy with the constitutional monarchy that they found in eighteenth-century England: 'a nation', in Montesquieu's (1989: 70) unmistakable reference, 'where the republic hides under the form of monarchy' (Rahe 1992: 524). And not only that. Many of those whom I would have to count as republicans did not describe themselves, whether for strategic or other reasons, in such terms. Like Montesquieu himself, they preferred to don less radical colours.

Republican themes found a particularly friendly climate when they began to appear in England in the seventeenth century. As the courts and the common law had developed from the middle ages in England (Berman 1983), they had assumed a decentralized, non-voluntaristic form and had given rise to firm assumptions about people's rights under the law—people's ancient rights, as they were often described— even their rights against the powerful; they had provided people with a sense that they lived under a constitution, an empire of law, of ancient and unquestioned standing (Blackstone 1978: 127–8; Pocock

1987; cf. Blom 1995: 49). This legal background may have been as important in the development of the eighteenth-century common-wealthman tradition as the independent republican ideas for which it provided such a nurturing climate. It meant that the newer republic-anism always had a juridical cast in which a central place was given to the notion of rights—customary, legal, and constitutional rights—as bulwarks against absolute power (Tully 1993: 261–2; see also Ingram 1994).

The remaining discussion in this chapter is in six sections. In Section II I show that there is philosophical space left unoccupied by the dis-tinction between negative and positive liberty, and that we can see room there for a third and distinct approach: the conception of free-dom as non-domination. In Section III, I introduce the republican conception, arguing in line with recent scholarship—and against the traditional orthodoxy—that it is not an example of the positive approach. Then, in Sections IV and V, I provide evidence for thinking that it was precisely the conception of freedom as non-domination, not the negative conception of freedom as non-interference, that was embraced among writers in the republican tradition. In Section VI, I show how the conception of liberty as non-interference came to replace the received republican notion at the end of the eighteenth cen-tury. And in Section VII I outline some considerations that played a role in undermining the republican way of thinking and in ensuring the triumph of the new conception.

The story I tell has a twist. It suggests that the originators of the neg-ative, purportedly modern idea of freedom as non-interference were not those who welcomed the American Revolution, and the bright new age that it seemed to announce, but rather those who opposed that revolution and sought to defend the interest of the British crown. Those who welcomed and defended the revolution were moved, on the contrary, by the republican conception of liberty as non-domina-tion which the modernist idea eventually came to replace.

II. A third conception: liberty as non-domination

The best way of introducing freedom as non-domination may be to observe that Berlin's taxonomy of positive and negative liberty fore-closes a more or less salient third possibility. He thinks of positive lib-erty as mastery over the self and of negative liberty as the absence of interference by others. Yet mastery and interference do not amount to the same thing. So what of the intermediate possibility that freedom consists in an absence, as the negative conception has it, but in an absence of mastery by others, not in an absence of inteference? This possibility would have one conceptual element in common with the negative conception—the focus on absence, not presence—and one element in common with the positive: the focus on mastery, not interference.

But it is one thing to observe that the syntax of Berlin's taxonomy allows this third possibility. It is quite another to establish that the possibility is meaningful. I maintain that it is, and I shall be arguing in the sections which follow that the republican tradition is associated with precisely this conception of freedom as non-mastery or, as I prefer to say, non-domination. Before coming to those arguments, however, I need to establish the prior claim that the conception does refer us to a meaningful possibility. In particular, I need to make clear that it refers us to a possibility that is distinct from those associated with the other two conceptions.

There is no problem in seeing how non-domination by others is distinct from the positive ideal of self-mastery, since the absence of mastery by others clearly does not guarantee the achievement of self-mastery. But there may be a problem in seeing how it is distinguished from the negative ideal of non-interference by others, for it may not be obvious that mastery or domination really is different from interference.

Domination, as I understand it here, is exemplified by the relationship of master to slave or master to servant. Such a relationship means, at the limit, that the dominating party can interfere on an arbitrary basis with the choices of the dominated: can interfere, in particular, on the basis of an interest or an opinion that need not be shared by the person affected. The dominating party can practise interference, then, at will and with impunity: they do not have to seek anyone's leave and they do not have to incur any scrutiny or penalty. Without going further into the analysis of domination or indeed interference—we turn to that task in the next chapter—a little reflection should make clear that domination and interference are intuitively different evils.

The difference between them comes out in the fact that it is possible to have domination without interference and interference without domination. I may be dominated by another—for example, to go to the extreme case, I may be the slave of another—without actually being interfered with in any of my choices. It may just happen that my master is of a kindly and non-interfering disposition. Or it may just happen that I am cunning or fawning enough to be able to get away with doing whatever I like. I suffer domination to the extent that I have a master; I enjoy non-interference to the extent that that master fails to interfere.

As I may suffer domination without interference, so I may undergo interference without being dominated: without relating to anyone in the fashion of slave or subject. Suppose that another person or agency is allowed to interfere with me but only on condition that the interference promises to further my interests, and promises to do so according to opinions of a kind that I share. Suppose that the person is able to interfere in the event of the interference satisfying that condition, but that otherwise they are blocked from interfering or are subject to a deterrent penalty for attempting interference. It may be that a third party polices the person's performance or it may be that I am in a position to contest it myself. In such a case it is not possible to see the interference as an exercise of domination; the person interferes with me but not on an arbitrary basis. The person envisaged relates to me, not as a master, but more in the fashion of an agent who enjoys a power of attorney in my affairs.

As we can have domination without interference, then, so we can have interference without domination. The first possibility is illustrated by the non-interfering master, the second by the non-mastering interferer. Domination can occur without interference, because it requires only that someone have the capacity to interfere arbitrarily in your affairs; no one need actually interfere. Interference can occur without domination, because interference need not involve the exercise of a capacity for arbitrary interference, only the exercise of a much more constrained ability.

Given that interference and domination are different evils, non-interference and non-domination are different ideals. The difference between them is summed up nicely in the different ways they would rank the four scenarios to which we are directed as we imagine that there is or is not interference and that there is or is not domination. Where there is neither interference nor domination, the two ideals will endorse the situation. Where there is both interference and domination, the two will disapprove. They come apart, however, when one evil is realized but not the other. If there is domination but no interference, as in the case of the non-interfering master, only the ideal of non-domination will find anything to denounce. If there is interference, but no domination, as in the case of the non-mastering interferer, only the ideal of non-interference will see anything to criticize. This counterpointing is a little glib, as we shall see in later chapters, but it may serve usefully as a first presentation of the difference between the ideals. Here it is, in summary form.

No interference, no domination: good under the two ideals.
Both interference and domination: bad under the two ideals.
Domination but no interference: bad only under the non-domination ideal.
Interference but no domination: bad only under the non-interference ideal.

There is a second way of bringing out the difference between the ideals and it may also be worthwhile mentioning this (Pettit 1993*a*; 1993*b*). To enjoy non-interference is to escape coercion in the actual world. For a relevant range of possible choices no one coerces you to choose one way or another; were you to face one of those choices, you could make your choice without hindrance, threat, or penalty. What will it take, then, for such a non-interference world to be a non-domination world? In one way it will take less: it will not compromise the fact of non-domination that you suffer some interference, provided that the interference is not perpetrated by an agent on an arbitrary basis and does not represent a form of domination. But in another, crucial way, it will take more for that non-interference world—specifically, the world without interference by arbitrary powers—to be a non-domination world; the world must be a non-interference world of that kind, not by accident, but by virtue of your being secured against the powerful.

You might enjoy the non-interference in the actual world, because of a quite precarious contingency: say, because it happens that certain powerful individuals have a liking for you or it happens that you are able to keep out of the way of such individuals or ingratiate yourself with them. In this sense, you might enjoy non-interference in the actual world but not enjoy it with any degree of security against the powerful: not enjoy it robustly or resiliently. Let this or that condition vary—let you become less likeable, less lucky, or less cunning—and immediately interference, in particular interference on an arbitrary basis, follows: the powerful begin to coerce you in any of a variety of ways. You enjoy non-interference from the powerful in the actual world, as we might say, but you do not enjoy it in the range of readily accessible worlds—a range of nearby possible worlds—where this or that contingent condition is varied; you do not enjoy it resiliently.

Where the ideal of non-interference involves this inbuilt contingency, the ideal of non-domination avoids it. For if you are not dominated by anyone else, if you are not subject to a capacity for arbitrary interference by anyone else, then it follows that the non-interference you enjoy in the actual world, you enjoy with a certain resilience or security. In the scenario just envisaged, the non-interference you enjoy is non-secure, precisely because there are powerful individuals about who can interfere with you: if they do not interfere, that is because they happen to like you, or you happen to be able to avoid them or placate them. But the most crucial difference between enjoying non-domination and enjoying mere non-interference is precisely that no individuals have this sort of power over you. Were other individuals to take against you—were you to become less likeable, less cunning, or whatever—still that would make no difference to the non-interference you enjoy; you would be protected against any interference that they might come to contemplate.

When you are not dominated, then, you enjoy the absence of interference by arbitrary powers, not just in the actual world, but in the range of possible worlds where contingencies of the kind mentioned have a different, less auspicious setting. Those who are attached to the ideal of non-interference value the fact of having choice—the fact of non-interference—whether the choice is dominated or not; those who embrace the ideal of non-domination value the fact of having undominated choice, but not necessarily the fact of having choice as such. They do not mind the lack of choice that results from non-arbitrary interference and they may despise the sort of choice that you enjoy by grace of your own cunning or charms or ingratiation, seeing it as a demeaning and despicable bequest. The first group focus on the quantity of choice available, no matter what kind of choice is involved; the second are interested only in choice of the right, undominated quality.

So much for my argument that the dichotomy between the ideals of non-interference and self-mastery leaves space, and indeed saliently leaves space, for a third possibility: the ideal of non-domination. But one further question. Is it plausible to think of this as an ideal of freedom or liberty: as an ideal, specifically, of political and social liberty? In particular, is this plausible for someone who is prepared to describe the conditions of non-inteference and self-mastery as ideals of freedom?

The plausibility of describing non-domination as an ideal of liberty appears in the fact that, as there are structural commonalities in the rival conceptions of free will (O'Leary-Hawthorne and Pettit 1996), so there is a structure in common to the conception of political liberty as non-domination and the negative conception of political liberty (see MacCallum 1967). When a person is free in the sense of negative liberty they are exempt from interference in the things they do—exempt from intentional coercion or obstruction—where exemption means that they enjoy the absence of such interference. When a person enjoys non-domination, they are exempt from arbitrary interference in the things they do, where exemption now means that others are unable to interfere with them in that way. The constraint from which exemption is given is not interference of any sort, just arbitrary interference. And the exemption given involves not just the absence of the interference but the incapacity of others to practise it: if you like, the resilient absence of the interference.

Do these variations on the condition of non-interference give us an alternative that it is also plausible to describe as an ideal of liberty? Is it plausible to say that there is a way of speaking of political and social freedom such that non-domination is both necessary and sufficient for freedom in that sense? The necessity claim is that if a person is dominated in certain activities, if he or she performs those activities in a position where there are others who can interfere at their pleasure, then there is a sense in which that person is not free. This can hardly be denied, especially by somone who thinks that it is also plausible to describe self-mastery as an ideal of freedom. It is similar to the claim that in order for someone to be free in doing something, they must be master of themselves; it requires, more weakly, that at least they must not be subject to anyone else's mastery.

The sufficiency claim is that if a person is not dominated in certain activities—if they are not subject to arbitrary interference—then however much non-arbitrary interference or however much non-intentional obstruction they suffer, there is a sense in which they retain their freedom. This can hardly be denied, especially by somone who thinks that it is also plausible to describe non-interference as an ideal of freedom. For it is only slightly stronger than the claim that in order for someone to be free in doing something it is sufficient that others do not intentionally get in their way: that it does not matter if they are subject to serious non-intentional obstacles, deriving from their own incapacities or the recalcitrance of the natural world. If non-intentional obstruction can be overlooked in one ideal of freedom, then why not allow that another ideal may overlook the sort of interference—the sort of intentional obstruction or coercion—that is non-arbitrary, being required to track the agent's interests and ideas? Such non-arbitrary interference, after all, is saliently different from the interference that someone can perpetrate at their own pleasure.[1]

---

[1] When someone is subject to natural or non-intentional obstacles, they may be described under the conception of freedom as non-interference as not free—if you like, as non-free—to do the things that are blocked, even though they are not strictly unfree to do them: they do not suffer interference (Pettit 1989*b*). And when someone is subject either to such obstacles or to corresponding forms of non-abitrary interference, then under the conception of freedom as non-domination, as we shall notice in the next chapter, they can also be said to be non-free—non-free but not unfree—in regard to the options in question.

I conclude that not only is there a third alternative that is intermediate between the ideals of non-interference and self-mastery. It is also perfectly plausible to think of this alternative condition, like the others, as an ideal of political and social freedom. With these points established, it is now time to return to the republican tradition, and to see why that tradition should be associated with this third conception of liberty and not with either of the other two.

III. The republican conception of liberty is not a positive one

The standard way of reading the republican tradition, in conformity to the Berlin–Constant framework, is as a tradition that prizes positive liberty above all else, in particular the liberty of democratic participation. But while the republican tradition places a recurrent, if not unfailing, emphasis on the importance of democratic participation, the primary focus is clearly on avoiding the evils associated with interference. This is a theme that has been developed recently in the work of Quentin Skinner and some other historians of thought.[2] We need to look into it before going on to raise the question of whether the stress on the evils of interference went with a belief in freedom as non-interference or, as I believe, with a belief in freedom as non-domination.

The emphasis on the evils of interference was there already in the originating, Roman conception of *libertas*. A number of writers make the point (Wirszubski 1968; Nippel 1994) but perhaps Hanna Pitkin (1988: 534–5) is the most emphatic. 'The Roman plebs struggled not for democracy but for protection, not for public power but for private security. Of course they sought public, institutionalised guarantees of that security. But *libertas* . . . was "passive", "defensive", "predominantly negative".' This refrain appears in the fact that while *libertas*, or freedom, was equivalent by all account to *civitas*, or citizenship (Wirszubski 1968: 3; Crawford 1993: 1), the Romans found no

[2] The point was first defended at any length by Skinner (1983; 1984), when he insisted that republicans like Machiavelli did not have a positive conception of liberty but rather one of a distinctively negative stamp (see too Spitz 1995*b*: ch. 4; Patten 1996). But for Skinner's work I would never have thought to look to the republican tradition for the third conception of liberty. My argument that republicans were concerned with non-domination fits well with the spirit of that work, even if he expresses his view of Machiavelli and other republicans by saying that they were concerned with liberty as non-inteference under distinctive assumptions about what that cause required. I am indebted to Skinner for drawing my attention to the writings of Price and Priestley on which I rely heavily in developing my argument; indeed, he also directed me to Paley's writing about liberty which figures importantly later in the chapter.

difficulty in acknowledging that people in distant colonies could be citizens, and could enjoy the freedom of citizens, without being able to vote: these were known as *cives sine suffragio*, citizens without the vote (Crawford 1993: 110).

The focus on the evil of interference remains in place in the work of Machiavelli, the principal architect of republican thought in the early modern world (Colish 1971: 349). The point has been argued trenchantly by Skinner (1983; 1984) and supported by other recent scholars (Guarini 1990). As the Roman plebs, according to Pitkin, sought protection or private security, so in general, Machiavelli says, people's eagerness for freedom comes of a desire, not to rule, but rather not to be ruled (Machiavelli 1965: 204). 'A small part of them wishes to be free in order to rule; but all the others, who are countless, wish freedom in order to live in security. For in all republics, in whatever way organised, positions of authority cannot be reached by even forty or fifty citizens' (Machiavelli 1965: 237).[3]

What is the benefit to a person of living freely, living in security? Machiavelli (1965: 236) answers: 'the power of enjoying freely his possessions without any anxiety, of feeling no fear for the honor of his women and his children, of not being afraid for himself'. This benefit may be best secured for Machiavelli under democratic conditions (1965: 315) but he is clear that it may also be attained in monarchies, as when he invites the contemporary prince to survey the times when things went well in post-republican Rome.

In those governed by good emperors, he will see a prince secure in the midst of his secure citizens, the world full of peace and justice; he will see the Senate with its authority, the magistrates with their honors, the rich citizens enjoying their riches, nobility and virtue exalted; he will see the utmost tranquillity and the utmost good, and on the other side all hatred, all license, corruption, and ambition wiped out; he will see golden days, in which every man can hold and defend what opinion he wishes. (Machiavelli 1965: 222; see too Colish 1971.)

This focus on avoiding interference rather than on achieving participation remains in place in the later republican tradition which Machiavelli did so much to shape. While James Harrington follows Machiavelli in regarding democratic controls as important for liberty, he clearly sees people's liberty as consisting in something distinct from participation in government. When freemen or citizens 'attain unto

[3] Pasquale Pasquino argues in a forthcoming work that Machiavelli has two conceptions of freedom, one for the powerful and one for the ordinary people. If he is right, then we should think of Machiavelli as embracing the non-positive notion of liberty only as an ideal for ordinary people. I am grateful to Pasquino for pointing out this possibility, and for drawing my attention to the work by F. W. Maitland that is mentioned later in this section.

liberty', he says, what they achieve is 'to live of themselves' (1992: 75; see too Maitland 1981: 109–10; Nippel 1994: 21). Sometimes Harrington actively downplays popular democracy. 'The spirit of the people is no wise to be trusted with their liberty, but by stated laws or orders; so the trust is not in the spirit of the people, but in the frame of those orders' (Pocock 1977: 737). The distrust evinced in this remark is echoed in contemporary republicans such as John Milton, who actively shuns 'the noise and shouting of a rude multitude' (Worden 1991: 457) and, a little later, Algernon Sydney (1990: 189) who says of 'pure democracy': 'I know of no such thing; and if it be in the world, have nothing to say for it.'

The emphasis on the importance of avoiding interference and attaining personal independence recurs in the writings of the commonwealthmen that Harrington influenced, including those who inspired and championed the American Revolution. A good expression of the emphasis is in *Cato's Letters*.

True and impartial Liberty is therefore the Right of every Man to pursue the natural, reasonable, and religious Dictates of his own Mind; to think what he will, and act as he thinks, provided he acts not to the Prejudice of another; to spend his own Money himself, and lay out the Produce of his Labour his own Way; and to labour for his own Pleasure and Profit.' (Trenchard and Gordon 1971: ii. 248)

In the later commonwealthman tradition, there is a growing stress on the importance of democratic decision-making: quite rightly, as I shall argue in the second part of the book. A Whig defender of the American cause, Richard Price (1991: 25), argued that, if those in government 'are subject to no control from their constituents, the very idea of liberty will be lost and the power of choosing representatives becomes nothing but a power, lodged in a few, to choose at certain periods a body of masters for themselves and for the rest of the community'. But neither Price nor anyone in this camp defined liberty by participatory access to democratic controls. It is true that Joseph Priestley, a close friend of Price's , described the democratic power of voting as political liberty; but he distinguished between political and civil liberty and argued, like Price, that such a power was a means, and not necessarily an indispensable means, to civil liberty: 'the more political liberty a people have, the safer is their civil liberty' (Priestley 1993: 33; cf. 141).

As it was for Priestley and Price, so it was for others. 'Republican government', Tom Paine (1989: 168) wrote in 1792 , 'is no other than government established and conducted for the interest of the public, as well individually as collectively. It is not necessarily connected with any particular form, but it most naturally associates with the representative form, as being best calculated to secure the end for which a nation is at the expense of supporting it.' The authors of the *Federalist Papers* built representative democracy into the definition of a republic (Madison *et al.* 1987: 126). But they too insisted that democratic representation was only one of a number of ways of furthering 'civil liberty'; like the separation of powers they placed it in the catalogue of 'powerful means by which the excellencies of republican government may be retained and its imperfections lessened or avoided' (Madison *et al.* 1987: 119).

The important point to notice, then, is that the writers at whom we have been looking, the writers who identify with the broad republican tradition of thinking, take liberty to be defined by a status in which the evils associated with interference are avoided rather than by access to the instruments of democratic control, participatory or representative. Democratic control is certainly important in the tradition, but its importance comes, not from any definitional connection with liberty, but from the fact that it is a means of furthering liberty.

One qualification. While it is true that republican thinkers in general regarded democratic participation or representation as a safeguard of liberty, not as its defining core, the growing emphasis on democracy did lead some individuals away from traditional alignments and towards the full populist position of holding that liberty consists in nothing more or less than democratic self-rule. However republican and attractive his views in other respects (Spitz 1995*a*), Rousseau is probably responsible for having given currency to such a populist view. The populist twist was a new development, and attained its full form only when the ideal of democratic self-rule came to be held up as the main alternative, or at least the main alternative among notions of liberty, to the negative ideal of non-interference. To think of the republican tradition as populist, as of course many have done, would be to sustain the very dichotomy that has rendered the republican ideal invisible.

In an early work, unpublished during his lifetime, the great historian F. W. Maitland told a story of the rise of the democratic emphasis which reinforces this claim nicely. He argued that the rising commitment to democracy from the seventeenth century on—the conventional theory of government, as he described it—was motivated by a concern to remove arbitrary power from the state, but that it tended to lead, ultimately, to an affirmation of majoritarian democracy which was inconsistent with such a concern.

If the conventional theory leads to an ideally perfect democracy—a state in which all that the majority wishes to be law, and nothing else, is law—then it leads to a form of government under which the arbitrary exercise of power is most certainly possible. Thus, as it progresses, the conventional theory seems to lose its title to be called the doctrine of civil liberty, for it ceases to be a protest against arbitrary forms of restraint. (Maitland 1981: 84).

IV. The republican conception of freedom as non-domination: the liberty-versus-slavery theme

So much by way of arguing that the main figures in the republican tradition were not concerned primarily with liberty in the positive sense of democratic participation but rather with liberty in a sense opposed to interference. We come now, however, to the crucial question. Did the republican emphasis on the importance of avoiding interference come of a belief in freedom as non-interference or of a belief in freedom as non-domination? I shall argue that it came of a belief in freedom as non-domination.

There are two grounds for thinking that the conception of liberty as non-domination is the view of liberty that we find in the republican tradition. The first is that in the republican tradition, by contrast with the modernist approach, liberty is always cast in terms of the opposition between *liber* and *servus*, citizen and slave. The condition of liberty is explicated as the status of someone who, unlike the slave, is not subject to the arbitrary power of another: that is, someone who is not dominated by anyone else. Thus, the condition of liberty is explicated in such a way that there may be a loss of liberty without any actual interference: there may be enslavement and domination without interference, as in the scenario of the non-interfering master.

In the present section I explore this ground for thinking that the conception of liberty as non-domination is the republican view. I turn to the second ground in the next section. The second ground is that liberty is explicated within the republican tradition in such a way that not only can liberty be lost without actual interference; equally, interference may occur, under the scenario of the non-mastering interferer, without people being rendered thereby unfree. The non-mastering interferer envisaged by republicans, as we shall see, was the law and government that obtains in a well-ordered republic.

The republican tradition is unanimous in casting freedom as the opposite of slavery, and in seeing exposure to the arbitrary will of another, or living at the mercy of another, as the great evil. The contrary of the *liber* or free person in Roman, republican usage was the *servus* or slave. Whereas the slave lived at the beck and call of a master, the free person enjoyed a status at the other extreme. The free person was more than a *servus sine domino*, a slave without a master, who might be picked upon by anyone; the *liber* was, of necessity, a *civis* or citizen, with all that that implied in the way of protection against interference (Wirszubski 1968). This opposition between slavery or servitude on the one hand and freedom on the other is probably the single most characteristic feature of the long rhetoric of liberty to which the experience of the Roman republic gave rise (Patterson 1991). It is significant, because slavery is essentially characterized by domination, not by actual interference: even if the slave's master proves to be entirely benign and permissive, he or she continues to dominate the slave. Contrasting liberty with slavery is a sure sign of taking liberty to consist in non-domination rather than in non-interference.

Machiavelli is one of those who gives pride of place to the liberty–servitude opposition, identifying subjection to tyranny and colonization as forms of slavery (Colish 1971: 333). We find him contrasting those cities that live in freedom, for example, and those that live in slavery. All cities and provinces that live in freedom anywhere in the world, he says, make very great gains.

They do so because their populations are larger, since marriages are freer and more attractive to men, and each man gladly begets those children he thinks he can bring up, without fear that his patrimony will be taken from him; he knows not merely that they are born free and not slaves but that by means of their abilities they can become prominent men . . . The opposite of all these things happens in those countries that live as slaves. (Machiavelli 1965: 33)

But it is in the English and American developments of the republican heritage that the polarized language of freedom and servitude, freeman and slave, really comes into its own. James Harrington (1992: 269) marks the contrast in the context of stressing the need for a person to have material resources if they are to be free: 'The man that cannot live upon his own must be a servant; but he that can live upon his own may be a freeman.' For Harrington, the ultimate in unfreedom is having to live at the will of another—the arbitrary will of another—in the manner of the slave; the essence of freedom is not to have to endure such dependence and vulnerability. He uses this language to mark the contrast between someone who lives in Turkey, subject to arbitrary rule, for example, and the citizen of republican Lucca: 'the greatest bashaw is a tenant, as well of his head as of his estate, at the will of his lord, the meanest Lucchese that hath land is a freeholder of both' (Harrington 1992: 20). The crucial phrase here is 'at the will of his lord': no matter how permissive the lord is, the fact of depending on his grace and favour, the fact of living under his domination, entails an absence of freedom.

The commonwealthman tradition that Harrington influenced gave a large role to the freedom–slavery opposition. Thus, Algernon Sydney (1990: 17), could write in the 1680s: 'liberty solely consists in an independency upon the will of another, and by the name of slave we understand a man, who can neither dispose of his person nor goods, but enjoys all at the will of his master.' And in the following century, the authors of *Cato's Letters* could give a characteristically forceful statement to the theme.

Liberty is, to live upon one's own Terms; Slavery is, to live at the mere Mercy of another; and a Life of Slavery is, to those who can bear it, a continual State of Uncertainty and Wretchedness, often an Apprehension of Violence, often the lingering Dread of a violent Death. (Trenchard and Gordon, 1971: ii. 249–50)

This theme was repeated, not just by others in this Whig tradition, but even in the work of Tories like Lord Bolingbroke. Whether for sincere or strategic reasons, he invoked most of the Whig themes in criticism of the Whig government of Sir Robert Walpole (Skinner 1974; Pagden 1987). Prominent among those themes was the insistence that the history of liberty is the history of enslavement and emancipation. As Quentin Skinner (1974: 117) writes in exposition of Bolingbroke: 'to study the cause of liberty and its loss is inevitably to study the history of the various European countries which have passed from a state of popular freedom into the slavery of absolutism.'

Most commonwealthmen in the early eighteenth century used the rhetoric of liberty and servitude in celebrating emancipation from Stuart absolutism and in criticizing the domestic machinations of government. It did not matter to the commonwealthman that the government he attacked was Whig; power was always dangerous and power always needed to be watched (Robbins 1959: 120). But as the eighteenth century developed, a new cause of commonwealthman concern came into view: the cause of the American colonies, and in particular their claims against taxation by a government over which they had no control. Here, clearly, were people who lived at the mercy of an alien and potentially arbitrary will: the will of the British Parliament. Here, as the votaries of the tradition saw it, were a people in the chains of slavery, a people unfree.

One of the more moderate spokesmen for this point of view was Joseph Priestley. Here is his statement in 1769 of the American complaint against new proposals for certain duties.

Q. What is the great grievance that those people complain of? A. It is their being taxed by the parliament of Great Britain, the members of which are so far from taxing themselves, that they ease themselves at the same time. If this measure takes place, the colonists will be reduced to a state of as complete servitude, as any people of which there is an account in history. For by the same power, by which the people of England can compel them to pay *one penny*, they may compel them to pay the *last penny* they have. There will be nothing but arbitrary imposition on the one side, and humble petition on the other. (Priestley 1993: 140)

If Priestley's statement seems extreme, it pales beside the writings of Richard Price, and beside the comments on the American side of the Atlantic. Price (1991: 85) saw the situation of the Americans in the most lurid of colours, contrasting it with that of free citizens who are subject to no arbitrary controls. 'Like cattle inured to the yoke, they are driven on in one track, afraid of speaking or even thinking on the most interesting points, looking up continually to a poor creature who is their master, their powers fettered, and some of the noblest springs of action in human nature rendered useless within them.'

What Priestley and Price were writing in England was complemented in full, and in the full-dress imagery of freedom versus slavery, in America (Bailyn 1965; Reid 1988). One passage must suffice to illustrate the theme; it is an instruction voted by the town of Boston in May 1772.

An exterior Power claims a Right to govern us, and have for a number of Years been levying an illegal tax on us; whereby we are degraded from the rank of Free Subjects to the despicable Condition of Slaves. For its evident to the meanest Understanding that Great Britain can have no Right to take our Moneys from us without our consents unless we are her Slaves. (quoted Reid 1988: 92)

This discussion of the liberty–servitude theme in the republican tradition should serve to support the claim that freedom is conceived of there as non-domination, not as non-interference. For it is a commonplace of the tradition that masters may be kindly and may not actually interfere with their slaves. Algernon Sydney (1990: 441) could write, for example, in the late 1600s that 'he is a slave who serves the best and gentlest man in the world, as well as he who serves the worst'. And Richard Price (1991: 77–8) could add in the century following: 'Individuals in private life, while held under the power of masters, cannot be denominated free, however equitably and kindly they may be treated.' But if even the slave of a kindly master—the slave who suffers no interference—is unfree, then freedom must require the absence of domination, not just the absence of interference.

This line of thought is more or less explicit in the complaint that Priestley brings on behalf of the American colonists. It is a proof of the unfreedom of the Americans, as he puts it, that the Parliament of Great Britain could arbitrarily tax them for their last penny, even though it now only taxes them for one penny and even though, he might have added, it is unlikely ever to try and tax them for their last penny. The mere fact of being exposed to such a capacity on the part of others, the mere fact of being dominated in that way, meant for Priestley that the Americans were unfree (see too Paine 1989: 24–5).

V. The republican conception of freedom as non-domination: the law-and-liberty theme

I have been arguing that under the republican conception of liberty, in particular under the republican way of contrasting liberty with slavery, it is possible for liberty to be lost without actual interference. This is a first ground for thinking that the conception casts liberty as non-domination, not as non-interference. We turn now to the second ground for holding by that view. This is that under the republican conception of liberty it is equally true that interference can occur without any loss of liberty. In particular, interference occurs without any loss of liberty when the interference is not arbitrary and does not represent a form of domination: when it is controlled by the interests and opinions of those affected, being required to serve those interests in a way that conforms with those opinions.

Where the domination-without-interference theme is associated with the republican belief in the domination exercised by the non-interfering master, the interference-without-domination motif comes out in the republican emphasis on the fact that while the properly constituted law—the law that answers systematically to people's general interests and ideas—represents a form of interference, it does not compromise people's liberty; it constitutes a non-mastering interferer. Republicans do not say, in the modernist manner, that while the law coerces people and thereby reduces their liberty, it compensates for the damage done by preventing more interference than it represents. They hold that the properly constituted law is constitutive of liberty in a way that undermines any such talk of compensation: any such talk of taking one step backwards in order to take two forward. According to the earliest republican doctrine, the laws of a suitable state, in particular the laws of a republic, create the freedom enjoyed by citizens; they do not offend against that freedom, even in a measure for which they later compensate.

The line taken by republicans comes out in their conception of freedom as citizenship or *civitas*. Citizenship is a status that exists, of necessity, only under a suitable regime of law: as one commentator on the republican tradition says, 'the main feature of the *civitas* is the rule of law' (Viroli 1990: 149). But citizenship and freedom are represented as equivalent to one another by all republicans, under the established Roman precedent: 'at Rome and with regard to Romans full *libertas* is coterminous with *civitas*' (Wirszubski 1968: 3; see too Crawford 1993: 1). And so freedom is seen in the republican tradition as a status that exists only under a suitable legal regime. As the laws create the authority that rulers enjoy, so the laws create the freedom that citizens share.

The laws only do this, of course, so long as they respect people's common interests and ideas and conform to the image of an ideal law: so long as they are not the instruments of any one individual's, or any one group's, arbitrary will. When the laws become the instruments of will, according to the tradition, then we have a regime—say, the despotic regime of the absolute king—in which the citizens become slaves and are entirely deprived of their freedom. Each of them lives, in Harrington's phrase, 'at the will of his lord'; each of them is wholly dominated by the unconstrained power of the individual or group in command.

The republican view that the laws create people's freedom makes sense if freedom consists in non-domination. Good laws may relieve people from domination—may protect them against the resources or *dominium* of those who would otherwise have arbitrary power over them—without themselves introducing any new dominating force: without introducing the domination that can go with governmental *imperium*. The political authorities recognized by the laws represent potential dominators, but the recurrent republican idea is that these will themselves be suitably constrained—they will have no arbitrary power over others—under a proper constitution: say, where suitable mechanisms of representation, rotation of office, separation of powers, and the like are in place (Oldfield 1990). While the law necessarily involves interference—while law is essentially coercive—the interference in question is not going to be arbitrary; the legal authorities will be entitled and enabled to interfere only when pursuing the common interests of citizens and only when pursuing these in a manner that conforms to the opinions received among the citizenry.

It is not only the republican equation of freedom with citizenship—and the view, therefore, that the laws help to create freedom—that makes good sense if freedom is non-domination. So does the associated republican claim that the conditions under which a citizen is free are one and the same as the conditions under which the city or state is free (cf. Harrington 1992: 8). Suppose the laws and customs suffice to constrain those within and without a society who would wield arbitrary power over others; and suppose that they do not introduce arbitrary powers in their own right. We may say that those who live under that dispensation are free. Or we may say, with equal justice, that the dispensation represents a free polity, a free mode of organization and government. It is perfectly intelligible why the concern of republicans should as often focus on how to achieve the free body politic as on how to achieve freedom for individuals.

The republican view that law is or can be creative of liberty was forcefully challenged in the seventeenth century by Thomas Hobbes. While he belonged to an absolutist tradition that had been developing for some time, Hobbes found a way of countering republican ideas that was quite original and, in the long run, influential (Tuck 1993).

Hobbes begins by presenting freedom, not as non-domination, but rather as non-interference. 'A Free-Man', he wrote in *Leviathan*, 'is he, that in those things, which by his strength and wit he is able to do, is not hindered to doe what he has a will to' (Hobbes 1968: 262). People are hindered and rendered strictly unfree for Hobbes only so far as they are physically coerced. But he allows that there is also a sense in which people are rendered unfree by bonds that coerce by threat, not by physical means: these are 'made to hold, by the danger, though not by the difficulty of breaking them' (Hobbes 1968: 264). The upshot, then, is that liberty consists in the absence of coercion: liberty proper in the absence of physical coercion, liberty in the broader sense—the liberty of subjects, as he calls it—in the absence of coercion by threat (on Hobbes on liberty, see Skinner 1990*a*).

This way of conceiving of liberty—and it was a great novelty in its time—led Hobbes to argue that law is always itself an invasion of people's liberty, however benign in the long term. He observes that freedom in the sense of non-coercion—freedom, as he sees it, in the relevant sense—is always invaded by the coercive laws imposed by a state, whatever the nature of that state. The upshot is that people only have freedom in the silence of the laws; they have freedom only where law does not intrude. 'The Liberty of a Subject, lyeth therefore only in those things, which in regulating their actions, the Sovereign hath pretermitted' (Hobbes 1968: 264).

This observation enabled Hobbes to ridicule the republican idea that there is some special sense in which the citizen of a republic is free and the subject of a despotic regime is not, or indeed a special sense in which the republic is a free body politic, the despotism an unfree one. In each of these two sorts of state, the subject has freedom in the same sense: in the sense of not being entirely coerced by the law. And each of these two sorts of state is itself free only in a shared sense: in the sense of being free to resist or invade other states. Hobbes makes the points in setting up a contrast between republican Lucca and despotic Constantinople.

There is written on the Turrets of the city of Luca in great characters at this day, the word LIBERTAS; yet no man can thence inferre, that a particular man has more Libertie, or Immunitie from the service of the Commonwealth there, than in Constantinople. Whether a Commonwealth be Monarchical, or Popular, the Freedome is still the same. (Hobbes 1968: 266)

Hobbes issued a powerful challenge to the republican tradition of thinking in setting out this understanding of freedom, and this implication for the relation between law and liberty. His own ultimate end was the defence of authoritarian government, and it served his purposes well to be able to argue that no set of laws was particularly associated with liberty; it meant that the laws of an authoritarian Leviathan could not be faulted on traditional republican grounds and that his case for such a state could be given a decent hearing: it would not be laughed out of court. Hobbes was widely read over the following century or so, but it is striking that most of his readers stuck with the republican way of thinking. The most outstanding exception is another authoritarian thinker, though one of a different stripe from Hobbes. Sir Robert Filmer held that perfect liberty would require the absence of laws, 'for it is no law except it restrain liberty' (Filmer 1991: 268). 'But such liberty', he then argued, 'is not to be found in any commonweal, for there are more laws in popular estates than anywhere else, and so consequently less liberty' (p. 275).

The challenge thrown out by Hobbes was taken up with confidence and gusto on the republican side, both by Harrington and by others (Gwyn 1965: 12). Harrington addressed it a few years after the publication of *Leviathan* in his *Oceana*. Having quoted the passage about Lucca and Constantinople, he goes on to ridicule what he took to be Hobbes's argument:

The mountain hath brought forth and we have a little equivocation! For to say that a Lucchese hath no more liberty or immunity *from* the laws of Lucca than a Turk hath from those of Constantinople, and to say that a Lucchese hath no more liberty *by* the laws of Lucca than a Turk hath by those of Constantinople, are pretty different speeches. (Harrington 1992: 20)

For Harrington, liberty in the proper sense is liberty *by* the laws—this is liberty in the sense of citizenship—whereas liberty *from* the laws is something of little significance. We can speak of liberty from the laws with any government whatsoever, he says, but we can speak of liberty by the laws only with some states: only, in effect, with republics and their like. He underlines his message with a contrast to which we have already drawn attention: 'it is known that whereas the greatest bashaw is a tenant, as well of his head as of his estate, at the will of his lord, the meanest Lucchese that hath land is a freeholder of both, and not to be controlled but by the law.' The idea is that in Lucca the law makes a citizen free, by ensuring that no one has arbitrary power over them; and this in stark contrast to what happens with the subject, even the bashaw, in Constantinople.

But what if the law of Lucca itself represents the imposition of arbitrary will? Harrington supposes, in the favoured, republican phrase, that the law of Lucca is an 'empire of laws, and not of men' (Harrington 1992: 8). More specifically, as he goes on to stipulate, it is a law 'framed by every private man unto no other end (or they may thank themselves) than to protect the liberty of every private man, which by that means comes to be the liberty of the commonwealth'. Harrington does two things in this added stipulation. First, he makes clear that if there is freedom by the laws in Lucca, then that is because the laws are framed by individuals for the protection or liberty of individuals: this, or they only have themselves to blame; this, in his own words, or they may thank themselves. And second, he makes clear that when we speak of the freedom of the commonwealth of Lucca, we do not mean, *pace* Hobbes, that the commonwealth is free to resist or defend other states, but that it is a state where the laws are fitted to create freedom for their citizens.

The Whig or commonwealthman tradition, and the tradition that led ultimately to the American Revolution, came down decisively on the side of Harrington in this exchange with Hobbes. In that tradition, as we have seen, it is domination or slavery, not just any sort of coercion, that is presented as the opposite of liberty. And in that tradition, as a consequence, there is little or no suggestion that law necessarily reduces the liberty of those who live under it; on the contrary, the right sort of law is seen as the source of liberty.[4]

[4] One apparent (and perhaps only occasional) dissident is Algernon Sydney. He sees liberty in the republican vein as 'an independency upon the will of another' (1990: 17) but he

John Locke is a good representative of the commonwealth tradition, though the originality of his rational, contractarian perspective gives him a special status (Robbins 1959: 58–67; Tully 1993). And Locke is clearly on Harrington's side in the debate about law and liberty. He argues for a 'freedom from Absolute, Arbitrary Power' as the essential thing, and the thing that marks the contrast with slavery (Locke 1965: 325). And in explicit opposition to Filmer, he sees law as creative of freedom: 'that ill deserves the Name of Confinement which serves to hedge us in only from Bogs and Precipices . . . the end of Law is not to abolish or restrain, but to preserve and enlarge Freedom' (Locke 1965: 348).[5]

Richard Price (1991: 27) is particularly forthright on the theme of law—or, more generally, government—and freedom. 'It is the end of all just government, at the same time that it secures the liberty of the public against foreign injury, to secure the liberty of the individual against private injury. I do not, therefore, think it strictly just to say that it belongs to the nature of government to entrench on private liberty.' And again: 'Just government, therefore, does not infringe liberty, but establishes it. It does not take away the rights of mankind but protect[s] and confirm[s] them' (p. 81). Price explicitly connects this view on the relation between law and liberty with the view of liberty as non-domination. 'It is not . . . the mere possession of liberty that denominates a citizen or a community free, but that security for the possession of it which arises from such a free government as . . . takes place, when there exists no power that can take it away' (Price 1991: 82).

Price's views on liberty and law, or more generally liberty and authority, were commonplace in eighteenth-century England and America. The general opinion was that without law there was no liberty—no liberty in the proper, civil sense—and that the legal dispensation under the received constitution of England was especially well suited to the production of liberty. Caleb Evans (1775: 20) put the point nicely. 'Such is the excellent nature of the British constitution that the voice of its laws is the voice of liberty. The laws of England are the laws of liberty'. Evans's sentiment would have been second nature to anyone familiar, as many were, with Montesquieu's comments on

appears to think that social life invariably compromises the sort of independency available outside of society (p. 31): this, perhaps, because he is unusual among republicans in holding that all governments have an 'arbitrary power' (p. 570).

[5] While Locke shows signs of being moved by the republican consideration mentioned in the text, his view that law does not infringe liberty may also be influenced by the view (*a*) that being free is being subject to reason and (*b*) that the law ideally represents the rule of reason.

England, published in the 1740s: 'the one nation in the world whose constitution has political liberty for its direct purpose' (Montesquieu 1989: 156). Montesquieu was widely read in eighteenth century England and America, and he had deeply influenced the canonical commentary on the laws of England that Sir William Blackstone had published in the 1760s. Blackstone (1978: 126) himself wrote: 'laws, when prudently framed, are by no means subversive but rather introductive of liberty; for (as Mr Locke has well observed) where there is no law there is no freedom.'

VI. The rise of liberty as non-interference

So much for the argument that the republican tradition conceived of liberty as non-domination, not as non-interference. Proponents of the two conceptions of freedom will agree that people are unfree where there is interference and domination and they will agree, equally, that people are free where there is neither interference nor domination. The cases that distinguish them are those in which interference and domination diverge: first, the non-interfering master scenario, where there is no interference but there is domination; second, the scenario of the non-mastering interferer—the ideal law—where there is interference but no domination. What we have observed in the argument of the last two sections is that republicans view both scenarios in the way that fits with freedom as non-domination. The kindly master does deprive subjects of their freedom, dominating them without actually interfering. The well-ordered law does not deprive subjects of their freedom, interfering with those subjects but not dominating them.

We have seen that Hobbes was the first to identify freedom, not with non-domination, as in the republican tradition, but with non-interference: with the absence of physical coercion and coercion by threat. And we have seen that, by doing this, he was able to challenge the republican idea that liberty is the product of republican—or if not republican, certainly non-authoritarian—laws. But I have mentioned only one person who followed Hobbes in this line of thought: another authoritarian, Sir Robert Filmer. So when did the Hobbesian notion of liberty gain popular currency? When did freedom as non-interference displace the ideal of freedom as non-domination?

The notion of freedom as non-interference first became prominent, so I suggest, in the writings of a group of thinkers who had an interest, like Hobbes and Filmer, in arguing that all law is an imposition and that there is nothing sacred from the point of view of liberty about republican, or even non-authoritarian, government. The group I have in mind were all opposed to the cause of American independence and, in particular, to the republican rhetoric in which that cause was articulated.

Perhaps the best example of someone who took this line is John Lind, who worked in the mid-1770s as a pamphleteering defender of the Prime Minister, Lord North. Lind argued systematically against the cause of American independence in a number of publications, including an attack on the views of Richard Price, published anonymously as *Three Letters to Dr Price* (Lind 1776). Although he does not mention Hobbes, his starting point is the central Hobbesian assumption that liberty is 'nothing more or less than the absence of coercion' (p. 16), where coercion may be physical or moral: may involve physical restraint or constraint, or the restraint or constraint associated with 'the threat of some painful event' (p. 18). Lind is quite clear that understanding liberty in this fashion means replacing the liberty–slavery opposition that he finds in Price's work with a quite different contrast between liberty on the one hand and restraint or constraint—in a word, interference—on the other.

The Hobbesian conception of liberty leads Lind, as it led Hobbes, to maintain that all law infringes on people's liberty. 'All laws are coercive; the effect of them is either to restrain or to constrain; they either compel us to do or to forbear certain acts. The law which secures my property, is a restraint upon you; the law which secures your property, is a restraint upon me' (p. 24). The supreme power in a free country— the legislature—protects the liberty of each, according to Lind, but only so far as it restrains or constrains others; by such restraint or constraint it gives each liberty 'against all other subjects upon whom the law does operate' (p. 70).

Hobbes used his conception of liberty to argue that the subjects of his *Leviathan* are going to be no worse off in terms of liberty—he thought they would be much better off in other terms—than the citizens of republican regimes; people in each dispensation would have freedom in the one and only sense of being left some areas of discretion by the law. And now Lind uses the conception to argue, in similar vein, that British subjects in the American colonies are no less, and no more, free than their counterparts in Britain itself. There is nothing inherently opposed to freedom in a colonial system of law.

He maintains that, in the American case, 'We are not enquiring into the authority which one state may exercise over another state, but into the authority which one part of a community, called governors, may exercise over another part of that same community, called subjects'

(p. 112). And he then points out that, far from its being the case that Americans are in the position of slaves, subject in Price's words to 'a dreadful power' that they can in no way control, they are in exactly the same pass as people in Britain itself. 'Dreadful as this power may be, let me ask you, Sir, if this same power is not exercised by the same persons over all the subjects who reside in all the other parts of this same empire?—It is' (p. 114).

Consistently with not making slaves of the American colonists, of course, British rule might not have done very well by those colonists; it might not have produced much security or happiness, as Lind observes (p. 73). But on this front too he is sanguine. He insists that British rulers have interests in common with American subjects, and that 'the interest of the British subjects, residing in America, must be as dear to the members of the British parliament as the interests of the British subjects, residing in Britain' (p. 124).

Lind was not the only pamphleteer to argue in such terms against Richard Price and, more generally, against the cause of American independence (see Hey 1776). But where did the ideas originate, given the dominance of the commonwealthman tradition, and given the fact that Hobbes was not a favoured authority: that Harrington had triumphed decisively over him in that respect?

The problem of origin may not be as dramatic as we have made it seem. It was customary in the eighteenth century, even within the republican tradition, to distinguish proper, civil liberty from natural liberty: from the liberty that people would enjoy in the state of nature with which Hobbes and Locke had made people familiar (Blackstone 1978: 125–6). It would have been easy for most commonwealthmen to admit that law restrains and thereby reduces natural liberty, because natural liberty was not regarded as liberty proper; on the contrary, it was associated with something taken to be inimical to the realization of liberty proper: viz. licentiousness (Reid 1988: 34). The availability of the category of natural liberty, however, may have made things straightforward for those of a Hobbesian bent. It meant that they could argue their point of view by identifying liberty with natural liberty and by sidelining talk of civil liberty. Let liberty be associated with natural liberty and Lind's line of argument becomes readily available.

But whether or not this observation is correct, it is worth noting that Lind and others were directly influenced in their anti-American writing by exposure to someone who thought that he had made a great breakthrough in coming to see liberty as the absence of coercion. This is Jeremy Bentham, who was himself an opponent of the American, and later the French, Revolutions (Hart 1982: essay 3). Referring to 'a very worthy and ingenious friend' (p. 17), Lind acknowledged Bentham's influence on his conception of liberty, and did so as a result of a complaint from Bentham that he had failed to mention him in an earlier article of April 1776. Douglas Long (1977: 54) has drawn attention to a letter from Bentham to Lind in which he asks to be recognized as the author of that conception of liberty, on the grounds that the conception is 'the cornerstone of my system'.

It may have been half a year or a year or more, I do not precisely recollect the time, since I communicated to you a kind of discovery I had made, that the idea of liberty, imported nothing in it that was positive: that it was merely a negative one: and that accordingly I defined it 'the absence of restraint': I do not believe I then added 'and constraint': that has been an addition of your own.

The fact that Bentham could think his conception of liberty a kind of discovery, and the fact that the conception appeared at a time when it could serve an important ideological purpose—the critique of the cause of American independence—suggests strongly that we were right in saying that Hobbes's notion of freedom had little influence prior to the late eighteenth century: that up to then, the republican notion of freedom as non-domination reigned more or less unchallenged in the English-speaking world. It is as if the Hobbesian notion had been put on the shelf of historical curiosities, only to be reclaimed at a time when suddenly it promised to do important, ideological work: to help in silencing complaints of servitude and domination—complaints of unfreedom—from those in Britain's American colonies.[6]

---

[6] Hobbes's notion of freedom may have been influential outside the political domain, as it certainly was in the work of Abraham Tucker, for example. Writing in the 1760s on matters of philosophy and theology, Tucker resorted to a Hobbesian conception of liberty—though he does not mention Hobbes by name—in order to try to overcome the problem of how 'the dominion of Providence' can be consistent with human freedom. Since liberty consists in the absence of 'restraint or force', he argues, it is consistent with divine planning and foreknowledge; such divine intervention does not represent the sort of coercion that is inimical to freedom (Tucker 1834: 541 ff.). This argument is reminiscent of Hobbes himself, (1968: 263), when he urges that there is no problem with free or unimpeded action having been rendered necessary by its causal origin. Tucker's use of the Hobbesian notion of freedom may have influenced Bentham and Paley, who are discussed below; he was a proto-utilitarian, after all, and he is recognized as a forerunner, even an authority, by Paley (1825: pp. xv–xvi).

VII. The triumph of freedom as non-interference

If the story so far is correct, then liberty as non-interference first appeared in the writings of authoritarians like Hobbes and Filmer and then achieved a certain popularity in the tracts of Tories who were opposed to American independence. Hardly an auspicious debut. But if the notion had relatively sordid origins, it quickly attained a respectable status, not just among authoritarians and reactionaries, but also among those who saw themselves as advancing the cause of democracy and freedom.

One source of respectability, of course, would have been Bentham himself. For as Bentham became more reformist and more progressive in his thinking, as he came to shape radical English political thought and as he came to think more positively of American independence, he retained his conception of liberty as just the absence of coercion; he may even be the one who did most to establish it as the modernist notion. As Douglas Long (1977: 43) notes, 'Bentham was to argue that there was a sense in which a sovereign might enhance the value of subjects' liberties by his acts of regulation, but he was never to lose sight of the fact that every act of regulation emanating from a sovereign was destructive of liberty.' Bentham remained emphatic on the point. 'As against the coercion applicable by individual to individual, no liberty can be given to one man but in proportion as it is taken from another. All coercive laws, therefore . . . and in particular all laws creative of liberty, are "as far as they go" abrogative of liberty' (Bentham 1843: 503).

A second figure who would have been responsible for giving currency and respectability to the new notion of freedom as non-interference was William Paley, another utilitarian thinker who had great influence in the nineteenth century. Paley may have been the only writer in his time to recognize clearly the shift that was taking place, the shift indeed for which he argued, from the received notion of freedom as non-domination, freedom as security against interference on an arbitrary basis, to freedom as non-interference. He sets out his view with admirable clarity in *The Principles of Moral and Political Philosophy*, first published in 1785 (Paley 1825).

Paley recognizes in this work that the usual notion of civil liberty, the one that agrees with 'the usage of common discourse, as well as the example of many respectable writers' (p. 357), is that of freedom as non-domination. 'This idea places liberty in security; making it to consist not merely in an actual exemption from the constraint of useless and noxious laws and acts of dominion, but in being free from the *danger* of having such hereafter imposed or exercised' (p. 357; original emphasis). He says that writers who understand liberty as security in this way tend to focus on the question of how best to guarantee against the relevant danger and, in rehearsing the possible answers, he provides us with an overview of contemporary republican thinking (pp. 358–9; cf. Madison *et al.* 1987: 119).

Instead of this received notion of civil liberty Paley defends a view that is clearly in the Benthamite camp. Laws are a restraint of private will, he says, though some laws are better than others, doing more for the public happiness: 'the laws of a free people impose no restraints upon the private will of the subject, which do not conduce in a greater degree to the public happiness' (p. 355). Thus Paley holds out a picture of liberty—or at least 'personal liberty', as he likes to say—in which liberty requires nothing more or less than the absence of restraint, in particular intentional restraint. He acknowledges that law is needed for advancing such freedom overall, as it is required for furthering freedom as non-domination, but he makes quite clear that when law furthers liberty it does so despite itself taking liberty away. He argues: '1st, that restraint itself is an evil; 2ndly, that this evil ought to be over-balanced by some public advantage; 3rdly, that the proof of this advantage lies upon the legislature; 4thly, that a law being found to produce no sensible good effects, is a sufficient reason for repealing it' (p. 355).

What are Paley's grounds for defending the view that liberty—personal liberty at least—is opposed to restraint of any kind, and that law as such represents an invasion of such liberty? The question is worth asking, because his book was so widely read in the nineteenth century and because the considerations he raises were clearly influential with others as well.

One line of argument used by Paley is that those who take the alternative view, those who see liberty as security against arbitrary interference, are confusing means and end: 'they describe not so much liberty itself, as the safeguards and preservatives of liberty' (p. 359). This echoes a complaint of Bentham's in one of his manuscripts: 'That which under the name of Liberty is so much magnified, as the invaluable, the unrivalled work of Law, is not liberty, but security' (Long 1977: 74).[7]

---

[7] In the course of defending a view of liberalism under which it encompasses the commonwealth tradition—see the Introduction—Stephen Holmes (1995: 245) argues that the idea of physical and psychological security was important to liberals, and quotes Bentham (1871: 97) to the effect that liberty is 'a branch of security'. But the context from which Holmes quotes makes it quite clear that Bentham is not there defending the view of liberty as non-domination. 'By creating obligations,' Bentham (1871: 94) writes in that context, 'the law to the same extent trenches upon liberty' (p. 94). Some liberals, Bentham included, may have been concerned with security of non-interference in the probabilistic sense of

A second theme that is present in Paley's advocacy of liberty as non-interference is also prominent in Bentham's considerations (Long 1977: ch. 4), and indeed in Lind's (1776: 25). This is the suggestion that defining liberty as non-interference is scientifically more satisfying than representing it as non-domination; it corresponds to the requirements of 'just reasoning or correct knowledge' rather than those of 'panegyric and careless declamation' (Paley 1825: 359–60). The definition does away with hyperbolic talk of slavery, for example: it rejects 'those popular phrases which speak of a free people; of a nation of slaves; which call one Revolution the era of liberty, or another the loss of it; with many expressions of a like absolute form' (p. 356). The new definition gives us an ideal which, unlike the established conception, is not always either fully present or completely absent but can be realized in degrees (p. 356). Lind's (1776: 25) ironic invective against Price's talk of slavery suggests a similar point. 'Things must be always at the maximum or minimum; there are no intermediate gradations: what is not white must be black; all must be absorbed, or all must be equally reflected' (see too Hume 1994: essay 11).

But the third complaint that Paley makes against the notion of liberty as non-domination is perhaps the most interesting from our point of view. He argues that the ideal in question is excessively demanding on government and does not represent a sensible goal to assign to the state:

those definitions of liberty ought to be rejected, which, by making that essential to civil freedom which is unattainable in experience, inflame expectations that can never be gratified, and disturb the public content with complaints, which no wisdom or benevolence of government can remove. (p. 359)

It is difficult to know exactly what Paley had in mind in putting freedom as non-domination in the 'too hard' basket. But the claim that the ideal is excessively demanding fits well with the line—the neo-republican line—that I mean to argue in the remainder of this book. I agree with Paley that the republican ideal of freedom as non-domination is indeed a very dense and demanding goal around which to orientate our social and political institutions; it would support radical changes in traditional social life and it would legitimate recourse

wanting to increase expected non-interference rather than in the modal sense discussed here: in the sense of wanting to increase people's immunity against (arbitrary) interference, even against the sort of (arbitrary) interference that the potential interferer—the person who is not blocked from interfering—is unlikely to practise. They may have been concerned with security in the sense of wanting to reduce involuntary risk—see Mill (1977: 294–5) for example—but not in the sense of wanting to reduce exposure to the power of another. This issue will come up again later.

to the law—to a non-dominating law—in the cause of making those changes. But I disagree so far as I think that the state—the contemporary state, not the sort of state that existed in his time—is well up to the task of realizing such an ideal.

The density of the ideal of freedom as non-domination would not have been a problem for premodern republican thought, since it went without saying among premoderns that the state could aspire to realize the ideal only for a small élite of males: the property-holding, and indeed mainstream, males who made up the citizenry. Harrington (1992: 269) was quite clear on the point: 'The man that cannot live upon his own must be a servant; but he that can live upon his own may be a freeman.' But the density of the ideal of non-domination must have seemed to represent a problem, as it came to be a more and more general assumption in the eighteenth century—the century of Enlightenment—that human beings are equal and should be equally well served by their social and political institutions.

How could anyone expect the state to ensure that employees— servants, as they were—would enjoy a non-dominated status, when the prevailing notion of employment or service entailed a subjugation to the master's will? The prevailing notion is well caught in a remark of Sydney's (1990: 548–9) in which he reveals why a servant cannot hope to enjoy non-domination. 'He must serve me in my own way, or be gone if I think fit, tho he serve me never so well; and I do him no wrong in putting him away, if either I intend to keep no servant, or find that another will please me better' (Sydney 1990: 548–9)

How could anyone expect the state to ensure that women would enjoy such an non-dominated status when the received view was that women were subject to the will of their father or husband (Pateman 1988)? How, for example, to meet the problem that Mary Astell (Hill 1986: 76) raised for republicans in the seventeenth century?

If all Men are born Free, how is it that all Women are born Slaves? As they must be, if the being subjected to the inconstant, uncertain, unknown, arbitrary Will of Men, be the perfect condition of Slavery? And, if the Essence of Freedom consists, as our Masters say it does, in having a standing Rule to live by?[8]

John Lind unwittingly emphasizes these points when, in criticizing Richard Price's ideal of freedom as self-legislation—essentially, the ideal of not being subject to the arbitrary will or legislation of another—he argues that it would have absurd results for women and

---

[8] On the significance of the charge, from Astell's own point of view, see Springborg (1995). My thanks to Jan Crosthwaite for suggesting I look at Astell's work.

servants. Arguing that Price cannot mean women to be 'degraded to slaves', he draws what seems to him to be a *reductio* of Price's position: that women too must legislate for themselves: 'Every woman is her own legislatrix,' as he puts it in a mock slogan that is meant to mark the absurdity of the proposal (Lind 1776: 40). And in another context he points out that for Price, absurdly, servants must count as slaves: must count as subject to the domination of their masters and governors, and therefore unfree. 'According to your own principles, what are servants but slaves?' (Lind 1776: 156). What indeed?

For thinkers like Paley and Bentham it would have been axiomatic that all human beings are equal, even if in practice they did not draw the full implications of this equality. 'Everybody to count for one, nobody for more than one', in the slogan ascribed to Bentham by John Stuart Mill (1969: 257). Given such an assumption of equality, any ideal for government would have to present itself as a universal ideal, not just as an ideal for an élite citizenry. And the ideal of universal non-domination, the ideal of securing a non-dominated status for every adult, might well have seemed a fantasy to thinkers who took for granted the subordinate status of women and employees.

Perhaps this explains in some part why the ideal of non-domination lost its place in the work of Bentham and Paley and, later, in the work of those who would have claimed the new name of liberal. As these thinkers enlarged the compass of their concern to include more and more people as citizens, it must have seemed less and less realistic to stick with the rich old ideal of freedom as non-domination. Much better to thin out the ideal of freedom and to orientate the state by the light of the new, modernist ideal, or by the light of some other goal entirely. Even securing the greatest happiness of the greatest number—the goal shared by Bentham and Paley—would have looked much more tractable and attractive than securing freedom as non-domination; it was taken to require the reduction of many forms of interference—and, in those ways, the furthering of freedom as non-interference—but it would not necessarily have seemed to require that no one be subject to the arbitrary will of another.

We have been looking at how the modernist ideal of liberty as non-interference came to achieve a respectable status via the work of Jeremy Bentham and William Paley: how it came to transcend its origins in the ideologically driven attempt to mock American complaints of slavery and unfreedom. The considerations which weighed with Paley in embracing freedom as non-interference must have weighed also with others of his ilk in the years that followed. For there is no doubt but that this notion did rapidly take over among those who identified with the cause of liberty and described themselves as liberals.

Liberals are a broad church, as emphasized in the introduction, but most of them unite in endorsing the modernist conception of liberty. Right-of-centre liberals who worry only about the formal realization of liberty focus fairly explicitly on non-interference; certainly the majority of them do so. And those on the left—those who embrace a concern to make liberty effective or to realize equality or welfare as well as liberty—generally seem to have their eyes on non-interference too. John Rawls (1971: 302) manifests a concern for liberty as non-interference, for example, when he writes: 'liberty can be restricted only for the sake of liberty.' Rawls's assumption is that law always represents a restriction of liberty, and reveals a conception of liberty that is directly continuous with that of Hobbes and Bentham (Skinner 1983: 11–12; see too Feinberg 1972: 23–4 and Spitz 1994).[9]

Not only did the conception of freedom as non-interference displace the republican idea in the new liberal tradition. It apparently succeeded in staging this *coup d'état* without anyone's noticing the usurpation that had taken place. When Constant delivered his lecture on the liberty of the ancients and the liberty of the moderns, he saw only the alternatives of positive liberty, in particular the liberty of democratic participation, and negative liberty: liberty as non-interference. And when Berlin came to present his own retrospective musings on these matters, he could suggest that those not attached to positive liberty allied themselves invariably with the Hobbesian tradition. 'Law is always a "fetter",' he said in exposition of the approach, 'even if it protects you from being bound in chains that are heavier than those of the law, say arbitrary despotism and chaos' (Berlin 1958: 8). Liberty as non-domination—republican liberty—had not only been lost to political thinkers and activists; it had even become invisible to the historians of political thought.

---

[9] F. A. Hayek sometimes suggests that the interference of a certain sort of law—a law that has been produced by a certain process of evolution, or a law that is inherently justifiable in a certain way—does not remove liberty (see Gray 1986: 61; Kukathas 1989: 132). For Hayek, then, freedom will not be the absence of interference as such but rather the absence of interference by agencies other than those favoured laws. It will be close to the sort of liberty that is sometimes described in the French juridical tradition as public liberty: liberty, as that is assured under the law (Morange 1979). Rawls can sometimes be read as endorsing a similar view of law and liberty, in which case the comment in the text would have to be revised; but this is not the place to go into such issues of interpretation.

CHAPTER 2

Liberty as Non-domination

The last chapter gave us a historical introduction to a conception of liberty—a distinctively republican conception, as I believe—that fits on neither side of the now established negative–positive dichotomy. This conception is negative to the extent that it requires the absence of domination by others, not necessarily the presence of self-mastery, whatever that is thought to involve. The conception is positive to the extent that, at least in one respect, it needs something more than the absence of interference; it requires security against interference, in particular against interference on an arbitrary basis.

I believe that this republican conception of freedom, this conception of freedom as non-domination, is of the greatest interest in political theory, and that it is important to put it back on the table in current discussions. My aim in this book is to try to identify the main features of freedom as non-domination, to show what it would mean to take the ideal as a political cause, and to indicate the institutional impact of organizing things so that the ideal is advanced. The book is an exploration of what a neo-republican politics would involve.

This chapter takes a more philosophical line on the material that we covered in a historical way in the last. I want to look in some detail at what is involved in construing freedom or liberty as the absence of domination by another (see Pettit 1996a).[1] First, I discuss what domination, as I understand it, comes to. Next, I go on to look at what the absence of such domination—what freedom as non-domination—

---

[1] The argument in the chapter, and in the book as a whole, is a development from a series of other works: for example, Pettit (1989a; 1993a; 1993b; 1993c; 1994c; 1996a) and Braithwaite and Pettit (1990). But the argument has been transformed in the course of its development and there are even differences with Pettit (1996a): I here connect arbitrariness more directly with the failure to track people's interests according to their ideas, for example, and I hold out less hope for the strategy of reciprocal power. For an excellent, sympathetic reconstruction of the position presented in the earlier articles, see Spitz (1995a: ch. 5).

would require. And then in the third section I return to Paley's three objections to construing freedom in this way and show why we need not be disturbed by them.

I. Domination

A definition

One agent dominates another if and only if they have a certain power over that other, in particular a power of interference on an arbitrary basis (Weber 1978; Connolly 1983). They have sway over the other, in the old phrase, and the sway is arbitrary. It is time now to try to give a more explicit account of what such domination, such arbitrary sway, involves.

In giving this account, I shall often speak as if there are just two individual persons implicated in cases of domination, but that is only for convenience. While a dominating party will always be an agent—it cannot just be a system or network or whatever—it may be a personal or corporate or collective agent: this, as in the tyranny of the majority, where the domination is never the function of a single individual's power. And while a dominated agent, ultimately, will always have to be an individual person or persons, domination may be often be targeted on a group or on a corporate agent: it will constitute domination of individual people but in a collective identity or capacity or aspiration.

There are three aspects to any relationship of domination. Putting the aspects starkly, and without yet adding glosses, someone has dominating power over another, someone dominates or subjugates another, to the extent that

1. they have the capacity to interfere
2. on an arbitrary basis
3. in certain choices that the other is in a position to make.

We need to look at this account of domination, clause by clause. What is it to interfere, then, in the manner postulated in the first condition? Interference cannot take the form of a bribe or a reward; when I interfere I make things worse for you, not better. And the worsening that interference involves always has to be more or less intentional in character: it cannot occur by accident, for example, as when I fall in your path or happen to compete with you for scarce goods; it must be at least the sort of action in the doing of which we can sensibly allege negligence (Miller 1990: 35). Were non-intentional forms of obstruction also to count as interference, that would be to lose the distinction between securing people against the natural effects of chance and incapacity and scarcity and securing them against the things that they may try to do to one another. This distinction is of the first importance in political philosophy, and almost all traditions have marked it by associating a person's freedom with constraints only on more or less intentional interventions by others (Spitz 1995*a*: 382–3).

But interference, as I understand it, still encompasses a wide range of possible behaviours. It includes coercion of the body, as in restraint or obstruction; coercion of the will, as in punishment or the threat of punishment; and, to add a category that was not salient in earlier centuries, manipulation: this is usually covert and may take the form of agenda-fixing, the deceptive or non-rational shaping of people's beliefs or desires, or the rigging of the consequences of people's actions (Pettit 1989*b*; Lukes 1992: 995).

The variables relevant to an agent's choice are the range of options presented as available, the expected payoffs that the agent assigns to those options, and the actual payoffs—the outcomes—that result from the choice. All interfering behaviours, coercive or manipulative, are intended by the interferer to worsen the agent's choice situation by changing the range of options available, by altering the expected payoffs assigned to those options, or by assuming control over which outcomes will result from which options and what actual payoffs, therefore, will materialize. Thus physical obstruction and agenda-fixing both reduce the options available; the threat of punishment and the non-rational shaping of desires both affect the payoffs assigned to those options; and punishment for having made a certain choice and disruption of the normal flow of outcomes both affect the actual payoffs. Where the removal of an option from the range of available alternatives is an on-or-off matter, of course, the other modes of interference come in degrees: the expected or actual costs of certain options may be worsened in a greater or a smaller measure.

Context is always relevant to determining whether a given act worsens someone's choice situation, since context fixes the baseline by reference to which we decide if the effect is indeed a worsening. This contextual sensitivity has important implications for the extent to which interference occurs. It means that acts of omission, for example, may count in some circumstances as forms of interference. Consider the pharmacist who without good reason refuses to sell an urgently required medicine, or the judge who spitefully refuses to make available an established sentencing option involving community service instead of prison. Such figures should almost certainly count as interfering with those whom they hurt. The contextual sensitivity will have other effects too. It may mean, for example, that exploiting someone's urgent needs in order to drive a very hard bargain represents a sort of interference. Consider the pharmacist who agrees to sell an urgently required medicine but not for the standard fee—not even for the fee that is standard in the circumstances of an emergency call—only on extortionate terms. Such a person interferes in the patient's choice to the extent of worsening what by the received benchmark are the expected payoffs for the options they face.

But though interference always involves the attempt to worsen an agent's situation, it need not always involve a wrongful act: coercion remains coercion, even if it is morally impeccable. I interfere with you if I obstruct your making a phone call by deliberately occupying the only kiosk available: and this, even though it is perfectly within my rights to occupy that kiosk. I interfere with you if I destroy your custom by deliberately undercutting your prices—assuming I have the required resources—whenever you try to sell your wares: and this, again, even if our market culture tolerates my behaviour. I even interfere with you if I stop you interfering with another, where my act is morally required, not just morally innocent. The notion of interference, as I employ it here, is entirely unmoralized: whether one person interferes with another is decidable without reference to whether any particular moral offence has occurred; it is decidable just in the light of the facts, albeit the facts as they are seen through the local cultural lens.

So much by way of explicating interference. But what is it to have the capacity to interfere, which the first clause requires? Remember the old joke. 'Can you play the piano?' 'I don't know, I've never tried.' The lesson of that joke is that the capacity to interfere must be an actual capacity, as we might call it—a capacity that is more or less ready to be exercised—not a capacity that is yet to be fully developed: not anything like the virtual capacity of the musically gifted person who has yet to try out the piano. Consider a collection of people who, if they were to constitute themselves as a coherent agent, would have a ready capacity to interfere with someone. Or consider the agent, personal or corporate, who would have such a capacity, did they only recognize the presence of the potential victim, or the availability of causal modes of contact. In such cases there is only a virtual capacity to interfere, not an actual capacity, and I shall not say that there is domination. There is virtual domination, we might say, but not actual domination.[2] Virtual domination may be something for republicans to

---

[2] My thanks to Dennis Robinson for pressing me on this point.

guard against, of course, because of the future dangers it represents. But it does not yet constitute the central evil to which they are opposed.

The second clause requires that the person have the capacity to interfere on an arbitrary basis if they are to dominate the other party fully. What makes an act of interference arbitrary, then—arbitrary, in the sense of being perpetrated on an arbitrary basis? An act is perpetrated on an arbitrary basis, we can say, if it is subject just to the *arbitrium*, the decision or judgement, of the agent; the agent was in a position to choose it or not choose it, at their pleasure. When we say that an act of interference is perpetrated on an arbitrary basis, then, we imply that like any arbitrary act it is chosen or not chosen at the agent's pleasure. And in particular, since interference with others is involved, we imply that it is chosen or rejected without reference to the interests, or the opinions, of those affected. The choice is not forced to track what the interests of those others require according to their own judgements.

Notice that an act of interference can be arbitrary in the procedural sense intended here—it may occur on an arbitrary basis—without being arbitrary in the substantive sense of actually going against the interests or judgements of the persons affected. An act is arbitrary, in this usage, by virtue of the controls—specifically, the lack of controls—under which it materializes, not by virtue of the particular consequences to which it gives rise. The usage I follow means that there is no equivocation involved in speaking, as I do speak, either of a power of arbitrary interference or of an arbitrary power of interference. What is in question in each case is a power of interfering on an arbitrary, unchecked basis.

Under this conception of arbitrariness, then, an act of interference will be non-arbitrary to the extent that it is forced to track the interests and ideas of the person suffering the interference. Or, if not forced to track all of the interests and ideas of the person involved—these may make inconsistent demands—at least forced to track the relevant ones. I may have an interest in the state imposing certain taxes or in punishing certain offenders, for example, and the state may pursue these ends according to procedures that conform to my ideas about appropriate means. But I may still not want the state to impose taxes on me—I may want to be an exception—or I may think that I ought not to be punished in the appropriate manner, even though I have been convicted of an offence. In such a case, my relevant interests and ideas will be those that are shared in common with others, not those that treat me as exceptional, since the state is meant to serve others as well as me. And so in these cases the interference of the state in taxing or punishing me will not be conducted on an arbitrary basis and will not represent domination.[3]

The tradition of thinking which we discussed in the last chapter took a distinctive view of what is required for an act of interference—in particular, an act of legal or government interference—to be non-arbitrary, and I follow that tradition in giving this account of non-arbitrariness. Consider Tom Paine's (1989: 168) complaint against monarchy. 'It means arbitrary power in an individual person; in the exercise of which, *himself*, and not the *res-publica*, is the object' (cf. Sydney 1996: 199–200). What is required for non-arbitrary state power, as this comment makes clear, is that the power be exercised in a way that tracks, not the power-holder's personal welfare or world-view, but rather the welfare and world-view of the public. The acts of interference perpetrated by the state must be triggered by the shared interests of those affected under an interpretation of what those interests require that is shared, at least at the procedural level, by those affected.

When is an interest or idea likely not to be shared with some members of the population and likely to be an inappropriate guide for state action? The operational test suggested by the tradition is: when it is sectional or factional in character. But how to test for what is sectional or factional? The only possible means is by recourse to public discussion in which people may speak for themselves and for the groups to which they belong. Every interest and every idea that guides the action of a state must be open to challenge from every corner of the society; and where there is dissent, then appropriate remedies must be taken. People must find a higher-level consensus about procedures, or they must make room for secession or conscientious objection or something of that kind.

This is to say that the identification of a certain sort of state action as arbitrary and dominating is an essentially political matter; it is not something on which theorists can decide in the calmness of their studies (Young 1990). But though it is political, I should stress that it is not essentially value-laden. There is a fact of the matter as to whether or not the state is effectively forced to track non-sectional interests and ideas when it interferes in people's lives. Politics is the only heuristic

---

[3] Notice that this means, under a conception of freedom as non-domination, that neither a tax levy, nor even a term of imprisonment, need take away someone's freedom. But while such burdens do not compromise someone's freedom, still, as I put it later in this chapter, they do condition it. And so, while they do not compromise someone's freedom as non-domination, they do allow us to say that the person is not free to spend or to travel as they wish.

available for determining whether the interference of the state is arbitrary or not, but the issue for which it provides a heuristic is still an issue of fact. What has to be established is whether people really are dominated, not whether domination is visible from within some privileged evaluative standpoint. As the facts of the matter, including facts about local culture and context, determine whether a certain act counts as interference, so the facts of the matter determine whether a certain act of interference counts as arbitrary.

Arbitrariness, as we have defined it, may be more or less intense, and this draws attention to the fact that the domination associated with a power of arbitrary interference may be more or less intense too. Suppose that an agent can interfere in the life of another more or less at will: they can act just as their own whim or judgement leads them; they can act at their pleasure. Suppose, moreover, that the agent is subject to no particular difficulty or cost in exercising this capacity to interfere with someone: there is no prospect, for example, of suffering retaliation. And suppose, finally, that the interference in question is the most effective available: it can remove any options that the agent does not like or it can impose unbearable costs on the person's choice of those options. Such an agent will enjoy an absolute power of arbitrary interference over that person. The only brake on the interference that they can inflict is the brake of their own untrammelled choice or their own unchecked judgement, their own *arbitrium*.

Such an absolute power of arbitrary interference may have been available to slave-holders over their slaves in certain dispensations—certainly not in all—and it may have been accessible in some regimes to despotic potentates over their subjects. But it is not likely to be realized in many contexts. Such power is often approximated, however, at lower levels of intensity, even in rule-governed societies. The husband who can beat his wife for disobeying his instructions and be subject, at most, to the mild censure of his neighbours; the employer who can fire his employees as whim inclines him and hardly suffer embarrassment for doing so; the teacher who can chastise her pupils on the slightest excuse or pretence at excuse; the prison warder who can make life hell for inmates, and not worry much about covering her tracks: all such figures enjoy high degrees of arbitrary power over those subject to them. They may not be as common in some societies today as they once were. But they are not as unfamiliar as the slave-holder or potentate, and even where they do not survive, they have often left somewhat less powerful, but still recognizable, progeny in their place.

There are two generic sorts of constraint that we might expect to call on in trying to reduce arbitrariness: that is, in forcing a powerful agent like the state to track relevant interests and ideas. The first sort would put preconditions of action in place which make sectional interference that much more difficult: this, say, in requiring government to follow certain parliamentary procedures or to meet certain legal conditions in the way they act. These constraints are designed to filter or screen out unsuitable acts; they mean, where they are effective, that the agent does not interfere at will. The other sort of constraint would put penalties in place rather than filters: penalties which mean that any agent who perpetrates certain types of interference—violence, fraud, and the like—or who perpetrates otherwise legitimate types of interference under certain conditions—as when a public official has an undeclared interest in the outcome of their decision—can be called to account and punished. These constraints are designed to expose unsuitable acts of interference to sanction, rather than screening them out; they mean, when they are effective, that the agent cannot interfere with a guarantee of impunity.

And so, finally, to the third clause in our characterization of domination. The main thing to notice about this clause is that it mentions certain choices, not all choices. This highlights the fact that someone may dominate another in a certain domain of choice, in a certain sphere or aspect or period of their life, without doing so in all. The husband may dominate the wife in the home, the employer dominate the employee in the workplace, while that domination does not extend further—not, at least, with the same level of intensity.

We saw in the discussion of the second clause that domination may be more or less intense: a dominating agent may be able to interfere on a more or less arbitrary basis, with greater or lesser ease, and in a more or less severe measure. We see here that domination may also involve a greater or lesser range; it may vary in extent as well as in intensity. This variation in extent will be important insofar as it is better to be dominated in fewer areas rather than in more. But it will also be important insofar as domination in some areas is likely to be considered more damaging than it is in others; better be dominated in less central activities, for example, rather than in more central ones (see Taylor 1985: essay 8).

Common knowledge

The three conditions given are sufficient, as I see things, for domination to occur, though perhaps only in a limited measure, and perhaps only over a restricted domain. But if the conditions obtain to any noticeable degree in a world like ours, for a species like ours, then a further important condition is likely in many cases to be fulfilled too. This is that it will be a matter of common knowledge among the people involved, and among any others who are party to their relationship—any others in the society who are aware of what is going on—that the three base conditions are fulfilled in the relevant degree. The conditions may not be articulated in full conceptual dress, but the possibilities involved will tend to register in some way on the common consciousness. Everyone will believe that they obtain, everyone will believe that everyone believes this, and so on. And so on, at least, in the following pattern: no one will disbelieve that everyone believes this, no one will disbelieve that that is not disbelieved . . . (Lewis 1983: 166).

Why is the obtaining of the three conditions likely to mean that it will be a matter of common knowledge that they do in fact obtain? Some plausible empirical assumptions support it. The question as to whether such conditions obtain is going to be salient for nearly everyone involved, since it is of pressing interest for human beings to know how far they fall under the power of others. And the fact that the conditions obtain, if they do obtain, is usually going to be salient for most of the people involved: this, since the kinds of resource in virtue of which one person has power over another tend, with one exception, to be prominent and detectable. There is a salient question, then, and a salient basis for answering the question. And this means, plausibly (Lewis 1969: 56), that in cases where the answer is 'Yes'—in cases where the conditions for subjugation are fulfilled—there is a basis for common knowledge, or at least for something approaching common knowledge, that they are indeed fulfilled. Everyone will be in a position, not just to see that the conditions are fulfilled, but to see that everyone else is in a position to see that they are fulfilled, and so on.[4]

The resources in virtue of which one person may have power over another are extraordinarily various: they range over resources of physical strength, technical advantage, financial clout, political authority, social connections, communal standing, informational access, ideological position, cultural legitimation, and the like. They also include the resource of being someone—say, being the only doctor or police officer around—whose help and goodwill the other may need in various possible emergencies. They even include the resource of perceived

[4] Lewis's argument, briefly, is this. The fact that the resources in question are available to the powerful person is compelling for everyone; it can be seen by everyone to be compelling for nearly everyone; and it serves for everyone to indicate that the conditions obtain. And so, assuming that people ascribe common information and inductive standards to one another, the fact that the resources are available will be seen by everyone to indicate that the conditions obtain, will be seen by everyone to be seen by everyone to indicate this, and so on.

intractability—at the limit, perceived irrationality—that enables someone to drive a hard bargain.

I said that with one exception such resources tend to be prominent and detectable by those to whose disadvantage they may be deployed, and that this helps ensure that where one person has any dominating power over another, in virtue of an inequality in such resources, it is a matter of common knowledge that that is so. The exception is the case where one person or group is in a position to exercise backroom manipulation, whether manipulation of the options, manipulation of the expected payoffs, or manipulation of the actual payoffs (Lukes 1974; Geuss 1981; Meyerson 1991; Philp 1985; Wartenberg 1990; West 1990). Where domination is achieved by such means, it will not be a matter of common knowledge, unlike most other cases, that in this respect some people fall under the power of others.

When I say that the existence of a certain sort of domination between two parties is going to be a matter of common knowledge amongst them, and amongst their fellows, I should mention that this does not entail that they will evaluate it negatively: it does not entail that they will be aware of the domination as something on a par in any way with slavery. It is possible for those who do the dominating, for example, to take their superiority so far for granted that it does not ever strike them that the parties they dominate may bristle under the yoke. Think of Helmer Thorvald, the husband in Ibsen's play *A Doll's House*. He is clearly aware of dominating Nora, his wife, and indeed clearly believes that this domination is good for her. But he is absolutely blind to the fact that this domination could come to seem irksome and demeaning to Nora herself. No problem there; and no challenge to the claim that such domination is generally a matter of common knowledge. The lesson is that, even where domination exists and is recognized, it may not be seen for what it is when the dominated parties cannot speak for themselves.

Given that the fulfilment of the three original conditions—their fulfilment in any noticeable degree—is generally going to be a matter of something approaching common knowledge, the domination to which the conditions bear testimony will have an important subjective and intersubjective significance. Domination is generally going to involve the awareness of control on the part of the powerful, the awareness of vulnerability on the part of the powerless, and the mutual awareness—indeed, the common awareness among all the parties to the relationship—of this consciousness on each side. The powerless are not going to be able to look the powerful in the eye, conscious as each will be—and conscious as each will be of the other's consciousness—of this asymmetry. Both will share an awareness that the powerless can do nothing except by the leave of the powerful: that the powerless are at the mercy of the powerful and not on equal terms. The master–slave scenario will materialize, and the asymmetry between the two sides will be a communicative as well as an objective reality (Ball 1993).

Conscious of this problem, John Milton deplored 'the perpetual bowings and cringings of an abject people' that he thought were inevitable in monarchies (Worden 1991: 457). And a little later in the seventeenth century Algernon Sydney (1990: 162) could observe that 'slavery doth naturally produce meanness of spirit, with its worst effect, flattery'. The theme is given a particularly interesting twist a century later, when Mary Wollstonecraft deplores the 'littlenesses' and 'sly tricks' and 'cunning' (Wollstonecraft 1982: 359) to which women are driven because of their dependency on their husbands: because of their slavery, as she also calls it (p. 354). 'It is vain to expect virtue from women till they are, in some degree, independent of man; nay, it is vain to expect that strength of natural affection, which would make them good wives and mothers. Whilst they are absolutely dependent on their husbands they will be cunning, mean, and selfish' (p. 299, cf. p. 309).

What contemporary relationships might illustrate the domination of some by others, with the associated effects on subjectivity and status? We have already got some sense of examples. In the absence of a culture of children's rights and appropriate guards against child abuse, parents individually or jointly will enjoy subjugating power over their children. In the absence of a culture of equal rights that is supportive of battered wives, husbands will enjoy such power over their spouses. In the absence of other employment opportunities and appropriate controls—say, those that a vigilant union might guarantee—employers and managers will enjoy subjugating power over their workers. In the absence of countervailing powers, creditors will often enjoy dominating power over their debtors (Ransom and Sutch 1977: ch. 8). In the absence of possibilities of appeal or review, bureaucrats and police will certainly enjoy that power over members of the public. And in the absence of some forums and procedures for dealing with minority grievances, a mainstream government may well dominate those in various marginalized groups.

Consent and contestability

It is important to notice that some of the relationships that I mentioned in illustrating domination will have originated historically in

consent, while others will not. Whether a relationship sprang originally from a contract or not, whether or not it was consensual in
origin, the fact that it gives one party the effective capacity to interfere
more or less arbitrarily in some of the other's choices means that the
one person dominates or subjugates the other (Spitz 1995*a*: 362–3,
397–8). Other considerations apart, this would have given traditional
republicans a good reason to be hostile, as they were consistently hostile, towards the slave contract: towards the contract whereby someone, for whatever gain, voluntarily submits to the domination of
another (Locke 1965: 325).

The fact that consent to a form of interference is not sufficient as a
guard against arbitrariness means that no one who is concerned about
domination can be happy about two developments that gathered
momentum about the turn of the nineteenth century. One development was the growth of the populist idea, as we described it in the last
chapter, that provided the majority rules, all is well. Majority rule may
seem to be blessed by its consensual character, but it can clearly
involve the domination of minority groups, and no one who resists
domination can endorse unconstrained majoritarianism.

The other development that opponents of domination must deplore
is the rise of the doctrine of free contract. This is the doctrine that the
freedom of contract means the freedom to decide on the terms of a
contract, not just the freedom to enter or refuse to enter into a contract, and that the free contract legitimates any treatment of one by
another that the parties agree to accept. The law of contract was
rapidly evolving and consolidating about the turn of the nineteenth
century (Stoljar 1975; Atiyah 1979). The development of the doctrine
saw freedom of contract invoked in defence of some fairly appalling
contractual arrangements, as people ignored the consequences for
domination—as they ignored the asymmetries of power established
under the contract—and argued that a contract that was not actively
coerced was free (MacDonagh 1980; Cornish and Clark 1989;
Horowitz 1977). This development is highly questionable from the
point of view of anyone who is worried about domination. It could
never have materialized, in all likelihood, had people remained
focused on that evil, in particular, had they continued to think that
freedom required the absence of domination, not just the absence of
interference.

But though consent to interference is not a sufficient check against
arbitrariness and domination, is it likely to be a necessary one? Should
we hold that any act of interference is arbitrary to the extent that those
affected have not consented to the exercise of that sort of power? The

belief in the necessity of consent for the legitimacy of government has spawned dubious doctrines of implied or virtual or tacit consent. It would be good if we did not have to think of the consent of those affected by certain acts of interference—say, by acts of law and government—as necessary for the non-arbitrariness and legitimacy of the interference. For that would mean that we did not have to look to such doctrines in the attempt to legitimate ordinary political realities.

Happily, a little reflection shows that what is required for non-arbitrariness in the exercise of a certain power is not actual consent to that sort of power but the permanent possibility of effectively contesting it. The state will not interfere on an arbitrary basis, by our earlier account, so far as its interference has to be guided by certain relevant interests and ideas and those interests and ideas are shared by those affected. This does not mean that the people must have actively consented to the arrangements under which the state acts. But what it does mean is that it must always be possible for people in the society, no matter what corner they occupy, to contest the assumption that the guiding interests and ideas really are shared and, if the challenge proves sustainable, to alter the pattern of state activity. Unless such contestability is assured, the state may easily represent a dominating presence for those of a certain marginalized ethnicity or culture or gender. The point is familiar from what is now often known as the politics of difference (Young 1990), and I make much of it in discussing democracy in the second part of the book.

Domination without interference

There are two final points about domination or subjugation that I want to stress, since they connect closely with themes in the last chapter. The first is that the possession by someone of dominating power over another—in whatever degree—does not require that the person who enjoys such power actually interferes, out of good or bad motives, with the individual who is dominated; it does not require even that the person who enjoys that power is inclined in the slightest measure towards such interference. What constitutes domination is the fact that in some respect the power-bearer has the capacity to interfere arbitrarily, even if they are never going to do so. This fact means that the power-victim acts in the relevant area by the leave, explicit or implicit, of the power-bearer; it means that they live at the mercy of that person, that they are in the position of a dependant or debtor or something of the kind. If there is common knowledge of that implication, as there usually will be, it follows that the power-victim cannot enjoy the psychological status of an equal: they are in a position where fear and deference will be the normal order of the day, not the frankness that goes with intersubjective equality.

Does this point mean that no difference is made by the fact, if it is a fact, that the power-bearer is benign or saintly? That depends. If being benign or saintly means that the person acknowledges that they are subject to challenge and rebuke—if it means that they make themselves answerable in the court of certain considerations—then that entails that they cannot interfere with complete impunity; they can be quoted, as it were, against themselves. Suppose that a power-bearer acknowledges a code of *noblesse oblige*, for example, or just aspires to be a virtuous person. That is going to mean, in itself, that the power they have over someone else is at least less intense that it might have been; there is a certain reduction in the domination they represent, by virtue of their being exposed to the possibility of effective rebuke. This observation is relevant to my argument in the final chapter that the virtue of others represents an indispensable element in the set of safeguards that protects a person from domination.

If, on the other hand, being benign or saintly simply means that the person happens to have inclinations that do no harm to anyone else—in the actual circumstances, they do not lead to interference with anyone—then it will not entail a reduction in the domination of those who are under this person's power. It will remain the case that the person can interfere on an arbitrary basis and that anyone under their power lives, and lives by common knowledge, at that person's mercy. Even when a dominating agent is benign in this sense, of course, the likelihood of interference will be that much lower. But it is important to see that domination goes with the accessibility of arbitrary interference to another, and that improbability of the kind in question here does not make for inaccessibility. Someone can be in a position to interfere with me at their pleasure, even while it is very improbable that they will actually interfere.

The observation that there can be domination without interference connects with the theme highlighted in the last chapter, that slavery and unfreedom is consistent with non-interference: that it can be realized in the presence of a master or authority who is beneficent, and even benevolent. As Richard Price (1991: 77–8) stated the point: 'Individuals in private life, while held under the power of masters, cannot be denominated free, however equitably and kindly they may be treated.'

Interference without domination

The second point I wish to emphasize about domination is that while the enjoyment of dominating power over another is consistent with never actually interfering, it is equally true that one agent may actually interfere with another without dominating that person. The public official or authority who interferes with people in a way that is forced to track their interests and ideas fails to enjoy subjugating power over the person affected. The official is subject to such screening and sanctioning devices, at least in the ideal, that they can be relied upon to act on a non-factional basis: on a basis that is supported by non-sectional interests and ideas. They interfere, since they operate on the basis of coercive law, but their interference is non-arbitrary.

The parliament or the police officer, then, the judge or the prison warden, may practise non-dominating interference, provided—and it is a big proviso—that a suitably constraining, constitutional arrangement works effectively. The agent or agency in question may not have any discretion in the treatment of a person affected, so that they cannot interfere at will, only under constitutionally determined conditions. Or if they have certain areas of discretion—for example, in the way in which the judge may have some discretion in sentencing—then their ability to exercise it to the intentional detriment of the person is severely limited: their actions may be subject to appeal and review, so that they are exposed to sanction in the event of using that discretion in a way that is not properly controlled by non-sectional interest and judgement.

Suppose that a constitutional authority—say, a judge or a police officer—operates under discriminatory laws and suppose that those laws severely constrain such agents in how they act. Do we have a complaint to make in the case of such constitutional discrimination? We certainly have. The fact that the laws are discriminatory means that they do not track the relevant interests or ideas of the group against whom discrimination is practised. Those who implement such laws, therefore, act on an arbitrary basis from the point of view of the group in question. It is true that they may have no option but to act in that way; by hypothesis they operate under severe legal constraint. But the fact that they are forced to interfere on an arbitrary basis with members of the group is consistent with their being able to interfere in that way; the fact that they are under a legal obligation to interfere on an arbitrary basis is consistent with their having the capacity to interfere on that basis.[5]

[5] An alternative line would be to say that while the constrained agents do not dominate members of the group, the legislators who make the laws or who are in a position to change the laws certainly do; they are the principal whose wishes are carried out by the constrained agents.

Like the first point made, this second one connects directly with the discussion in the last chapter. It bears on the question of whether law itself represents an abrogation of liberty: a restriction on people's pre-existing liberty which is justified by the effect it has in realizing a greater liberty and happiness overall. It should be clear that the law need not itself represent a form of domination, under the account of domination advanced here, and that the relation of law to liberty need not be represented in Hobbesian or Benthamite terms. There will be systems of law available, at least in principle, which are entirely undominating and entirely consistent with freedom: not only will they inhibit potential dominators and reduce unfreedom, they will do so without representing a form of domination in their own right. And equally there will be systems of law that do introduce arbitrary control at some point and that do thereby embody domination and unfreedom: systems that are more or less authoritarian, in the fashion of Hobbes's Leviathan, or America's British legislature. These, in the old republican phrases, will represent the empire of men, not the empire of law (Harrington 1992: 8).

II. Non-domination

The absence of domination

The absence of domination may mean the absence of domination in the presence of other people: the status associated with living among other people, none of whom dominates you. Or it may mean the sort of status that can also be realized through the absence of other people: through living in isolation from society. Non-domination, as that is valued in the republican tradition, means the absence of domination in the presence of other people, not the absence of domination gained by isolation. Non-domination is the status associated with the civil role of the *liber*: *libertas* is *civitas*, in the Roman way of expressing the idea; liberty is civil as distinct from natural freedom, in the idiom of the eighteenth century. It is a social ideal whose realization presupposes the presence of a number of mutually interactive agents (Pettit 1993*a*: ch. 3); we return to the point in the next chapter.

In this respect, freedom as non-domination contrasts in an interesting way with the alternative ideal of freedom as non-interference. That ideal is linked to the notion of natural rather than civil liberty. And the linkage suggests that it may be enjoyed in isolation from society, so that non-interference means the absence of interference, whether in the presence of other people or in their absence: whether by design or by default. Where freedom as non-domination represents the freedom of the city, freedom as non-interference tends to represent the freedom of the heath: 'the right of common upon a waste', in a nice phrase from Paley (1825: 355).

Non-domination in the sense that concerns us, then, is the position that someone enjoys when they live in the presence of other people and when, by virtue of social design, none of those others dominates them. Such a status, as we shall see, may come in one or another degree, but it will often be convenient to speak as if it were an on–off matter. Someone enjoys non-domination, we can say, when they live among others and when no other satisfies the conditions discussed in the last section; no other has the capacity to interfere on an arbitrary basis in their choices.

Strategies for achieving non-domination

How might we enable a person who is in danger of being dominated to achieve non-domination? What social designs might help to advance non-domination? There are two broad approaches conceivable. One is the strategy of reciprocal power, as we might describe it, the other the strategy of constitutional provision.

The strategy of reciprocal power is to make the resources of dominator and dominated more equal so that, ideally, a previously dominated person can come to defend themselves against any interference on the part of the dominator. If each can defend themselves effectively against any interference that another can wield, then none of them is going to be dominated by another. None is going to be subject to the permanent possibility of interference on an arbitrary basis by another.

The strategy of reciprocal power is rarely going to be available in this ideal, defensive form. Usually the only thing feasible will be to enable each of the parties involved, if not to defend themselves against interference by another, at least to threaten any interference with punishment and to impose punishment on actual interferers. But such punishment and threat of punishment are themselves forms of interference, as we know, and forms of interference that do not track the interests and ideas of those who are affected. Thus, under this non-ideal version of the strategy, arbitrary interference and domination may be reduced, but it is not ever going to be eliminated.

The strategy of constitutional provision seeks to eliminate domination, not by enabling dominated parties to defend themselves against arbitrary interference or to deter arbitrary interferers but rather by introducing a constitutional authority—say a corporate, elective agent—to the situation. The authority will deprive other parties of the power of arbitrary interference and of the power of punishing that sort of interference. It will thereby eliminate domination of some parties by others and if it does not itself dominate those parties, then it will bring an end to domination. The reason that the constitutional authority will not itself dominate the parties involved, if it does not dominate them, is that the interference it practises has to track their interests according to their ideas; it is suitably responsive to the common good.

Suppose we are starting from a position where one party dominates others. Is it really plausible that the strategy of constitutional provision could work here? Given the original difference of power, is not the dominating party going to believe that any inhibiting authority, no matter how it is elected or constituted, fails to track their particular interests, as they were served in the status quo?

If the previously dominant party does believe this, then under a regime that is genuinely non-dominating, it has to be possible for them to voice their complaint and to contest the interference of the authority in their affairs. And if they are not satisfied with the judgement that the interference which inhibits them is not dominating, then it has to be possible for them to withdraw from the arrangement and encounter the authority, under a balance-of-power scenario, just as an agency for defending others against interference and for deterring interference by threatening and imposing punishment on interferers. Otherwise it is indeed the case that the arrangement, however well it serves the previously dominated parties, will not serve the interests of the previously dominant one: it will be a dominating form of interference from that agent's point of view.

This concession need not worry us at this stage, since we are merely illustrating ways in which domination can be reduced and perhaps eliminated. But it is worth remarking that actually it is not entirely outlandish to think that the previously dominant party might accept the constitutional arrangement. After all that arrangement is going to be justified in response to contestation by the claim that everyone is capable of becoming vulnerable to others, and that they each have a common interest in being protected from others in a constitutionally assured manner. The stronger party can reject that claim only to the extent of believing that their current advantage is more or less assured and that they are not as other men and women. And that belief is hardly compelling, especially since henceforth the authority is going to protect others by all the defensive and deterrent means at its disposal.

Non-domination as a form of power

Whether it is furthered by courtesy of constitutional provision, or in virtue of an equal distribution of relevant resources, it should be stressed that non-domination is itself a form of power. It represents a control that a person enjoys in relation to their own destiny and such control constitutes one familiar type of power: the power of the agent who can prevent various ills happening to them (see appendix to this chapter).

Another way of stressing the power-involving aspect of non-domination, to return to a theme of the last chapter, is to emphasize that non-domination involves a sort of immunity or security against interference on an arbitrary basis, not the mere absence of such interference. Suppose that for a certain range of choices I happen to enjoy the absence of all interference by arbitrary powers in the actual world: no one with such a power gets in the way of my making my preferred choice, and no one of that kind would get in the way had I chosen differently among the relevant options. It is possible, consistently with this supposition, that the non-interference I enjoy is extremely insecure and that I am a relatively powerless individual. I may enjoy it only for the very contingent reason that while there are agents around who dominate me—agents with an arbitrary power of interference—it happens that they like me and leave me alone; or it happens that I am able to ingratiate myself with them and placate them as they become ill-disposed towards me; or it happens that I am cunning and manage to keep out of their way when trouble is brewing; or whatever. In such a world, the price of my liberty is not eternal vigilance but, as Gore Vidal once said, eternal discretion.

To enjoy non-domination is to be in a position where no one has that power of arbitrary interference over me and where I am correspondingly powerful. It is to be possessed, not just of non-interference by arbitrary powers, but of a secure or resilient variety of such non-interference. Let the agents in question take against me; let me fail to be good at toadying to them; let me lose the cunning required to keep out of their way. None of this matters if I really enjoy non-domination: if I really benefit from the reciprocal power or the constitutional provision required for non-domination. It will still be the case that I enjoy non-interference at the hands of the agents in question, for that blessing comes to me securely, and not just by courtesy of one of the contingencies mentioned. I will count by any criteria, then, as a relatively powerful individual; I do not have to depend on my luck for avoiding the relevant sort of interference.[6]

---

[6] To enjoy non-interference is not to be interfered with in the actual world where I choose

Common knowledge

We have seen that non-domination comes about through the absence of domination in the presence of other people: through living among other people none of whom satisfies the three conditions for domination in your regard. And we have seen that non-domination in this sense may be realized via the strategy of reciprocal power or the strategy of constitutional provision, but that in either case it involves a positive control over your own life: a security in the possession of non-interference. There is one more point that I need to make by way of general introduction to the idea. This is that wherever someone comes to enjoy non-domination, this is something of subjective and intersubjective significance. As domination or subjugation usually becomes a matter of common knowledge among those who are party to the relationship, so non-domination will also tend to connect with common awareness.

We saw in the last section that if the three conditions for subjugation are satisfied in any noticeable degree then, in most cases, it is going to be a matter of more or less common knowledge amongst parties to the relationship that the conditions are satisfied. This argument started from the fact that it is always a salient question whether one person has dominating power over another—whether the three conditions are fulfilled—and that the inequality of resources that gives rise to such power is usually going to be a salient datum: the exception will be the case where resources of covert manipulation are used to make people incapable of registering, for example, that others deprive them of certain options.

Suppose now that measures are put in place to defeat the conditions for domination in some relationship. Suppose that the measures help to ensure that neither of two parties has dominating power over the other or, equivalently, that each enjoys non-domination in relation to the other. The question of whether either has dominating power over the other will remain a salient issue. And the measures taken to redress the imbalance of resources that gave one such power over the other—including, now, measures designed to control manipulation—will

what I want and, equally, it is not to be interfered with in those related worlds where my wants vary and I choose some other options; this is a modal or counterfactual aspect of freedom that often receives mention. To enjoy the same non-interference with the security of non-domination is to satisfy that condition plus a further modal condition: it is also not to be interfered with in those possible worlds where the attitudes of powerful agents vary, or my ingratiating capacities are lessened, or my native cunning is not what it was, and so on. It is to remain resiliently possessed of non-interference across this range of possible worlds, as well as in the worlds originally considered. See Pettit (1993*a*; 1993*b*).

almost certainly constitute a salient datum. Thus, by the style of argument mentioned before, we may be sure that it will be a matter of nearly common knowledge among parties to the relationship that the conditions for domination fail, and that non-domination rules. Or at least we may be confident that this will happen when other things are equal: when there is no concerted attempt, for example, to persuade people of the opposite.

This point is of the greatest importance, because it connects non-domination with subjective self-image and intersubjective status. It means that the enjoyment of non-domination in relation to another agent—at least when that agent is a person—goes with being able to look the other in the eye, confident in the shared knowledge that it is not by their leave that you pursue your innocent, non-interfering choices; you pursue those choices, as of publicly recognized right. You do not have to live either in fear of that other, then, or in deference to them. The non-interference you enjoy at the hands of others is not enjoyed by their grace and you do not live at their mercy. You are a somebody in relation to them, not a nobody. You are a person in your own legal and social right.

The association of freedom with subjective and often intersubjective status—the association of freedom with a feeling of independence and immunity—goes back a long way in the republican tradition (Wirszubski 1968: 159). It is even there in Machiavelli, who is more tolerant of coercion and terror than most writers. 'The common benefit gained from a free community', he says, 'is recognised by nobody while he possesses it: namely, the power of enjoying freely his possessions without any anxiety, of feeling no fear for the honor of his women and his children, of not being afraid for himself' (Machiavelli 1965: 236). Montesquieu (1989: 157) seems to offer a gloss on Machiavelli when he writes, over two centuries later: 'Political liberty in a citizen is that tranquillity of spirit which comes from the opinion each one has of his security, and in order for him to have this liberty the government must be such that one citizen cannot fear another citizen' (see too Spinoza 1951: 259).

John Milton stressed the intersubjective rather than just the subjective aspects of enjoying republican freedom. 'They who are greatest', he says of the 'free commonwealth', 'walk the streets as other men, may be spoken to freely, familiarly, without adoration' (Worden 1991: 457). This theme assumes rhapsodic dimensions in the writings of Richard Price (1991: 84–5) and Joseph Priestley. I quote Priestley (1993: 35–6) at length, though his references are unfortunately (and, I believe, unnecessarily) sexist.

A sense both of political and civil slavery, makes a man think meanly of himself. The feeling of his insignificance debases his mind ... On the other hand, a sense of political and civil liberty, though there should be no great occasion to exert it in the course of a man's life, gives him a constant sense of his own power and importance; and is the foundation of his indulging a free, bold, and manly turn of thinking, unrestrained by the most distant idea of control. Being free from all fear, he has the most perfect enjoyment of himself, and of all the blessings of life.

The subjective and intersubjective aspect of freedom as non-domination marks a contrast with the way in which freedom as non-interference is normally construed within the liberal tradition. Far from being associated with any particular psychological profile, freedom is contrasted within this tradition with the feeling of freedom and, more generally, with subjective or intersubjective status. Berlin (1958: 43) expresses the point forcefully.

When I demand to be liberated from, let us say, the status of political or social dependence, what I demand is an alteration of the attitude towards me of those whose opinions and behaviour help to determine my own image of myself ... Yet it is not with liberty, in either the 'negative' or in the 'positive' senses of the word, that this desire for status and recognition can easily be identified.

Many liberals worry about the good involved in feeling free, but the point is that they think of that good as something detachable and detached from the good of liberty itself, as that is ordinarily understood (Weinstein 1965: 156–7; Shklar 1989: 28; but see Holmes 1995: 245).

It is understandable why liberals should detach non-interference from the common recognition of non-interference. I cannot escape domination without the presence of protective institutions that testify to my non-domination. But I can escape interference, I can escape even the likelihood of interference, without the presence of such eloquent devices. The actual or expected non-interference that I enjoy may come to me by good fortune alone: the good fortune, for example, of being vulnerable only to agents who like me or only to agents whom I am able to outwit. And such good fortune will not tend to be a matter of common recognition.

We saw at the beginning of this discussion that the ideal of freedom as non-interference is not generally taken as a social ideal; it is represented as a status that can be enjoyed, not just in the presence of people, but also in their absence: not just by design—institutional design—but by default. We see now that, equally, the ideal is not usually depicted as a subjective or intersubjective ideal, but as something whose realization may or may not have psychological significance. In both social and psychological dimensions, then, it contrasts with the ideal of freedom as non-domination.

III. Paley's objections

This analysis of what domination and non-domination involve should give us a good appreciation of the ideal of freedom as non-domination. But William Paley, as we saw in the last chapter, made three widely supported objections to defining freedom as non-domination. It will be useful for us, in conclusion, to see how far the ideal of freedom as non-domination can be made proof against those complaints.

The means–end objection

The first of Paley's objections was a charge of confusion: those who espouse liberty as non-domination 'describe not so much liberty itself, as the safeguards and preservatives of liberty' (Paley 1825: 359). If seeking non-domination involves seeking a certain sort of security against a certain sort of interference, then of necessity it involves a concern for how to safeguard and preserve such non-interference. Paley's view is that republicans lose sight of the value of non-interference and fetishize the institutions that are meant to promote it. They focus on the means—the devices for securing non-interference—when they should really have their eye on the end: as he sees it, the non-interference itself.

But Paley misrepresents in two ways the tradition that we have been discussing. First, the theorists of freedom as non-domination seek security against only a certain sort of interference: that which materializes, whether to good or ill effect, on an arbitrary basis. Second, and more important, what those theorists seek is a specific sort of security against that interference, in particular the sort of security which means, not just that people with a power of arbitrary interference probably will not exercise it, but that the agents in question lose that power: they are deprived of the capacity to exercise it or at least their capacity to exercise it is severely reduced.

This second point needs emphasis. Republicans do not value the absence of arbitrary interference that is achieved by courtesy of an 'indulgence', as Richard Price (1991: 26) puts it, or 'an accidental mildness'. Trying to secure the absence of arbitrary interference, then, is not trying to promote it by no matter what means. After all, it might just happen that the most effective means of promoting non-interference by certain powerful people would be to devise institutions that flatter them and give them reason to think that those with whom they might otherwise interfere regard them as paternalistic deities. Trying to secure the absence of arbitrary interference means trying to promote it, then, but only under this important constraint: that none of the means adopted, no matter how unlikely they would make arbitrary interference, can leave the threatening agents with the unhindered capacity to interfere. The point is not just to make arbitrary interference improbable; the point is to make it inaccessible.

The best explanation of Paley's misrepresentation of republicans may be that there is an ambiguity in the notion of safeguarding or securing something. Trying to secure a good may mean acting so as to maximize its expected realization. In this usage 'secure' has a purely probabilistic sense and is equivalent to 'promote'. Alternatively, trying to secure a good may mean trying to ensure that no one can take it away from you: trying to devise things so that others are not able to deprive you of it. In this usage 'secure' does not mean 'promote', since the means of maximizing the expected realization of the good may involve leaving control of the good in the hands of another. Rather what it means is something like 'protect it against others'. Paley's mistake may be to imagine that when republicans speak of wanting to safeguard or secure non-interference—in particular, to secure the absence of arbitrary interference—they mean that they want to promote it, not protect it.[7]

The black-or-white objection

Paley's second complaint against the ideal of freedom as non-domination is, in effect, that it comes only in black or white, at a maximum or at a minimum: that it does not admit of degrees in the way that we would expect. He complains of absolutist talk of free and enslaved peoples when such expressions 'are intelligible only in a comparative sense' (Paley 1825: 356). This complaint might have been justly entertained under the sting of the rhetoric employed by Richard Price and

---

[7] To try to secure non-interference in the protection sense is to try to reduce interference in those possible worlds where other people take against you or you are not so cunning or whatever; and to do this regardless of the probability of those worlds. To try to secure non-interference in the promotional sense is to try to reduce interference in various possible worlds, but in a way that takes account of how probable it is that those worlds are ways the actual world may be; it will be to ignore a world where some powerful agent decides to turn nasty, for example, to the extent that such a change is improbable.

others, for it is certainly true that they painted their pictures in stark black and white. But the question is whether the complaint tells essentially against the conception of freedom as non-domination.

I think that the discussion in this chapter makes it clear that it does not. We saw in the first section that the domination of one person by another may vary both in intensity and in extent. On the one side, the interference of which the dominator is capable may be more or less arbitrary, the cost and difficulty of interfering may be more or less great, and the interference accessible may be more or less severe. And on the other side, the dominator may be able to interfere in the affairs of the dominated across a wider or narrower range of activities, and in more or less important areas.

These variations in the intensity and extent of domination ensure that there must also be differences in the intensity with which someone can enjoy non-domination, and in the extent of the non-domination enjoyed. Such differences will appear with differences in the extent to which, and in the intensity to which, domination is reduced. People will enjoy more and more non-domination both as dominators come to dominate them less intensely and as they come to dominate them across a smaller extent.

Nor, crucially, is that all. The furthering of non-domination is not strictly equivalent to the reduction of domination, whether that be a reduction in its intensity or a reduction in its extent. We can expand non-domination, not just by reducing existing domination, but by novel extensions of the area over which, and the ease with which, a subject can exercise undominated choice, at whatever level of intensity. We can introduce or facilitate undominated choices in areas where they do not currently exist or are very costly. The choices may be unavailable because the relevant options are not culturally accessible— not accessible in the way reading is not accessible in a non-literate culture—or because the options are curtailed by an excessively constraining law or because the hard facts of life put them beyond reach.

Suppose I am a physically handicapped person for whom getting around my home town is impossible or difficult. My non-domination would be increased, at whatever level of intensity, by my being provided with the means of locomotion, for I would thereby be facilitated in the enjoyment of certain undominated choices. And my non-domination would be increased, even though no one currently dominates me on matters of where I go; it is just that I am unable to go anywhere.

The expansive way of increasing the extent of people's freedom as non-domination can be nicely identified in terms of a distinction between factors that compromise liberty and factors that condition it.

Freedom as non-domination is compromised by domination and by domination alone. But while my freedom is not compromised, therefore, by a limitation in my ability to exercise it, that limitation is still significant; it conditions the freedom that I enjoy. We can increase the intensity and extent of people's freedom as non-domination by reducing the compromises to which they are subject: that is, by reducing domination by others. But we may also increase the extent of people's freedom as non-domination by reducing the influence of conditioning factors and by expanding the range or ease of the undominated choices that they enjoy. As we may say that someone is unfree so far as their freedom is compromised by domination, so we may say that they are not free in this or that respect—they are non-free, though not strictly unfree (Pettit 1989*b*)—insofar as their freedom is subject to certain conditioning factors.

The claim that we need to think about reducing the influence of conditioning factors parallels an assumption that is often made by adherents of freedom as non-interference. Many such theorists take it for granted that in advancing the cause of freedom as non-interference it is important, not just to reduce the interference that people suffer in their given range of choice, but also to increase as far as possible the choices available to them by liberating them from unnecessary natural or social limitations; it is important not just to make freedom as non-interference a formal reality, as it is said, but also to make it effective.[8]

The assumption that more choice is always better than less, or that easier choice is better than harder, has rightly been questioned, and the questioning needs to be internalized in discussions of freedom as non-domination as well as in discussions of freedom as non-interference (Dworkin 1988: ch. 5). But the point is that the two conceptions of freedom are on a par in each arguing that, other things being equal, we

[8] It is worth noting that to want to make negative liberty effective is distinct from wanting to replace it with a positive notion of liberty. The two moves are sometimes confused with one another. Both negative liberty and republican liberty can be realized in a purely formal or in an effective way; and the desire for the effective realization of each is different from an attachment to a positive ideal of liberty. The project of making negative liberty effective has been invoked to support some quite radical policies. See e.g. Waldron (1993: essay 13) and Van Parijs (1995); on the measurement of effectiveness, relevant also for republicans, see Sugden (1996). Arguments from the need to make non-interference effective represent an interesting twist in liberal thinking, but they depend on an assumption which those who regard non-interference as the only good cannot easily accept. This is the assumption that the interference practised by the state in the attempt to make non-interference effective—in the attempt to help people overcome, not interference, but natural or non-intentionally imposed limitations—is justified by that increase in effectiveness. Here, of course, there is a direct contrast with the republican approach; provided that it is not arbitrary, state interference will not count as a serious loss—as a way of compromising liberty—in the republican's book.

ought to expand the range or ease of favoured choice as well as its intensity: we ought to try and reduce influences that condition freedom as well as influences that compromise it. The difference between the conceptions is that they draw the boundary between compromising and conditioning influences at different points. For the conception of freedom as non-inteference, only non-intentional influences such as those of natural obstacles condition rather than compromise freedom. For the conception of freedom as non-domination, intentional interferences that are non-arbitrary are similar to natural obstacles in conditioning but not compromising freedom. Thus the first conception puts law on the compromising side of the compromising/conditioning divide, while the second conception holds that a non-arbitrary law belongs on the conditioning side.

If we endorse the ideal of freedom as non-domination, to return to Paley's objection, we are not committed to thinking that all is fair or all is foul: that freedom is fully realized or entirely frustrated. We may advance non-domination in incremental stages, by reducing the degree to which a dominator can interfere on an arbitrary basis, or by restricting the range of choice across which the dominator may exercise control, or by resorting to the expansive sorts of measures just canvassed. There will be difficulties in measuring the progress achieved in such partial stages, of course, as there are difficulties in measuring progress achieved in advancing the cause of freedom as non-interference (Pettit 1989*b*); there will be issues to do, for example, with how intensity should be traded off against extent—more on this later—and with whether liberation in some areas of activity is more important than liberation in others (Taylor 1985: essay 8). But there can be no doubt that there is progress to be won in such incomplete steps. The discourse of freedom as non-domination is not inevitably tied to the dichotomous rhetoric of total emancipation or complete enslavement.

The too-hard objection

Paley's last and most important objection was that the ideal of freedom as non-domination is too demanding to be sensibly given to the state: that it would 'inflame expectations that can never be gratified, and disturb the public content with complaints, which no wisdom or benevolence of government can remove'. What have we to say in answer to this, if we choose to embrace the ideal and treat it as a universal value?

We certainly have to admit that there is a charge to answer. There are two respects in which our expectations of the state are going to increase greatly if we think that the state should be designed to advance freedom as non-domination, not freedom as non-interference. The ideal of targeting only forms of dominating interference, not interference as such, means that we are going to be relatively well-disposed towards giving the state considerable power; we are going to look more fondly on state interference, provided that such interference can be bound by constraints that make it non-arbitrary. And the ideal of targeting all forms of domination, not just those in which there is actual interference, means that we are going to be relatively ill-disposed towards tolerating relations of domination, even relations of domination where the stronger party may usually be expected to stay their hand; we are going to look less fondly on the traditional relationship of husband to wife, for example, or employer to employee.

The shift from freedom as non-interference to freedom as non-domination is going to have two effects, then, that might have disturbed Paley and that might have motivated his third criticism. The shift is going to make us potentially more radical in our complaints about the ways in which social relationships are organized. And it is going to make us potentially less sceptical about the possibilities of rectifying those complaints by recourse to state action.

But does this increase in social radicalism and this decrease in social and political scepticism give good ground for rejecting the republican approach and for embracing instead the modernist, liberal ideal of freedom as non-interference? The remainder of the book can be read as an argument in favour, precisely, of being more radical in relation to policy, less sceptical in regard to the state. It can be seen to that extent as an extended response to Paley's final objection. What I have done so far is toidentify and articulate the republican notion of freedom as non-domination. What I shall be doing in the chapters to come is to make the case for treating that notion as a political ideal, and to examine the institutional significance of establishing it as an ideal. I hope that the upshot will be a vision of public life in which the republican ideal does not have the destabilizing, subversive effects that turned the likes of Paley away from it.

APPENDIX: DOMINATION AND OTHER FORMS OF POWER

It may be useful to relate dominating or subjugating power, as we have characterized it here, to the other, very different conceptions of power that are found in political theory (Clegg 1989; Wartenberg 1990; Patton 1994; Hindess 1996). Those who are not interested can move directly to the next chapter.

All conceptions of power, roughly speaking, make different choices at the choice points—the points marked by 'OR'—in the following schema.

1. Power is possessed by an agent (person/group/agency) OR by a system
2. so far as that entity exercises OR is able (actually or virtually) to exercise
3. intentional OR non-intentional influence,
4. negative OR positive,
5. in advancing any kind of result whatever OR, more specifically, in helping to construct certain forms of agency OR shape the choices of certain agents.

This schema allows us to see what unifies the different conceptions of power deployed when we speak at one extreme of the power of the effective agent to make things happen or, at the other, of the power of the system to keep revolutionary options off the agenda and so perpetuate itself. Our schema even lets us see how it is possible to think of power on the model that makes it as inescapable as gravity; there is always some factor that exercises or is able to exercise some influence on the sorts of agent we are or on the sorts of thing we do.

Most importantly from our point of view, however, the schema allows us also to situate subjugating or dominating power relative to such alternatives. Power of this general kind exists when there is

1. an agent, personal or corporate
2. that is able (actually able) to exercise
3. intentional influence
4. of a negative, damaging kind
5. in helping to shape what some other person or persons do.

Dominating power in this sense is interactive, because it requires an agent as bearer and an agent as victim (clauses 1 and 5). It is capacity-based, because it is able to exist without being exercised (clause 2). It is an intentional sort of power, because the things which the bearer can do are things that the bearer can be blamed or praised for doing: they are not beyond the agent's control, as we say (clause 3). And it is a negative kind of power, insofar as it is a capacity to damage the victim, not a capacity to improve the victim's lot (clause 4). The conception contrasts in one or more of these dimensions with the other forms of power that political theorists countenance.

CHAPTER 3

Non-domination as a Political Ideal

We saw in Chapter 1 that when people spoke of freedom and the value of freedom in the republican tradition, they were focused on what we have been describing as non-domination: the condition under which you live in the presence of other people but at the mercy of none. We saw in Chapter 2 what exactly, or more or less exactly, non-domination involves; in particular, we looked at the features of freedom as non-domination that mark a contrast with the now more established idea of freedom as non-interference. The differences all stem from the fact that you can be dominated by someone, as in the case of the lucky or cunning slave, without actually suffering interference at their hands; and you can be interfered with by some agency, as in the case of subjection to a suitable form of law and government, without being dominated by anyone.

But the republican tradition did not just offer a distinctive interpretation of what freedom involves. It cast freedom as non-domination in the role of supreme political value, and gave support to the assumption that the rationale for a coercive and potentially dominating state is simply that, properly constituted, such a regime serves to advance that value. 'Liberty is the Chiefest Good of Civil Society' (Gwyn 1965: 88). The tradition countenanced no other end for the state—no other justified end—besides that of furthering this freedom. It depicted the ideal of non-domination as the one and only yardstick by which to judge the social and political constitution of a community.

I turn in this chapter and the next to the consideration of why, faithfully to the republican tradition, we should recognize non-domination as a value with a distinctive claim to the role of yardstick for our institutions. This chapter makes out the basic case for why and how non-domination can figure as a political ideal, and the next chapter looks at the attractive features of the ideal. This chapter is in three sections. First I show why freedom as non-domination is a personal good that practically everyone has reason to want and, more generally, to value. Then I argue that it is something which inherently concerns political institutions, not something that can just be left to individuals to further by other means. And third, I maintain that non-domination is a goal which such institutions should seek to promote, not a constraint that they have to honour in the pursuit of other goals; I defend a consequentialist version of republicanism. This republican doctrine, as we shall see, is a consequentialism with a difference: it allows us to say that the institutions which promote people's freedom as non-domination go to constitute that freedom, not to cause it; the doctrine does not countenance any temporal or causal gulf between civic institutions and the freedom of citizens.

There is nothing in this book to support explicitly the traditional assumption that freedom as non-domination is the only goal with which our political institutions need to be concerned. But my own view is that once we fully understand the demands of promoting non-domination, once we appreciate the extensive but attractive reshaping of those institutions that it would require, we shall find the claim quite congenial. Those who hail freedom as non-interference and who think that the minimal state is not normatively satisfactory generally invoke other values as independent criteria of political evaluation: values like equality, or welfare, or utility, or whatever. Freedom as non-domination does not call for the same sort of supplementation since, as we shall see, it already requires institutions that perform well in regard to values like equality and welfare; thus those values do not have to be introduced as distinct desiderata.

In arguing for the attractions of freedom as non-domination, I shall be comparing it exclusively with the negative ideal of non-interference, not with the positive ideal of self-mastery. If positive freedom is interpreted in populist fashion as democratic participation, then this neglect will scarcely need explanation: such a participatory ideal is not feasible in the modern world, and in any case the prospect of each being subject to the will of all is scarcely attractive. But in comparing freedom as non-domination just with the negative ideal of non-interference, I shall also be ignoring those versions of the positive ideal of self-mastery that equate it with personal autonomy. And I need to say something in explanation of this restriction of focus.

Freedom as personal autonomy may be a very attractive value, perhaps even an intrinsic good (Raz 1986); indeed I am myself committed to a version of the autonomy ideal that I describe as 'orthonomy' (Pettit and Smith 1990; 1996). Freedom as personal self-mastery, however, is a richer ideal than that of freedom as non-domination; there can certainly be non-domination without personal self-mastery, but there can hardly be any meaningful form of self-mastery without non-domination. Moreover, freedom as personal self-mastery ought to be facilitated, if not actively promoted, under a state that assures freedom as non-domination; it is bound to be easier for people to achieve autonomy once they are assured of not being dominated by others. It would not be a useful exercise, then, to compare the attractions of these two freedoms. For consistently with thinking that the state should be orientated towards the promotion of freedom as non-domination, and not just towards the promotion of freedom as non-interference, I can happily admit the attractions of freedom as personal self-mastery.

There is a difference, of course, between the republican viewpoint that I defend and the position of someone who thinks that the state should explicitly embrace the richer ideal of promoting people's personal autonomy. Such an opponent will argue that the sort of state required for the promotion of non-domination is too austere an agency to be attractive or compelling, and that we need to ascribe the richer ideal to the state if we are to justify the political expectations that we are entitled to entertain. But it is not possible at this stage to respond to that argument. I can only hope that once opponents of this kind see the full profile of the republican state that I defend, and once they perceive that that state will facilitate the realization of the autonomy that they treasure, they may be persuaded that there is no need to give the state explicit responsibility for promoting people's personal self-mastery. They may be persuaded that people can be trusted to look after their own autonomy, given that they live under a dispensation where they are protected from domination by others.

I. Non-domination as a personal good

Almost everyone assumes that freedom as non-interference is a good. It is the sort of thing that anyone will desire for themselves and, generalizing to the case of others, will admit as desirable for anyone. I go along with that assumption, and I intend to argue for the value of freedom as non-domination—to argue for its status as a personal good—by showing how well it compares with the other sort of freedom in various regards. I will argue, in particular, that it compares very favourably with freedom as non-interference in its claim to be an instrumental good: a good that generates other benefits for the individual who enjoys it. I have no quarrel with someone who argues that

freedom as non-domination, or indeed freedom as non-interference, is
an intrinsic good, but I shall not address that claim here.

An instrumental good

The main instrumental benefit that we associate with the enjoyment of
non-interference is the benefit of not having your choices blocked or
inhibited by others, at least not in an intentional or quasi-intentional
manner. Consistently with enjoying a total absence of interference
you may find yourself constrained by all sorts of natural obstacle—by
your own lack of power or wealth or by the unfriendliness of the environment—but you will not be constrained by obstacles of an intentional sort, for such obstacles would represent interference. If your
actual non-interference is maximized, then, or if your expectation of
non-interference is maximized, you will be assured of the maximal
enjoyment available of this benefit.

We saw earlier that the cause of advancing freedom as non-
interference in a society may be taken to include not just reducing the
factors that compromise it—acts of interference by others—but also
the factors that condition it: natural obstacles. To advance freedom as
non-interference will be to remove interference as far as possible, and
to expand as far as possible the sphere of uninterfered-with choice.
Should we count the reduction of natural obstacles, as well as the
reduction of intentional interference, as a benefit associated instrumentally with enjoying freedom as non-interference? I argue not.

The absence of natural obstacles is not a benefit that flows instrumentally from the enjoyment of non-interference, since you can enjoy
perfect non-interference in the presence of such obstacles. The connection with non-interference comes about more indirectly. If you
believe that non-interference is a value, say because of associated
benefits, then it is natural, not just to want to promote the intensity of
its enjoyment in a society, but also—so far as this is consistent—to
expand the range of choice over which it is enjoyed. While the project
of aggregatively advancing non-interference does involve reducing
natural obstacles to choice, therefore, the link with reducing natural
obstacles is premissed on the independent value—say, the instrumental value—of non-interference; it is not itself part of what makes non-
interference valuable.

If this treatment of freedom as non-interference seems unfair, then
I should say that the parallel lesson goes for freedom as non-
domination. The project of advancing non-domination, assuming that
it is a suitable value, naturally involves both promoting the intensity

of non-domination—removing factors that compromise this freedom—and expanding the domain of undominated choice: removing
factors, like natural or legal or cultural obstacles, that condition it. But
the assumption that non-domination is a value, say an instrumental
value, has to be vindicated independently of the effects that might go
with expanding the domain of undominated choice. The lesson that
applies to establishing the value of freedom as non-interference also
applies here.

We have seen, then, that the main instrumental benefit associated
with freedom as non-interference is the enjoyment of choice that is not
affected by intentional blocking or inhibition by others. We now turn
to the question of how freedom as non-domination compares in this
respect. Does it provide the same instrumental benefit? And if it does
not, does it offer benefits that are suitably compensating? I shall argue
that it provides something short of the same instrumental benefit but
that it compensates, and more than compensates, by providing three
further benefits as well.

Freedom as non-domination promises, not exemption from intentional interference, but exemption only from intentional interference on
an arbitrary basis: specifically, exemption from a capacity on the part of
others for arbitrary interference. It is consistent, unlike freedom as non-
interference, with a high level of non-arbitrary interference of the sort
that a suitable system of law might impose. What it sets itself against is
not interference as such—in particular, not interference of that non-
arbitrary kind—but only the sort of interference that occurs under such
a lack of checking and constraint that, for all the victim can tell, it may
be guided by hostile, unshared interests and hostile, unshared ideas.
Devotees of non-interference look for a sphere of action for the individual that is untainted by any actual or expected coercion. Devotees of
non-domination look for a sphere of action that is untainted by coercion—or the capacity for coercion—from arbitrary quarters only.

The difference between the two ideals on this front connects with
their different views of law. Devotees of freedom as non-interference
view legal or state coercion, no matter how well bounded and controlled, as a form of coercion that is just as bad in itself as coercion
from other quarters; if it is to be justified, then that can only be because
its presence makes for a lesser degree of coercion overall. Devotees of
freedom as non-domination view state coercion, in particular coercion
that occurs under a suitable form of law, as something that is not so
potentially unobjectionable, being on a par with obstruction by natural obstacles rather than with coercion by arbitrary powers. As I put
it in the last chapter, the first group put every system of law on the

compromising side of the compromising/conditioning divide, while the second argue that a suitably non-arbitrary form of law belongs on the conditioning side of that distinction.

In promising actual or expected exemption from all interference, the ideal of freedom as non-interference may look more attractive than its rival. Better, it seems, to be exempt from all interference, or as much interference as possible, than to be exempt just from interference—or even from a capacity on the part of others for interference—that occurs on an arbitrary basis. But there are three other benefits that the rival ideal of freedom as non-domination is likely to bring in its train, and these should serve to establish its greater value.

The first of the further benefits becomes visible when we reflect on a salient way in which arbitrary interference is worse than non-arbitrary. To suffer the reality or expectation of arbitrary interference is to suffer an extra malaise over and beyond that of having your choices intentionally curtailed. It is to have to endure a high level of uncertainty, since the arbitrary basis on which the interference occurs means that there is no predicting when it will strike. Such uncertainty makes planning much more difficult than it would be under a corresponding prospect of non-arbitrary interference. And, of course, it is also likely to produce a high level of anxiety.

Freedom as non-domination requires us to reduce the capacities for arbitrary interference to which a person is exposed, while freedom as non-interference requires us to minimize the person's expectation of interference as such. But this means that, while the non-domination ideal would tend to require conditions where certainty is high, the non-interference ideal is consistent with a great loss on this front. It is quite possible that the maximal non-interference possible for someone will be available under an arrangement where that person has to suffer much uncertainty. But it is hardly conceivable that the same is true for the maximal non-domination that they might achieve.

Imagine that we have a choice between leaving employers with a lot of power over employees, or men with a lot of power over women, and using state interference to reduce such power. Maximizing overall non-interference is perfectly compatible with taking the first option. While we do not guard against interference by the stronger under that option, we may not think that it is very likely to occur; and because we do not guard against interference by the stronger, we will count the absence of state interference as a great boon. Thus maximizing overall non-interference is perfectly compatible with forcing the individual employee or the individual woman to have to live with much uncertainty.

What is true at the overall or aggregate level may also hold at the individual level. For related considerations may mean that maximizing the individual's own non-interference would require exposing them to a high level of uncertainty. Perhaps the recourse to the law would be so interventionist in their own lives and so ineffective in stopping interference by others that it would mean more interference, not less. Perhaps the way to maximize the person's expected non-interference is to leave them in subjection to others, then, in a position where they suffer much uncertainty. Their expectation of non-interference would be at a maximum, but at the maximal point envisaged the interference to which they are exposed would be the arbitrary sort that induces uncertainty: the sort that occasions anxiety and makes planning difficult.

The project of increasing a person's freedom as non-domination could not tolerate this uncertainty, because it would baulk at accepting any degree of subjection to another. Devotees of freedom as non-domination emphasize the advantage of their ideal in this respect when they say that the unfree person is exposed to the inconstant, uncertain will of another and consequently suffers anxiety and wretchedness. 'Having always some unknown evil to fear, though it should never come, he has no perfect enjoyment of himself, or of any of the blessings of life' (Priestley 1993: 35). Their assumption is that if we try to further someone's freedom as non-domination then we will remove the spectre of such uncertainty. Maybe the person has to live by the standing rule of a constitution and a law, a rule that makes for a degree of coercion in their lives. But they do not have to live under constant fear of unpredictable interference, and so they can organize their affairs on a systematic basis and with a large measure of tranquillity.

The second benefit associated with freedom as non-domination, and not with freedom as non-interference, becomes visible when we reflect on another way in which arbitrary interference is worse than non-arbitrary. To suffer the reality or expectation of arbitrary interference is not only to have to endure a high level of uncertainty. It is also to have to keep a weather eye on the powerful, anticipating what they will expect of you and trying to please them, or anticipating where they will be and trying to stay out of their way; it is to have strategic deference and anticipation forced upon you at every point. You can never sail on, unconcerned, in the pursuit of your own affairs; you have to navigate an area that is mined on all sides with dangers.

Advancing someone's freedom as non-domination means reducing other people's capacities for arbitrary interference in their lives, and will reduce their need for strategic deference or anticipation, as it will reduce the level of uncertainty with which they have to live. But advancing someone's freedom as non-interference is not guaranteed to have this effect. For it may very well be that the best way to maximize someone's expectation of non-interference is to rely in good part on their native wit and cunning: to get them to look after their own freedom by forcing them to develop and exercise strategies of placating and anticipating the powerful. A world in which strategic flattery and avoidance is rampant—a world in which women become adept at placating their men folk, for example, or at not crossing their paths—may represent the best prospect for keeping interference as such at a minimum.

Having to practise strategic deference and anticipation, however, like having to live with uncertainty, is a serious cost. For the strategic disposition imposed requires the agent to curtail their own choices: to tug the forelock at appropriate moments and, when that promises not to be enough, to keep out of sight. Such enforced self-denial, of course, does not represent a form of interference, even of arbitrary interference, for interference has to be intentionally perpetrated by another; that, indeed, is why the cause of freedom as non-interference can be promoted by an arrangement involving a lot of strategic deference and anticipation. But nonetheless it is clearly bad that people should have to resort to denying themselves various choices in order to achieve non-interference. And it is a clear advantage of the ideal of freedom as non-domination that in targeting arbitrary interference as the enemy, and in seeking to reduce the capacities of others to interfere arbitrarily in anyone's affairs, it presents a picture of the free life in which the need for strategy is minimized.[1]

The third benefit associated with freedom as non-domination but not with freedom as non-interference is one that I have already highlighted in arguing that the fact that someone enjoys non-domination is likely to become a matter of common knowledge and to generate associated subjective and intersubjective benefits. While someone's freedom as non-interference may be at a maximum in a situation where they have to recognize that they are vulnerable to the whim of another, and have an inferior social status to that other, the enjoyment of freedom as non-domination goes with the possibility of their seeing themselves as non-vulnerable in that way and as possessed of a comparable social standing with the other. They can look the other in the eye; they do not have to bow and scrape.

---

[1] I am grateful to John Ferejohn, Liam Murphy, and Quentin Skinner for helping me to see this point.

That two people enjoy the same freedom as non-interference, that they even enjoy the same expectation of such freedom, is consistent with one of them, and only one of them, having the power to interfere in the life of the other. Consistently with possessing the power to interfere, the more powerful may have no interest in interfering; this may be because of indifference or preoccupation or devotion: it may even be because the less powerful people are good at keeping them happy or at keeping out of their way. Thus the powerful person may be as unlikely to interfere with others as the less powerful. But even if both parties enjoy equal non-interference, and an equal expectation of non-interference, they are likely to develop a shared awareness of the asymmetry of power, and indeed an awareness shared with others in the community: this was a major theme of the last chapter. And once it is a matter of common awareness that one of them is powerful enough to be able to interfere more or less arbitrarily in the life of the other, then that is going to affect their relative status. It is going to be a matter of common knowledge that the one is weaker than the other, vulnerable to the other, and to that extent subordinate to the other.

Why should I be forced to think of myself in this way, it may be asked, if the other person is really no more likely to interfere with me than I with them? The answer takes us back to a consideration already mentioned in the last chapter. Seeing an option as an improbable choice for an agent, even as a vanishingly improbable choice, is different from seeing it as a choice that is not accessible to the agent: seeing it as a choice that is not within the agent's power. Thus the fact that another person is unlikely to interfere with me, just because they happen to have no interest in interfering, is consistent with their retaining access to the option of interfering with me. Now it is the attribution of accessible choices, not the attribution of probable choices, that determines how I and others view a person and, in particular, whether we view them as someone on whom I depend for enjoying non-interference (Pettit and Smith 1996). And so it is quite possible for me to be forced to think of myself as subordinate to someone who is no more likely to interfere with me than I am to interfere with them. More generally, it is possible for this way of thinking to be established as a matter of common recognition, so that my status, my standing in public perception, becomes that of a subordinate.

Advancing someone's freedom as non-domination is bound to mean reducing this sort of subordination, as it is bound to mean reducing the uncertainty with which they have to live, and the strategy to which they have to have recourse. For while it is possible to enjoy the highest degree of non-interference available in a situation where you are subordinate to another, every increase in your non-domination is going to mean decreasing the subordination to which you are exposed. After all, increasing your non-domination means reducing the capacity of others for interfering with you on an arbitrary basis, and that means reducing their access to such interference.

To sum up these reflections, then, freedom as non-domination may seem to do less well than freedom as non-interference in servicing unrestricted choice; after all, it is opposed only to arbitrary interference—specifically, to others having the capacity for such interference—not to interference as such. But freedom as non-domination does much better in three other respects, all of them of intuitively great importance. It promises to do better in delivering a person from uncertainty, and from the associated anxiety and inability to plan; from the need to exercise strategy with the powerful, having to defer to them and anticipate their various moves; and from the subordination that goes with a common awareness that the person is exposed to the possibility of arbitrary interference by another: that there is another who can deploy such interference, even if they are not likely to do so.

As against my line of argument so far, it may be said that those who espouse freedom as non-interference are not generally known for welcoming or even acknowledging the uncertainty, the strategy, and the subordination I have been documenting. How to explain this? The answer may be that those who espouse the ideal often take it for granted that it is best furthered by traditional, non-dominating institutions—say, by the institutions of the common law—that are most readily justified, as they were traditionally justified, by the desire to avoid arbitrariness. Thus what the people in question effectively embrace is not what they officially embrace: it is not freedom as non-interference, neat, but rather freedom as non-interference under the rule of such a common law.[2]

This constrained version of the non-interference ideal is close enough to the ideal of freedom as non-domination to make it seem that uncertainty, strategy, and subordination are ruled out. They are ruled out, it is true, in the forum where people's relations are effectively directed by the relevant legal injunctions. But the constrained ideal still falls short of freedom as non-domination, since it is consistent with allowing domination—and the attendant uncertainty, strategy, and subordination—within those spaces where the relevant legal injunction leaves people to other devices. Thus it is consistent, in a

[2] As indicated in the last chapter, Hayek may be an example of someone who takes this view. See Gray (1986) and Kukathas (1989).

way that freedom as non-domination would not be, with domination occurring in the workplace or in the home or in any of a multitude of so-called private spaces.

I do not think that anyone can be indifferent to the benefits that freedom as non-domination promises. To be able to live your life without uncertainty about the interference you will have to endure; to be able to live without having to stay on your toes in dealing with the powerful; and to be able to live without subordination to others: these are great and palpable goods and they make a powerful case for the instrumental attractions of freedom as non-domination.

A primary good

They make a case, indeed, not just for the instrumental attractions of the ideal but for its status, in John Rawls's (1971) phrase, as a primary good. A primary good is something that a person has instrumental reasons to want, no matter what else they want: something that promises results that are likely to appeal to them, no matter what they value and pursue.

The considerations rehearsed so far show that advancing someone's freedom as non-domination is likely to help them escape from uncertainty, strategy, and subordination; certainly, it is more likely to do this than advancing their freedom as non-interference. But something stronger also holds true. Suppose we take steps to reduce a person's uncertainty about interference, to reduce their need for exercising a strategy of deference and anticipation with others, and to reduce the subordination associated with vulnerability. It is hard to see how we could take such steps without at the same time advancing their freedom as non-domination. Freedom as non-domination appears to be, not just a more or less sufficient instrument for promoting those effects, but a more or less necessarily associated factor. There is no promoting non-domination without promoting those effects; and there is no promoting those effects without promoting non-domination. This may not hold in every possible world, but it certainly seems to hold under plausible assumptions about how the actual world works.

Given that freedom as non-domination is bound up in this way with the effects discussed, how could anyone fail to want it for themselves, or fail to recognize it as a value? Short of embracing some religiously or ideologically motivated doctrine of self-abasement, people will surely find their ends easier of attainment to the extent that they enjoy non-domination. Certainly they will find those ends easier of attainment if they are ends conceived and pursued under the pluralistic conditions that obtain in most developed democracies and, of course, in the international world at large. Freedom as non-domination is not just an instrumental good, then; it also enjoys the status, at least in relevant circumstances, of a primary good.

This point is easily supported. For almost all the things that a person is likely to want, the pursuit of those things is going to be facilitated by their having an ability to make plans (Bratman 1987). But short of enjoying non-domination, the person's ability to make plans will be undermined by the sort of uncertainty we discussed. Hence, to the extent that it involves a reduction in uncertainty, non-domination has the firm attraction of a primary good.

But the primary-good status of freedom as non-domination can also be supported by reference to the reduction of strategy and subordination that it makes possible. To be a person is to be a voice that cannot properly be ignored, a voice which speaks to issues raised in common with others and which speaks with a certain authority: enough authority, certainly, for discord with that voice to give others reason to pause and think (Pettit 1993*a*; chs. 2, 4; Postema 1995; Pettit and Smith 1996). To be treated properly as a person, then, is to be treated as a voice that cannot be dismissed without independent reason: to be taken as someone worth listening to. The condition of domination would reduce the likelihood of being treated as a person in this way, so far as it is associated with a need for strategy and a subordinate status.

The dominated, strategy-bound person is someone with reason to watch what they say, someone who must be assumed always to have an eye to what will please their dominators. And equally, the dominated, subordinate person is someone, by common assumption, who has reason to impress their dominators and try to win a higher ranking in their opinion. Such a person will naturally be presumed to lack an independent voice, at least in the area where domination is relevant. They will fail to make the most basic claim on the attention of the more powerful, for they will easily be seen as attention-seekers: they will easily be seen in the way that adults often see precocious children. They may happen to receive attention but they will not command attention; they may happen to receive respect but they will not command respect.

It seems reasonable to hold that, no matter what their other commitments, everyone—or at least everyone who has to make their way in a pluralistic society—will want to be treated properly as a person, as a voice that cannot be generally ignored. But that being so, it follows that every such person has reason to want freedom as non-domination;

in the absence of such freedom, they will be the strategy-bound, sub-ordinate sorts of creature who cannot expect to be treated properly as persons. Thus the connection with avoiding strategy and subordination, like the connection with avoiding uncertainty, shows that freedom as non-domination has the status of a primary good.

II. Non-domination as a political concern

So much on why non-domination is a personal good or value. But the argument does not yet show that non-domination is a value that the state ought to try and advance. We all know that friendship is a great value in human life, but few of us believe that the state should give itself the task of furthering friendship. Why is freedom as non-domination different, as republicans have always taken it to be?

Although friendship is something that all of us pursue and value, we probably think that most of us can pursue it fairly effectively for ourselves and that the state is unlikely to do better. If republicans take a different view of freedom, that is because it contrasts in these respects with friendship. It is also a good that most of us pursue and value, as we have just been arguing. But unlike friendship it satisfies two crucial conditions, one negative, the other positive. It is not something that individuals can satisfactorily pursue by private, decentralized means and it is something that the state is able to pursue fairly effectively.

The discussion in the remainder of this book amounts to a sustained argument that freedom as non-domination satisfies the positive condition. The book is designed to show how institutions can be designed—specifically, designed in a republican pattern—so that people's enjoyment of non-domination is more or less smoothly maximized. It remains in the present section, then, to indicate why freedom as non-domination satisfies the negative condition: why it is not something that individuals can satisfactorily pursue by relying just on their own private efforts.

Against the decentralized pursuit of non-domination

One more or less obvious argument against leaving non-domination to the care of individuals is that doing so would be likely to lead to a very unequal distribution of non-domination. Suppose that people do pursue their own non-domination, each in their own private way. They individually seek to defend themselves against interference from others, to punish any interference that occurs—thereby showing that no one can interfere in their affairs with impunity—and to deter or deflect possible acts of interference. It should be clear that such individual efforts can lead in a very undesirable direction. Inequalities of physical health and prowess, social connection and influence, environmental location, and the like are inevitable in any real-world situation. And such inequalities are bound to accumulate under any real-world history, as the strong use their strength to accumulate more and more resources and thereby to become stronger still. Thus, the inevitable result of people's pursuing non-domination in a decentralized way will be that most find themselves at the mercy, here of this stronger person or group, there of another. We may expect a society where petty despotisms are rampant: where men lord it over women, the richer lord it over the poorer, insiders lord it over outsiders, and so on. We must countenance even the possibility that the dynamics will produce all-powerful despots, each with a region or domain of their own.

Some may argue that this view of things is excessively pessimistic, and that a decentralized system of promoting non-domination would not necessarily lead to a very poor distribution of non-domination. In order to persuade those in this category, a further argument is needed. We need to be able to argue that, pessimism aside, it is generally going to be bad for the cause of non-domination to rely on people's having reciprocal powers sufficient to check one another's interference; in particular, that the strategy of constitutional provision—the strategy of having a state that seeks to promote non-domination by non-dominating means—is much more promising.

While a constitutional authority will not dominate people, it must invariably limit the choices available to them or make those choices more costly. Any system of law and government is bound to mean that certain options are no longer available to agents, or at least no longer available on the previous terms. It will put coercive pressures in place in an attempt to remove a variety of choices. And since it must rely on taxation for its own existence, it will ensure that various choices that remain available become more costly. While it will not make people unfree, in the sense of dominating them, it will reduce the range and ease of undominated choice that they enjoy: it will make them relatively non-free.

But though the strategy of constitutional provision does have this disadvantage, it is more promising in that regard than wholesale recourse to the strategy of reciprocal power. Under the strategy of reciprocal power, as that works ideally, each achieves non-domination through having resources sufficient to ensure that every act of

interference by another can be effectively resisted; defence is so effective that there is no need to resort to deterrent measures. But the
scenario where there is no constitutional provision for universal protection, and where each asserts himself or herself in individual resistance, still approximates to permanent civil war. While people might
enjoy non-domination under such a scenario—assuming that no one
person or group becomes dominant—the range and ease of undominated choice would be savagely reduced. No one would be able to
trade or travel, for example, without having to equip themselves with
costly resources of resistance and defence. The choices available to
people might be undominated, but they would be very expensive and
very restricted.

This disadvantage of the strategy of reciprocal power in relation to
the alternative strategy of constitutional provision can be expressed in
our language of compromising and conditioning factors. Both strategies mean that while people's liberty may not be directly compromised, it is seriously conditioned: in the one case, by the inhibiting
effects of everyone's being their own defender, in the other by the
coercive and fiscal costs of the law. The disadvantage of the reciprocal-
power strategy is simply that it promises to have a much more severe
conditioning effect. Almost any other way of achieving a life without
domination would seem to be better than having to endure the restrictions imposed by a war of all against all.

But even this argument against relying on the strategy of reciprocal
power is flattering to that strategy. For it assumes that people have
resources sufficient to be able to resist interference effectively, and that
they do not have to rely on threatening others with retaliation in order
to deter them: they do not have to rely on coercing others and thereby
interfering with them in a manner that does not track their interests
and ideas. But this assumption is itself quite unrealistic. For it is
inevitable, under any such scenario, that people will depend on the
deterrent value of threatening retaliation, not just on their defensive
resources. And to the extent that they do rely on such mutual coercion, they will continue in the scenario envisaged to interfere with one
another on an arbitrary basis. The best that is really feasible under the
strategy of reciprocal power is a balance of deterrence, not a defensive
equilibrium.

The decentralized arrangement envisaged under the strategy has all
the disadvantages canvassed in the state of nature that is demonized,
ironically, by Hobbes (Tuck 1989). Hobbes's argument is that if everyone seeks to protect themselves against interference from others, in
particular to protect themselves pre-emptively, then the result is

bound to be a war of all against all. Each will naturally prefer a strategy of self-protection, including pre-emptive self-protection, to a strategy involving unilateral disarmament. This is going to be a better strategy than disarmament, after all, no matter what others do: if others self-protect then it is going to be an essential defence measure, and if others disarm it is going to be a useful insurance. But if everyone follows a strategy of self-protection, including pre-emptive self-protection, then everyone will be worse off in terms of non-domination than if everyone disarms. People will dig themselves into a hole; they will individually act in a way that is collectively self-defeating (Parfit 1984: pt. 1).

It does not take much reflection to become persuaded that whatever the limiting effects of constitutional provision on the choices available to people, they are nothing compared with the disadvantages associated with wholesale recourse to the strategy of reciprocal power. And yet constitutional provision promises to do at least as well in reducing domination by others. Thus the strategy of constitutional provision, the strategy of having recourse to a state, looks by far the more attractive option. It may be a good idea to rely on the reciprocal-power strategy within the framework of a constitutional state. The trade union movement almost certainly advanced the non-domination of workers in the industrial world of the nineteenth century. And that movement increased workers' non-domination precisely by giving them collective powers with which to confront the powers of employers. But there is very little reason to be attracted to the strategy of reciprocal power as a general means of advancing people's freedom as non-domination.

Freedom as non-domination, then, is not an ideal that should be left to individuals to pursue in a decentralized way. The strategy of reciprocal power holds out the prospect of too many problems to be taken seriously. The lesson is that we should explore the alternative and more promising strategy of relying on constitutional provision, and the remainder of the book is given to that pursuit.

Non-domination and the modern, pluralistic state

The exploration of the strategy links us with the project that was pursued over many centuries by thinkers in the republican tradition. But it is important to stress that we shall be looking to political institutions with quite a different attitude from that of premodern republicans. We saw in the first chapter that traditional republicans would have thought that freedom as non-domination was attainable via the political system only for a propertied élite of mainstream males: the élite who would constitute the citizens. As we explore the requirements of non-domination, we shall naturally break with the élitism of traditional republicans and assume that our concern must be universal in scope. The brand of republicanism that we shall be developing is in this respect a characteristically modern or inclusive brand: one that shares with the liberalism to which the likes of Bentham and Paley gave birth the assumption that all human beings are equal, and that any plausible political ideal must be an ideal for all.

The proposal to take non-domination as a supreme ideal for the state will give rise to misgivings of the kind that standard liberalism attracts when it hails the ideal of non-interference, or some combination of non-interference and other values, as the supreme political good (Sandel 1984). Like the liberal project, our proposal—our republican proposal—is motivated by the assumption that the ideal is capable of commanding the allegiance of the citizens of developed, multicultural societies, regardless of their more particular conceptions of the good. Communitarians will maintain against this assumption that the ideal of non-domination is not as neutral as it seems—it is distinctively Western or characteristically masculinist or whatever—and that, neutral or not, it is incapable of motivating people across the familiar divisions of race, religion, gender, and the like.[3]

Those who take these lines of criticism are offering, in effect, a counsel of despair about contemporary, developed society. They are saying that there is no possibility of morally motivating allegiance to a polity, other than on the basis of a fairly homogeneous community grouping; that is why they are well described as communitarians. But such thinkers are also offering, in my opinion, a counsel of ignorance. People in some traditions may display an ideologically nurtured desire to subject themselves to this or that subgroup: to those, for example, of noble birth, priestly role, or patriarchal status. But to my eye this requires the suppression of a deep and universal human desire for standing and dignity, and the elimination of a robust and healthy disposition to feel resentment at such pretensions of superiority. And even if I am wrong about that, what is certainly true, as I argued in the last section, is that someone who is content to live in the mainstreams

[3] Contemporary liberals claim to satisfy neutrality by looking for a state in which each individual is enabled to pursue their own conception of the good. Republicans satisfy neutrality through having the state acknowledge only the ecumenical or non-sectarian good represented by the freedom of its citizens. Christine Korsgaard (1993) makes the point in her discussion of old liberals (in effect, republicans) and new liberals. Contemporary liberals tend to embrace, not just non-interference, but other more contentious ideals as well—equality, welfare, or whatever—and this may explain their interpretation of neutrality.

of a contemporary, pluralistic society is bound to treasure the ideal of not being dominated by others. Embrace the life of a sect who abase themselves before some self-appointed guru and you will see little in the ideal of freedom as non-domination. Embrace the life of a contemporary, pluralistic society and you will see much.

No doubt it will be said that, even if this is true, still the universally recognized ideal of non-domination is too faint a light to guide a society and polity: that the motivationally effective shaping of shared institutions requires recourse to less neutral, culture-bound beacons (MacIntyre 1987). But this sustained despair about contemporary society should merit only limited sympathy. It may ultimately prove impossible to identify a neutral political ideal, such as I believe freedom as non-domination to be, which is capable of commanding the allegiance of people in different subcultures; it may transpire that no such ideal can sustain the demands that people are likely to entertain in relation to the polity. But let that prove impossible, after the effort has been made; don't let the proclamation of impossibility inhibit the making of the effort. I see the argument in this book as an effort along precisely the path that these critics would block. I respond to their criticism by inviting them to follow that argument—especially as it is developed in the last chapter of each part—and to locate the points at which their world-weary, theory-weary lights, ultimately their ultra-conservative lights (Holmes 1989), predict failure.

III. Non-domination as a goal, not a constraint

Assuming that non-domination is indeed a value, and a value relevant to the political system, the next question is how the value should shape that system: how it should serve to guide it. There are two salient if not strictly exclusive possibilities (Pettit 1997). The first is that the value or good or ideal should serve as a goal for the state to promote, the second that it should serve as a constraint on how the state is to pursue other goals.

Consequentialism and non-consequentialism

A good will be a goal for an agent or agency if and only if the task is to promote the good: to maximize its expected realization. Take the good of peace. This will be a goal for an agent or agency if and only if the task is to do whatever is required for maximizing expected peace: whatever is required, notice, even if this includes breaking the peace, as in fighting the war to end all wars. A good will be a constraint for an agent or agency, on the other hand, if and only if the task is not necessarily to promote it, but to bear witness to its importance or to honour it. Honouring the good, so we may suppose, will mean acting in the way that would maximize the expected value, if everyone else did the same as you: it will mean doing your part in the promotion of the value on the assumption that others look after their parts (Pettit 1991; 1997). Peace will be a constraint on an agent or agency, then, if the task is always to act in a peaceable way, rather than doing whatever would maximize peace.

Bertrand Russell went to prison during the First World War, as did many others, for pacifist beliefs. He argued forcefully that the value of peace required the allies to withdraw from that gruesome and useless conflict. But there was a difference between Russell and some of his pacifist friends which only appeared at the time of the Second World War. For where they continued to adopt a pacifist stance in 1939 and to oppose the allies' resort to war, Russell took the view that this war was justified: in particular, that it was justified by the fact that the cause of peace would be forever compromised if Hitler was not opposed. The difference that came out in these varying stances was that whereas the other pacifists took the value of peace as a constraint on the behaviour of a state—as something that could not be breached even for the sake of maximizing peace itself—Russell revealed a consequentialist attitude to the value of peace. He was passionately devoted to peace, but saw it as a goal that a state ought to promote, even if promoting it meant going to war, not as a constraint that it was bound to honour.

Freedom as non-interference features in some theories as a goal for the state and in others as a constraint on how the state may behave. Suppose you think that the main or unique political good is freedom as non-interference. What institutions ought you to regard, then, as politically right for a society? The answer which makes non-interference a goal is, roughly: those institutions whose presence would mean that there is more non-interference enjoyed in the society than would otherwise be the case; those institutions which do best at promoting such liberty. The answer is rough, because this formula does not yet say whether promoting a property like liberty means maximizing its actual or expected realization and, if the latter, whether the probabilities that should determine the expectation are subject to any constraints. But we need not worry here about such details.

It may seem that this first answer—this consequentialist or teleological answer—is the only possible theory of right institutions for someone attached to the value of freedom as non-interference. But a little thought shows that this is not so. An alternative approach would start from the fact that the state is itself a source of interference, since law is necessarily coercive, and that in this respect the state offends against the value of non-interference: it fails to honour non-interference in the way in which someone fighting for the cause of peace fails to honour the value of peace. Someone taking this approach is likely to invoke the language of rights, and to say that the point is not to promote overall non-interference as well as possible but to respect the allegedly natural and fundamental rights of people not to be interfered with. This approach would represent a deontological version of liberalism, where the other represents a consequentialist or teleological form of the doctrine.

Deontological or rights-based liberalism raises questions about whether it could ever be legitimate to have a state; it may seem to make anarchism the only option. But those who take the approach have presented various arguments for why it is consistent with at least a minimal state: a state that serves only the nightwatchman functions of internal order and external defence. One of the best known of these arguments is that given by Robert Nozick (1974), according to which any state of anarchy in which people's rights to non-interference are respected would more or less inevitably lead, and lead without any breach of those rights, to the establishment of something close to a minimal state.

The choice that arises with peace and with freedom as non-interference arises also with freedom as non-domination, as indeed it arises with all values. It is possible to think of non-domination either as a goal that the state should promote or as a constraint that it should honour. In the first case, we think that the state should be designed so that expected non-domination among those who live under the system is at a maximum. In the second case, we think that it should be designed so that, whether or not expected non-domination is maximized, the system unambiguously testifies to the value of non-domination: this, through assuming the form required to promote expected non-domination in the ideally compliant world; this, in particular, through not involving the slightest taint of domination in the state's own constitutional arrangements.

Republican consequentialism

What attitude does the republican tradition take to non-domination? It is not possible to quote text and verse on the point, as the choice between teleological and deontological attitudes to freedom as non-domination was never articulated as such within the premodern tradition. But there is one aspect of the tradition that suggests a fundamentally teleological outlook. This is that almost all the main figures treat the question of which institutions do best by freedom as an open, empirical issue, not as a question capable of a priori resolution (Oldfield 1990). Machiavelli is willing to concede, for example, that where people are already corrupt, and unlikely to sustain a suitable form of law, the best way to promote freedom as non-domination may require a prince with fairly absolute power (Rubenstein 1991: 54). Locke (1965: s. 2.221) is ready to justify both a royal prerogative and a right of popular resistance by reference to the doctrine—also used in absolutist *raison d'état* arguments (Tuck 1993)—that the safety of the people is the highest law: *salus populi suprema lex.* And Montesquieu (1989: 204) is even prepared to admit, for empirical reasons, that the cause of liberty may occasionally justify the bill of attainder—the law directed against a particular individual—that was anathema to most republicans: 'the usage of the freest peoples that ever lived on earth makes me believe that there are cases where a veil has to be drawn, for a moment, over liberty, as one hides the statues of gods.'

The question of which institutions do best by freedom would not be open, or at least would not be very open, on a deontological approach. If certain institutions instantiate and honour non-domination in one context, then they will tend to do so in each of a range of plausible contexts. To honour non-domination in any such context will be to take the form that would be required for the promotion of non-domination if every other agent and agency did its part also; and this will be to take the same form, regardless of context. Thus the assumption that the question is open probably manifests a view of non-domination as a goal for the state to promote by those means, whatever they are, that prove empirically most effective.

Certain eighteenth-century thinkers like Hume and Burke would have regarded many of the republican masters as excessively dogmatic about which institutions did best by freedom (Haakonssen 1994: p. xvii). But if those masters were dogmatic on certain points—say, on the desirability of a citizen militia or on the evil of faction—they always offered empirical reasons for their preference: like Machiavelli, they usually returned to the lessons of republican Rome in order to defend their point of view.

A good example of the experimental attitude to institutions appears in the *Federalist Papers* when the authors—in this case, Hamilton—discuss the main institutional forms that republicans endorse (see too Paine 1989: 167–70).

The regular distribution of power into distinct departments; the introduction of legislative balances and checks; the institutions of courts composed of judges holding their offices during good behavior; the representation of the people in the legislature by deputies of their own election: these are wholly new discoveries, or have made their principal progress towards perfection in modern times. They are means, and powerful means, by which the excellencies of republican government may be retained and its imperfections lessened or avoided. To this catalogue of circumstances that tend to the amelioration of popular systems of civil government, I shall venture, however novel it may appear to some, to add one more . . . I mean the enlargement of the orbit within which such systems are to revolve, either in respect to the dimensions of a single State, or to the consolidation of several smaller States into one great Confederacy. (Madison, *et al.* 1987: 119)

But one word of caution. The republican approach became intertwined in the commonwealthman tradition with a habit of jurisprudential, natural-rights thinking, and had a deontological aspect. Locke and those commonwealthmen who followed him (Haakonssen 1995) saw natural rights in the image of the ancient rights of Britons, as means whereby republican goals could be advanced (but see Zuckert 1994); 'the primary use of rights by Locke and republican-Whig writers', as James Tully (1993: 261) puts it, 'is to constrain or limit the king or parliament to act within a known and recognized constitutional structure of lawfulness: to subject their governors to the rule of law by exercising their rights' (see too Tuck 1979; Worden 1991: 443; Ingram 1994). The influence of this natural-rights focus is clear also in various later documents, otherwise of a republican cast, like William Blackstone's *Commentaries on the Laws of England*, published in the 1760s, and indeed the *Federalist Papers* (Lacey and Haakonssen 1991). My inclination is to think that when republicans spoke of natural rights, however, they generally meant to argue that certain legal rights were essential means of achieving freedom as non-domination, and that the description of such rights as natural did not have more than rhetorical significance for them. In particular, it did not imply that the rights were fundamental norms that called to be honoured in deontological fashion.[4]

---

[4] One way of linking rights-talk with republicanism would be to recognize certain natural, perhaps absolute, rights not to be interfered with on an arbitrary basis; these would be different from natural rights not to be interfered with on any basis, and would not raise problems for legitimating the state: in practice, they would be rights against interference other than by a suitable law. Such an approach would amount to a programme of honouring non-domination, and would constitute a deontological version of republican thought. It is possible that, wittingly or unwittingly, some eighteenth-century figures may have been deontological republicans in that sense.

But, whatever is true of the historical tradition, I believe that a teleological orientation is clearly the better one to adopt, at least in the first instance, towards a value like non-domination. There are all sorts of ways in which it may be quite natural to tolerate a political failure to honour non-domination, if the failure represents the most effective means of increasing non-domination overall. It may be that the cause of maximizing non-domination requires giving parliament special unfettered powers in some area, for example, or giving judges a lot of sentencing discretion for a certain sort of offence. And if the cause of maximizing non-domination does require such departures from the perfect constitution—from the constitution that exemplifies non-domination in each and every feature of its design—then it would seem only natural to tolerate those departures; it would be precious, even fetishistic, to insist on remaining faithful to the abstract ideal.

I say that it is better in the first instance to adopt a consequentialist orientation with a value like non-domination. The reason for the qualification about the first instance is that if the promotion of non-domination required resort to institutional arrangements and strategies that proved intuitively repulsive to our moral sense, then we might well wonder whether non-domination really was an adequate political ideal or, if we remained confident on that point, whether the appropriate policy really was one of promoting the ideal rather than honouring it.

The relevant test, here as in other aspects of a political theory, is that of reflective equilibrium. The aim of political theory is to find a yardstick for political institutions that it is hard for anyone to question but that proves on examination to prescribe all the measures and patterns that it seems proper, by our considered judgements, to require: an ideal that proves, on reflection and perhaps after revision on both sides, to equilibrate with our judgements about proper political responses, and to help in the extrapolation of those judgements to new cases (Rawls 1971; Swanton 1992: ch. 2). A teleological republicanism would fail to satisfy reflective equilibrium if it required intuitively objectionable arrangements. As it happens, I do not believe that such a republicanism, such a consequentialist commitment to freedom as non-domination, does fail the test of reflective equilibrium. On the contrary, I think that it makes requirements that reform our considered intuitions only in ways which prove on reflection to be compelling: it is in equilibrium, in this reflective way, with considered intuitions about how things should be politically organized. The point should emerge in the course of the book.

Maximizing extent and intensity

How can freedom as non-domination serve as a unified goal for the state, how can it serve as an effective measure of political performance, given that extent and intensity represent separate dimensions of freedom? Are there not two goals here, rather than one? In raising this question, I abstract from the further complexity, that the measurement of extent may itself be problematic, given that kinds of choice matter as well as numbers of choices; this may require us to weight different areas differently (Taylor 1985: essay 8). I also abstract from the extra difficulty that in increasing non-domination overall we may make its distribution—its extent in another sense—very unequal; we deal with that complexity in the next chapter. Those issues aside, will there not be choices between increasing the intensity of non-domination enjoyed by someone over a certain area, or enjoyed by a group of people over that area, and increasing the extent of the non-domination in question: increasing the number of areas where they can enjoy such non-domination? And does that not make for a serious difficulty?

Strictly speaking, no. We might assume that there are distinct mixes of intensity and extent between which the republican can be indifferent, consistently with thinking that some mixes are better than others. It is possible for republicans to think that there are indifference curves in the space of intensity and extent but that one indifference curve is better than another; it represents equally valued mixes, any one of which is better than any of the equally valued mixes on the other curve (Barry 1965). If republicans do think this, then the maximization of non-domination for a person or group will involve locating that person on the best available indifference curve, by means of giving them this or that particular mix of intensity and extent.

But while the two dimensions of freedom as non-domination do not necessarily make for a theoretical difficulty, they do make for an unappealing indeterminacy. It appears, if we go along with the indifference-curve representation, that in seeking such and such a level of non-domination for someone our target may be any one of a large number of mixes: in this mix the person enjoys very intense non-domination but over a narrow extent; in that mix the person enjoys a less intense non-domination but over a wider extent; and so on. Such indeterminacy does not fit well with the intuition from which republicans begin: that domination is a salient evil, and that removing it or reducing it is a more or less unambiguous enterprise.

I believe that, consistently with acknowledging that there are two dimensions to non-domination, we can substantiate this republican attitude. There are a couple of assumptions that hold in the actual world, and they serve to make the target of maximizing non-domination considerably more determinate than the indifference-curve representation would suggest.

The first assumption is that when the state reduces or removes domination in one area that will not make it more difficult—indeed, it may even make it easier—to remove it in others. This becomes plausible once we take account of the measures whereby the state acts and, if it is to be non-dominating, is bound to act. The police who are established to protect someone against assault or theft can also serve to protect them in other ways. The education that is provided in order to guard someone against exploitation is likely to serve that person well in guarding them against other forms of manipulation too. More generally, an investment of state resources that enables people to avoid one sort of danger is likely to help them at the same time to avoid others. Thus the attempt to reduce domination in a given area of choice, the attempt to intensify the non-domination enjoyed by an agent or group in that area, will not typically raise obstacles to the project of reducing domination in other areas.

This first assumption means that the attempt to maximize freedom as non-domination involves, in the first instance, an attempt to identify the areas where the relevant agent or agents are dominated, and an effort at intensifying non-domination in those areas. There is no particular need for the state to have to worry about whether it may be better to concentrate on this or that area, and no issue about how different modes of concentration will serve respectively the intensity and extent of non-domination that people are to enjoy. The state can feasibly give its attention to all the areas where people are currently exposed to domination.

While this first assumption rules out one sort of indeterminacy that might complicate the project of promoting freedom as non-domination, there is a second that it does not rule out. We know from previous discussions that any system of law, however effective in countering domination, imposes constraints and costs on people and in that way reduces the extent of their undominated choice; it does not compromise freedom, as we put it, but it does condition it. The state may have a choice, therefore, between being more restrictive on the extent of choice, thereby giving people a more intense degree of non-domination, and being less restrictive and giving them a lower degree of non-domination. And so far as the first assumption goes, these options may represent equally potent ways of maximizing non-domination.

The choice in question here involves a less permissive state that is more effective in intensifying non-domination and a more permissive state that is less effective. But there are other choices too that involve this second sort of indeterminacy. Not only may a state vary in how permissive it is, we also know that it may vary in how far it seeks to expand people's choices into new areas by removing physical and cultural obstacles. The state may or may not offer the physically handicapped person a means of getting about, for example, and it may or may not offer ordinary people means of overcoming their more ordinary limitations. This observation suggests that, as republicans may face a choice between having a less or more permissive state, so they may face a choice between having a state that is less or more expansive. In each case, it seems, there will be an indeterminacy as to whether republicans will go for greater intensity of non-domination over a smaller extent or for lesser intensity over a larger extent.

This second sort of indeterminacy is effectively removed, however, under a further plausible assumption. As the state seeks to reduce domination—to make non-domination more intensive—it has to have recourse to devices that protect the vulnerable from the dangerous or that redress the balances of resources between them. But there is a limit, and a fairly accessible limit, on what such devices can achieve by way of intensifying non-domination. In particular, there is an accessible limit on what such devices can achieve without the state itself becoming the most dangerous of all dominating presences. One of the recurrent lessons of republican thinking, addressed and sustained in the later part of this book, is that as a state gains the powers necessary to be a more and more effective protector—as it is allowed a bigger and bigger army or police force or intelligence service, for example—it becomes itself a greater threat to freedom as non-domination than any threat it seeks to remove. There is an accessible limit on how intense the state can hope to make people's non-domination, then, in any area of activity.

But if there is an accessible limit on how intense the state can make a person's or a group's non-domination, then that is going to minimize the need for the sorts of trade-off just described. Assume that the cause of non-domination, in particular the cause of increasing the intensity of non-domination, is certainly going to require a system of law. We will not have to face hard choices between less permissive and more permissive systems of law, to the extent that no non-dominating system of law can fail too badly on the score of permissiveness. Any restrictive or non-permissive system is going to make domination by the state more likely and is not going to be attractive. Assume again that the cause of non-domination, in particular the cause of increasing intensity, is certainly going to require the protection of a person against dominating forces. We will not have to face hard choices between increasing the level of that protection and expanding what people can do under the umbrella of such protection, for the cause of more effective protection will not generally make substantial demands on the resources that expansion would require. Expansion may not be an attractive project, of course, but the case against it will not often be that the resources required can be put to better use in protecting the person more effectively.

The two assumptions discussed make the republican target of promoting freedom as non-domination more determinate, and more intuitive, than it would otherwise be, for they ensure that intensity is given priority over extent. The aim assigned to the state will be to do all it can to increase the intensity with which people enjoy non-domination and then, having achieved that goal, to look to the permissive and expansive means whereby it may increase the extent of undominated choice. I defended the state in the last section on the grounds that, even if it does no better than the war of all against all in increasing the intensity of people's non-domination—actually we saw reason why it does do better here—it promises to do much better in increasing the extent of undominated choices; it does not involve the same need for precautions and the same costs. But we are also committed to arguing, of course, that if there are two states that do equally well in intensifying non-domination and one of them is more permissive or expansive than the other, then we should prefer that which gives people a greater extent of undominated choice.

This prioritizing of intensity over extent promises to serve us well in political policy-making; it holds out a prospect of reflectively equilibrating republican views with received intuitions. But it also fits well with natural predispositions. We start from the evil of domination, as all republicans do, and we identify freedom by the absence of that domination. It is only natural that we should seek in the first place to remove or reduce all actual domination—that is, to increase the intensity of non-domination in the areas actually under threat—and seek in the second to maximize the range and ease of choice, often more or less novel choice, with which people can enjoy such non-domination.

Non-domination institutionally constituted, not caused

There is more to be said in favour of the teleological, and against the deontological, way of thinking in ethics and politics, but this is not the place to explore such considerations (Braithwaite and Pettit 1990: ch. 3; Pettit 1991; 1997). In concluding this discussion, however, there is a further and important point I want to make. This is that, though the ideal republic will be designed to promote freedom as non-domination, this does not mean that the institutions of the state will be causally detached from the non-domination they realize. It does not mean that the institutions will relate in a standard cause–effect fashion to the non-domination that they help to bring about. On the contrary, the institutions will constitute, or help to constitute, the very non-domination which citizens enjoy under them (see Spitz 1995*b*: chs. 4 and 5).

Suppose that we have civic institutions in place, maybe these, maybe those, which confer a perfectly undominated status, over whatever area, on each and every adult in the society. Although there are other people around—although there is no shortage of potential dominators—no one is subject to the arbitrary interference of another; the institutions distribute power and protection in such a way that the only interference accessible is non-arbitrary: it is not interference that may be guided by unshared interests or ideas. Now, assuming that we have such perfect institutions in place, what is the relationship between them and the non-domination which they serve to establish?

The relationship between such institutions and the non-interference that people may enjoy under them—the non-interference, not the non-domination—involves a familiar causal element: the institutions themselves interfere with people, but they also have the effect of inhibiting others from interfering, and so the actual level of non-interference that people enjoy is a function of this causal impact. The striking thing about the relationship of the institutions to the non-domination that they put in place, however, is that it does not have the same causal character. The people who live under the institutions do not have to wait on the causal effect of the institutions in inhibiting potential interferers before they enjoy non-domination. To enjoy such non-domination, after all, is just to be in a position where no one can interfere arbitrarily in your affairs, and you are in that position from the moment that the institutions are in place. True, it is bound to take time and some causal interaction for your non-domination to become a matter of common awareness, and for potential offenders to be deterred. But the non-domination as such precedes such causal sequences. It comes into existence simultaneously with the appearance of the appropriate institutions; it represents the reality of those institutions in the person of the individual.

But though the relation between state and non-domination is not causal, neither is it mysterious. The presence of certain antibodies in your blood makes it the case that you are immune to a certain disease, but it does not cause your immunity, as if the immunity were something separate on which we had to wait; the presence of those antibodies constitutes the immunity, as we say. By analogy, the presence in the polity of such and such empowering and protective arrangements makes it the case that you are more or less immune to arbitrary interference, but it does not cause that immunity; it constitutes it. To be immune to a certain disease is to have antibodies in your blood— maybe these, maybe those—which prevent the development of the relevant virus. The presence of the antibodies represents a way of realizing the immunity; it is not something that causally leads to it. To be immune to arbitrary interference, to enjoy non-domination, is to have inhibitors present in your society—maybe these, maybe those— which prevent arbitrary interference in your life and affairs. And the presence of suitable inhibitors—suitable institutions and arrangements—represents a way of realizing your non-domination; it is not something that leads by a causal path to that non-domination.

Montesquieu (1989: 187) implicitly recognizes this point when he talks of liberty as it exists, now in the constitution, now in the citizen. More generally, anyone who thinks of freedom as coterminous with citizenship, as republicans have traditionally done, is bound to take freedom to depend in a constitutive rather than a causal way on the institutions that support it. If freedom consists in being a citizen of a polity and a society in which each is protected against arbitrary interference by others, then freedom is not brought causally into existence by the institutions that characterize that polity and society. Like citizenship, it involves nothing over and beyond the status of being suitably incorporated within those institutions.

Some people may think it an ominous feature of freedom as non-domination that it is an institutional reality, in the sense explained. They may say that, if freedom is conceived of as something that the state constitutes or helps to constitute, then it is not going to represent a criterion by which the state can be judged. But that is nonsense. Freedom as non-domination is an institutional reality in the sense that it is constituted, not caused to exist, by the institutional arrangements that put it in place. But we can still compare the freedom as non-domination that different sets of institutions may constitute, and we can still find that one set does better than the other in respect of such freedom: we can do this in just the way as we could compare the kinds and levels of immunity against a certain disease that different sorts of antibody might conceivably provide.

There might be a problem of the kind suggested if freedom as non-domination were defined in terms of certain institutions: defined in terms of them in the way in which a positive, populist concept of freedom is defined by reference to institutions of democratic participation. The definition of freedom in terms of direct democracy makes it logically impossible to rank other institutions above direct democracy in the dimension of freedom. And the definition of freedom as non-domination in terms of the local political institutions would have a similar disabling effect. But the fact that certain local institutions constitute the freedom as non-domination that people enjoy does not mean that freedom is to be defined by reference to those institutions. Freedom as non-domination is defined by reference to how far and how well the bearer is protected against arbitrary interference. Even if it is assumed that the only protections available are institutional in character, this definition still enables us to judge different sets of institutions, local ones included, by reference to their promotion of non-domination. And it makes it possible to do this while allowing us to recognize that the non-domination produced by any set of institutions is produced in the constitutive, not the causal, sense of that term.

CHAPTER 4

Liberty, Equality, Community

We saw in the first chapter that those in the republican as distinct from the more recent liberal tradition thought of domination, not of interference, as the antonym of freedom; and I tried in the second chapter to articulate a precise conception of freedom as non-domination. We have been looking in the last chapter, in a rather abstract way, at the capacity of non-domination to serve as an ideal for the orientation of the political system. I argued that it is an important human value; that it is something with which the polity should be concerned; and that it naturally serves as a goal for the polity to promote, not as a constraint for it to honour.

We move on now to look briefly at two of the very considerable attractions that non-domination possesses, when considered as a political ideal. These are that the ideal is distinctively egalitaran and communitarian: it supports the French connection between *liberté* on the one hand and *égalité* and *fraternité* on the other. It will be useful to consider these attractions before we go on to look at the institutional ramifications of freedom as non-domination. The recognition of the attractions may lead otherwise sceptical readers to take the discussion of the institutional ramifications more seriously. And the identification of the attractions will make that discussion smoother, enabling us to take for granted certain observations that would otherwise have to be spelled out at a number of different points.

I. An egalitarian ideal

The inclusivist assumption that each is to count for one, none for more than one—the assumption that marks off the republicanism explored here from premodern varieties—already embodies a sort of egalitarian commitment: it means that the polity is required to treat people as equals. But treating people as equals does not necessarily involve equal treatment: it does not necessarily imply, for example, that each will get an equal share in whatever is taken as the good that the polity tries to provide (Dworkin 1978).

Suppose that we think of well-being or utility as the goal of the polity. The utilitarian will say that each is treated as an equal to the extent that no one is favoured in the political decision about where to deploy utility-increasing resources, whether in this person's life or in that; resources will always be deployed wherever they do most good in the overall maximization of utility. The upshot is that the allocation of utility which the utilitarian defends may turn out to be a very unequal one; it may just be, for example, that some people are very difficult to make happy and that they are systematically ignored in the political allocation of utility-increasing resources.

Freedom as non-interference is inegalitarian in the same way as utility. People differ from one another in at least two respects that are relevant to maximizing non-interference. Some are more likely to interfere with others, in the absence of legal interference with them. And some are more likely to be interfered with by others, in the absence of legal interference with those others. Some are more dangerous than others, some more vulnerable. This means that the way for the legal regime to maximize non-interference overall may be to concentrate its restraining efforts on those who are more likely to interfere, and to concentrate its protective efforts on those who are less likely to be interfered with. Thus non-interference may be maximized under a regime that actively takes away the freedom as non-interference of those who are more likely to be offenders—say, by interning them— and that fails to invest resources in the protection of those who are more likely to be victims.

The inegalitarian character of utility and of non-interference makes them relatively unattractive as political goals, since it is in tension with the thought that each is to count for one and none for more than one. The point is acknowledged implicitly by the devotees of freedom as non-interference, who insist that the goal is not liberty as such but rather equal liberty (Rawls 1971). There is no way of maximizing the enjoyment of equal liberty, as a matter of logic, without distributing liberty in equal measures, and the qualification has the effect of turning non-interference into an egalitarian goal.

By contrast with freedom as non-interference, and with utility, freedom as non-domination displays a significantly egalitarian character. A quick argument shows, for example, why it is vanishingly unlikely that freedom as non-domination can be maximized under an arrangement like selective internment and selective underprotection. The government that does badly by the particularly dangerous and the particularly vulnerable may itself do quite well by others in terms of non-interference and expected non-interference; while it has the power to interfere with them, as shown by its treatment of the disadvantaged, it may be very unlikely to interfere in that way. That, essentially, is why the arrangement is liable to maximize expected non-interference. But things are crucially different from the point of view of freedom as non-domination.

I assume that measures like selective internment and selective underprotection are bound to represent an arbitrary exercise of power by the government or by the majority which constitutes the government's principal. Such measures are so outrageous that no constraints could ever make them less than the arbitrary acts of a ruling will: they manifestly fail to track interests and ideas that are shared, not just by those whom they benefit, but also by those whom they affect. But then the government which does so badly in non-domination terms by those affected—by the dangerous and the vulnerable—does badly at the same time, and regardless of probabilities of actual interference, by all the other individuals in the society.

By virtue of its treatment of the dangerous and the vulnerable, the government establishes itself—or the majority establishes itself—as a collective agent which has the capacity to interfere arbitrarily in the affairs of any individual. It establishes itself as a dominating presence which dramatically reduces the freedom as non-domination of everyone in the society. The public abuse of *imperium* implicit in such an initiative does far more damage to the case of non-domination than the private abuse of *dominium* that it is designed to reduce. There is little prospect that the positive differences made by the measures of selective internment and underprotection will be enough to compensate for the loss to non-domination on the other side.

This argument is important, since the plausible initiatives whereby the distribution of non-domination might be made unequal are likely to represent acts of government domination. But it is one thing to argue that if they are themselves acts of domination, as many clearly can be, no anti-equality initiatives are likely to maximize non-domination overall. The more interesting question may be whether the maximization of non-domination supports its more equal distribution even if the initiatives taken, including anti-equality initiatives, are all non-dominating. What if the anti-equality initiatives consist, for example, just in letting natural differences of resources go uncompensated? Could such initiatives—such non-dominating, anti-equality initiatives, as we may take them to be—serve to increase the overall level of non-domination enjoyed in the society?

There are two salient questions to consider. The first bears on initiatives that seek to give some people more intense non-domination than others, the second bears on initiatives that seek to give some people more extensive non-domination than others: they endow or leave some people with a greater range or ease of undominated choice. The first question is whether it might be possible to promote overall non-domination by allowing some people more intense non-domination than others. The second is whether it might be possible to do so by allowing some people to enjoy a larger extent of undominated choice: by allowing them to enjoy undominated choice over a greater number of issues or under circumstances of fewer costs; by allowing them, in effect, to be materially better off than others.

I shall argue that a republican regime which seeks to maximize non-domination is bound to avoid initiatives that leave the intensity of non-domination unequal, but that no such stricture applies to its leaving the extent of non-domination—in effect, leaving material resources—unequal. Without necessarily having to embrace a material egalitarianism, then, republican consequentialism is required to support what we can describe as structural egalitarianism. There may be many reasons why republicanism should seek to reduce material inequalities, of course, as we shall see in the next chapter; but the connection with material egalitarianism is not as tight—not as independent of empirical contingencies—as the connection with structural egalitarianism.

Structural egalitarianism

The primary consideration that leads me to defend structural egalitarianism is that the intensity of freedom as non-domination which a person enjoys in a society is a function of other people's powers as well as of their own. Take a person's powers to include all those factors that are liable to affect political, legal, financial, and social clout. The intensity of someone's freedom as non-domination—if you like, the level of their protection—is not just a function of the powers that enable the person to resist or deter arbitrary interference by others. It is also a function of the powers at the disposal of those others, for, depending on the nature and size of the powers of others, what their own powers enable them to achieve in the way of resistance and deterrence will vary. In the land of the blind, the one-eyed man is king. The point is that a person's absolute score in relation to the intensity of non-domination is a function of their relative score in regard to powers: it is a function of their power-ratio in the society as a whole.

The fact that each person's freedom as non-domination is a function of their relative powers has an immediate impact on the possibility of increasing the overall intensity of non-domination by introducing a greater inequality in its distribution. Any anti-equality initiative will make at least two parties less equal in their intensity of non-domination. It will do this either by increasing the advantaged person's powers or by decreasing the powers of the other party or by doing both at once: in whatever way, it will worsen the power-ratio of the disadvantaged party. But if the initiative is intended to raise the overall intensity of non-domination by the same margin by which it raises the intensity of non-domination of the favoured party, it is ill-designed. For the shift in the power-ratio that raises the advantaged party's absolute intensity of non-domination by interval A (for advantage) will serve at the same stroke to lower the disadvantaged person's intensity of non-domination, in absolute terms, by interval D (for disadvantage). The weaker party's absolute intensity of non-domination is a function of their relative powers, and the anti-equality initiative is bound to worsen it.

An anti-equality initiative can succeed in maximizing the expected intensity of non-domination, then, only if the margin or margins by which it increases the expected non-domination of the advantaged compensate for the margins by which it decreases the expected non-domination of the disadvantaged. But there is no reason to think that A-margins are generally going to be larger than D-margins. There is no reason to think that those who benefit in absolute terms from an anti-equality initiative are going to enjoy an increase that compensates for the loss to those who suffer in absolute terms from that initiative.

This observation already teaches us a relevant lesson. It means that, in the unlikely event that we are starting from an egalitarian base where everyone enjoys the same intensity of non-domination, it will make little or no sense to think of resorting to anti-equality initiatives in order to increase the overall intensity of non-domination enjoyed. The chances are that such a resort will reduce the overall intensity of non-domination at the same time as it makes its distribution less equal.

But what if we are starting, as it is more plausible to suppose, from an inegalitarian base? Is there any reason, then, to think that anti-equality policies may increase the overall intensity of non-domination? No, there is not. On the contrary, there is every reason to believe that in general any anti-equality intervention will be inferior to some pro-equality one. Here I am moved by a consideration additional to the consideration that a person's absolute intensity of non-domination is a function of their relative powers. The secondary consideration is, as we may put it, that the capacity of a person's power-ratio to produce intensity of non-domination is subject to diminishing marginal productivity.

Where someone's power-ratio is poor, any improvement in their position will make for a comparatively large increase in their intensity of non-domination. Where the starting ratio is good, any improvement will make for a comparatively small increase in their intensity of non-domination. More generally, as the ratio in question improves, the function from ratio to intensity will decrease; it will take more and more of an improvement in the ratio to produce a given increase in non-domination. Improvements in the ratio are subject to diminishing marginal productivity in regard to the intensity of non-domination that they make possible.

Imagine that we are dealing with just two individuals, A and B. Suppose that A is sufficiently well resourced to be generally able to resist interference from B or to deter B from interfering. Suppose, in other words, that A enjoys a high intensity of non-domination in the society constituted by A and B, not being subject to interference at will and with impunity from B. In such a case, it will not do much for A's non-domination to increase their powers even further; in fact, it may do nothing at all: A may be at a point where extra powers have zero marginal productivity.[1] The increases may be more or less redundant, providing A with powers that are not really needed for the purposes of non-domination. The case contrasts with what those increases would have achieved had A been comparatively powerless and generally unable to resist B's interference or deter B from interfering. In such a situation, the value of the increases would have been much greater.

The fact that improvements in a person's power-ratio are subject to diminishing marginal productivity in regard to intensity of non-domination means that if we are starting from an inegalitarian base, then no anti-equality initiative can hope to do as well in the

---

[1] Might there be a point where further increases in the resources-ratio have a negative effect, reducing the person's non-domination relative to others? Might the marginal productivity of increasing the resources-ratio be negative, not just zero? It may seem so, since further increases in the resources available to a person could certainly make them a target of resentment and thereby facilitate collective action by others. But that is to say that the further increases in the resources of the person are more than compensated for by increases in the resources of the others: the increases that go with the facilitation of collective action. And that means that the increases in the resources of the person in question do not make, after all, for an increase in their resources-ratio.

production of overall non-domination as a corresponding pro-equality one. Any anti-equality intervention has to increase the difference in intensities of non-domination enjoyed by at least two individuals. That implies that it has to improve the power-ratio of a better-off individual rather than improving the power-ratio of a worse-off one. But since the function from power-ratio to intensity of non-domination is subject to diminishing marginal productivity, the anti-equality intervention must be generally expected not to do as well as the rival intervention that would have improved the power-ratio of the worse-off individual.[2] The anti-equality intervention involves an expenditure in power-conferring resources that is designed to increase overall intensity of non-domination, and it appears that those resources would have been more efficiently spent on the less well-off individual than on the better-off.

Think of your attempts to improve the overall intensity of non-domination as steps up a stairway. Every upward step will have a negative as well as a positive effect if it involves worsening someone's power-ratio; at the same time as it increases this or that person's intensity of non-domination, it will decrease another's. We can think of this negative effect as the stairway's falling lower by a certain margin with every upward step that is taken. The effect of any such attempt to improve the overall intensity of domination can be represented, then, as the net change in your altitude as a result of going up a step and at the same time having the stairway fall. What we have argued is that the net change in altitude that is achieved by any anti-equality initiative is bound to be less beneficial than the change that could have been achieved under some corresponding, pro-equality step. The more promising step is always the step that makes for greater equality.

Our arguments show that the maximization of non-domination is unlikely in many circumstances to require further departures from equality of intensity: that in respect of equality, as in so many other respects, there is a stark contrast between the value of freedom as non-domination and the value of freedom as non-interference. For all practical purposes, the goal which we set for ourselves in espousing the republican ideal of freedom is the promotion of equally intense non-domination. The general presumption can be that non-domination will not be furthered unless there is an increase in the equality with which the intensity of non-domination is enjoyed.

---

[2] I assume, plausibly, that the productive effects of that rival intervention on the person favoured will not be outweighed by damaging effects on the non-domination of the other individual.

In affirming this egalitarian aspect of freedom as non-domination, we make contact once again with the long republican tradition. For while that tradition was certainly élitist in its premodern incarnation, restricting its concerns to propertied, mainstream males, it asserted the importance of equality among the citizenry from its earliest beginnings (Wirszubski 1968: ch. 1). The equality sought required an equality before the law and before whatever instruments were available for asserting people's freedom as non-domination; it did not entail material equality. But republican thinkers were prepared to argue that it might be necessary to restrict the wealth of the very rich and powerful in order to ensure equal freedom for all; it might be necessary to have severe restrictions on sumptuary or luxury levels of affluence (Oldfield 1990). Their commitment to equal freedom was not an empty posture; it went to the heart of their value-system.

Some may not be persuaded that the connection between non-domination and equally intense non-domination is as tight as I take it to be. If they are to be substantively faithful to the republican tradition, then—and, more inclusively, to the idea that each is to count for one, and none for more than one—such thinkers will have to do with freedom as non-domination what Rawls and many liberals do with freedom as non-interference. They will have to take equal freedom—strictly speaking, equally intense freedom—to be the central concern. Myself, I do not think this move is necessary, given the egalitarian character of the fundamental value, and so I shall continue to take non-domination as such to be the goal of the republican polity. But I have no great objection if others are unpersuaded and wish to cast the goal explicitly as equally intense non-domination.

Material egalitarianism

But if the project of maximizing freedom as non-domination is committed to equalizing the intensity with which people enjoy such freedom, or at least to avoiding any anti-equality initiatives, what of its implications for equality in the extent of people's undominated choices? Does it mean that at any point where people differ in the range or ease of choice available to them—at any point, in effect, where they differ in material resources—it is always better for overall non-domination that there should be equality? Does it mean, more specifically, that if a state has the choice between allowing a certain inequality in extent of undominated choice or imposing such equality, it should always go the egalitarian way?

No, it does not. It may be that the overall level of non-domination in a society is maximized at a point where some people enjoy a larger extent of undominated choice than others, say because they work harder and have more resources. I shall be looking in the next chapter at ways in which the promotion of freedom as non-domination is likely in the actual world to require the reduction of material inequalities. But the point to register here is that, if there is a connection between maximizing non-domination and ensuring material equality, it is not the tight sort of connection that ties the consequentialist project to structural equality; it does not obtain in such a large range of possible worlds.

We are supposing that the state which equalizes people's holdings does so in a non-dominating way. Even such a state will have to impose legal limits on the growth of the holdings of the richer, and therefore on the extent of their undominated choices, in order to lift the extralegal limits on the holdings of the less rich and on the extent of the undominated choices available to them. But that means that any increase in extent of undominated choice that it achieves on the part of the less rich is liable to be offset, and perhaps outweighed, by the decrease in the extent of undominated choice that it imposes by its legal interventions on those who are richer. There is no reason to think that by equalizing holdings, and by equalizing extent of undominated choice, the state may expect to maximize the overall level of non-domination in the society; even supposing that its equalizing initiatives do not have a dominating character—and this, of course, is quite controversial—they may well have the effect of imposing more limits than they remove.

The difference between the situation here and the situation with intensity is interesting. The extent of people's undominated choices may be a function, not just of their own holdings, but also of the holdings of others: this is because of the interactive effect of holdings on demand and price, and thereby on the costs of choice. That makes for a parallel with the claim that the intensity of people's non-domination is a function, not just of their own powers, but of the powers of others. But the parallel breaks down in a further crucial respect. For whereas a person's power-ratio is subject to diminishing marginal productivity in its effect on their intensity of non-domination, nothing similar holds as between a person's holdings-ratio and their extent of undominated choice.

The money that will enable me to do something, poor as I am, will enable you to do exactly the same things. The utility derived from money may diminish with wealth, but its capacity to buy things, and its capacity therefore to extend undominated choice, does not. Thus there is no reason to think that for any extra choice that it allows to those who are well off already, and already have a larger extent of choice, the state would have done better to ensure that the extra choice went to the less well off. Any resources, and any choices, that it gives to the less well off it must take from the well off, and there is not going to be any necessary advantage, from the point of view of maximizing the extent of undominated choice, in that transfer. On the contrary, we can imagine many situations where there would be a loss: situations where, even though the state remains non-dominating, the attempt to impose equality involves costs that reduce the total quantum of undominated choice.

The upshot is clear. While the republican project of promoting over-all freedom as non-domination does imply equally intensifying non-domination, it does not necessarily involve equally extending undominated choice. While the project is committed to structural egalitarianism, as I put it, and while it scores well in this regard, it is not essentially committed to any sort of material egalitarianism. There may be a case for instituting certain material equalities—that is matter for the second part of the book—but it is subject to more empirical contingencies than the case for establishing structural equality: the case for establishing equality in the intensity with which people enjoy freedom as non-domination.

Equality and children

One final query. It is all very well to argue that promoting the intensity of non-domination will tend to equalize it, when we have competent, adult individuals in mind. But how far will that goal be consistent with treating children, for example, as equal members of the society? I think that it is important to recognize that children, and perhaps some other categories of people, are in a special position relative to the state and society. Children cannot be given the same opportunities as adults if they are to be enabled, when they become adults, to enjoy the sort of non-domination which a republic would confer: they must be subjected to the disciplines inherent, as any parent knows, in fostering education and development. But how then would children be treated under a regime for promoting freedom as non-domination? Would they be reduced to living at the mercy of their guardians and teachers?

Absolutely not. The republican point of view would suggest that children should enjoy the standard intensity of non-domination, in the sense of being protected as well as anybody else against arbitrary power. The disciplines of education and child-rearing would reduce the areas of choice that are open to children, but such reductions in the extent of undominated choice, necessary though they are, would not legitimate any compromise in the intensity of the children's non-domination.

While giving parents and teachers special powers over children, then, as the law gives the authorities powers over ordinary adults, the disciplines would not give them any right of arbitrary interference. Parents and teachers would be subject to such constraints, and exposed to such possibilities of sanction, that two things, ideally, are assured: first, they will seek to advance the relevant interests of the children; and second, that they will seek to promote those interests by non-idiosyncratic lights. Parents and teachers would be allowed to exercise considerable interference in the lives of children, in other words, but the interference would be designed to track the children's interests according to standard ideas, and it would not constitute a form of domination.

II. A communitarian ideal

In contemporary political theory, liberalism and communitarianism are often presented as the main alternative approaches. Liberalism emphasizes the importance of individual freedom—freedom as non-interference—where communitarianism insists on the equal, even prior, importance of communal belonging. Liberalism looks for a state that will abstract from people's different communal and cultural affiliations—a state that will be neutral between such commitments—and deal even-handedly with all individuals. Communitarianism, at least in some of its versions, looks for a state that will be grafted closely onto a community's way of life, at whatever cost in neutrality, and that will generate attachment and commitment in its citizens.

We saw in the last chapter that in seeking a relatively neutral brief for the state—a brief that is not tied to any particular conception of the good—republicanism joins with liberalism against communitarianism. But the feature of non-domination which I now want to emphasize means that there is still solid hope that communitarians may be attracted by the republican project. The feature, in a word, is that freedom as non-domination is an inherently communitarian ideal. Communitarians focus on communitarian goods, assuming that such ideals are invariably tied up with particular, sectarian conceptions of how people should live. I argue that freedom as non-domination is precisely the sort of communitarian ideal that ought to appeal to them, while rejecting the assumption that it must therefore fail on the count of neutrality; as already argued, it remains a sort of good that almost anyone, or at least anyone in a pluralist society, can be expected to want and value.

A good will be a communitarian ideal, in my sense, just so far as it displays two features: it is a social good and a common good. A good will be social to the extent that its realization presupposes the existence of a number of people who display intentional attitudes and perhaps intentional activities (Pettit 1993*a*: ch. 3); as a matter of logic it goes and comes, like solidarity or status, with the comings and goings of people's interactive dispositions (see Miller 1990). A good will be common to the extent that it cannot be increased (or decreased) for any member of the relevant group without at the same time being increased (or decreased) for other members of the group: it has the sort of non-excludability that economists ascribe to goods like clean air and external defence. It will be a partially common good to the extent that it cannot be increased for one without being increased for some; it will be a perfectly common good to the extent that it cannot be increased for one without being increased for all.

Among the basic values canvassed in contemporary political philosophy, most are not communitarian goods. Many are not social goods and, whether social or not, most do not display any degree of commonness. I am thinking of goods like utility or happiness, relief from misery or poverty, justice as fairness, and of course freedom as non-interference (Pettit 1993*a*: 304–7).[3] Such goods do very badly on the commonness criterion, because it is clearly possible in principle for someone to do well in such terms while their fellows fare ill. That others are unhappy or impoverished or unfairly treated or much interfered with does not in itself mean that I am badly off on those criteria. And that others are likely to suffer such a fate does not in itself mean that I am likely to suffer the same misfortune: probabilities are too much a function of individual circumstances.

The non-communitarian nature of those goals may account for the hostility with which they are viewed by many critics of contemporary liberal theory. If the state has the job of promoting such goods, then it is essentially an institution of compromise that looks for the best way of reconciling the conflicting ends of different people. When I am required to honour such a state, conforming to its laws and

[3] Explicitly egalitarian goods—material equality, equality of opportunity, etc.—fare better. Although it is possible to improve one person's position in regard to equality without improving the position of others, it is impossible to attain perfect equality for one person without at the same time attaining it for all.

expectations, I will not be invited to identify with any group or groups that the state serves in common, for its very rationale emphasizes my separateness from others and my competition with them. Perhaps that is the sort of argument that sets communitarians against liberalism. But however well-placed in that connection, the argument cannot be directed against a republican theory that starts from the value of freedom as non-domination. For this value has a strikingly communitarian character (see Philp 1996). It is both a social and a common good.

We saw in Chapter 2 that freedom as non-domination is a social good that comes about, not by virtue of the absence of other people, but by virtue of checks on the capacity of other people to exercise domination. You cannot enjoy freedom as non-domination by default, as we put it; you cannot enjoy it just because there are no other people about. Freedom as non-domination comes about only by design: only because there are legal and social arrangements in place which ensure that the other people who are about cannot interfere with you on an arbitrary basis. Freedom as non-domination requires the freedom of the city, not the freedom of the heath. We shall see now that this social good is also a common good, and thus that it ought to have great appeal for communitarian thinkers.

To enjoy non-domination is to be in a position where others are unable to interfere on an arbitrary basis in your affairs. But no one will be able to interfere arbitrarily in your affairs just to the extent that no one is able to interfere with those of your ilk, in particular those of your ilk in matters of resistance and exposure to interference: in matters of vulnerability. To the extent that those others are exposed to arbitrary interference, you too are exposed; to the extent that they are dominated, you too are dominated. You will only enjoy non-domination, therefore, so far as non-domination is ensured for those in the same vulnerability class as you. Those of you in each class sink or swim together; your fortunes in the non-domination stakes are intimately interconnected.

For all that this observation entails on its own, of course, your vulnerability class may be a singleton; it may consist of you alone. But those who interfere arbitrarily with others, if they are not absolutely random in their choices, do so on the basis of certain markers: this is my wife, this is a black youth, this is an immigrant worker, this is someone old and frail, and so on. And that means that each person, in all likelihood, will belong to a significant vulnerability class or to a number of such classes. They may be well situated relative to other members of the class and do slightly better in the protections that are available to them. But if the class has a salient unity, then they must recognize that there is no way of achieving the best in the way of non-domination—the best that non-members can achieve—short of eliminating the domination of all members of the class.

Suppose that women are not protected, either by law or culture, from physical abuse by their husbands. You may be a fortunate woman whose husband is very unlikely to abuse you, say because of being deeply in love, but that difference between your situation and those of other married women does not mean that your fate in the non-domination stakes is quite independent of theirs. On the contrary. To the extent that any woman can be abused on an arbitrary basis by her husband, womanhood is a badge of vulnerability in this regard; in particular, it is a badge of vulnerability that you, fortunate though you are, must bear in common with others. You can only hope to escape domination in this respect to the extent that all women are enabled to escape domination. Your fate is intertwined with theirs.

Why say that your freedom as non-domination depends on how other women are situated but not, or at least not necessarily, your freedom as non-interference? The reason goes back to the fact that you are dominated insofar as your husband has the capacity to interfere with you—insofar as interference is an accessible option for your husband—and regardless of whether he is actually likely to interfere. The republican will say that, while you may be unlikely to suffer actual interference at the hands of the loving husband, still you are dominated by him, and there is no way of removing that domination without altering the conditions under which women generally relate to men. Freedom as non-domination requires the inaccessibility of arbitrary interference to your husband, not just the improbability of his having recourse to such interference.[4]

Someone concerned about non-interference will be forced to take quite a different line. Suppose it happens that the loving husband is entirely unlikely to interfere with you. The devotee of non-interference will have to say that this situation is desirable in the highest possible degree. There is no probability of interference by your husband, and such expected non-interference is achieved without

---

[4] It will be better of course to have a loving husband than a non-loving husband, even though both are dominating presences. This situation will be better, indeed, by reference to the value of non-domination itself. With a loving husband a woman is going to be given more choices in which to enjoy the non-domination that she possesses in relation to other agents; the enjoyment of that non-domination will not be pre-empted by actual interference on the part of the husband. Thus if a woman is allowed by a dominating but loving husband to spend her money as she wishes she will at least be able to enjoy whatever non-domination she possesses in relation to agents in the market-place; the extent of her non-domination relative to those agents will be increased.

relying on protective coercion or interference by legal or cultural authorities. It will not matter in the books of this theorist that you are dominated—that your husband has the capacity to interfere on an arbitrary basis—and so there is no particular cause or grievance that you will share, by the accounting in those books, with less fortunate women. If you take up the grievance of those women, that will have to be an altruistic act; you cannot take up their grievance on the basis of recognizing a common cause with them.

The line of thought that we have followed up to this establishes that freedom as non-domination is a partially common good: a common good from the point of view of each vulnerability class. The goal of freedom as non-domination gives a common cause to each of the salient vulnerability classes in any contemporary society: to each of those groups who are rendered particularly vulnerable by virtue of gender or ethnicity or colour or sexual preference or whatever; to each of those groups who, in this sense, count as relatively oppressed (Young 1990: ch. 2). If we attach ourselves to the promotion of non-domination in any contemporary society, then one of the first things to recognize will be that the politics required for that enterprise cannot be just an atomistic project; it will have to be articulated at the level of group grievance and group assertion, as well as at levels involving individuals as such. If I am a member of an indigenous population in contemporary Australia or Canada, for example, then how far I achieve non-domination is intimately tied up with how far other indigenous people do so; there is a single, solidaristic cause here, not just a sum of individual causes.

But if non-domination is a common good to this extent, is it ever likely to be a perfectly common good? Is it ever likely to be such that it cannot be increased for one without being increased for all? Yes, to the extent that a special, empirical assumption is satisfied. This is the assumption that people in the society at large belong to the same vulnerability class. They are permutable in the vulnerability stakes, so that if one sees another suffer interference, they can truly say, 'There but for the will of god—there but for brute fortune—go I.'

The permutability assumption is clearly not going to be satisfied, certainly not satisfied in respect of every form of interference, in a polity that gives formal or informal significance to caste or class or colour or whatever. Whites need not belong to the same vulnerability class as blacks in a racist society. But the permutability assumption will have to be better and better satisfied as we approach the society where the enjoyment of non-domination is maximized. By the argument given in the last section, non-domination is an egalitarian goal that requires more or less equal distribution for its optimal promotion. That means that as non-domination is promoted, factors like caste and class, colour and culture, should decline in political significance: in significance as markers of vulnerability to interference. The community as a whole should approach the point of being a single vulnerability class. Non-domination would tend to be a fully common good in those circumstances, for it would become more or less impossible for any individual to increase their enjoyment of the good without everyone else increasing their enjoyment at the same time. The closer we approximate to the enjoyment of perfect non-domination, then, the more common that ideal will become: the more it will appear that our fortunes in the non-domination stakes are intimately interconnected.

It is a very important observation that non-domination is a communitarian good. It means that the cause of freedom as non-domination will always have the dimension of a social and common cause for the people involved in pursuing it. Contrary to the line of argument mentioned earlier, the fact of recognizing the state as an institution that promotes such a good will give us reason to identify with other people, and ultimately with the polity in general. It will not lead us to see ourselves as set apart, in essential competition.

We can speak of the liberation or emancipation of a society or class or caste, under the republican approach, without indulging in excessively collectivist rhetoric. The freedom of a society—and not just its freedom *vis-à-vis* other societies (Hobbes 1968: 266)—is as basic a notion as the freedom of individuals, to return to a theme that we have already mentioned; we can refer as properly to the freedom of Florence as to the freedom of Florentines (Harrington 1992: 8). Freedom is not the atomistic good associated with non-interference. It can be enjoyed by individuals, at least in the real world, only so far as it can be enjoyed by the salient groups to which those individuals belong. I return to this theme in the final chapter of the book.

The argument in this chapter should begin to make salient the attractions of freedom as non-domination in the role of a political ideal. When the leaders of the French Revolution spoke of freedom, equality, and fraternity, they do not have to be seen as going beyond the traditional republican ideal of freedom alone. They were committed to extending citizenship and freedom beyond the traditional élite, of course; influenced by Rousseau and Enlightenment thinkers, they had already broken—however incompletely—with the exclusivist aspect of premodern republicanism. But the only value we need see them as espousing is the value of freedom as such. For it is clear from the observations deployed here that there can be no hope of advancing the cause of freedom as non-domination among individuals who do not readily embrace both the prospect of substantial equality and the condition of communal solidarity. To want republican liberty, you have to want republican equality; to realize republican liberty, you have to realize republican community.[5]

[5] The themes explored in this chapter connect closely with the main thesis of Jean-Fabian Spitz's (1995*a*) illuminating study of political liberty. That thesis is that in the republican sense of liberty—he explicitly relates this to my own work—there is no liberty without equality and justice. I connect with that thesis again at various points in the second part of the book, especially in the last chapter.

PART II

REPUBLICAN GOVERNMENT

CHAPTER 5

Republican Aims: Causes and Policies

My interest in the republican conception of liberty comes of the hope that it can persuasively articulate what a state ought to try to achieve, and what form it ought to assume, in the modern world. I have wanted to find a new republican philosophy of government in the rich materials of the old, premodern tradition. I share the enthusiasm of historians for trying to establish the lost systems of coordinates by which past thinkers may have navigated, and I believe that identifying such exotic systems of reference may help us to see more clearly the landmarks by which we take our own bearings. But this book has not been driven by that motivation. It has been written, not out of a desire to retrieve a lost vision of public life, but out of a wish to explore a new vision of what public life might be.

The traditional republic is described in a moral language whose provenance is centuries old, of course, and the images in which the language is given substance derive from decisively premodern regimes: for example, the northern Italian cities of the Renaissance, the seventeenth-century English Commonwealth, and Britain's American colonies in the eighteenth century. This makes for a challenge to my project. Republican ideas about good citizens and good constitutions, so it will be alleged, even republican ideas as to what freedom means, are intimately tied to characteristically premodern suppositions: the supposition that the citizens constitute a propertied gentry, for example, or that they are bound by lost, artistocratic notions of honour or virtue, or that they are few enough to be able to assemble and vote at regular intervals, or whatever. The challenge posed is to show that we can hold onto the old republican ideal, as it has been articulated here, and build a modern image of republican institutions on that basis; 'the question for Pettit', as Alasdair MacIntyre says, 'is: in what kinds of institutions can the republicanism which he advocates be embodied?' (1994: 303)

This second part of the book is an attempt to meet that challenge. I want to give an idea of what it would mean to take the ideal of freedom as non-domination seriously, and to build modern institutions of government around it. And in doing this, I want to show that the institutions required are not so distant from what we have that republicanism looks utopian, nor so close to what we have that it seems uncritical. I want to show, in John Rawls's (1971) phrase, that republican political philosophy does well on the test of reflective equilibrium. It has institutional implications that prove, at least on reflective consideration, to equilibrate with our firmer intuitions. It represents a philosophy that we can live with and act on.

The first thing that needs to be made clear in a discussion of the institutional ramifications of republicanism is its significance for the causes that the state should take seriously and the policies that it should try to advance. I take up that task in this chapter. I argue first that a broad range of plausible causes can and will be given a hearing within the republican standpoint. And I try to show, second, that the policies that a republican standpoint would lead the state to espouse are wide-ranging and attractive: they are not confined to the narrow agenda that premodern republicans and classical liberals would have countenanced.

In discussing the causes and policies which a modern republic has to take seriously, this chapter focuses mainly on things that a republic must do in order to counter the dangers associated with different levels of *dominium*, different levels of resource and control, in everyday social life: these are the dangers that ordinary people face in their dealings with one another, individually and in the context of collective and corporate organization. The chapter following then considers the measures that are necessary if the state is to do this successfully, in particular to do this without coming itself to represent the form of domination that can go, not with *dominium*, but with *imperium* (Kriegel 1995). Where Chapter 5 looks at the aims that the republican state must espouse in combating the first danger, Chapter 6 looks at the forms that the republican state must assume if it is to combat the second.

I. Republican causes

A republican language

I argued in the introduction to this book that politics has a conversational, deliberative aspect, and that the role of political philosophy is to interrogate the languages in which such conversation is carried forward and, if necessary, invent or reinvent terms and idioms that may aid clarification and facilitate convergence. Of course, politics inherently involves interest and intrigue, power and struggle, and it would be quite utopian to suggest otherwise. But the most dominant interest, and the most aggressive power, still has to speak and still has to make a case for its hegemony. In particular, it has to find words that can reach the minds—if only the muted and mastered minds—of those in other camps and other quarters. Conversation is inseparable from politics, even if it sometimes degenerates into the one-way conversation of the aggressive publicity machine.

In seeking to facilitate political conversation, each political philosophy will look for a language that, ideally, does two things. First, it employs only conceptual distinctions and inferential patterns that no one in the community has serious reason to reject; it offers a medium of debate which no one has a priori ground for dismissing. In other words, the language connects with intellectual icons and paradigms that are recognized in common across the society. Second, the ideal language offers a medium which enables those in every quarter of the society to give a satisfying articulation of their particular grievances and goals. It answers to the fact of difference at the same time as it builds on a base of common ideas. It makes it possible for the significantly different voices in the society to express themselves in a way that others have to hear and honour.

Some thinkers may take issue with the idea of looking for a political language in which to articulate the grievances of different groups. They may say that the quest for a political *lingua franca* intrudes an assumption of a fundamental homogeneity among citizens, and that it will serve in practice to impose on different groups an image of their situation and their dissatisfaction that is not true to their experience. It is certainly reasonable of critics to warn of the permanent possibility that the search for a common language may not be as successful as some think: that the allegedly common language may construct some grievances in a way that distorts them. But it cannot be right that the search for a common language of articulation is inherently flawed. For unless different groups can find a common language in which to talk of their problems, the complaints of each group will be nothing but noise in the ears of the others; they will have the status, and the insignificance, of inarticulate mewlings.

It should be clear how a political philosophy may fail to provide a satisfactory language of debate. Take the classical liberal philosophy that makes freedom as non-interference the be-all and end-all of political good. In connecting with the almost ubiquitous idiom of liberty, that philosophy may do well by the first condition, offering a language that few can dismiss out of hand. But the philosophy clearly fails to offer a medium in which the palpable grievances of different groups can be reasonably articulated. Consider the grievance of the dominated worker or woman or tenant or debtor who does not actually suffer interference but who has to fawn and toady and look with a degree of apprehension on a master who holds power—perhaps only informal, legally unrecognized power—over them. Anyone in such a position has got a complaint to make: their position is saliently inferior to that of others. But, as we already know, no one in such a position will be able to make that complaint in the language of freedom as non-interference. For in terms of non-interference, in terms even of expected non-interference, there is no grievance audible; the language silences those whom it ought ideally to be serving.

The reason why classical liberalism fails in this respect is that the language of non-interference does not reach beyond the sector of opinion and interest with which it was in the first place associated. The liberal ideal of being let alone, in particular of being let alone by the state, took wing in the early days of industrial capitalism, as an ideal for the new class of profit-seeking entrepreneurs and professionals. For these individuals and their champions, the notion of freedom as non-interference articulated an indispensable precondition for competitive success, and it was easy for them to think—certainly it was convenient for them to think—that the notion represented a universally attractive ideal. They could ignore the fact that freedom as non-interference is consistent with insecurity, with lack of status, and with a need to tread a careful path in the neighbourhood of the strong; they were not themselves beset, after all, with such difficulties. They could neglect the fact that in holding up such freedom as the supreme ideal, therefore, they were denying women and workers a language in which they could protest at the insecurity, the need for strategy, and the lack of status that went with their particular social location.

I want to argue that, in contrast to the manner in which freedom as non-interference remains tied to the sector of interest and opinion that first gave it prominence and currency, freedom as non-domination transcends its origins—it reaches beyond its founding communities—and holds out the prospect of a language that satisfies our two conditions. As an idiom of freedom in which enslavement and subjection are the great ills, independence and status the supreme goods, this language has a claim to validity across the full spectrum of contemporary society, at least contemporary society in the pluralist, democratic mould. And as a language that enables us to express complaints of domination, so I argue, it has a claim to be able to articulate grievances which far outrun the complaints of its founding communities.

Those founding communities were very varied, as we know. In its earliest days, the ideal of freedom as non-domination appealed to those in the ancient world who claimed a position at the extreme opposite from that of a slave; in particular, those in the Roman Republic who claimed a position in which they did not have to acknowledge subjection to any monarch or master. Later, among populations that consciously aligned themselves with the Roman precedent, it had related attractions. It appealed to the citizens of Italian Renaissance cities, as an ideal that expressed the independence to which they aspired, individually and collectively, in relation to grandees and princes. It appealed in seventeenth-century England to those who prized a legal culture that gave them rights against the king, and who wished to banish every spectre of absolute, arbitrary power. It appealed in the eighteenth-century American colonies as an ideal that expressed their shared desire not to have to depend and wait on the dictate, however friendly, of a distant parliament. And it appealed in revolutionary France to those who rejected a regime in which monarchical caprice was the supreme law and aristocrats enjoyed an arbitrary system of privilege and dominance.

There are commonalities, and indeed restrictive commonalities, among the constituencies that cared in this way for freedom as non-domination. The individuals involved were always male, they were always men of substance—men of trade, men of land, men of property—and they were always, of course, members of the mainstream culture. In espousing the ideal of freedom as non-domination they identified heights, as they saw it, which were within their individual and collective reach, provided only that things did not go institutionally amiss: provided only that the king was removed or contained; provided only that the particularly rich and powerful did not secure too much influence for themselves; provided only that their numbers did not factionalize or that the factions did not gain unfettered control of the collectivity; and so on. The heights that they identified held out the prospect of a way of life within which none of them had to bow and scrape to others; they would each be capable of standing on their own two feet, they would each be able to look others squarely in the eye.

But despite these highly particular associations, I want to argue that the republican language of freedom as non-domination offers a medium in which a variety of grievances can be articulated, including the grievances of groups who are far removed from the founding communities. Not only does it have potentially universal appeal as a language of freedom; it has relevance to a variety of highly specific, even particularistic, causes.

There are two respects in which the ideal may seem unable to respond to some grievances. First, it focuses on human beings as distinct from the cosmos in general, and it is ill-equipped on the face of it to articulate the demands of those who reject anthropocentric perspectives: those who espouse radical forms of green political theory, for example. Second, and more significantly, it focuses, or has at least traditionally focused, only on some human beings: those who are male, those who are well off, and those who are situated in the mainstream culture. I propose to make my case for the republican language of freedom as non-domination—my case for its ability to articulate difference grievances and causes—by showing that it can cope with such demands. I will try to show that environmentalism, feminism, socialism, and multiculturalism can be cast as republican causes.

In arguing that republicanism can give a hearing and a voice to these and other causes, I do not mean that being a republican necessarily involves going along with everything that the movements in question have advocated. On the contrary. Republicanism enables us, and enables those within those movements, to give voice to relevant concerns. But it does not do this in an uncritical way; it does not do it in a such a way that it becomes hostage to the movements served. In constructing the grievances and demands put forward, it gives specific and distinctive accounts of the causes involved, though accounts that will, I hope, be found persuasive. Republicanizing the causes certainly means validating them, but it means validating them, inevitably, within the logic of republican ideas.

While I focus on the concerns of more or less radical movements in trying to substantiate the republican language of freedom as non-domination, I assume that the language can also serve to articulate the concerns of more mainstream groups; indeed, it is because of making this assumption that I focus on radical movements. I assume in particular that those entrepreneurs and professionals who were well served by the classical liberal ideal would also find the ideal of freedom as non-domination suited to their purposes. It might not enable them to raise the same, routine points against government interference, for such interference will be unobjectionable to the extent that it is not itself dominating and serves in other respects to promote non-domination. But the ideal of freedom as non-domination would still answer well to the interests of such individuals. As we saw in discussing the attractions of non-domination, it would offer them a way of defending the scenario in which they know where they stand and can advance their economic and related projects without apprehension or uncertainty.

There is one specific way, indeed, in which the ideal of non-domination might answer better than the ideal of non-interference to the interests of such conservative parties. Suppose we imagine a social world in which institutions of private property are not established or are capable of being politically eliminated. The ideal of non-domination might make it easier to support the introduction or reinforcement of private property in such a situation.

The ideal of non-domination suggests that, while the private-property move would require the non-dominating interference of the state—and while the move would thereby reduce in one respect the extent of undominated choice available to people at large—it would more than compensate by increasing the extent of such undominated choice in other respects. It would make choices and courses of action accessible—for example, those that involve owning and selling and giving things away—that would not otherwise exist even as possibilities. The ideal of non-interference does not make the argument for institutions of private property so straightforward. It suggests that if such institutions are justified, that must be because they make it possible for people to avoid interference in a greater measure than the measure in which they themselves require the interference of the state; or, even less convincingly, that the extent of non-interfered-with choice that they facilitate is so large that it compensates, by some intuitive weighting of extent against intensity, for the direct state interference that the institutions require. If defenders of private property want a really plausible case for politically recognizing their preferred institutions, then they might do better to embrace the ideal of freedom as non-domination rather than the ideal of freedom as non-interference.

Environmentalism

Green political theory sometimes assumes the radical form of arguing, not that people's interests will be betrayed unless the state adopts a certain ecological perspective, but that the interests of non-human subjects and systems—together, no doubt, with the interests of people—require the state to assume this or that form (Sylvan 1984–5). Such an ecological theory is bound to find republicanism excessively anthropocentric. After all, republicans believe that the state ought to be designed with a view to the promotion of people's freedom as non-domination alone, not with a view to the good of anything non-human. And that neglect of the non-human is going to be anathema to the sort of environmentalism envisaged here.

Is it possible to defend republicanism as an approach for environmentalists to take? There may be no particular problem with less radical forms of the environmental approach (Goodin 1992*b*; Passmore 1993). But is it possible to make a case for republicanism—to make a case for the resort to republican language—that will appeal to radical environmentalists? I believe that it is.

The first thing that needs to be said is that radical environmentalism, according to which the state should be shaped with a view to non-human as well as human interests, does not itself offer a language of grievance and claim that has any chance of reaching the ears of those outside the green movement. The language is too specialized, too intimately associated with a particular perspective on the world, to have the sort of general validity for which we should look in a medium of political debate. It may help believers to articulate their outrage—often their perfectly justified outrage—and to develop a philosophy that may yet gain wider acceptance, even the acceptance of the community at large. But as things stand at the moment, short of such widespread acceptance, it offers them no hope of making an impact on the political scene generally. Articulated in the terms considered, radical environmentalism will present itself as a sectarian movement, on a par with familiar religious groupings, and its concerns will make no particular claim in the public world. Why should I be moved by your arguments if you argue from premises that I do not accept? Why should people generally be moved by the arguments of radical environmentalists if they do not accept the premises from which those thinkers insist on starting?

The lesson is that politics, certainly politics in a pluralist society, inevitably requires pragmatism (Larmore 1987); or, if not pragmatism, at least the acknowledgement that there are reasonable differences of opinion which political argument must try to reach across (Rawls 1993). It requires those who are committed to various political causes to be able to articulate the concerns they want the state to take up in terms which others can understand and internalize. Unless the devotees of a cause are prepared to do this, they cannot reasonably expect their fellow citizens to listen, let alone to go along.

The pragmatism required may not appeal to purists, but, apart from being ineffective, the purist attitude is also exceedingly precious. Why should devotees of a certain cause shrink from presenting that cause in terms that have general appeal, on the grounds that the cause appeals to them in different, more particular ways? There is no inconsistency in admitting that a cause may appeal to different people on different grounds; one and the same conclusion may be supported by distinct sets of premises. And there need be no deception of others, and of course no self-deception, involved in arguing for a cause on grounds other than those on which you find the cause appealing; you need make no secret of the fact that the cause appeals to you in a distinctive way, even as you seek to display its attraction in publicly more accessible terms.

If this lesson is accepted, then I can begin to make a case for articulating environmental concerns in republican language. While republicanism, like almost all mainline political philosophies, is decisively anthropocentric, it gives us salient reasons why we should be concerned about other species and about our ecosystem more generally; in particular, it gives us reasons why we should want our state and our laws to try to advance such concerns.

These reasons are not hard to find. The ecosystem, with the other species of animals that it contains, offers us our place in nature; it is the space, ultimately, where we belong. We are what we eat. And equally we are what we breathe, we are what we smell, we are what we see and hear and touch. We are all that it is given to us to identify with in that world, worked and unworked by humans, that we see as our own. We are none of us a social island, in Donne's memorable metaphor. And neither is any one of us a natural island. We live in physical, biological, and psychological continuity with other human beings, with other animal species, and ultimately with the larger physical system that comes to consciousness in us.

These linkages between us and our environment mean that when you degrade that enviroment you hurt me and mine, you hurt us and ours. You may affect our collective chances of survival, our individual prospects of a long and healthy life, or our opportunities for affirming our conaturality with other species, and for identifying with the planet that we share with them. Or if you do not affect us, the current representatives of our species in those ways, you may well affect future generations of human beings, including the future citizens of the society and state that we constitute.

We are each physically vulnerable, then, not just in our own individual bodies but in our shared environment and world. But if that is the case, then it is clear why the republican state has to espouse environmental concerns. That any damage is done to the environment—the environment of subgroups, of the society as a whole, or of all societies on earth—means that there is an assault on at least the range of our undominated choice. The damage is bound to mean that the costs of our exploiting various opportunities are raised or that certain opportunties are closed to us: at the limit, as in nuclear devastation, it may mean that few opportunities remain. Even if the damage comes about inadvertently, then, or as the aggregate outcome of individually innocent actions, it counts as a loss in the ledger-book of republican liberty. And, of course, if the damage does not come about inadvertently, if it represents interference by some agency that manages to cover its tracks or to assert its way, then it represents an even greater loss. It means that the agency which assumes the right to inflict that environmental damage exercises a form of domination over those who are affected; they live, at least in some part, at the mercy of that agency: it can harm them or not harm them, interfere in their lives or not interfere, at its pleasure.

The upshot should be clear. The republican state that we envisage here, the state that is dedicated to promoting freedom as non-domination, is bound to espouse what we may loosely describe as the environmental cause. The fact that it starts from an anthropocentric concern may mean that it cannot directly endorse the more ecocentric philosophies of radical environmentalists. But it does not mean that environmentalists will find it an alien, uncomprehending instrumentality. On the contrary, the republican philosophy should give environmentalists a particularly persuasive and effective way of stating their central demands. The republican state should be a polity in which environmentalists can feel at home.

Feminism

So much for the capacity of republicanism to make sense of a non-anthropocentric cause such as environmentalism often appears to be. I now want to consider three causes that are certainly anthropocentric but that seem to create difficulties for republicanism on a different score. Traditional republicans envisaged a citizenry of men, of men of substance, and of men in the mainstream. What needs to be established is that, notwithstanding these gendered and propertied and unicultural associations, the ideal of freedom as non-domination can have appeal for people who live beyond such boundaries. It can serve as an ideal for feminists, for socialists, and for multiculturalists. I argue the case for feminism first.

While the image of the person who need not fear or defer to others, the image of the person who knows no master, is traditionally a male ideal, that image has always had a presence in the literature of feminism. It has been there, in the margins, as the image of what might be realized, not just for men, but for women too. Even while freedom as non-domination looked accessible only to males, it held out a prospect that made sense also for females.

Consider the remark from Mary Astell that we quoted in the opening chapter. 'If all Men are born Free,' she asked in the 1690s, 'how is it that all Women are born Slaves? As they must be, if the being subjected to the inconstant, uncertain, unknown, arbitrary Will of Men, be the perfect condition of Slavery? And, if the Essence of Freedom consists, as our Masters say it does, in having a standing Rule to live by?' (Hill 1986: 76). Mary Astell's rhetorical intentions in making this remark are complex and difficult to discern (Springborg 1995), but the very fact that the passage is so often quoted testifies to the appeal of non-domination as a feminist ideal. The force of the question is palpable. There is indeed something awry in an arrangement that saves men from a dominated status, and that represents that status as degraded and demeaning, while exposing women to precisely that sort of standing in relation to men.

The ideal of a woman's not having to live at the beck and call of husband or father, the ideal of her not having to beg their leave or curry their favour, is present a century after Astell in the influential writings of Mary Wollstonecraft (1982). It is there also in the polemic waged by John Stuart Mill (1970) in the nineteenth century, under the influence of Harriet Taylor, against what they called the subjection of women. 'No slave is a slave to the same lengths, and in so full a sense of the word, as a wife is' (Mill 1970: 159) And it is a salient motif of contemporary feminist writings, surfacing in the work of Carole Pateman (1988), for example, as the ideal implicit in her assault on the subordination of women (see too Young 1990). Jane Mansbridge and Susan Okin (1993: 269) are absolutely clear on the point. 'Throughout its plurality, feminism has one obvious, simple and overarching goal—to end men's systematic domination of women.'

The connection between the republican tradition of thinking and the articulation of feminist ideals is nicely marked in the way that William Thompson (1970) chose to define the situation of women when he wrote in the last century of marriage as the white-slave code (see Pateman 1988: 123). For if the main problem for women is that cultural, legal, and institutional pressures combine to put them in a position akin to that of slavery—combine to place them under the thumb of men—then the ideal for women is precisely that of being secured against arbitrary interference: being given freedom in the sense in which this connotes, not just an absence of interference, but an absence of domination.

I argued in the case of environmentalism that relevant demands, however conceived among environmentalists themselves, can be given a republican voice. The historical association between feminism and republicanism—or at least between feminism and the republican ideal of non-domination—means that something stronger is true in this case. Not only can republicanism offer a persuasive articulation of the central feminist claims, it also provides an articulation that has had a continuous history within the ranks of feminists themselves.

It must be admitted, of course, that republicanism has not always proved attractive to feminists. But that is not because of any essential quarrel with the republican ideal. It is rather because of the association of republicanism, partly under the influence of a bad, populist history, with more or less masculinist images of democratic participation and public activism. But such an association, as we know, is misplaced. And once we recognize that, we should be able to see that in principle the institutional means of furthering freedom as non-domination can be designed as much with women in mind as men; they can be made to accommodate women's voices and women's concerns as well as men's voices and men's concerns (James 1992).

There is much to be done on this front. Whatever the progress made in modern states, women still have to endure a special vulnerability in many homes, in various workplaces, and on the streets of different cities. That vulnerability is not the product of lesser physical prowess so much as of a deeply entrenched set of assumptions about the role of women, about the competence of women, and about what women are after if they walk the streets at night. And when women look to the improvement of their situation, individually or collectively, they often find that the institutions of their society are against them. Child-minding and educational institutions may make it next to impossible for them, in the context of established assumptions, to organize a career. Workplace practices may make it hard for them to gain influence or make an impact in their place of employment. And the world of politics may make it extremely difficult for them to force an entry or make a mark: it may be a world suited to males without family cares and a world organized around habits of male dealing and male bonding. Such grievances are probably going to be audible in any of a number of philosophical forums, but they are bound to have a particular resonance in the auditorium of republican politics.

Socialism

So much for the claim that the ideal of freedom as non-domination is not inherently gendered—in particular, is not tied to a masculinist picture of social and political life. Now to the issue of whether it is likely to appeal, not just to feminists, but also to socialists. Is the ideal associated with a picture of life that is suited only to people who enjoy independent economic security, such as property would have traditionally provided? Or does it represent an ideal that can also have an attraction for ordinary workers?

The answer to this question, I believe, is a resounding affirmative. As capitalism began to develop in the nineteenth century, and as the grievances of an industrial working class began to mount and multiply, one of the main ideas that served to articulate the disaffection of socialists was that of wage slavery (Marx 1970: ch. 19). The image of workers as wage slaves casts them as dependent on the grace and mercy of their employer, and as required to court paths of caution and deference in dealing, individually or collectively, with their bosses. If that image is to serve as a way of showing what is objectionable in the condition of workers, then it is premissed on the appeal of its opposite: on the appeal of the idea that workers should not be exposed to the possibility of arbitrary interference, that they should enjoy freedom as non-domination.

If the employers in any area are collectively capable of blacklisting someone who displeases them, as many nineteenth-century employers certainly were, and if unemployment effectively means destitution, then it is clear why socialists should have thought that workers were nothing more than wage slaves. Perhaps it was true, as classic liberals might have thought, that employers were not often likely to exploit the vulnerability of their workers: perhaps their economic interests generally counselled them against petty harrassment of the kind that workers would not have dared oppose, for example, and perhaps those interests counselled them equally against capricious practices of hiring and firing. In other words, perhaps the workers whose cause gave rise to the socialist movement were not particularly subject to interference. But that was clearly not to the point in the reckoning of workers.

What they must have found objectionable, and what led socialists to indict early capitalism as a system of wage slavery, is the fact that, however little interference workers suffered, it was still the case that they lived under permanent exposure to interference, in particular to arbitrary interference. Economic rationality may have argued for gentleness among their masters, but it remained objectionable from the socialist point of view that workers lived in subjection to those masters: that their employers were, precisely, masters.

If this line of thought is right, we should certainly expect that the ideal of freedom as non-domination will appeal to socialists. Socialism was nurtured on an attachment to that republican ideal, applying it to more or less revolutionary effect in criticism of the emerging employment relationship. Socialists refused to endorse the credentials which liberals believed that that relationship received, for example, from its origin in the free contract of employment. They maintained that it was unjust of an employer to fire a worker for arbitrary reasons, and rejected what a current defender describes as 'the traditional negative libertarian "at-will" doctrine that, consistent with contractual obligations, an employer may fire an employee for "good cause, no cause or even for cause morally wrong" ' (Levin 1984: 97; see too Cornish and Clark 1989: 294–5). They saw individual employer–employee contracts as a form of the very slave contract which republicans had always repudiated, and they railed against the domination which was realized under the terms of such contracts.

Besides giving them grounds for such complaints, the ideal of freedom as non-domination would also have enabled socialists to defend the use of the strike weapon—the only instrument to which workers were able to have recourse. The ideal of freedom as non-interference has always been invoked, usually in the context of free contracts of employment, to make a case against collective industrial action by workers. Such action is a form of interference, of course, since it involves coercion or active obstruction. And on the face of it the strike is a form of interference that is unprovoked on the employer side: after all, employers impose their wishes only in negotiating free contracts, not necessarily by any form of coercion or force or even manipulation. Thus the ideal of non-interference naturally makes collective industrial action look illegitimate.

The ideal of freedom as non-domination gives a very different cast to collective action. Let us suppose that individual contracts of employment are wrested from workers under the spectre of destitution, and that they put the employer in a position of domination relative to employees. The resort to collective action, in such a situation, may represent the only hope of winning freedom as non-domination for those who are employed. It may be the only way of giving the workers sufficient power to enable them to be able to stand up, individually, to their employer.

I hope that these observations should indicate that, as it fits well with feminist goals, so the ideal of freedom as non-domination ought also to be congenial to socialists. It is implicit in the complaint about wage slavery; it makes sense of socialist impatience with the doctrine of free contract; and it supports the socialist belief in the legitimacy, where required, of resort to collective industrial action. But there is also one further point to make in arguing for the socialist attractions of the republican ideal. This is that the folk tradition of socialism, the tradition embodied in the pamphlets and verses and slogans of the working-class movement, has often expressed a desire for precisely the sort of status associated with freedom as non-domination. The point is supported by the popularity of the complaint about wage slavery, but it is also vividly borne out in the resentment that the tradition displays towards the petty pretensions of employers and the debasement that such pretensions imply for workers.

This resentment can be found among the Chartists in England in the 1830s and 1840s, and among those who identified a decade or so later with the free labour movement in the United States (Foner 1970). It is well expressed in two verses from 'A Bushman's Song', a popular ballad in which Banjo Paterson (1921) tried to catch the sentiments of a rural, Australian worker in the 1890s:

I went to Illawarra, where my brother's got a farm;
He has to ask his landlord's leave before he lifts his arm:
The landlord owns the country-side—man, woman, dog, and cat,
They haven't the cheek to dare to speak without they touch their hat.

It was shift, boys, shift, for there wasn't the slightest doubt
Their little landlord god and I would soon have fallen out,
Was I to touch my hat to him?—was I his bloomin' dog?
So I makes up for the country at the old jig-jog.

Multiculturalism

We have seen that, though the premodern beneficiaries of freedom as non-domination, the traditional champions of republican ideals, were all well-resourced males, there is every reason why freedom as non-domination should appeal also to feminists and socialists; we have seen, indeed, that that ideal is implicit in much feminist and socialist writing. These points connect with the suggestion advanced in the first chapter, that the retreat from the ideal of freedom as non-domination was occasioned precisely by a recognition that if women and workers were to assume the status of equal citizens, then the state would have to give up on the project of furnishing citizens in general with freedom in the traditional sense. The state might seek to maximize freedom as non-interference but it would be impossible, short of a total transformation of the contemporary society, for it to promote widespread freedom as non-domination.

But there is one other feature that marks the premodern beneficiaries of freedom as non-domination, apart from the fact that they were all men and, in particular, all men of substance. This is that they all also belonged to the mainstream culture of the societies in which they lived. The citizens of the polities in question did not include the Jews, for example, who lived throughout Europe and the New World; and the citizens of a Protestant polity like Britain did not include the Catholics who lived among them. This observation raises the question as to whether the ideal of freedom as non-domination can appeal, not just to women and workers, but also to those who belong to ethnic minorities and who exist outside the mainstream culture of a society: whether it can appeal, for example, to immigrant groups or indigenous, postcolonial populations.

The argument here has to be different from the argument in the case of feminism and socialism, for the tradition of defending minority or indigenous rights—the multicultural tradition, for want of a better term—does not have the same documentary history. I cannot argue here that multiculturalism has traditionally espoused an ideal like that of freedom as non-domination; I can only hope to show that multicultural concerns can be supported by an appeal to that ideal. Multiculturalism relates to republicanism more in the fashion of environmentalism than in the manner of feminism and socialism.

The main multicultural complaint is that the modern state is generally organized around presuppositions associated with one mainstream culture: it conducts its business in the language of that culture; it authorizes the habits of the religion of that culture; it projects an image of normal life that is drawn from that culture; it works via laws that may make sense only relative to the practices of that culture; and so on. The challenge raised by that complaint is whether the modern state can be given a rationale and a form that will enable it to serve the interests of those in minority cultures equally with the interests of those in the mainstream. The point that I want to make here, in defence of republicanism, is that if the modern state is orientated around the promotion of freedom as non-domination, then it will have a reason and a capacity to cater for the claims of those in minority cultures.

We saw earlier that freedom as non-domination is a communitarian ideal. If someone is dominated, if someone is exposed to arbitrary interference by others, then that is always in virtue being of a certain kind or class; the person is vulnerable insofar as they are black, or female, or old, or poor, or whatever. That means that to the extent to which we advance a person's freedom as non-domination, we must advance the freedom as non-domination of some relevant vulnerability class or classes to which they belong. And it means that if a person is to take up the cause of their own liberation, their own protection against domination, then they have to identify with the cause of others in their vulnerability classes. There may be no way, for example, whereby a woman or a worker can achieve an improvement in their freedom as non-domination short of achieving something for women or workers in general, or at least for women or workers in their particular situation.

The lesson of this observation is that so far as membership in a minority culture is likely to be a badge of vulnerability to domination, the members of that culture, and the state that assumes concern for their fortunes, must address the needs of the culture in general. It is not going to be enough to claim to be concerned with individuals in the culture, without any particular reference to what binds them together.

This lesson means that, just as a state may have to be focused on matters of gender in determining the requirements for advancing freedom as non-domination, so it may have to be alert to issues of cultural membership. In each case it must be sensitive to the possibility that, if someone of the relevant gender or culture is to enjoy freedom as non-domination—if such a person is to share in this common good—then they may have to be furnished with resources that are tailored to their special position. No one baulks at the fact that those in remote regional areas often have to be provided with special resources if they are to enjoy the same benefits as their urban counterparts; rural schooling and transport and communication, for example, may be much more expensive per head than urban counterparts. And, equally, no one should baulk at the possibility that if those in certain groups are to share in the common republican good of non-domination—the common good, if you like, of citizenship—then their special position may require that they be given special attention and support.

All of this said, the important point to register is that the special provision required for a minority culture may be quite radical, consistently with an overall republican vision. Suppose that the culture is an indigenous one, for example; that members see others, reasonably, as invaders of their traditional land; and that they view assimilation with those others, or even subjection to one and the same jurisdiction with them, as inherently objectionable and offensive. There is no hope in such a case that members of the minority culture can be assured of enjoying freedom as non-domination, short of very radical measures.

It may be necessary for representatives of the mainstream culture to acknowledge the dispossession imposed on the minority and, assuming that restitution or full compensation is impossible, to make some form of reparation in token of renouncing the past assumption of domination. And assuming that secession is not feasible, it may be necessary for them to treat members of the minority culture as conscientious objectors to mainstream ways, and to allow them various forms of exemption from otherwise universal obligations. It may be necessary to allow members of the minority culture to have a limited jurisdiction over their own territories, for example, and to organize their own affairs in a collective manner.

There are difficult issues to be resolved in considering the detail of such multiculturalist initiatives, and this is not the place to address them properly (see Kymlicka 1995). The point that I want to stress is that as the republican ideal is perfectly congenial from a feminist or a socialist perspective, or indeed from an environmentalist, so it can appeal also to those whose main concern is with catering for the special needs of minority cultures. Freedom as non-domination is a pluralistic ideal, and may be expected to command allegiance across a wide spectrum of contemporary interest and opinion.

The dynamism of the republican ideal

There is one last point to make that bears on the pluralistic character of the republican ideal. An ideal will be capable of appealing to the very different sorts of groups and movements that I have been discussing only insofar as it lends itself at every point of interpretation and implementation to further glosses and to further applications. It must be a dynamic ideal that is always rich in further possibilities of extrapolation and development, not a static ideal that is tied mechanically to a fixed pattern of institutional life. The ideal of freedom as non-domination displays precisely this sort of dynamism and that is why it can appeal so much more widely than the ideal of freedom as non-interference.

Freedom as non-domination requires that a person not be exposed to the possibility of interference on an arbitrary basis. The person must not be in a position where others can interfere in their lives in a manner that may be guided, for all the checks available, by interests or ideas that they do not share at any level. This ideal is dynamic, because there is never a final account available of what someone's interests are or of whether certain forms of interference—certain forms of state interference, in particular—are guided by ideas that they share. As people interact, and organize, and affirm certain identities—say, identities as women or workers or members of an indigenous population—they are always liable to see what had been unquestioned, barely visible patterns in their relations with certain others as indices of a dominating relationship. They are always liable to reaffirm old interests or ideas, or to espouse new interests or ideas, that make routine impositions assume the profile of arbitrary power.

The notion of what makes an exercise of power arbitrary, then, is systematically developmental: it is systematically open to possibilities of discursive reconstrual, as people discover novel affiliations and are able to make a case for viewing received forms of treatment in a new, critical light. And as the notion of arbitrary power, ultimately the notion of domination, is developmental, so too is the complementary ideal of freedom as non-domination. The requirements of such freedom are not fixed once and for all, as on tablets of stone. They are subject to constant reinterpretation and review as new interests and ideas emerge and materialize in the society.

It is this dynamic aspect of freedom as non-domination which explains how it can articulate diverse grievances of the kind surveyed here. To endorse republican freedom is not to accept a ready-made ideal that can be applied in a mechanical way, now to this group, now to that. It is to embrace an open-ended ideal that gains new substance and relevance as it is interpreted in the progressively changing and clarifying perspectives of a living society. I return to the point in the next chapter when I consider the role of democracy within a republican regime.

II. Republican policies

The republican posture on policy

It is impossible to give any detailed sense of the policies that a modern republican state would be likely to support. Knowing the overall goal you want to promote—in our case, freedom as non-domination—is not a sufficient base for policy development; nor indeed is knowing the broad sorts of cause with which you identify. What is also needed is an informed sense of the various institutional means available for promoting that goal, of their respective advantages and disadvantages, and of the circumstances under which the policies are to be implemented. As a consequentialist philosophy, republicanism is not dogmatic or doctrinaire. It presents us with a programme for developing policy, not with a policy blueprint. It recognizes that there has to be a division of labour in policy research, and that at a certain point the political theorists have to make way for the lawyers, the social scientists, and the other policy experts.

One obstacle to presenting a full account of republican policies is particularly worth remarking. In any society the role that the state is going to play in advancing people's freedom as non-domination has to depend on the role played in this respect by the civil society: by that form of society that extends beyond the narrow confines of family loyalty but that is strictly independent of the coercive state (Taylor 1995: essay 11; Gellner 1994: 5). Where there is a lively and tolerant civil society, where individuals and groups form the sorts of infra-political commitment that reduce or directly challenge possibilities of domination, then there is going to be less for the state to do; where such a rich civil society fails to materialize, but where it is still sufficient to make a state possible, there is going to be more (see Machiavelli 1965: 241). I return to this issue in the final chapter.

But though I have to abstract from detailed policy recommendations in this discussion, the very notion that freedom means non-domination, not just non-interference, implies that there is bound to be a big difference between the republican posture on state policy and the posture that is likely to appeal to those who cherish freedom as non-interference.

Because republicans cherish non-domination, they will differ in two relevant ways from those who cherish non-interference. In language that we introduced earlier, they will be less sceptical of the possibility of state intervention and they will be more radical in their view of the social ills that the state ought to rectify. They will be politically more optimistic and socially more radical. Their lesser scepticism about the state will come of the fact that they do not view state action, provided it is properly constrained, as an inherent affront to liberty: as itself a form of domination. And their greater radicalism about social ills will come of the fact that they do view any form of domination, even one in which the dominator may generally be expected to stay their hand, as such an affront; they do think of it as a relationship that essentially compromises liberty.

Consider the lesser state scepticism first. For someone concerned with non-interference as such, taxation is an inherent bad—it is itself a form of interference, after all—and any tax-supported policy must deliver a high expected benefit in non-interference terms if it is to make up for the certain cost, in those very same terms, of taxation. For republicans whose concern is with non-domination, not non-interference, taxation is not nearly so bad or objectionable in itself— at least not on the face of it—as the domination against which it is designed to protect. When a government taxes people under a well-ordered system of law, it need not dominate them, since the interference involved should not be arbitrary; it should be designed to track people's interests according to their ideas. The taxation will restrict the area in which those who are taxed enjoy undominated choice, for it deprives them of certain resources, but that is a much lesser offence than domination itself. Hence republicans will be better disposed than believers in freedom as non-interference to rely on tax-supported measures; they will be less sceptical about the desirability of having recourse to state intervention.

But not only will republicans tend to be less sceptical in regard to state action; they will also be more radical in relation to social policy. The liberal whose concern is maximizing expected non-interference will not worry about the fact that an employer is in a position to interfere more or less arbitrarily with an employee, for example, if it seems that the employer's interests will keep the level of interference low; certainly the liberal will not worry much about this situation if the only prospective remedy itself involves recourse to state interference. But republicans will be concerned about any possibility of arbitrary interference, since the fact that such interference is accessible to certain agents means that they dominate others; and of course they will be all the more concerned about the possibility to the extent that they see a way of remedying it by a state intervention that does not involve domination. Hence republicans will be scandalized by social circumstances that are likely to leave unmoved those liberals whose only concern is non-interference. They will take a more radical view of the ills that government is called upon to rectify.

We can see from these observations that, however detailed empirical matters turn out, republicanism is likely to give us a very different posture on issues of policy from that which a liberal attachment to freedom as non-interference would tend to support. Of course, it may just be that empirical constraints prove so demanding that republicans have to retreat towards the sorts of minimal governmental policy that their opponents favour. Suppose it is established that state welfare encourages dependency among welfare recipients, as a certain orthodoxy has it (on this see Fraser and Gordon 1994), and that such dependency undermines the capacity of recipients to achieve non-domination. That would have important implications for the way in which welfare—if 'welfare' remains the appropriate word—ought to be made available under a republican regime, and would push republicans towards minimal policies. But the point is that only special empirical constraints are likely to persuade republicans to adopt such a position. Their first inclination is going to be politically more optimistic and socially more radical.

Does this mean, in that much-used phrase, that republicans generally favour big government? Yes and no. They will be well disposed towards a form of government that gives the law and the state a considerable range of responsibilities. They will be very ill-disposed, on the other hand, towards a form of government that gives authorities, or even majorities, a high degree of power and discretion; they will look for the legal and democratic controls discussed in the next chapter. While they will look with optimism towards the possibility that the state may be able to reduce the dominating effects of private *dominium*, they will remain alert to the danger of giving the state the sort of licence that would introduce a dominating form of public *imperium*. Perhaps government should have a large range of responsibilities assigned to it, and perhaps in that sense it should be big. But government should not have a large range of independent powers and in that sense it should be decidedly small.

One final comment. While republican government may tend to be big in the range of responsibilities which it assumes, it is important to recognize that if it becomes too big in this dimension then it is liable to become big also in the range of independent powers that it can exercise: it is liable to become a dominating presence in its own right. There is a built-in brake, then, on how much republicanism is going to want the state to do. The ideal of non-domination is not the sort of monstrous ideal that is liable to require ever more intensive degrees of state interference in the lives of ordinary people. Whatever optimism it encourages in regard to state action, it is an inherently satiable or moderate goal (Braithwaite and Pettit 1990).

Assuming that no unusual empirical constraints impose themselves on the state, it may be worth trying to give a rough impression of the sorts of policy that the modern republic is likely to favour. There are five broad areas of policy-making in which we can expect such a state to involve itself: external defence; internal protection; personal independence; economic prosperity; and public life. I shall say something under each of these heads, in an attempt to convey a sense of the capacity of republicanism to serve as a plausible, policy-making perspective. I shall not relate my suggestions directly to the foregoing discussion of republican causes—those causes each bear on a number of different policy-making areas and the connections should be more or less obvious.

External defence

The modern republic, like any form of state, is bound to concern itself with issues of defence against external enemies. Unless the country or city in question is adequately defended, after all, there is going to be a live and continuing prospect of domination from outside. Indeed, to the extent that the country is not adequately defended, another country may dominate it, and thereby dominate its citizens, even without actually intefering; it may be in a position to interfere—to invade or threaten, for example—at will and with relative impunity. Republicans will shrink, not just from interference, and from likely interference, but from the situation where more or less arbitrary interference is within the power of another state.

But if republicans see a major policy challenge on the defence front, it should be clear that they need not think that the proper response is for the republic to arm itself to the teeth or, even worse, to strike pre-emptively against potential opponents. What the proper response is will depend on how the republic can best improve the prospects for non-domination on the international front. And the experience of history surely teaches that the best response is not likely to be bellicose or aggressive. The experience is that, as states rely more and more on their arms and their armies to inhibit each other, they become hostage to military pressures and logic. There may not be the spectre of the army coup that haunted traditional republican thinking and led republicans to favour the citizen militia over the standing army; in many countries the division of the military into different armed services, and the development of a democratic ethos, has reduced that prospect considerably. But there certainly will be a sustained prospect of war, as the generals on the different sides assume responsibility for national security and impose on the polity at large a militaristic image of how to discharge that responsibility.

When war becomes a sustained prospect, and when states defend themselves against one another by threat and counter-threat, then the cause of non-domination is compromised. Even if war does not eventuate—and in war ordinary people suffer the worst extremes of domination—the fact of threat and counter-threat means that each state is actively coercing others. And in any case the logic of threat and counter-threat means that the different sides have to spend more and more on military defence, that the citizens of the countries in question have to bear those costs, and that the extent of undominated choice that they can then enjoy is severely reduced. We saw earlier that there is a powerful republican case in favour of resort to the strategy of constitutional provision and against resort, or at least wholesale resort, to the strategy of reciprocal power; this, ultimately, provides the basis for the republican argument in favour of having a state. What we now see is that a similar logic applies in the international arena. The strategy of reciprocal power, at least in its military version, looks very unattractive, and republicans must naturally look for more constitutional provisions.

What provisions to seek? Here there is only a little that we can say that is not exceedingly vulnerable to empirical fortune. It is going to be attractive for the republican state to establish cultural, economic, and legal networks to the extent that such regional or global systems of relationships inevitably discipline members in the manner of constitutional commitments. It is also going to be attractive for the republican state to support a body like the United Nations, insofar as it promises to be able to contain conflicts and ultimately to make conflicts more and more unlikely. More generally, it is going to be in the interest of the republican state to encourage different layers of multinational cooperation and institutionalization. The emergence of institutional order, regional and global, promises to serve the cause of defence more effectively than exclusive reliance on military capacity.

The republican state will have to establish itself as a good international citizen, of course, if it is to foster the development of this sort of order. It will need to maintain a military capacity as a last resort. But it had better not flout the shared regional and international sense of what sort of capacity is reasonable. It will need to maintain limits on immigration, if it is to retain its current republican character and if it is to sustain the republican ethos that that requires. But it had better not show itself indifferent to the the plight of immigrants and refugees, or to the difficulties endured by those countries who are struggling to cope with the movements of peoples. It will need to look to its own interests in the development of trading and financial arrangements with other countries. But it had better not adopt a posture of being prepared to give up on every commitment it makes, at the first sign of an unforeseen cost. And so on.

If republican defence policy points us in the direction of multinational cooperation and institutionalization—if it suggests, indeed, that the well defended republic has to be a good international citizen—then it is worth noting that such a policy is likely to merge with republican requirements on other fronts. While the republican state represents an indispensable means of furthering people's non-domination, there is nothing sacred from the republican point of view about the state or about the state's sovereignty. Given the existence of multinational bodies of various kinds, there are some domestic issues on which it may be better from the point of view of promoting freedom as non-domination to give over control to those bodies and thereby to restrict the local state.

The more distant an agency is from a given issue, it is true, the less well informed it will be on certain aspects. But, equally, the more distant an agency is from an issue, the more likely it is to represent an impartial arbiter. That being so, it may be quite a good thing from the republican point of view that various domestic issues should be taken out of the realm of local decision-making and given over to international adjudication. Should development be allowed in a particular wilderness area? Should homosexuality be legally permitted and homosexuals allowed full civic rights? Should women have the right to work in certain industrial sectors and to earn the same wages as men? It is fairly obvious that on such questions international bodies, and indeed informal international movements, may promise to counter local factional interests in a more reliable manner than the domestic state. They may promise to do better in the promotion of freedom as non-domination among the citizens of that state than the state itself. The best republican policy may well be to expatriate domestic sovereignty in such cases and to give a certain guaranteed weight, if not absolute discretion, to relevant international agencies. In supporting multinational cooperation and institutionalization, republican defence policy would cohere well with what republican policy may require in such other areas.

Internal protection

Where defence policy points us towards the international arena, policy related to the protection of individual citizens and groups points us towards the internal forum. And it points us, in the first place, towards the criminal justice system. Criminal laws are an absolute prerequisite for the protection of citizens; they serve to identify offences, to deter offenders, and to vindicate victims by exposing offenders to legal penalty. Thus Montesquieu (1989: 188) is led to say: 'the citizen's liberty depends principally on the goodness of the criminal laws.'

Of course the good customs or norms of a society are also important in protecting individuals. Indeed, there is considerable evidence that criminal laws only work well when combined with such forces (Braithwaite 1989; Tyler 1990); I return to this theme in the last chapter. But if criminal laws need cultural forces, equally cultural forces are going to need reinforcement from criminal laws. First, there may be some individuals who are not responsive to ordinary norms and who can only be deterred or countered by the threat of legal sanction. Second, many individuals who are responsive to ordinary norms might cease to be responsive if they became aware that there was no great sanction attendant on breaking the norms. Which of us would remain virtuous if we had access to the ring of Gyges—the ring that makes a wearer invisible—and could commit a variety of offences with complete impunity? And third, many individuals who are responsive to such norms might cease to be responsive did they lose assurance, as the absence of legal sanction might cause them to lose assurance, that others are responsive too.

But however essential it is to the cause of non-domination, a system of criminal laws can do more harm than good if it is ill-designed. Republicans have always stressed that the system will greatly reduce people's freedom as non-domination, for example, if it leaves room for arbitrary arrest or detention; *habeas corpus*, as that was established in English law, became a treasured republican principle. And republicans have usually recognized that unless the system is properly run and tempered it can come to represent, in Montesquieu's (1989: 203) words, a 'tyranny of the avengers'.

What is the message of republicanism, then, for the design of criminal law? A first, obvious lesson is that, since the laws should only criminalize where criminalization promises to further overall non-domination—that is the core republican logic—and since criminal laws are both delicate and dangerous weapons, there should be a presumption in favour of parsimony. The state should be willing to resort to criminalization only reluctantly, and only to the extent that criminalization is clearly necessary for the protection of citizens (Braithwaite and Pettit 1990; see Montesquieu 1989: 191).

Why say that criminal laws are delicate and dangerous weapons, as this argument for parsimony has it? Criminal laws are delicate weapons because they only work well, as we mentioned, when they combine with other cultural forces; they cannot be expected to work miracles all on their own. Criminal laws are dangerous weapons because, as they may help to promote freedom as non-domination, so they can also have a negative effect on that ideal; they are two-edged swords. Criminal-law sanctions have a negative impact on the non-domination of those convicted of offences, imposing fines or prison sentences that reduce their scope for undominated choice and even serve—if not ideally, at least in practice—to expose them to domination. Criminal law processes often terrorize the innocent as well as the guilty, raising a spectre that haunts every corner of the society. And criminal-law agents represent potential forces of domination that it is difficult for even the most conscientious republican regime to keep in check.

This last point is worth particular emphasis. The main agents of the criminal-justice system are the police, and modern police represent the salient sort of threat to republican values that the standing army was taken to constitute among traditional republicans. Charged with the job of ensuring public order, guarding against crime, and apprehending criminals, police forces are nowadays given enormous powers, they are exposed to huge temptations to abuse those powers, and their use of the powers is subject only to very imperfect controls. The powers in question include the power to charge or not to charge, perhaps even the power to frame; the power to harass and make life miserable for someone; the power to spread rumours and ensure someone's defamation; and, of course, the power to threaten such ills and thereby coerce people to do what they want. The temptations include the age-old temptation just to assert yourself and command attention; to realize an identity as part of a powerful, self-reinforcing group; to achieve influence and impact in certain areas; and, perhaps above all, to bribe and blackmail your way to affluence: this temptation is particularly salient in any society that insists on prohibiting activities like the taking of alcohol or the use of even soft drugs. To expect people to remain incorruptible under such conditions of power and temptation is unrealistic and any republican is going to want to have the police operate under more demanding constraints, and answer to a more restricted brief, than is generally the case in contemporary democratic societies.

The controls currently employed for the regulation of police are clearly inadequate, as is borne out by the widespread evidence of police corruption in modern states, and as is obvious from even a little reflection (Caplow 1994). Police forces have generally been able to survive scandals without having to make deep organizational changes, police chiefs have been able to maintain a pattern of internal rather than external investigation of most problems that arise, and individual officers have been inhibited from whistle-blowing by an ethos of loyalty to colleagues that is stronger than any more impartial ethics of policing. Here in republican terms is a recipe for disaster: a recipe for ensuring that the police may become a greater force of domination that any which they seek to counter. *Quis custodiet custodes?* Who will guard against the guardians? Who indeed?

If the first lesson of republicanism for criminal justice is a parsimony in criminalization—and ultimately, therefore, an inhibition about allowing the criminal-justice system to grow too large—a second is that, if we are to avoid Montesquieu's tyranny of the avengers, then the punishment of criminals must be radically rethought (Braithwaite and Pettit 1990). Most criminal-justice systems impose penalties without any regard to compensation or reparation for the harm done in the offending act and without any thought of bringing the offender to appreciate and regret that harm. The received idea is that victims can seek compensation by recourse to civil law—this is clearly not substantiated in practice—and that the criminal law only has to do, in the old phrase, with imposing the King's peace. Given that the point of punishment is just to impose the King's peace—or, as it may, the people's peace—criminal-justice systems tend to let the nature and level of punishments be dictated, now by this set of pressures, now by that. Some theorists of those systems have claimed to find a deterrent logic implemented in the pattern of punishments imposed, others a logic of blame and retribution. But the truth is that in most countries the pattern of criminal punishments looks more like the random product of press attention, moralistic fashion, and the fluctuating taste for vengeance. There is no hard evidence that it is an optimal, even a reliable, means of deterring actual or potential offenders, and no evidence that it represents a systematic way of communicating blame or of punishing crimes in proportion to degree of blame.

What would a republican state do in regard to sentencing and penal policy? Here is a sketch suggestion. Every act of crime, provided the act is criminalized on a proper republican basis—provided that it is the sort of act that ought to be a crime in the republican's book—does mischief in three different ways. It denies the status of the victim as non-dominated or free: as not liable to arbitrary interference by another. It reduces the extent of the victim's undominated choices, removing certain options, or raising their cost, or even eliminating the possibility of choice, as in the limit case of homicide. And, finally, it damages the dispensation of non-domination in the society as a whole, holding out the sort of interference perpetrated as a permanent possibility for the victim and for everyone in the victim's vulnerability class. These observations argue that what punishment should be designed to do in a republican regime is to put right such damaging effects and thereby to promote overall non-domination.

What would the rectification of the ills ideally require? Subject to the constraint of thereby increasing non-domination overall—and, in particular, respecting general limits on the treatment of offenders—the rectification should pursue the three Rs of republican sentencing, as John Braithwaite and I have described them elsewhere. It should seek to elicit *recognition* by the offender of the status of the victim as non-dominated and free; *recompense*—restitution, compensation or at least reparation—from the offender for the harm done to the victim and/or the victim's family; and a *reassurance* for the victim and the community at large that the offender will not continue to be the threat that they proved to be in committing the crime (Pettit with Braithwaite 1993; 1994; Pettit forthcoming). What recognition, recompense, and reassurance are going to require will depend in any instance on the nature of the crime and the circumstances of the criminal and victim. Reassurance may be obtained indirectly, for example, if the offender was injured in the course of the crime and made incapable of reoffending; or it may be obtained more straightforwardly, insofar as the sanction imposed should serve to deter the offender—and, it may be hoped, others too—from committing similar crimes in the future. But this is not the place to go into such details.

I have identified the likely shape of republican policy on criminal justice by two principles: parsimony in criminalization and a reconceptualization of criminal punishment as a means of rectifying the effects of crime. I have suggested that such a reconstrual of the criminal-justice system is continuous with Montesquieu's desire to avoid a tyranny of the avengers, and that it has good traditional credentials. But I should mention, in conclusion, that traditional republicans have only a patchy record on matters in this area. Their main concern was to get rid of the pattern of arbitrary arrest and punishment associated with absolute monarchies; and in their desire to provide a systematic basis for the criminal-justice system, they did not give much thought to the question of how that might be best done: in particular, how it might be best done from the point of view of liberty. We may feel that we are among fellow spirits when we read something like the eighth amendment to the US Constitution: 'Excessive bail shall not be required, nor excessive fines imposed, nor cruel and unusual punishments inflicted.' But then we may well begin to wonder, when we consider that even Montesquieu was tempted to endorse a system for determining punishment that looks akin to the eye-for-an-eye of the *lex talionis*. 'It is the triumph of liberty when criminal laws draw each penalty from the particular nature of the crime. All arbitrariness ends; the penalty does not ensue from the legislator's capriciousness but from the nature of the thing' (Montesquieu 1989: 189).

So much for republican policy on the provision of internal protection. It remains only to note that not only have we looked sketchily at the policies that are likely to be required, we have not even looked at all the areas of state activity that are relevant to those policies. Thus the protection of individuals and groups is served, not just by criminal law, but also by the law of tort. Republican values would certainly have implications for such areas of state initiative but it is impossible to devote any time to those implications here.

Personal independence

The third of our five areas of policy-making bears, not on what should be done by way of providing the collective goods of defence and protection, but rather on what it is necessary for the state to do in fostering the independence—the socioeconomic independence—of each individual person. To be independent in the intended sense is to have the wherewithal to operate normally and properly in your society without having to beg or borrow from others, and without having to depend on their beneficence. It is, in Amartya Sen's (1985) illuminating account of these things, to have the basic capabilities that are required for functioning in the local culture. Or if it is not always to have the capabilities themselves, it is at least to have the things that those capabilities normally enable a person to secure (Cohen 1993).

The basic capabilities required for functioning in one society may be different from those required in another (Sen 1983; cf. Smith 1976: 870). You need to be able to provide yourself with enough to eat in any society, as you need to be able to keep yourself in clothes and to provide yourself with shelter. But what it is to have enough to eat and what it is to have adequate clothing or shelter will vary from one sort of society to another. And in any case there are all sorts of things that are necessary for functioning in one society which are not necessary in another.

The necessities of life in a contemporary developed society, for example, far outstrip what would have been required in a more traditional community. To function properly in a contemporary society you have to be able to read and write, to do basic mathematics, to have access to information about matters like work opportunities, medical facilities, transport services, weather forecasts, and to have the resources—a postal address or a telephone number—to make yourself available for contact by others—say, by potential employers. And to function properly in such a society you need also to know how to ascertain and assert your legal rights in dealing with the police, with your children's school, or with your spouse; to know where you can bank your money and how you can use credit facilities; and to have the means of getting about in your local environment and of availing yourself of opportunities for work and leisure. As society has become more complex, and as the demands of successful social living have multiplied, so the standard necessary for assured access to a decent quality of life—the standard necessary for socioeconomic independence—has risen too.

If a republican state is committed to advancing the cause of freedom as non-domination among its citizens, then it must embrace a policy of promoting socioeconomic independence. I may be dependent on others for access to some of the things necessary for a decent quality of life without necessarily being dominated by them. I may not be dependent on any given individual or group, for example—my dependence may be anonymous, as it were—and so may not be exposed to domination by any agent in particular. But in general the fact of not enjoying socioeconomic independence is going to lessen my prospects for the enjoyment of freedom as non-domination.

A first way in which this is true relates to the extent of non-domination rather than its intensity. Insofar as I lack the physical or personal or financial resources for doing something, the extent of undominated choice that is available to me is limited. Thus by providing such resources, by providing in such a way for my socioeconomic independence, the state would do well by my freedom as non-domination. It would put certain undominated choices within my reach for the first time, or it would reduce the costs of pursuing those choices.

But there is a second and more important way in which a lack of socioeconomic independence will lessen my prospects for the enjoyment of freedom as non-domination; this relates to the intensity of non-domination I enjoy, not its extent. Suppose I lack the wherewithal to get by under ordinary day-to-day circumstances: I cannot read or write, for example, or cannot adequately provide for my more basic needs, or cannot access important information, or cannot depend on cultural support against the assumptions of husband or employer. In any such case it is manifest that the unscrupulous are in a position to make free with me. Banking on my ignorance of relevant standards and expectations, they may mislead, manipulate, and exploit, almost without check. And even where they do nothing so outrageous, they may still exercise a high degree of domination. If I am lucky enough to have a job, for example, my employer may still be able to interfere at will and with impunity in my affairs; the employer will be able to depend on my terror of getting the sack, or on my ignorance, or just on my cultural powerlessness, for an assurance that such interference will not be resisted or punished.

Or suppose that I suffer, not such general ills, but the conditional ills associated with being unable to cover medical costs in the event of falling sick or legal costs in the event of a criminal charge or in the event of needing to go to law in order to defend my interest. A medical or legal emergency would open up possibilities of domination of the kind just discussed. It would mean that I had to throw myself on

the mercy of another—say, on a doctor or lawyer or on a rich bene-
factor—and thereby expose myself to arbitrary interference by that
other; I would be unlikely to resist or punish various exploitative or
manipulative responses, after all, if doing so meant being medically or
legally abandoned or meant leaving a child or spouse abandoned. But
even if no emergency actually arises, a lack of medical or legal cover
would expose me to domination. A lack of either sort of cover would
dispose me to tolerate a degree of arbitrary treatment from those on
whom I am likely to have to depend in the event of an emergency. And
a lack of legal cover would expose me to the sort of arbitrary treatment
against which the normal mode of protection involves going to law.

Or suppose, finally, that I am handicapped in some manner. I cannot get around in the ordinary way because I have lost, or I have never
had, the use of my legs. Or I cannot see. Or I cannot perform routine
intellectual tasks. It scarcely needs arguing, if only because of the
literary treatment that has been given to the theme, that in such an
event I am going to be exposed to a degree of domination by those on
whom I depend for managing my life. If I desperately need the help of
some particular other or others, as I surely will, then I am going to be
in a position where I will not complain against any arbitrary, perhaps
petty, forms of interference by such agents. I will be disposed to placate them at any cost, putting myself in the classic position of the dominated supplicant (see Goodin 1984).

We have distinguished two republican reasons for wanting the state
to promote people's socioeconomic independence. One is the inten-
sity-based argument that by doing this the state will guard the socio-
economically dependent against forms of domination that otherwise
they will almost certainly have to endure. The other, mentioned
earlier, is the extent-based consideration that by doing this the state
will facilitate undominated choice on the part of the socioeconom-
ically dependent.

How radical are the policies that such a republican way of thinking
would support? That depends. It depends, first, on how serious the
problems are, which in turn depends on the quality of the civil society
in question; in a well-ordered civil society the effects of a given level
of deprivation will not be so bad as in an ill-ordered one. And it
depends, second, on how effective are the means that the state can
identify for dealing with the problems: for example, it depends on how
far the state can identify means of dealing with the problems that do
not foster the dependency mentality or the dependency culture of
which critics of the welfare state sometimes complain. Depending on
how these essentially empirical questions are answered, republicans

will require the state to provide more or less assistance for those in need; to provide it entirely in cash or at least partly in kind; to provide it directly or by means of independent civil agencies; to provide it subject to means-testing or as part of a universal form of provision; and so on. There is no direct argument from the republican ideal to decisions on such specific matters of policy; the policy decisions will be determined by empirical considerations as well as by philosophical.

But notwithstanding the need to rely on empirical assumptions in the development of policy, there are two likely features of republican policy in this area that are worth mentioning. The first is that the policy is almost certain to fall short of strict material egalitarianism, however interpreted. And the second is that the policy is bound to require that welfare be made available under well-established routines, even law-like constraints, not at the discretion of particular authorities.

The goal of intensifying the non-domination of the needy, lessening the prospects of their being exploited or manipulated or intimidated by others, requires that they have what Sen describes as the basic capabilities for functioning in society: thus it would require the substantial reduction of certain material inequalities. But it is clear that a person can have sufficient capabilities not to be exposed to domination—it is clear that they can have the basic capabilities required—without necessarily having the same resources as others. I do not have to be as wealthy as you, my employer, in order to be wealthy enough—and assured of being wealthy enough—not to put up with any petty, arbitrary interference.

If the goal of intensifying non-domination does not argue for ensuring strict material equality, neither does the goal of increasing the extent of people's undominated choices. The reason for this, as we saw in the last chapter, is that even if the equalizing initiatives do not involve the state in a dominating role—and that is a big 'if'—there is no reason to think that the extent of undominated choice can be maximized at the limit of egalitarian transfers. In order for the state to provide one person with extra resources, and thereby to extend their undominated choices, it must deprive another person of those resources, and must thereby reduce the extent of that person's undominated choices. There is no reason to think that the transfer will make for a gain. On the contrary, the costs of the state intervention will almost certainly mean that less is given to the second person than is taken from the first and that the transfer makes for a decrease in the extent of undominated choice overall.

Apart from being hostile to material egalitarianism, there is also a second feature that republican policy on socioeconomic independence is almost certain to display. However the welfare needs of people are serviced under a state that promotes overall freedom as non-domination, they must not be serviced in a manner that itself involves certain forms of domination. Whatever level of income support is given to the needy, for example, it must be given so far as possible in the fashion of a right (see Ingram 1994). It must not have the aspect of a gift that may be withdrawn at anyone's whim: not at the whim of a subsidized employer, not at the whim of a street-level bureaucrat, not even at the whim of an electoral or parliamentary majority.

Withdrawing the gift is going to constitute interference by the benchmark of what is normal, and the unchecked power to withdraw it will amount to a power of arbitrary interference. And even if withdrawing the gift is not itself to count as interference, the claimant's fear that the gift will be withdrawn may lead them, and lead them as a matter of common knowledge, to be willing not to resist or complain about a variety of other acts of interference that the powerful may perpetrate. Unless the income support comes under conditions that guard against such whim, then the claimant is denied freedom as non-domination in the very act whereby that freedom was meant to be promoted.

This requirement on the mode of providing welfare argues in favour of a more or less constitutional guarantee of welfare provision, with some independent, depoliticized means of determining levels of provision. It argues for a mode of delivering welfare that is independent of political vagaries and bureaucratic whims, for example, and independent equally of the caprice of any other agents that may be involved. Consider the employer who is given incentives to hire otherwise unemployed people, for example. The requirement we are discussing would argue against giving such an employer the right to hire and fire at will, with all the other arbitrary powers of petty intrusion that such a right would bestow. And it would argue for this restriction, even though employers might be willing to take on more employees in its absence.

In conclusion, a historical comment. The premodern republican tradition assumed that there was nothing that could be done to give independence to those who did not already have it, and so it did not support the sort of state envisaged here. But, still, those affiliated with republican thought did always display an interventionist spirit, and the proposals I have been sketching are not entirely foreign to that tradition. Where traditional republicans thought that intervention in the economic fortunes of citizens could aid the overall cause of freedom as non-domination, they proved themselves more than willing to call for it. Thus the tradition was often associated with a belief in special tax-ation on luxury or sumptuary goods and a commitment to ensuring that no one was allowed the sort of wealth that might enable them to corrupt public officials and lord it over lesser citizens. In Harrington (1992), indeed, the tradition became linked with a redistributive, agrarian proposal, designed to ensure that land did not come exces-sively under the control of a few. The existence of such precedents should make it clear that calling for a welfare state need not make for an altogether radical break with the older republican tradition.

Economic prosperity

The republican state will concern itself with matters of economic prosperity to the extent that it can thereby lessen the prospects of domination—raise the intensity of non-domination enjoyed in the society—or improve the range or ease of undominated choice: that is, increase the extent of non-domination in the society. Both goals pro-vide reasons for economic interventions.

They suggest, for example, that the republican state will concern itself with the level of employment and the stability of the financial system. When employment is high, and when the financial system enjoys substantial confidence and robustness, then other things being equal there are fewer opportunities for people to be exploited and manipulated and the prospects for freedom as non-domination are improved. The republican goals also suggest that, other things being equal, the state will concern itself with providing a good infrastructure for industry and commerce, with facilitating productivity in the work-place, with fostering market development and choice, and with establishing trade linkages with other countries. If not directly related to reducing prospects of domination—that is, to intensifying non-domination—the realization of such advances would serve at least to extend the undominated choice that people enjoy in the society.

The development of republican economic policy is bound to be of interest when we are addressing specific policy situations and dilem-mas. There will be challenging questions to do with exactly what sorts of state interventions are best designed to further people's freedom as non-domination in such circumstances, and there is every reason to expect that republican answers may be quite different from the answers supported by other approaches. But there is not much of interest that can be said about republican economic policy in the abstract. Whatever brand differentiation it displays, this is only likely to appear when we look at concrete issues.

The cause of economic prosperity is related, not just to economic policy, strictly so called, but also to various areas of legal policy; the state can further economic prosperity, after all, by introducing any of a number of legal instruments. One example is the legal instrument whereby companies were enabled to become more or less autonomous agents, with assets and liabilities independent of the personal assets and liabilities of their owners (Coleman 1974). Another was the development of the law of contract, early in the nineteenth century, that enabled economic players to be innovative in the arrangements to which they could bind themselves. Under earlier law, most relationships into which individuals voluntarily entered—that of husband to wife, servant to master, passenger to sea-captain, and so on—were governed by more or less standing rights and obligations; under the new law of contract, people were not shackled by established practice in this way and were entitled to bargain their way individually towards a set of mutually agreeable expectations (Atiyah 1979; Stoljar 1975).

It should be clear that the republican state is bound to look carefully at legal instruments of these kinds, since the gain that they may make possible in economic prosperity is liable to be offset by losses in other areas that connect with freedom as non-domination. I have already mentioned, for example, that the law of contract as it emerged in the nineteenth century suggested that if a contract is entered freely, then the conduct that occurs under the terms of the contract is unimpeachable. Such a suggestion must be entirely unacceptable to a republican. The striking feature of a contract, even a free contract—a contract that is not the product of coercion or manipulation, for example—is that it may give one party a power of domination over the other. The force of circumstance may drive a person into making a contract that exemplifies or approximates the slave contract that was roundly condemned in the commonwealth tradition (Locke 1965: 325). From a republican point of view, then, the free contract cannot serve the role of automatic legitimator—even prima facie legitimator—of what happens under the terms of the contract. The idea of free contract loses the authorizing capacity that it was given in the classical liberal tradition.

A law of contract is obviously going to have a place, and an important place, in any modern society; it is a prerequisite for economic activity and prosperity. So how would the republican state be likely to cast it? In any contract, no matter how freely undertaken, one party gives a certain hostage to the other: they expose themselves to the damages that the other may seek in the event of their not performing as promised; if you like, one party runs the risk of domination by the other. That being so, the republican state which wants to promote non-domination is bound to expect contract law, not just to facilitate voluntary agreements among different agents, but to play a regulative role in disallowing contracts that involve terms under which one party has the possibility of dominating the other.

This point of view on contract was not fully developed among pre-modern republicans, as contract only assumed a major role in the organization of social life from the nineteenth century on. But what I think of as the republican viewpoint is well represented in the theory that contract confers sovereignty on one party over another and that the law of contract, although it belongs to private law, can serve a public-law role by increasing people's security in the contractual aspect of their lives. The view is outlined in a path-breaking article by Morris R. Cohen (1933: 587).

Adherents of the classical theory have recognized that legal enforcement serves to protect and encourage transactions that require credit or reliance on the promises of others. But we also need care that the power of the state not be used for unconscionable purposes, such as helping those who exploit the dire need or weaknesses of their fellows. Usury laws have recognized that he who is under economic necessity is not really free. To put no restrictions on the freedom to contract would logically lead not to a maximum of individual liberty but to contracts of slavery, into which, experience shows, men will 'voluntarily' enter under economic pressure.

Public life

The final area of policy-making that I want to consider bears on the public life of the polity and the society. When I speak of public life, I mean the life of the community as that is based in matters of common knowledge or belief. Something occurs in public life just so far as it does indeed occur; it is generally believed that it occurs; it is generally believed that it is generally believed that it occurs; and so on.

What is it for something to be generally believed to occur? And what is it for the pattern that is described in the words 'and so on' to be realized? It will be generally believed that something occurs, I assume, if nearly everyone believes this or at the least—and this alternative is important—if nearly everyone is in a position to learn that it occurs in the event of seeking such knowledge: if there is some record available, for example, that will lead them to such a belief. And, to turn to the other issue, the 'and so on' clause will be fulfilled, we can suppose, if at any higher level there is at least an absence of belief that the condition of the previous level is unfulfilled; there is no need to require positive belief, as distinct from an absence of disbelief, at successive levels (Lewis 1983: 166). At the third level, for example, there may be an absence of disbelief that it is generally believed that the event occurred, and at the fourth level an absence of disbelief in the third-level absence of disbelief.

The public life of a community is of the utmost importance for the enjoyment of non-domination. Everything that happens in relation to politics is going to be part of public life, and it is essential for people's freedom that that public sphere is well-ordered: it is essential, in particular, that there is no domination associated with the *imperium* of government. One of the major aims of the republican state, then, must be to try and promote the forms of government—the forms of legal and democratic control—for which I argue in the next chapter. But apart from looking to governmental tasks that are covered in that later discussion, we can already see at this stage that public life is going to present a republican state with important policy challenges.

Let us suppose that the republican state has ensured that few people are exposed to domination, whether on the side of *dominium* or *imperium*. We know from earlier considerations that at least when other things are equal—at least, for example, when no one tries to induce the contrary opinion—this will tend to become a matter of common belief and so to be registered in public life. And we also know that if this does become a matter of common belief, then people's non-domination will give them the great benefits discussed earlier. They can be confident about what is within their power of choice and what not, they can cease to worry about exercising care and strategy in relation to the powerful, and they can savour the sense of enjoying an equal status with others in the society: they can look all those others in the eye, conscious of a shared consciousness that no one can interfere arbitrarily in their lives.

But if people's non-domination secures those benefits only so far as it becomes established in common awareness and public life, then it is of the first importance for the republican state, in particular the state that has actually secured a high degree of non-domination for its citizens, to make sure that people's non-domination is registered in public life. Suppose that a state secured non-domination but allowed its enemies, internal or external, to persuade many citizens that it had not been secured. The upshot would be tragic and poignant. Having brought its people into the promised land, as it were, the state would have failed to persuade them that they were there.

Not only should the state concern itself with public life in order to make sure that people enjoy the benefits of the non-domination that has been secured; the cause of non-domination itself gives the state reason to focus on public life. What is registered in the public life of a community can have important effects on how far people's non-domination is promoted. If it is registered as a matter of common belief that a person is protected, then the protections, whatever their previous value, will be all the more effective. If it is registered that the person is not protected, then the protections will be all the less effective. If it is registered that this or that measure is required to promote non-domination, then this will help or hinder the cause of non-domination to the extent that the beliefs are reliable or unreliable. And so on. The goal of producing non-domination, not just the goal of realizing the benefits associated with the non-domination produced, gives the state reason to be concerned with the public life of the community.

How is a republican state likely to further its vision of public life? There are a great number of issues relevant to policy in this area. They become visible as soon as we reflect on the difficulties that plague the public life of many contemporary democracies.

A first difficulty that is very striking is the loss of public space, urban, rural, and wild, in many societies. Consider the pattern of residential and commercial life, for example, that has begun to emerge in many American cities. The middle class feel threatened by the level of violence in the city centres and respond to it by withdrawing from public places. The home or street or suburb is intensively secured, perhaps placed under the surveillance of a private security firm, and is cast as a place of retreat from the hostile city. And the office or workplace, even if it is situated in the city, is increasingly insulated from it; there is direct access from private parking areas and lunchtime services are provided within its walls. The emerging pattern is one that bodes extremely ill for public life, for it ensures that the view which people have of others in their society, in particular the view that they have of those who do not belong to their own class and coterie, becomes hostage to fantasy. Lacking direct experience and contact across the different divides in their society, people can easily lose any sense of what is a matter of general belief and expectation in that society.

But if the contraction of public space is one problem, it is exacerbated by the related difficulty that the information which people get about the environment in which they live is often highly biased. Newspaper and television reporting in contemporary democracies is driven by the search for sales and, relying on the appeal of the sensational, concentrates more and more on inducing the horror that produces voyeuristic outrage and the terror that guarantees voyeuristic thrills. Undoubtedly, and unhappily, the image presented of the surrounding society is well enough grounded in the way things are not to attract refutation and rejection. But the image is so one-sided that it often borders on a nightmare fantasy.

A third area of difficulty for public life comes of the way in which public opinion, so called, is generally represented—and in being represented, realized—in our democratic societies. Again, the media have a major role here and, again, the media often fail their societies badly. Sometimes they venture accounts of public opinion that are entirely speculative, and often motivated by sectional ends. And sometimes they give accounts of public opinion that are based on outrageously rigged polling. But even if the media rely on more or less well-designed polls, they can still be seriously misleading. The reason is that the person polled often has no motive to think seriously about what they say: it is not as if they will affect anything by their individual response and it is not as if they will have to answer for that response (Brennan and Lomasky 1993; Fishkin 1991; 1995). The person polled may well have a motive just to use the opportunity for giving expression to frustration or exasperation or malice or something of the kind.

I have mentioned problems associated with public space, public information, and public opinion-polling. Such pressures on public life reduce the prospects for promoting freedom as non-domination and, in particular, for creating a firm awareness of the non-domination actually available. What policies should the republican state adopt in response to such difficulties? I have nothing to report in the way of policy research, as already stressed, but it may be useful if I mention some initiatives for which there is at least a prima facie case.

The problems of a contraction in public space call, on the face of it, for radical action. They require a political commitment to building a shared, public environment of a kind that has been eroded in recent years by a creeping libertarianism. The assumption has often been that it is an unconscionable imposition on taxpayers for the state to commit itself to improving public space, and that in any case it is not clear that public space is what the public really wants: the evidence quoted here, ironically, is the growing retreat to private space and the increased search for private security. But I hardly need to stress that a republican perspective would offer a completely different view of things. Of course the state can reasonably impose on taxpayers if the benefit sought is a more accessible public space, and of course we may presume that such a public space is desirable from the point of view of citizens: it is, after all, a precondition for the full realization of their freedom as non-domination.

What should the state do about the poor quality of information that the public gets on what is happening in the society at large? It is important, first of all, that there should be many different voices in the media. This entails that media ownership and control should not be allowed to concentrate in a few hands. And it entails that the state should set up or subsidize media that are governed by different interests from those that dominate in commercial life: it should support semi-autonomous state broadcasting services, for example, and encourage as far as possible the growth of community-based media. The state should also assume responsibility, of course, for media regulation, though the best line here will almost certainly be to encourage a serious degree of self-regulation among media organizations (Ayres and Braithwaite 1992).

What is to be done, finally, about the problems that arise with the formation of public opinion? A recent proposal for dealing with the problem of opinion polling, and opinion formation, is worth mentioning. James Fishkin (1991; 1995) argues that the media should at least occasionally attempt to conduct what he calls a deliberative opinion poll. This would involve taking a random sample of people, bringing its members together for some days in order to deliberate about the issues in question, broadcasting some of their debates and then polling participants at the end. The evidence is that people's opinions change in the course of such deliberation, and it would surely be preferable if public opinion were represented, and shaped, by the evidence of deliberative polls, not just by the evidence of ordinary polling. 'An ordinary poll models what the public thinks, given how little it thinks, how little it knows, how little it pays attention. A deliberative opinion poll, by contrast, models what the public would think, if it had a better chance to think about the questions at issue' (Fishkin 1995: 45).

In conclusion, one further line of thought about policy in relation to the public sphere. John Rawls has argued that one of the desiderata of any political ideal is something that he describes as publicity. The ideal must be capable of being publicly avowed and endorsed as a yardstick by which institutions and initiatives are reasonably assessed (Rawls 1971: 130–6; 1993: lecture 6). There must be nothing about it that requires a degree of secrecy, nothing about it that is likely to alienate any significant group—in particular any group that is willing to tolerate other groups (Scanlon 1982; Young 1990; Barry 1995)—and nothing about it that makes it incapable of measuring the performance of the polity. The ideal should represent an effective criterion that is capable of being justified, and of being seen to be justified, by the lights of everyone in the society (Gaus 1990; D'Agostino 1996).

There is no difficulty about the republican ideal serving as a measure for the performance of public institutions, as the considerations advanced in this chapter should have begun to make clear. And neither is there any difficulty about the state's being justified in pursuing that ideal; as I argued in the first part of the book, freedom as non-domination is a very attractive goal for the polity to promote. But not only is the ideal of freedom as non-domination capable of satisfying the publicity requirement. What I now want to remark is that the republican state which is given to the promotion of the ideal is bound to want to establish this as a fact of public life. It is bound to want to prove, not just that people enjoy non-domination under its institutions—this has been our focus up to now—but also that non-domination is an effective and in particular a justifiable measure of political and institutional life.

The reason, very simply, is that if the state can establish the credentials of the republican goal in this way, then it can promote that goal all the more effectively (Spitz 1995*a*; Philp 1996). Let it be a shared opinion that freedom as non-domination is desirable and that the state is justified in pursuing it. In that case the desirability of enjoying non-domination will be all the more palpable, as the benefit in question is more deeply appreciated. And in that case it will become all the more likely, and all the more likely by people's own lights, that they do enjoy non-domination at one another's hands. As their moral appreciation of the benefit of non-domination grows, they will presumably each find increased reason not to offend against it. They will each have an extra moral motive for not offending, and they will each have an extra motive of a kind related to their reputation. If the moral desirability of non-domination is established as a matter of common belief, then it is going to be matter for shame if you are found to offend against it.

We saw earlier that the republican state is bound to want the fact of people's non-domination established in public life, and we looked at some of the policies it may have to pursue to that end. What this final consideration shows us is that that state will try to establish not just the legal and cultural reality of non-domination but also its moral desirability. I shall return to this important line of thought in the last chapter, when I consider the relation between the republican state and civil society.

CHAPTER 6

Republican Forms:
Constitutionalism and Democracy

I looked in the last chapter at the things that we may expect the republican state to try to do in order to cope with the problems that arise in people's dealings with one another: the problems associated with variations in levels of *dominium* or control. But, as I have stressed time and again, the state can itself become an agent of the sort of domination associated with *imperium* rather than *dominium*. I look in this chapter at the forms which the republican state should realize if its pursuit of republican aims is not to be compromised in this way. The distinction between aims and forms is not canonical or clear-cut, of course, but it gives a fair sense of the shift of focus involved.

The agencies of the state, including the state that is devoted to republican causes and policies, interfere systematically in people's lives: they coerce the people as a whole through imposing laws in common upon them, and they coerce different individuals among the populace in the course of administering that law and applying legal sanctions. If the interference that the state practises in these ways is allowed to be arbitrary, then it will be itself a source of unfreedom. And so the question with which we shall be concerned comes immediately into relief. How can the state be organized so that state interference involves little or no arbitrariness?

The question is how things can be arranged so that the presence of arbitrary will in the apparatus of state coercion is minimized. We are not concerned at this stage with how to guard against human weakness—that is the issue in the next chapter—but with how to guard against the possibility that government agents, even perfectly public-spirited agents, can make coercive decisions on an arbitrary basis. It has to be remembered, after all, that even if government agents always respected the interests and ideas of ordinary citizens in their decision-making, the fact that they had the capacity not to do so—the fact that they had the power to interfere on an arbitrary basis—would imply that they dominated such citizens. Or at least it would imply this, so far as their virtue offered only an imperfect guarantee that they would track the interests and ideas of ordinary people.

My answer to the question raised connects at various points with a consensus on institutional matters that we find among traditional republican writers—so at least I believe—and I shall try to indicate the extent to which it fits with that tradition. But the discussion is intended, I should emphasize, as a theoretical exercise, not a historical one. The fact that the sketch provided turns out to accord with a traditional consensus is a welcome but incidental result. It is welcome, because it provides evidence that the main concern of republicans was indeed the promotion of freedom as non-domination; it is incidental, because the primary focus is not the reconstruction of detailed republican beliefs but the exploration of what it would mean to take seriously the republican goal of freedom as non-domination.

But while the views defended in the discussion fit with traditional republican tenets, they are not platitudinous in character. They endorse established institutional ideals like the rule of law, the separation of powers, and democratic accountability, but they support those ideals on a distinctive basis and sometimes offer quite unorthodox reformulations of their content. As I shall try to highlight continuities with the republican tradition, so I shall also try to indicate these points of difference with more or less established ways of thinking.

My discussion is divided into two sections. In the first section I discuss the need for constitutionalist constraints in the ideal republic; in the second I consider the way that decision-making power should be democratically controlled within the republican state. My case for constitutionalist constraints is that republican instrumentalities should not be manipulable by those in power, and the key to my conception of democratic control is the claim that everything done by a republican government should be effectively contestable by those affected.

I. Constitutionalism and non-manipulability

If we want the republican state to avoid assuming an arbitrary, dominating form, then what should we seek in the means whereby it tries to advance its republican aims? Assuming that the means are otherwise successful—assuming that other things are equal on that front—a first desideratum must be to ensure that they leave as little room as possible for the exercise of arbitrary power. There will be no point in establishing institutions or in taking initiatives that reduce the domination associated with *dominium* if those very instruments make room for the sort of domination associated with *imperium*; what is gained on the one side will be lost, and perhaps more than lost, on the other.

The lesson is that the instruments used by the republican state should be, as far as possible, non-manipulable. Designed to further certain public ends, they should be maximally resistant to being deployed on an arbitrary, perhaps sectional, basis. No one individual or group should have discretion in how the instruments are used. No one should be able to take them into their own hands: not someone who is entirely beneficent and public-spirited, and certainly not someone who is liable to interfere for their own sectional ends in the lives of their fellow citizens. The institutions and initiatives involved should not allow of manipulation at anyone's individual whim.

How to make republican instrumentalities maximally non-manipulable? Here, as on questions to do with republican aims, it is essential to take account of empirical realities, and it is impossible to devise a complete blueprint on a purely philosophical basis. But under any plausible scenario there are three broad conditions that a non-manipulable system will need to satisfy and I shall concentrate on these. The first condition is, in James Harrington's (1992: 81) phrase, that the system should constitute an 'empire of laws and not of men'; the second, that it should disperse legal powers among different parties; and the third, that it should make law relatively resistant to majority will. The empire-of-law condition bears on the place and content of the laws, the dispersion-of-power condition on their operation in day-to-day life, and the counter-majoritarian condition on the ways in which the laws may be legitimately altered.

All of these conditions serve to thwart the will of those who are in power; they make government more difficult to organize, not less. In this sense they operate like formal constitutional constraints and represent a belief in what we may call constitutionalism. We find constitutionalism in place wherever there are legally established ways of constraining the will of the powerful, even if the constraints are not recorded in a formal constitution. The historian F. W. Maitland argued in the last century that the most important achievement of democratic government was its contribution to such constitutionalism.

The introduction of a democratic element into governments has rendered us less subject to the 'inconstant, uncertain, unknown will of others', not because we are now under fewer laws to which we have not given our consent, but because the friction of the governmental machine has been increased, because it has become too unwieldy to be used in a capricious way. The exercise of arbitrary power is least possible, not in a democracy, but in a very complicated form of government. (Maitland 1981: 84–5)

The empire-of-law condition

There are two aspects to the empire-of-law condition. The first prescribes that laws should assume a certain sort of shape: roughly, that they should conform to the constraints described by contemporary rule-of-law theorists (Fuller 1971; Ten 1993). They should be general and apply to everyone, including the legislators themselves; they should be promulgated and made known in advance to those to whom they apply; they should be intelligible, consistent, and not subject to constant change; and so on.

It should be clear why republicans will want laws to conform to constraints of these kinds. If the laws do not satisfy such constraints, then those who make, execute or apply the law may easily be given arbitrary power over others. The legislators who can make laws without being subject to them, for example—say, the British Parliament in relation to the American colonies—will have arbitrary power. Again the legislators who can make retrospective laws or laws that apply, like the bill of attainder, to particular individuals or families will be able to interfere more or less arbitrarily in people's lives. And similarly, the administrators or judges who can choose at will to apply unpromulgated laws, or who can exploit the obscurity or inconsistency of the law for their own purposes, will represent an arbitrary regime. If the rule-of-law constraints are breached, then the law becomes a playground for the arbitrary will of the authorities.

The second aspect of the empire-of-law condition presupposes that the first is satisfied, and that any laws which are introduced will have a satisfactory shape. It prescribes that where government has a choice between acting on a legal basis—that is, legislating about the case on hand—and acting in a more particularistic way it should always prefer the first, principled approach. There is no suggestion that government action, provided that it is legal, is bound to be for the good. The idea is that, assuming that government action is indeed needed, that action should always operate via law-like decisions, in particular via decisions that honour the rule-of-law constraints: via decisions, for example, that are not ad hoc or *ex post*.

The republican rationale for this idea is that where the particularistic decision can be governed on an arbitrary basis by the will of the decision-makers, the principled piece of legislation is not so readily manipulable. The legislation will be of concern to people generally, including potentially the decision-makers themselves, and it is not going to be easy for them—though, unfortunately, it may still be possible—to guide it on an arbitrary basis.

Think of the contrast that Joseph Priestley (1993: 140) saw between the significance of British tax-collecting in America and in Britain itself. The Americans complain, he said, that when the Members of Parliament tax them they 'are so far from taxing themselves, that they ease themselves at the same time'. The British have no such complaint, he suggests, for the Members of the British Parliament fall under the laws they pass for Britain, as is only proper according to the empire-of-law condition. And so the members of the British Parliament cannot impose a tax on the people of Britain without imposing it on themselves.

The idea of extending the rule of law as far as possible—the idea, specifically, of preferring principled to particularistic decision-making—has far-reaching ramifications for how government is conducted. It means that parliament must always seek to legislate, under the usual rule-of-law constraints, about any issue that comes before it. But the empire-of-law condition also means that other agencies of government should be forced to act always in a principled, law-like way. They should be permitted to act only under the authority of law, and only in a way that accords with the requirements of law. Those agencies will have to conform to established protocols and procedures, for example, in the arrest, accusation, and adjudication of those believed to have committed a crime; or in the identification of those in need of welfare and in the provision of welfare to them; or in the determination of where certain government agencies are to be based and of where associated benefits are to flow; and so on. An empire of law requires fidelity to due process on a wide range of political fronts.

We can give importance to due process, however, without having a dedicated, detailed rule for every situation. If the law were codified in such dedicated detail, then that might make it non-manipulable. But codifying the law in that detail would mean denying all discretion to government agents, and thereby denying all possibility of fitting government action to the needs of particular cases. And such a regimentation of official response would almost certainly undermine the capacity of government to do much good in the furthering of the republican aims that I discussed in the last chapter. This observation suggests that the best sort of law may have to leave some discretion in the hands of government agents, relying on further measures—say, the measures of contestability that we consider later in this chapter—for ensuring that those agents cannot act on a wholly arbitrary basis. The best sort of law will always require government agents to satisfy certain constraints—it will always impose some measure of due process—but it may also have to allow a substantial degree of discretion.

The republican case for having an empire of law, therefore, need not entail the rule of the book; it need not commit us to an extreme proceduralism (Schauer 1991; Campbell 1996). The empire of law involves a regime where government agents are always required to act according to law, even if the law allows them to exercise a degree of discretion within the procedural boundaries that it establishes. The best system of law may allow various forms of discretion—even discretion that reduces predictability (Waldron 1989)—provided that the discretion is exercised under constraints that help guard against arbitrariness.

The necessity of the empire-of-law condition, in both of its aspects, was much emphasized in the republican tradition. 'Nothing can be more absurd', wrote Algernon Sydney (1990: 440, cf. 465), for example, 'than to say, that one man has an absolute power above law to govern according to his will, for the people's good, and the preservation of their liberty: For no liberty can subsist where there is such a power.' The condition was recognized as essential to ensuring that government action was not just a front behind which an individual or a group could exercise arbitrary power. It meant that the law was 'a standing Rule to live by', in the phrase imputed by Mary Astell to 'our Masters', and it helped to ensure that government would not represent 'inconstant, uncertain, unknown, arbitrary Will' (Hill 1986: 76).

The republican belief in an empire of law is generally endorsed among liberal theorists but has attracted criticism among Marxists and among many in the critical legal studies movement (Kelman 1987; on Marxism and rule of law, see Krygier 1990). The criticism has usually been that rule-of-law constraints can never be effective, and that they may serve only to cover up the fact that the law is often class-based and biased. We can concede, of course, that the requirement on government to act according to law may not be sufficient to guard against arbitrary power; it is because of assuming this, after all, that we go on to consider the need for democratic contestability in the next section. The question is whether the requirement is useful in any measure, not whether it is completely effective, and the evidence on that issue is overwhelming.

The work of leftist historians like E. P. Thompson shows that while law has often been abused by the powerful, for example, it has also served as a buttress for the protection of the poor and defenceless.

He writes of the resort that the powerful made to the rule of law in eighteenth-century England:

it was inherent in the very nature of the medium which they had selected for their own self-defence that it could not be reserved for the exclusive use only of their own class. The law, in its forms and traditions, entailed principles of equity and universality which, perforce, had to be extended to all sorts and degrees of men. (Thompson 1975: 264)

This verdict on law is borne out by the experience in the twentieth century of just what governments are capable of doing, and in partic- ular of how far they can dominate their citizens when law ceases to sat- isfy the constraints in question. Philip Selznick (1992: 64) makes the point strongly.

High on the agenda in the struggle for freedom—in Eastern Europe, for example, or South Africa—is the building, or rebuilding, of legal institutions capable of resisting political manipulation. For those who suffer oppression, criticism of the rule of law as 'bourgeois justice' or 'liberal legalism' can only be perceived as naive or heartless, or both.

Blandine Kriegel (1995: 49) generalizes the lesson when she writes: 'The idea of individual liberty was the grand innovation of the state under the rule of law, the foundation of the first body of law and poli- tics that rejects slavery.'

The dispersion-of-power condition

The second condition associated with the desirability of having a non- manipulable, constitutionalist system of government requires that the powers which officials have under any regime of law should be dis- persed. Where the empire-of-law condition bears on the place and con- tent of law, this condition bears on the way in which the law operates.

Where there is law there are, of necessity, different roles to be fulfilled. In the taxonomy that finally got established only in the eight- eenth century—most famously in the work of Montesquieu (1989)— there is the function of making law, of executing or administering law, and of adjudicating those controversial cases where the law has to be applied. The dispersion of power requires that these functions be pretty well separate. And the reason, at least from a republican point of view, is more or less obvious. A consolidation of functions in the hands of one person or group would be likely to allow that party to wield more or less arbitrary power over others; it would mean that they could play around with the law in a relatively unfettered way. As Madison put it in Federalist 47: 'The accumulation of all powers, legislative, executive, and judiciary, in the same hands, whether of one, a few, or many, and whether hereditary, self-appointed, or elective, may justly be pronounced the very definition of tyranny' (Madison *et al.* 1987: 303).

If legislators are to be allowed to legislate only in a way that is consistent with certain existing laws or principles, therefore, it is important that those who judge on whether the legislation does conform to those constraints are not the legislators themselves. Again, if those who execute the law are to be required to conform to existing laws in their mode of execution, then it is important that they are not their own judges; it is important that the relevant judicial power lies in other hands (see Montesquieu 1989: 157). The powers of legislation, execution, and adjudication must be distributed among different parties and bodies.

Although the full taxonomy of powers was only set out in the eighteenth century, when the so-called separation of powers became perhaps the outstanding theme in the republican tradition, republicans had insisted on the dispersion of power from much earlier (Vile 1967). Marchamont Nedham did not strike a particularly novel note, for example, when in 1657 he described the confusion of legislative and executive powers—executive powers would have included judicial—as a great error of government:

in all Kingdoms and States whatsoever, where they have had any thing of Freedom among them, the Legislative and Executive Powers have been managed in distinct hands: That is to say, the law-makers have set down Laws, as Rules of Government; and then put Power into the hands of others (not their own) to govern by those Rules. (In Gwyn 1965: 131)

We have concentrated, so far, on the separation of law-related functions. But the dispersion-of-power condition has significance in other areas too. The republican rationale for dispersing power is, other things being equal, to increase the non-manipulability of the law and to guard against government exercising arbitrary sway over others. The assumption is that if power is localized, in the sense of accumulating in this or that person, then power is potentially dominating. Given this rationale, the dispersion of power for which we should look may well support other measures besides the separation of legislative, executive, and judicial power.

One measure it may well support is the bicameral arrangement under which there are two houses of parliament, each with a distinctive base; indeed such bicameralism, as we shall see, is likely to appeal to republicans on a number of counts. And another, equally familiar, measure is the decentralization of power that is achieved by having a federal system under which a number of constituent states share power with the central government; it is no accident that republicans have been traditionally partial to federations. Yet another measure, this time a novel one, is the dispersion of power that can be realized in the contemporary world so far as governments agree to be bound by certain international covenants or conventions; this has the effect of giving over power to the international bodies that interpret those covenants. Such a policy is likely to be welcomed by someone who wants official power to be so dispersed that people's freedom as non-domination is safe in its presence (Majone 1996).

When I say that the dispersion of power may require more than the separation of legislative, executive, and judicial functions, I remain faithful to the older republican tradition. Within that tradition, the functional division was part of a larger project of dispersing power. This project was encapsulated in the ancient ideal of a mixed government in which different sectors are represented and power is given in part to this representative body—perhaps this house of representatives—and in part to that (Gwyn 1965; Vile 1967). The project supported a hostility, not just to compromising the division of functions, but also to anyone's being judge in their own case, for example, and to anyone's being both judge and jury.

The republican rationale for dispersing power, in particular the rationale for dividing functions, should be contrasted with other possible grounds for supporting it. Suppose you are a populist, who believes that the people should be the only makers of law; suppose you are of a parliamentarian mentality, for example, and think that the people's representatives are the one and only legal sovereign (Dicey 1960). In that case you will want to insist that law-making power should never drift elsewhere, in particular never drift into the hands of an unelected judiciary. On the letter of what the separation of power requires, you will be very exacting, at least in regard to law-making power. But your commitment to those requirements will come of a very different spirit from that which animated and animates the republican attitude. Indeed, it will come of a spirit that is directly anathema to republicanism, being complacent about the possibility of a majority imposing its will on others.

The contrast between the republican and the populist rationales for separating legislative, executive, and judicial functions comes out in a difference of view about how exact that separation should be. Republicans are likely to think that no exact division is really feasible: it is surely inevitable, for example, that in interpreting law the courts will effectively wield a degree of law-making power. Republicans may even believe that no exact division is likely to be desirable; the required regimentation of functions would be liable to compromise the ability of government to advance its republican aims. But that need not concern them, provided that power still remains effectively dispersed. Thus it did not concern the authors of the *Federalist Papers* who defended the US Constitution against the anti-federalist objection that it allowed an unwonted degree of leakage across functional boundaries (Manin 1994).

Populists, however, are bound to take a different view. They must think that any leakage of law-making power, whether in the direction of the judiciary or the executive, has to represent an inherent evil; it means that the law is made by someone other than the people or their representatives. Thus they have to insist on a separation of powers—or at least on an isolation of law-making power—that is as exact as possible; they have to look for a watertight compartmentalization. It may have been this populist attitude that inspired the anti-federalist objections to the US Constitution. If it was, then we can see the anti-federalists as figures whose enthusiasm for democracy led them to betray the essential republican concern: the concern to ensure against arbitrariness in power, even against arbitrariness in the power of the people.

The counter-majoritarian condition

We have urged that, other things being equal, a republican system of government should be maximally non-manipulable by arbitrary will, and that this requires that the system should meet the empire-of-law and the dispersion-of-power conditions. All the things that are done by government should be done according to law, in particular a law that satisfies rule-of-law constraints. But all the things that are done by government should not be done by the same individual or group; the powers and the doings of government should be dispersed among different agents.

We come now to a third condition that appeals on the same, constitutionalist grounds. If we are to make a system of government non-manipulable, then not only should we require an empire of law under which power is effectively dispersed, we should also try to ensure that the laws which rule in that empire are not subject to excessively easy, majoritarian change. Every law must be capable of being amended, of course, since there is no guarantee, even with the most plausible of laws, that it will continue to make republican sense: that it will continue to promote non-domination. But the counter-majoritarian condition insists that at least where the more basic and important laws are concerned—more basic and important from the point of view of non-domination—it should not be easy to change these laws. In particular, it should require more than the mere fact of majority support in the parliament or even in the population.

The more that is required, of course, may vary from one jurisdiction to another and from one area of law to another. The counter-majoritarian protection may involve just a general presumption against putting a law up for statutory amendment, as when it enjoys an established common-law status, or a strict requirement that it be put up for amendment only in the event of a special condition being satisfied. Or it may require that if the law is put up for amendment, the amendment has to have more than regular majority support in order to succeed: it must be passed in two differently constituted houses of parliament, for example, or it must be passed by a majority of electors in a majority of states, or it must command a two-thirds majority. We may think of the laws as democratic creations, but we should require democracy to work on different tracks and insist, with Bruce Ackerman (1991), that amendments to the more basic and important laws should have to pass along a particularly difficult route.

The republican case for having counter-majoritarian protection of at least some laws is fairly straightforward. Majorities are easily formed—they easily become actual rather than virtual agents—and majoritarian agents will exercise more or less arbitrary power if their will is unconstrained. Let the laws be subject to ready majoritarian amendment, then, and the laws will lend themselves to more or less arbitrary control; they will cease to represent a secure guarantee against domination by government. Most of us belong to a salient minority in some respect and most of us, therefore, have an interest in seeing that we do not live at the electoral mercy of the corresponding majority.

Modern republicans are bound to support some institutions, then, that serve to guard against majoritarian threats. They are bound to look favourably on those counter-majoritarian measures with which premodern republicanism has been associated, for example, such as the bicameral division of parliament, the recognition of constitutional constraints on law, and the introduction of a bill of rights. Which counter-majoritarian measures should be adopted will depend on local circumstances, of course, and is a matter for empirically informed debate. But it is scarcely conceivable that republicans would not endorse any.

The belief in counter-majoritarian protections requires a jurisprudence under which good law—good law, not necessarily law as such—is identified by some criterion other than the benchmark of having majority support. Republicanism, of course, finds such a criterion in the ideal of freedom as non-domination. Good law is law that promotes overall non-domination: law that reduces the domination to which *dominium* may lead without introducing the domination that can go with *imperium*. Perhaps good law in this sense is bound to have democratic support of some kind; we touch on that issue in the next section. But the fact of having majority support is certainly not a criterion of good law. Thus we must reject those nineteenth century, populist initiatives that, in Harold Berman's (1994: 1735) words, 'located the ultimate source of law in public opinion and the will of the legislature'. What legitimates law has got to be something other than the fact of enjoying popular majority support.

What view did historical republicans take on the legitimation of law and on its counter-majoritarian protection? Some were less worried than others about making the laws responsive to democratic decision-making bodies: this, perhaps, because of the view that democratic decision-making would be likely to embody considerations of the common good and not to impose arbitrarily on any minority. Machiavelli (1965: 315) holds out in this vein against 'the common opinion, which says that the people, when they are rulers, are variable, changeable, and ungrateful'. But even those who were happy to make the laws democratically responsive, such as Machiavelli, still thought it important that besides the laws or *leggi* that the people were likely to change there were the institutional or constitutional arrangements—the *ordini*—that offered a relatively fixed and constraining framework for legislation (Machiavelli 1965: 241; Rubenstein 1991: 49).

As the republican tradition evolved from the sixteenth century, it became more and more associated with a viewpoint that suggested reasons why good laws were not identified by majority support and should not be overly responsive to majoritarian opinion. A major influence here was the integrative jurisprudence, as it has been called, that was developing in England in the work of lawyers like Sir Edward Coke and Sir Matthew Hale (Berman 1994; see too Kelly 1991: 72–3). This style of jurisprudence ascribed to law the authority of a tradition that had been historically tested for its answerability to the expectations of the community and for its capacity, as we would say, to sustain freedom as non-domination. The tradition was embodied in the ancient, unwritten constitution which most English commonwealthmen praised in Britain, and it was the inspiring source—if not the unique source (Haakonssen 1991)—of the constitution that American republicans forged for the arrangement of their own affairs.

II. Democracy and contestability

So much by way of arguing that a system of government that meets the constitutionalist conditions discussed is going to be necessary for the promotion of freedom as non-domination. If government is not mediated by law, on the pattern of those conditions, then it will be readily manipulable by arbitrary and perhaps sectional will. Government must be carried out by means of an empire of law; the powers recognized under that law must be dispersed across different individuals and bodies; and the more basic and important laws must not be subject to straightforward majoritarian amendment.

But if a constitutionalist system of law is necessary for the promotion of freedom, then it should be clear that something else is needed too. However well designed, any system of law will leave certain decisions in the hands of different individuals and groups. Legislators will have discretion over the content of the laws, of course, and the problematic nature of legal interpretation means that administrators and judges are bound to have a lot of discretion when they come to execute and apply those laws: 'no law can be so perfect as to provide exactly for every case that may fall out' (Sydney 1990: 465). Besides, as already mentioned, the promotion of republican aims may often argue for leaving discretion over certain issues in the hands of executive and judicial authorities; even if it is possible, it may not be profitable to legislate in detail for how such officials should behave.

But if any system of law leaves decision-making power in the hands of various public authorities, then the advancement of non-domination requires that the decisions in question should be made on a basis that rules out arbitrary power. Otherwise freedom as non-domination will not be available to those whom those officials can affect: they will be subject to domination at the hands of the authorities. How then to rule out decision-making on an arbitrary basis among legislators, administrators, and judges? How to stop the *imperium* of government representing a form of domination?

Contestability

The authorities will exercise arbitrary power if the decisions they make can be based on their private, perhaps sectional, interests or on their private, perhaps sectional, ideas as to what their brief—their brief qua legislator, administrator, or judge—requires. If private inclination or private opinion can rule, then people will live at the mercy of the officials. The authorities will have the power, not just to interfere—that is inherent in a system of law—but to interfere on a relatively arbitrary basis. They will be in a position where they dominate ordinary people and, this being a matter of common knowledge, they will be in a position where ordinary people may be expected to have to bow and scrape to them.

The promotion of freedom as non-domination requires, therefore, that something be done to ensure that public decision-making tracks the interests and the ideas of those citizens whom it affects; after all, non-arbitrariness is guaranteed by nothing more or less than the existence of such a tracking relationship. The decision-making must not represent an imposition of their will on us, as the citizens are likely to think about the matter. It must be a form of decision-making which we can own and identify with: a form of decision-making in which we can see our interests furthered and our ideas respected. Whether the decisions are taken in the legislature, in the administration, or in the courts, they must bear the marks of our ways of caring and our ways of thinking.

What is required for one of us to be able to own a public decision in this way? A traditional line would say that we can own a decision in that manner only if we have consented to it, or to the policy it incorporates, in an explicit or at least an implicit fashion. But this comment is not much help. If explicit individual consent is required for non-arbitrariness, especially if the consent has to be unforced, then non-arbitrariness in public decisions becomes an inaccessible ideal. If implicit individual consent is thought to be enough, however, and an absence of protest is taken as evidence of implicit consent, then non-arbitrariness in public decisions becomes an ideal that is so accessible as to be empty: any decision that fails to drive me to the barricades will count as non-arbitrary from my point of view. Will it help if we move from individual to collective consent and stipulate that any public decision that attracts majority support, or that is in accord with a policy that attracts such support, is non-arbitrary? Surely not. Certain decisions and policies may attract majority support while representing the most arbitrary interference in the lives of various minorities.

We have already seen in Chapter 2 that there is very little connection between non-arbitrariness of interference and consent to that interference, so that these observations should not come as a surprise. What I suggested in that earlier discussion is that non-arbitrariness requires not so much consent as contestability. Imagine that another agent can and does interfere with me but that I am able effectively to contest any interference that does not answer to my relevant interests and ideas. It is only if I can effectively contest any such interference— it is only if I can force it to account to my relevant interests and ideas— that the interference is not arbitrary and the interferer not dominating.

The idea of contestability gives us a cue for the right response to our question. What might enable one of us to own a public decision? What might make it possible for such a decision not to have the aspect of an arbitrary act of interference? The answer which suggests itself is: the fact that we can more or less effectively contest the decision, if we find that it does not answer to our relevant interests or relevant ideas. The decision may materialize, like most public decisions, on a basis that is consensual only in a vanishingly weak sense. That does not matter, provided that it materializes under a dispensation of effective con- testability. The non-arbitrariness of public decisions comes of their meeting, not the condition of having originated or emerged according to some consensual process, but the condition of being such that if they conflict with the perceived interests and ideas of the citizens, then the citizens can effectively contest them. What matters is not the his- torical origin of the decisions in some form of consent but their modal or counterfactual responsiveness to the possibility of contestation.

Democracy

To require public decision-making to be contestable, in particular to be contestable from within every quarter in the society, is to insist that the decision-making satisfy a certain democratic profile. Democracy, as ordinarily understood, is connected with consent; it is almost exclu- sively associated with the popular election of the personnel in govern- ment, or at least with the popular election of the members of the legislature. But democracy may be understood, without unduly for- cing intuitions, on a model that is primarily contestatory rather than consensual. On this model, a government will be democratic, a gov- ernment will represent a form of rule that is controlled by the people, to the extent that the people individually and collectively enjoy a per- manent possibility of contesting what government decides (Shapiro 1990: 266).

Consider an analogy. Whatever existentialists may have thought, individual autonomy or self-rule cannot conceivably require that peo- ple should have considered and endorsed each of their particular beliefs and desires in a historical process of self-construction; if it did, then no one would be autonomous. What it requires, more plausibly, is that people are capable of exposing each of their beliefs and desires to appropriate tests, especially in the event of problems arising, and that whether or not they maintain such a commitment depends on how it fares in the tests (Pettit and Smith 1990; 1996). The index of individual autonomy is modal or counterfactual, not historical. People are autonomous in virtue of what can be—in virtue of what they can do in checking their beliefs and desires—not in virtue of what has been: not in virtue of a record of self-checking and self-construction.

Democracy refers us, at least etymologically, to the self-rule of a people. And as individual self-rule or autonomy can be modelled in a modal rather than a historical way, so plausibly can the self-rule of a people be modelled in that way. The self-ruling individual may run on automatic pilot much of the time, acting on beliefs and desires that originate in forgotten times and pressures. What makes them self-ruling is the fact that they are never just the victim of those beliefs and desires: they are able to examine them at will and, depending on how the examination goes, able to maintain or amend them. By analogy, the self-ruling demos or people may also often run on automatic pilot, allowing public decision-making to materialize under more or less unexamined routines. What makes them self-ruling or democratic is the fact that they are not exposed willy-nilly to that pattern of decision-making: they are able to contest decisions at will and, if the contestation establishes a mismatch with their relevant interests or opinions, able to force an amendment.

Preconditions of democratic contestability

I have argued that, while government should be conducted according to a form of law that makes it as non-manipulable as possible, this still leaves room for a great deal of discretionary decision-making and that such decision-making has to satisfy a condition of contestability if it is not to represent a form of domination. We have seen, furthermore, that imposing this condition is tantamount to insisting that the decision-making be democratic, in a certain sense of that term; it means that the decision-makers are accountable to the ordinary people whom they affect. But I have remained studiously vague on what exactly democratic contestability requires, and we need to turn now to that matter.

In order for public decision-making to be contestable, there are at least three general preconditions that have to be satisfied. The first is that decision-making is conducted in such a way that there is a potential basis for contestation. The second is that not only is there a potential basis for contestation, there is also a channel or voice available by which decisions may be contested. And the third is that not only is there a basis and a channel for contestation, there is a suitable forum in existence for hearing contestations: a forum where the validity of the claim is assessed and a suitable response determined.

A basis for contestation: the deliberative republic

What form does public decision-making have to take if it is to allow people a basis for contestation? There are two possible forms, in the rough, that it might assume (Pettit 1993*a*: 288–302). It might be a bargain-based form of decision-making, in which different interest groups try to secure a mutually beneficial agreement, with each looking for the agreement that will demand the smallest possible concession from them (see Gauthier 1986). Or it might be a debate-based form of decision-making, in which different parties try to agree on what arrangement answers best to considerations that they can all recognize as relevant, where one of the relevant considerations is that they should indeed reach an agreement (see Scanlon 1982; Barry 1995). In bargain-based decision-making, people come to the table with predefined interests and ideas—their hearts and minds are closed—and they hammer out an agreed arrangement by trading concessions with one another. In debate-based decision-making, people recognize certain relevant considerations in common, and they move towards an agreed outcome by interrogating one another about the nature and import of those considerations and by converging on an answer to the question of which decision the considerations support. In bargain-based decision-making, preferences are given, in debate-based decision-making preferences are formed (Sunstein 1993*a*).

Bargain-based decision-making offers one type of basis for contestation, debate-based decision-making offers another. The bargaining basis for contestation is that the public decision does not correspond to the bargain struck among relevant interest groups, or that it requires a concession which some interest group, perhaps one not represented properly in the decision-making, is unwilling to make. The debating basis for contestation is that the public decision is based on unsuitable considerations, or that it does not answer well to all the considerations relevant: it neglects the reality or the force of one or another of them.

If we want public decision-making to be contestable in a republican manner, if we want it to be contestable in such a way that people can be assured that it tracks relevant interests and ideas, then what form should we want that decision-making to take? Clearly, we should want it to be of the debate-based kind. The trouble with bargaining contestations is that they are only available to those who have sufficient negotiating power to be able to threaten other parties effectively; if you want to force a change of bargain, then you had better represent an interest group which pulls some weight. The attraction of debating contestations is that they are open to anyone who can make a plausible case against the line of public decision-making; you do not have to have any particular weight or power, at least not in principle, in order to be able to mount a reasonable challenge to a reasoned decision.

What might it mean for public decision-making, in particular for republican decision-making, to be debate-based and to allow of debating contestations? It would mean that at every site of decision-making, legislative, administrative, and judicial, there are procedures in place which identify the considerations relevant to the decision, thereby enabling citizens to raise the question as to whether they are the appropriate considerations to play that role. And it would mean that there are procedures in place which enable citizens to make a judgement on whether the relevant considerations actually determined the outcome: the decisions must be made under transparency, under threat of scrutiny, under freedom of information, and so on.

In a republic in which no one is to be dominated, and in which public decision-making is to track everyone's relevant interests and ideas, the considerations relevant will be required to have a characteristically neutral cast: they will be constrained not to favour any one sector of opinion or interest over another. In legislative decisions, the considerations relevant are likely to be whatever considerations can be brought forward as reasons that all have to countenance as pertinent, under accepted canons of reasoning. In administrative and judicial decisions, they will be the more specific considerations that are established as relevant under the laws that govern the operation of those arms of government, though in hard cases—in cases where the laws are relatively silent—they may extend to include the more general considerations that would be relevant to legislators. In every case there will be a requirement on the authorities to decide on the basis of suitable considerations and to make clear which considerations are moving them.

In arguing for an arrangement in which public decisions are taken in a deliberative way, I make contact with the ideal of a 'republic of reasons' that Cass Sunstein (1993*a*; 1993*b*; 1993*c*) finds in the American founders and defends in his own right. According to Sunstein, the traditional republican vision, in particular the vision which inspired Americans in the eighteenth century, is that of a polity within which citizens have equal claims and powers, public matters are decided by deliberation on the basis of considerations that have common appeal—they are not biased in favour of any group, or even in favour of the status quo—and agreement serves as a regulative ideal as to how things should be decided; the vision, in a word, is that of a deliberative democracy (see too Cohen 1989; Habermas 1994; 1995).

Quentin Skinner (1996: 15–16) supports Sunstein's reading of traditional republicanism. He has argued that one of the central themes of the classical and Renaissance humanism in which republican ideas were nurtured was a belief in dialogical reason: 'our watchword ought to be *audi alteram partem*, always listen to the other side.' 'The appropriate model', he says, 'will always be that of a dialogue, the appropriate stance a willingness to negotiate over rival intuitions concerning the applicability of evaluative terms. We strive to reach understanding and resolve disputes in a conversational way.'

This dialogical model was warmly embraced by those legislators who saw themselves as exemplifying the republican ideal in the late eighteenth century. In particular, it was used to defend an image of the legislative representative, not as a deputy under instructions from their constituents, but as someone charged to deliberate with the interests of the citizenry at heart. Consider the words of Roger Sherman in the first US Congress: 'when the people have chosen a representative, it is his duty to meet others from the different parts of the Union, and consult, and agree with them to such acts as are for the general benefit of the whole community. If they were to be guided by instructions, there would be no use in deliberation' (in Sunstein 1993*a*: 22). Or consider what the Abbé Sieyes told the French National Assembly in September 1789:

the deputies are present in the National Assembly, not to announce the already established wish of their constituents, but to deliberate and to vote freely according to their actual opinion, when that has been illuminated by the lights that the assembly provides for each. (Rials 1983: 13)

As there is little doubt of the republican pedigree of Sunstein's notion of deliberative democracy, there is no doubt of the republican case that can be made for it. The ideal of freedom as non-domination, and more specifically the ideal of making government power contestable by the citizenry, ensures that republicans are going to have to embrace such a vision of how democracy should work. Unless the public decision-making is designed to answer to suitable considerations, in a debate-based manner, there is not going to be an assured basis on which different people within the population can contest it. There will be no way of distinguishing arbitrary from non-arbitrary government.

Before leaving the theme of deliberative democracy, it is worth emphasizing one feature of the case made here in its support. This is that the value of such democracy is not contingent on the possibility that people will generally achieve a high degree of consensus about the matters that have to be decided in parliament, in the executive, or in the judiciary. Even if there is no imminent consensus on offer in such areas, it remains the case that effective contestability requires that the decisions should be made on the basis of reasoned deliberation.

The situation is parallel to that which we find in ordinary conversation. Short of being at a point where we agree about everything, I can be in a position to mount a conversational challenge—and indeed a potentially effective challenge—to the things that you say and do; what is required is simply that there should be enough common ground between us for conversation not to have reached utter stalemate. Similarly, short of the people in a society being at a point where they do or might agree about what should be done in some area by government, they can be in a position where there is still room for arguments that are recognized as relevant on all sides. So long as people are in that position—so long as they have not completely lost touch with one another's minds—contestation can represent an effective intervention and an effective discipline.

A voice for contestation: the inclusive republic

So much—and so much, admittedly, at a very abstract level of consideration—for what is required in order that people enjoy a basis for contesting public decisions. But having a basis for contesting such decisions will not be of much use if there is not also a means available for voicing contestations. What does the contestatory image of democracy require under this aspect?

What it requires is that for any way in which public decision-making may offend against someone's interests or ideas, there are means whereby those interests or ideas can be asserted in response. The democracy must be, not just deliberative, but inclusive. Suppose that a legislature is inclined to take a line that is inimical to a particular group within the society. The group will have a voice for contestation only insofar as they are enabled to speak out against that line, and speak out in a way that is liable to affect the proposed legislation. Or suppose that the administration or judiciary manifests an inimical pattern of decision-making. Again, the group offended will have a voice for contestation only insofar as they are capable of protesting against the pattern in question in a potentially effective manner: they can make themselves heard in decision-making quarters.

What is needed to give potential contestators voice? What is needed to enfranchise them in more than a purely formal or ceremonial sense? At the level of legislative decision, it is clearly going to be necessary that there are voices that can speak with credibility to the concerns and opinions of every significant group, and that can force those concerns and opinions on the deliberative attention of law-makers. In order to speak with credibility, such voices will have to come from the sector represented, not just resonate in sympathy with that sector (Pettit 1994*a*); and so ideally the group will achieve representation, not by grace of senatorial spokespersons, but via the presence of some of its own members (Phillips 1995). The reliably inclusive legislature will have to incorporate, in their own right, all the voices of difference that are found within the community (Young 1990). It will have to ensure that as the assembly of law-makers debates its way towards decision, it takes account of the considerations that are salient, not just from a restricted set of privileged viewpoints, but from the full range of social perspectives.

The inclusiveness requirement on the legislature will radiate, depending on circumstances, into a number of recommendations on the selection and structuring of the legislative arm of government. The obvious way for members of the legislature to be selected is by means of direct election, since that increases the chances that they will have the credence of the groups they represent. But a mode of election that reflects just regional constituencies may not ensure that significantly different groups are given a distinctive voice. And so it may be necessary to look to other measures too. If there is a bicameral system, as other considerations suggest there should be, then it may be useful to use a different method of election for each of the two houses. If there is a problem with the representation of women, it may be a good idea to require each of the major parties to field at least 40 per cent women. If there is an indigenous population which is more or less evenly spread, then it may be essential to have some seats allocated specifically to their representatives. If there is a minority of electors who find it difficult or unattractive to register and vote, let alone to stand for office, then it may be desirable to introduce a system of compulsory registration and voting. And so on.[1]

---

[1] Notice that this conception of contestatory democracy does not presuppose that when people go to the polls, they assume a deliberative profile and express their considered,

So much for making the legislature inclusive. But what about ensuring inclusiveness in the administrative and judicial arms of government? This is not the place to discuss how far officials in these areas should be popularly elected and how far appointed: that is, appointed by parliament or by bodies appointed by parliament. But it is clear that popular election can only play a small part, and it is equally clear that could it play a larger part, that would not be desirable. Administration and adjudication are primarily governed by legislation, and require qualities of competence and professionalization that are not going to be reliably identified under the pressure of popular election. So how can the administration and the judiciary be inclusive if they are not elected?

Corresponding to elective representation, one factor that should make for inclusiveness in these areas—it is not the most important requirement, as we shall see in a moment—is a certain minimum of statistical representation for the major stakeholder groupings. Consistently with requiring a body like a jury to be deliberative, making its decision on the basis of considerations as to whether the defendant is guilty beyond reasonable doubt, we naturally want it to represent a variety of different community backgrounds, including backgrounds that are shared, and backgrounds that are unshared, by the defendant. The reason is manifest. We recognize that even if a socially unrepresentative jury does its deliberative job as conscientiously as possible, it may not fully understand all the relevant factors, not being capable of reaching across certain divides; and we recognize that even if it does achieve such understanding, it may not have the same credibility in the community at large as a more representative body. If the people in a community are to believe that their interests and ideas will be fully understood and respected, in the event of their coming before a criminal court, or in the event of someone who offends against them coming before the court, they need to know that the jury that looks at the case will not be stacked against them: it will not be controlled by those who in one way or another are not of their kind.

detached judgement on what is for the best overall (See Coleman and Ferejohn 1986; Cohen 1986; Brennan and Pettit 1990). It might be good for republican purposes if people did vote in such a judgement-based way—it would provide an extra guard against the domination of minorities—and indeed there is some evidence that that is what they do in considerable measure (Kinder and Kiewiet 1979; 1981). But even if people vote for their representatives on the most self-regarding of grounds, the model that we have described can still work reasonably well. Nowhere in the description of the model do we presuppose that ordinary electors have to be public-spirited assessors of different policies and parties.

What holds of a body like the jury holds equally of every institution associated with the administrative and judicial arms of government. Even if the people who exercise administrative and judicial functions are not elected to the offices they discharge, it is important for republican purposes that they are not statistically unrepresentative in regard to major social groupings. It is important that they are not statistically dominated, for example, by the members of one religion, one gender, one class, or one ethnicity. Let the administration or the judiciary become statistically unrepresentative of major stakeholders and there is no longer a guarantee that members of unrepresented groups can make their voices heard in appropriate circles.

I have been discussing the requirements of inclusion that are necessary if people are to have a voice with which to contest public decisions. I have mentioned that inclusion will require elective representation in the legislature and statistical representation of major groupings in the administration and judiciary. But being included, having an audible voice, does not just reduce to being satisfactorily represented. What is even more important, especially with the administration and judiciary, is that there is room for you and those of the relevant kind to protest to the representative bodies in question, in the event of your believing that things have not been properly done. You must be able to complain and appeal; you must be able to state a grievance and demand satisfaction.

There are many channels whereby this aspect of inclusion can be realized. They include the opportunity of writing to your Member of Parliament, the capacity to require an ombudsman to make an inquiry, the right to appeal against a judicial decision to a higher court, and less formal entitlements such as those involved in rights of association, protest, and demonstration. As with most of the measures canvassed in the discussion, it is difficult to say anything in assessment of these measures independently of empirical realities. But we can make one observation with some degree of confidence. This is that the channels of contestation will be more effective to the extent that there are social movements, such as the green movement, or the women's movement, or the consumer movement, to which you can take your complaint in the first instance. Such movements should help to keep the channels of complaint free of noise, since they can serve as an initial clearing-house where complaints are sifted and consolidated. And such movements can be very effective in pressing those complaints that they do take up, since they command an audibility which individual citizens cannot hope to match. We return to the importance of such social movements in the final chapter.

Before leaving this discussion of what inclusive democracy requires, there is one last and very important point to make. Perhaps the greatest problem with making any democratic system of government truly inclusive comes of the fact that politicians need funds in order to win election, and that they and the parties they form have to depend on certain individuals and companies to finance their activities. Such dependency is bound to leave the politicians particularly alert to the interests of their financial supporters, and it means that, however formally satisfactory, the parliament and the government are going to cease to be substantively inclusive. Those who fund politicians and political parties can expect to have a greater voice in government than those who do not; those who do not contribute, or who have nothing to contribute, do not have the same chance of having their interests and ideas properly represented in the corridors of power.

What to do in order to guard against this problem? There is no easy solution, but it is clear where policy researchers should be looking. The questions that have to be investigated are issues like the following. Is there a way of limiting private campaign contributions and of making allowable contributions effectively public? Is there a way of publicly funding political candidates, say on the basis of their past performance, the performance of their party, or the degree of community support that they can demonstrate? Is there a way of enabling citizens to direct a limited portion of the tax they pay, or of a state allowance due them, to the party of their choice? And finally, is there a means of banning or limiting political advertising, given that such advertising is particularly costly and not particularly desirable: as we well know, it easily reduces political debate to a Punch and Judy farce (Sunstein 1993*b*)?

The problem of controlling the influence of the economically powerful on politicians, and more generally on government, is at once an age-old issue—it led some traditional republicans to propose severe limits on individual wealth—and a pressing contemporary problem. It comes up most strikingly in relation to campaign funds, but of course it also has a presence elsewhere. Economically powerful individuals and corporations can gain a special voice in the halls of government, for example, not just as a result of providing party funds, but also by virtue of the fact that their initiatives—say, initiatives in the location of industry—can have a dramatic effect on the fortunes of government. One of the greatest challenges for republican research must be to identify measures for effectively separating the worlds of government and business.

A forum for contestation: the responsive republic

I come finally to the third precondition that must be fulfilled if a polity is to realize the condition of contestability and to be democratic in the contestatory sense. If the polity is deliberative, then there will be a basis for citizens to contest any public decision, be it legislative, administrative, or judicial. And if the polity is inclusive, then there will be a voice available to people in every part of the community for expressing their contestations. The third precondition of contestability is that people must not only be assured of a basis and a voice for contestation, they must also be guaranteed a forum where the contestations they make can receive a proper hearing. The polity must be deliberative and inclusive, for sure, but equally clearly it must also be responsive.

This third precondition raises two broad questions. First, what procedures are sufficient to guarantee that people get a proper hearing for the contestations they raise? And second, what outcomes are likely to satisfy those who make such contestations? I shall consider these in turn.

When we think of a group of people getting a hearing for some challenge to public decision-making, then the image that suggests itself is that of popular movement, widespread controversy and debate, and progressive, legislative adjustment. We think of the hearing given in recent years to the women's movement, the green movement, the gay rights movement, and the movements in assertion of the claims of ethnic minorities and indigenous peoples. This image is not inappropriate. It is absolutely necessary in a contestatory democracy that people should be able to coalesce around group identities that were previously suppressed, for example, or espouse various causes that were not previously salient, and that they should have the opportunity to bring public opinion and political life around to their point of view. Any democracy that is going to serve republican purposes has to be able to give a hearing to evolving allegiances and commitments; it has to be open to deep and wide-ranging transformations.

But while this image has a central place in the picture of a responsive republic, it is important to recognize that there should also be other, less heroic procedures available for giving a hearing to contestation. Thus there should be such procedures available in order to ensure a hearing for more or less routine contestations of administrative and judicial decisions. There should be procedures that ensure, for example, that the bureaucracy or the police or the courts cannot ignore certain challenges that are raised against them. Such bodies should be required to answer for how they behave, at least in response to complaints that have passed an initial clearing and at least up to a certain level of appeal. There is no possibility of systematically ensuring such a hearing if the only procedures available involve the tumult of informal, popular protest.

But the need to have more formal and more routinized procedures is not just based on the infeasibility of frequent recourse to heroic debates. There are a variety of contestations where popular debate would give the worst possible sort of hearing to the complaints involved. In these cases, the requirement of contestatory democracy is that the complaints should be depoliticized and should be heard away from the tumult of popular discussion and away, even, from the theatre of parliamentary debate. In such instances, democracy requires recourse to the relative quiet of the parliamentary, cross-party committee, or the formal bureaucratic inquiry, or the standing appeals board, or the quasi-judicial tribunal, or the autonomous, professionalized body. It is only in that sort of quiet—it is only when political voices have been gagged (Holmes 1988)—that the contestations in question can receive a decent hearing.

This lesson has been learned in relation to at least some issues: witness the independence usually enjoyed, for example, by central banks. But it has not been learned on nearly enough fronts, and a republican philosophy would call for a radical examination of current practice. Consider what often happens, for example, in the area of crime. It is common wisdom among criminologists that heavy and strict sentencing options do not serve the community well in reducing crime levels; on the contrary, they may ensure that offenders constitute themselves as a class apart and establish effective networks and groupings (Braithwaite 1989). But, despite a rash of contestation to criminal-justice practice, there has been little or no movement away from such sentencing patterns in recent years; on the contrary, politicians in many countries have been pushing for ever more severe policies.

One plausible reason for this is that challenges to criminal-justice practice are generally heard in a public, politicized forum, with a variety of bad effects. When those convicted in the courts are harshly dealt with, and locked away for a lengthy period, then there is little or no possibility of a scandal in that forum. But when those convicted are treated leniently, or when those in prison are given remission for good behaviour, or are allowed out on parole, then there is always a possibility of scandal and always a possibility of public opinion being activated. Let one such person commit another crime, in particular a crime that has lurid aspects, and there is every chance that the press will seize on the fact, that there will be public outrage, and that the government will be called upon to put an end to the leniency in question.

Under the pattern described, failures on the side of harshness are unsanctioned by public opinion, while failures on the side of leniency—even a few failures among thousands of cases—are liable to attract an enormous public response. The false positives of excessive punishment are neither detected nor deplored; the false negatives of lenient punishment are blazoned abroad and are denounced in every corner (see Macdonagh 1958 and Pettit 1992). And this unbalanced pattern of triggering controls is exacerbated by the fact that the politicians who are called upon to respond to any outrage are expected to manifest concern in a manner that can communicate itself in the newspaper headline or in the television sound-bite. They will give little satisfaction, then, if they talk of long-term policies and the good effects of leniency on recidivism rates. They will be tempted to speak the more vivid body language of concern by sounding tough on crime and by calling for the ever harsher treatment of criminals.

If there is a solution to this sort of problem, if a republican democracy can hope to provide a better hearing for the persuasive challenges that have been brought against criminal-justice practice, that requires resort to a very different sort of hearing from that which those challenges currently receive. It would be silly of me to try to draft an alternative institution for hearing the challenges, but this much at least is clear: if criminal-justice practice is not to continue on its present, dominating pattern, then the responses that shape the practice must be decided by autonomous, professionally informed bodies that are not exposed to the glare and the pressure of public debate; the responses must be determined in a depoliticized way. In a case like this, contestatory democracy requires that the demos, and the legislative representatives of the demos, generally tie their hands and gag their mouths.

I have been discussing the question of what procedures should be in place for hearing the contestations that will be brought under a deliberative, inclusive democracy. A second question bears on the sorts of outcome that such hearings must deliver if the responses are to be satisfactory: that is, if they are to establish that government does not dominate the contesting parties.

A response will always be satisfactory, of course, if it supports the contestation and requires the public body to alter its decision and perhaps provide some compensation. It is in the nature of things, however, that not every contestation can be satisfied. And so the question is how the contesting party can still be assured that they, or those for whom they speak, are not subject to an arbitrary authority and are not dominated by government.

There are two reasons why a contestation may not be satisfied. The first is that it represents—understandably represents—the self-interest of the contesting individual or group, and that the judgement made is that the common interest requires the frustration of that particular party. Consider the appeal by someone convicted of an offence against the conviction or against the sentence; or consider the appeal by a group of local residents against having a road or an airport located in their area. In such a case, it is clearly possible for a contesting party to be confident of enjoying freedom as non-domination even when the judgement goes against them. All that is necessary is that they be assured that the judgement is made according to their ideas about proper procedures and that it is dictated, ultimately, by an interest that they share with others: an interest in the order secured by the criminal-justice system or an interest in the possibilities of travel realized by roads and airports. They may bitterly regret the fact that the judgement disadvantages them, but under the assurance described they can look on that disadvantage as a misfortune on a par with a natural accident; they do not have to see it as a token of domination by the state or by other groups within the state.

The second reason why a contestation may not be satisfied is that it represents, not the self-interest of the party in question, but a minority judgement as to what is in the common interest. This is a tricky case in which to try and ensure that the judgement does not present itself to the disappointed individual or group as a token of domination. It comes in two variants, one easier to resolve, the other harder.

In the easier variant, the issue is not of the greatest personal or cultural import to the party in question. The contestation may be about whether to subsidize private schooling, whether to build a transport system around road or rail, or whether to allow the continued growth of existing cities. The disappointed party in a contestation like this should be able to recognize that reasonable people differ on the matter in question. And so, under an appropriate institutional setting, such a party may be capable of assurance that the judgement against them materializes via procedures of which they approve—in awareness, for example, of the considerations that they themselves regard as persuasive—and that it represents a genuine attempt to determine the common interest. If they are assured of this—if the way things are done allows them to be assured of it—then they can accept the judgement without any sense of suffering domination.

This observation is borne out by empirical research. Tyler and Mitchell (1994: 746) summarize a review of relevant studies as follows:

research indicates that the key factor affecting the perceived legitimacy of authorities is procedural fairness. Procedural judgments have been found to be more important than either outcome favorability—whether the person won or lost—or judgments about outcome fairness

(see too Lind and Tyler 1988). One of the most difficult issues in contemporary democracy concerns the legalization of abortion on demand. And here these researchers found, in support of the studies summarized, that US citizens regard the Supreme Court as legitimate in its handling of abortion decisions, and defer to those decisions, in a measure that is mainly determined by whether they think that the decision-making procedures followed by the Court were fair. 'Institutional legitimacy is more important than is agreement with either past Court decisions in general or past Court decisions about the specific issue of abortion' (Tyler and Mitchell 1994: 789).

But suppose, to move to the difficult variant of our second case, that the contestation in question is of really pressing import, personal or cultural. The issue may have to do with whether a person will or will not be forced to do something that is offensive on religious grounds, or something that goes against a deep conviction of conscience. Or it may have to do with whether to recognize the traditional law of an indigenous population or whether to introduce an institutional arrangement that is passionately desired, say, among homosexual men or women. How can the disappointed party feel that they are not dominated in such a situation?

Let us assume, as a worst-case scenario, that the disappointed individual and group really cannot view the judgement against them as anything other than an exercise of arbitrary power. From their point of view, the judgement given on their contestation supports a form of interference that is not dictated, at any level, by an interest that they share in common with others; or if the interference is dictated by such a common interest, it is not directed by procedures which they can accept. What can be done to make government non-dominating in relation to such individuals and groups?

At the limit, the ideal of non-domination may require in relevant cases that the group are allowed to secede from the state, establishing a separate territory or at least a separate jurisdiction; that possibility has to be kept firmly on the horizon. But secession is not always possible and not always desirable overall, even from the point of view of the seceding parties. Thus it is important to register that, short of the secessionary limit, it may still be possible to boost the freedom as non-domination of radical dissenters. The measures that can help to achieve this result may be described, in an umbrella term, as measures of conscientious, procedural objection.

There should be room in any republican society for dissenting individuals and groups to claim a special treatment under the law. The special treatment allowed should not create the possibility of some individuals exploiting others—and thereby interfering on an arbitrary basis with them—through being able to escape the burdens of a system of coercion from which they continue to benefit. But there are a variety of ways in which individuals or groups might receive special treatment, on the basis of conscientious procedural objection, without looking for such an exploitative benefit. Think of the arrangements that are often canvassed by indigenous peoples in postcolonial societies. Think of the accommodations made to cater in the United States for religious groups like the Amish. Or think about the rules under which those who object to military service have been allowed to serve in other capacities instead. As so often before, I can only gesture here at possibilities that need careful empirical investigation. But it is clear that there are possibilities out there to be investigated, and that republican policy-making should make their investigation a matter of the greatest importance.

The emerging conception of democracy

We saw in the first part of this chapter that a non-dominating, republican government is bound to operate in accordance with constitutionalist constraints that help insure against the manipulation of political instrumentalities by sectional interests. But we have seen in the second part of the chapter that under any system of government, no matter how constitutionalist and non-manipulable, there are going to be sites at which public authorities make decisions and exercise power. And we have argued that if such decision-making is not to jeopardize people's freedom as non-domination, then it must be effectively contestable. Specifically, it must be subject to the constraints of a contestatory form of democracy: a democracy that follows deliberative patterns of decision-making, that includes all the major voices of difference within the community, and that responds appropriately to the contestations raised against it.

Although we discussed constitutionalist constraints, and indeed the likely aims of a republican state, prior to introducing the notion of a contestatory democracy, the notion of democracy has an important primacy. The account of republican aims, and the account of constitutionalist requirements, is a provisional, theoretically driven story about the shape that a successful republic is likely to have to take. But once a contestatory democracy is in place, then of course everything is up for grabs. If the operation of that democracy leads to the emergence of different aims from those that we outlined, or if it forces a rethinking of constitutionalist constraints, then it is obviously the dictates of that democratic process that should prevail. Again, if the operation of that democracy occasions a restructuring of the paths of contestation itself, then again the democratic process must prevail.

No text and no tradition is more important than the precipitates of the local democratic process. If the institutions that are selected under the development of that process are ruled out by reference to such an impersonal authority, then the polity is not effectively tracking people's interests and ideas. The claim that the democratic process is the last court of appeal, of course, has a very different resonance here from that which it might have in populist circles; the process envisaged is essentially one of contestation, after all, not one that necessarily involves majority decision-making. There is no suggestion that the people in some collective incarnation, or via some collective representation, are voluntaristically supreme. Under the contestatory image, the democratic process is designed to let the requirements of reason materialize and impose themselves; it is not a process that gives any particular place to will.

How far does the emerging conception of a contestatory democracy fit with the received republican tradition? The republican tradition, at least in the form it assumed in the English-speaking world, tended to lay great stress, as we have seen, on the fact that certain laws were tried and tested over a long history of challenge: they were part of an ancient and venerable constitution of freedom. 'The law that the friends of liberty trusted to protect liberty', as one commentator puts it, 'was not a code of substantive rules or guiding principles. It was, rather, restraint upon arbitrary power— the old law, the folk law, the good law, the customary law of the community' (Reid 1988: 63).

This emphasis on the attractions of well-tested, long-tested law makes sense in terms of our conception of democracy. For what is important under that conception is precisely that democracy provides an environment for the selection of laws which ensures that survivors are generally satisfactory; to the extent that survivors have proved capable of withstanding the contestations made against them, they may be presumed to answer to the interests and ideas of people at large. The main contrast between the conception of democracy in which the central notion is contestability and the standard, consent-centred conceptions is precisely that ours relies on a process of selection whereas those conceptions rely on a process of design. And the ancient-constitution idea makes contact with this selectional aspect of the contestatory approach.

But the contestatory approach also has a further anchorage in the republican tradition. John Locke (1965) is well known as a thinker who put considerable emphasis on the notion of contract and consent as a basis of government. But Locke introduced a second legal metaphor in characterizing government, arguing that, while government had a contractual aspect, it also had the aspect of a trust that the rulers were required to discharge on behalf of the people (Finn 1993). This idea had an important influence on the commonwealthman way of thinking, surfacing, for example, in Tom Paine's (1989: 168) comment that what is arbitrary about monarchy is that an individual holds power 'in the exercise of which, himself, and not the *res-publica*, is the object' (cf. Sydney 1996: 199–200). 'Republican government', Paine argued, 'is no other than government established and conducted for the interest of the public as well individually as collectively.'

The idea that government is a sort of legal trust—the idea that government is a more or less well-defined brief to which the rulers have to remain faithful—goes with the further idea that the people are entitled to challenge the government about how far and how well it is discharging that trust. And at the limit it goes with the idea, explicitly defended by Locke (1965) and the commonwealthmen, that if the government fails to do its job, then the people have the right to resist and overthrow it. This line of thought clearly belongs with the contestatory image of what democracy is about, and it shows that that image is not foreign to the republican tradition. It offers a picture of where the sovereignty of the people lies—not in electoral authorization but in the right of resistance (Pasquino 1996)—that fits naturally within the contestatory vision.

The contrast with interest-group pluralism

The contestatory conception of democracy marks a decisive rupture with some established ways of thinking. It breaks with any notion of democracy that would consecrate majority opinion, whatever the terms in which majority views are celebrated. It offers a particularly stark contrast to the interest-group pluralism that Cass Sunstein (1993*a*) has so effectively criticized, and I would like to conclude by considering it against the foil of that pluralist image.

The contestatory republic would foreground reason, in the sense of requiring public decision-makers to make their decisions, and to make them transparently, on the basis of certain neutral considerations. The interest-group paradigm would background, not foreground, reason. It would argue that the best way to organize things in public life is to have a framework which means that things will happen according to reason—in particular, things will happen so as to produce maximum preference satisfaction—if people within that framework each look only to the furthering of their own interests.

The paradigm starts from the invisible hand which economists have lauded for two hundred years. In the free market, so it is argued, the fact that buyers look for goods on the best terms available and the fact that sellers try to undercut competitors in the search for buyers—the fact, in short, that buyers and sellers each behave in an utterly self-regarding way—means, as by a beneficent, invisible hand, that goods generally become available at the competitive price: at the lowest price that is consistent with the sellers staying in business. The free market is a framework that does the work of reason in generating a result that is for the best overall, and in generating that result despite the fact—indeed, as a result of the fact—that agents within the framework each seek only their own ends.

The interest-group paradigm suggests that under an appropriate framework, the same sort of magic can be realized in politics as in economics. Think of the state as providing goods and services like law and order, external defence, public health, and other things that are not provided in the market. How are we to arrange things so that the consumers of such services—the citizens—are to achieve the highest level of preference satisfaction? How are we to achieve the ends, as they are taken to be, of reason? The interest-group idea is that we should design a framework of election, appointment, and decision-making— often it is imagined that we already have one—which ensures that if people behave like good self-seeking consumers, and if officials behave like good consumer-focused providers, then the outcome will be the highest possible level of preference satisfaction. Let citizens vote for the candidates and the policies which promise to satisfy their personal interests best. Let legislators vote for the policies that will give them the best chance of re-election. And let government and judicial officials act in the manner that best answers to the legislative or perhaps popular will that keeps them in office. In an appropriate framework of election and appointment, so it is suggested, the result will be that the citizens enjoy a greater level of preference satisfaction—or the same level with greater assurance—than they could expect under any alternative regime: in particular, under any republican regime (see Truman 1951; Dahl 1956; Stigler 1971).

While it has attained the status of a near-orthodoxy only in this century, the interest-group or invisible-hand way of thinking about politics was first sharply articulated by Bernard Mandeville (1924) in the early eighteenth century when he argued, contrary to republican orthodoxy, that private vice was to the public benefit (Hayek 1978: ch. 15). The way to get the best public results was not to have the citizens and the people internalize the common good and deliberate about how they could individually promote it; rather it was to encourage people each to seek the best for themselves and to rely on the social framework to ensure that this would lead, however indirectly, to the maximization of that good. Adam Smith built on Mandeville's ideas in the course of developing his economic views, and explicitly introduced the term 'invisible hand' into the literature (Smith 1982: 184–5). While he was in other ways of a republican cast of mind (Winch 1978), and while he was anxious to distance himself from Mandeville's attitudes, he may have done more than anyone else to bolster this way of thinking about politics. With the idea of the invisible hand in prominent circulation, it was inevitable that sooner or later people would think of using it to conceptualize politics as well as economics.

There are many questions—surprisingly many questions—that can be raised about how far the interest-group picture is capable of realization. There are questions about how far we can expect even self-seeking individuals to vote their interests in electoral outcomes, given that the chance of affecting that outcome is negligible, and that there are other, 'expressive' interests that voting can serve (Brennan and Lomasky 1993); there are questions about how far we can expect any voting system that is capable of coping with the different possible profiles of preferences to satisfy plausible constraints (Arrow 1963); and there are questions about how far we can expect public officials, elected and unelected, not to avail themselves of opportunities to satisfy pressures that are inappropriate under the pluralist picture (McLean 1987). But those questions apart, the republican perspective gives us an independent reason to reject the interest-group ideal.

However desirable maximizing overall preference satisfaction may seem, the invisible-hand way of seeking to achieve that end would mean that individuals were exposed on a variety of fronts to the spectre of arbitrary power. If I consider public officials and find in them a determination to do whatever will keep them in office, regardless of the considerations of non-domination that I or others can raise against their conduct—'Never mind your arguments; we have the numbers'—

then I must see them as people who hold a degree of arbitrary power over me. If I examine the courts and find a commitment to interpreting the law without regard to the telos of the constitution in establishing impartial government—with regard only to majority will, as available in the pubic record—then insofar as the majority will can disadvantage me and my ilk I must see the courts as means whereby I am left at the mercy of that will. And so on.

The backgrounding of reason which interest-group pluralism would recommend, therefore, is inherently inimical to the goal of promoting freedom as non-domination. Even if the preference-satisfaction way of reading reason's needs were not questionable, it should be clear that republicans are bound to hold out against the way in which such pluralism wants to have self-seeking or 'naked' preference (Sunstein 1993*a*: 25) become the motor of political life. To make naked preference into the motor of social life is to expose all weakly placed individuals to the naked preferences of the stronger: to make them hostage to whatever ill the stronger would do to them. Nothing could be further from the republican ideal. In arguing for the foregrounding of reason, the republican conception of a contestatory democracy sets its face squarely against the pluralist idea. That paradigm is anathema.

Do republicans have to oppose the free market as, by this argument, they have to oppose the proposal that would organize politics on market lines? No, they don't. It is true that in the free market, as theorized by economists, individuals face one another as the bearers of naked preferences and try each to do as well as they can in satisfying those preferences. But short of great differences of bargaining power, this arrangement does not mean that anyone is exposed to the possibility of arbitrary interference by any other or any group of others. One seller may be able to interfere with another by undercutting the other's price, but the second should be free, above the level of the competitive price, to undercut that price in turn; thus there is no question of permanent exposure to interference by another. The problems of majority preference formation that plague the political arena need not have analogues in the market, and so I do not find here the same possibilities of domination to which pluralist politics would give rise. The ideal of a contestatory democracy is revisionary, but not so revisionary as to be hostile to every form of market arrangement.

CHAPTER 7

Checking the Republic

In discussing republican institutions up to this point, I have concentrated on what aims the republican state should espouse and on what forms it should instantiate. I have tried to identify the things that a republican state should try to do in order to counter the domination that can go with private *dominium*. And I have attempted to spell out the measures that it should adopt in order to reduce the presence of arbitrary will in its own coercive arrangements and so to guard against domination by state *imperium*.

But these recommendations, for all I have said, may only have the character of an unattainable wish-list. Perhaps only creatures of an unattainable cast of mind—god-like creatures, machine-like creatures, or whatever—could sustain the republican regime described. Perhaps only such subjects would be able to identify effectively with republican aims and reliably to avoid the abuse of republican forms: the constraints of constitutionalism and democracy notwithstanding, such abuse is always going to be possible. Perhaps the regime would not be proof, in other words, against the vagaries of ordinary human nature. Who is to say that human beings have the capacity to sustain the patterns of behaviour required for the emergence and stabilization of such a state? Who is to say that the republic I have sketched is a feasible ideal?

This issue of feasibility might be discussed in relation to citizens in general or in relation to the narrower constituency of those citizens who occupy positions of authority. But I shall assume that citizens in general can be adequately motivated by the sanctions of the law, given a modicum of the civic virtue described in the next chapter. I shall concentrate here on the feasibility of our republican proposals in relation only to those in power. The question is whether we have reliable reason to think that those who hold office under the republic will behave in the manner that our proposals suppose. Can we really expect republican authorities to conform in a stable or reliable way to the patterns required for the promotion of freedom as non-domination? Can we really expect them to act in the manner that is needed for the advancement of republican aims and the preservation of republican forms?

Even this question, however, is not unambiguous. One issue, surprisingly enough, is whether we can expect compliance among moralistic authorities who zealously embrace the republican ideal. And another issue is whether we can expect compliance among those, on the contrary, who fail to embrace the ideal fully. The first is a question of the moral feasibility of republicanism, the second is a question of its psychological feasibility. I concentrate in the remainder of this chapter on the second, psychological question, and I should say a little here on the moral issue.

Republicanism is a consequentialist doctrine which assigns to government, in particular to governmental authorities, the task of promoting freedom as non-domination. But suppose that the authorities endorse this goal in a zealous, committed manner. Does that not raise the problem that they may seek in the name of the republican goal to breach the very forms that we, as system designers, think that the goal requires (Lyons 1982)? Does it not mean that they may often be motivated to take the law into their own hands—to dirty their hands (Coady 1993)—and to advance republican ends by non-republican means? It is often said that a utilitarian sheriff who is committed to promoting overall happiness might be required to frame an innocent person in order to avoid the worse consequences associated with a riot (McCloskey 1963). Is there not a parallel reason for thinking that republican officials who are committed to promoting overall non-domination will be subject to similar rule-breaking requirements? It would be a very serious problem if republicanism was morally infeasible in this way, for it would undermine the capacity of constitutional and institutional designers—ultimately it would undermine the capacity of a people—to plan for the effects they want to achieve.

Whatever is to be said of the utilitarian goal of overall happiness, however, the republican goal of freedom as non-domination does not raise a serious problem of moral infeasibility (Braithwaite and Pettit 1990: 71–8). People enjoy freedom as non-domination to the extent that no other is in a position to interfere on an arbitrary basis in their lives. The zealous agents who break faith with an assigned brief in order to promote non-domination assume and achieve resources of arbitrary power, for they behave in a way that gives their own unchallenged judgement sway over others. And this assumption of resources affects, not just the non-domination of those affected in this or that case, but the non-domination of most of the society; zealous agents set themselves up over all, not just over some. If certain agents think that they can maximize non-domination by transgressing the obligations of their brief, then, they are almost certain to be mistaken. Whatever non-domination they hope to bring about by departing from their brief, it is unlikely to be greater than the massive domination they thereby perpetrate over the population in general.

Against this, it may be objected that the sort of domination that official agents exercise over me and my like in virtue of covertly interfering with someone else is not itself harmful, so long as we remain unaware of the fact of being dominated. The agents may have reason to think, therefore, that it will be worth their while interfering if the chances of the interference becoming recognized are sufficiently small. I reply that no agent will ever be certain of not being caught out, and that the cost of being caught out is so enormous that, still, there is very unlikely to be a case for transgression sufficient to move a zealous agent. The cost of being caught out is that someone else will come to see that their lives are subject to the more or less arbitrary interference, not just of the agent in question, but of any other official agent: and, if someone else, then everyone else, since anyone who detects transgression is more than likely to make it public.

What if the chance of being caught out is really very small indeed? Why shouldn't a zealous agent conclude that however great the cost of being apprehended, the improbability is such that he or she should bend the law in this case: bend the law, for example, as in covering up the offences of an important public personage, and seeking thereby to advance the interests of the country? There may be the very exceptional circumstances where zealotry is pardonable—pardonable and perhaps even commendable—but a very serious consideration argues against there being many. This is that the more unlikely it is that an agent will be apprehended, the clearer it will be to people at large that this case is an acid test of whether they are living under a proper rule of law or under the arbitrary sway of officials who put themselves, out of whatever high motives, above that law. Let apprehension be likely and people may well reckon that the errant official just nodded. Let apprehension be unlikely and they will all the more certainly think that the errant official typifies a general, dominating frame of mind.

Short of catastrophic circumstances, then, there is unlikely to be any serious reason why a zealous agent should be tempted in the name of non-domination to break with the very rules of behaviour—the republican forms of government—that are designed to promote it. The considerations I have raised show that, given the power of official agents, and given their potential for domination, there is every reason why zealous agents should want to go out of their way to show people at large that there is no possibility of their taking the goal of non-domination into their own hands. There is every reason why they should look for institutional means of making it salient and credible that they are pre-committed to sticking with their brief, and to sticking with their brief even in cases where there is a prima facie case for zealous opportunism. There is every reason why they should want to make it salient and credible that their hands are tied: that they are agents with little or no independent discretion.

So much for the issue, as I described it, of moral feasibility. There is nothing about the republican goal, so it transpires, that would make it difficult to establish and stabilize republican institutions among moralistic agents who zealously internalize it. But the more important issue is that of psychological feasibility, not moral feasibility, and I turn to that in the remainder of the chapter. The question is whether the realization of republican institutions would place an impossible strain on the psychological capacities of ordinary, non-moralistic agents. In particular, the question is whether we can really expect such agents to carry out the functions that will be accorded to them if they occupy positions of authority within a republican state. Can we identify measures that promise to keep potentially wayward officials in line?

As in discussing earlier institutional proposals, I shall draw attention throughout the chapter to the linkages between the measures explored here and the views maintained, broadly speaking, within the republican tradition. But I should emphasize that the aim of the chapter is not to describe the republican heritage of ideas, and not to try to vindicate it. The aim is to look at how we may best hope to stabilize a republican regime—or indeed any similar, non-minimal dispensation—in the light of contemporary regulatory theory. If it turns out that this enterprise often connects with the republican tradition, then that is a happy result, but not a result that is sought in its own right.[1]

---

[1] This chapter draws on ideas in Pettit (1996*b*), but with some changes. The two most important are: first, that I now equate measures for screening out options with sanctions: this affects the interpretation of the deviant-centred and complier-centred strategies of regulation that I go on to distinguish; and second, that I here recognize that certain sanctions which the deviant-centred strategy may deploy do not impose a knavish assumption on the agents regulated: they can be, as I say, neutrally motivated.

I. The regulatory challenge

If the ideal republic that we have described is not likely to be a feasible or stable dispensation, then it may be a big mistake to try to introduce it in the first place. For those who are given power under the republic may prove, on its decay or transformation, to be worse tyrants than any that might otherwise have emerged. The problem of stabilizing the republic, stabilizing the sort of ideal described in the last chapter, is one of the age-old themes in the tradition (Pocock 1975). And no wonder. To set up an unstable republic, a republic that is sensitive to the smallest fall from grace among its rulers, might be just to pave the path towards despotism.

The challenge, then, is to identify devices whereby we might make the republic a resilient or stable phenomenon: an institution which is fit to survive the worst that nature and culture can confront it with. Or if not fit to survive the very worst possible—after all, as we shall see, such a regime might not be very attractive—at least fit to survive the worst that stands a reasonable chance of materializing. But what is the worst that stands a reasonable chance of materializing? The answer we give to this question depends on the view that we take of human nature, and in particular of the capacity of human beings to abuse power.

The republican tradition has always taken a pessimistic view of the corruptibility of human beings in positions of power, while being relatively optimistic about human nature as such. It generally downplayed the Augustinian fear of an inherently wayward people who require strong leadership if anarchy is to be avoided. But it enthusiastically countenanced the Ciceronian spectre of a corruptible leadership which requires careful containment if there is not to be tyranny or despotism (Bradshaw 1991: 117–18). As Richard Price (1991: 30) put it, 'There is nothing that requires more to be watched than power'. The view was, in Machiavelli's words (1965: 201), that the law-giver has to make pessimistic assumptions about people in positions of power: viz. 'that they are always going to act according to the wickedness of their spirits whenever they have free scope'.

There are two different interpretations of what this sort of assumption means. One is that people in power are inevitably corrupt: that is, in republican terms, that such people inevitably make their decisions by reference not to considerations of the common good but rather to more sectional or private concerns. This attitude represents a general cynicism about people, in particular about those individuals who seek and get power. The other interpretation is that people in power are not inevitably corrupt but are inherently corruptible: while they may actually make their decisions on a proper, impartial basis, they cannot be relied upon to continue to do so if there are no blocks or checks on the abuse of their power. This attitude is not so much a cynicism about those who happen to have power as a realism about what power can do to anyone who gets it. Consider the ring of Gyges, which would render a person invisible and enable them to do ill with absolute impunity. The idea on this second interpretation is that, as few of us would be able to resist the temptation to misuse the ring, so few people will be able to resist the opportunity to abuse power. Those in power may not be corrupt, but they are always corruptible.

I find the corruptibility assumption more compelling than the assumption of actual corruption. I also think that the corruptibility assumption is the more plausible interpretation of the view generally adopted within the republican tradition. But those considerations apart, there is good methodological reason to prefer approaching the challenge described on the basis of this assumption. It is granted on all sides that if we design institutions on the best-case assumption that people in power are all uncorrupt, and perhaps incorruptible, then the institutions may not work well in face of vice. But it is equally true that if we design institutions on the worst-case assumption that people are all corrupt, then the institutions may not work well in face of virtue: as we shall see later, for example, the institutions may actively serve to corrupt the uncorrupt! If we design institutions, however, on the middling-case assumption that people in power are corruptible, then we shall have to design institutions that work well both for agents who are not actually corrupt and, as a second line of defence, for agents who are. It is good to be given reason to cover both eventualities, and so I propose to conduct the discussion on the basis of this middling-case assumption.

Assuming that people in power are corruptible, what can we do to make sure that a republican dispensation is stable or resilient? Can we rely on education, socialization, professionalization, and the like? Can we put our trust in the effects of the citizen virtue that we shall be discussing in the next chapter? We shall get nowhere without such influences, as I argue in that chapter. But no one can seriously believe that those influences are sufficient on their own to guard against corruptibility. In the best-ordered society, with the best-disposed citizens, it still remains the case that as no one is proof against the ring of Gyges, so no one is proof against the temptations of unconstrained power. Thus, even if things are as good as they can be on the virtue front, there is still more to do in guarding against corruption. Madison makes the point in Federalist 10, when discussing the form of corruption that consists in joining a faction and preferring the faction's interest to that of the society as a whole. 'The inference to which we are brought is that the causes of faction cannot be removed and that relief is only to be sought in the means of controlling its effects' (Madison *et al.* 1987: 123).

The republican tradition has always embraced this conclusion, however much it may have insisted on the importance of virtue. It has embraced the need, not just for a republican pattern of law and democracy, but for a regime of checks and balances, as they came to be called. The commonwealthman, John Trenchard, put the point nicely in discussing constraints on magistrates or rulers.

Only the Checks put upon Magistrates make Nations free; and only the Want of such Checks makes them Slaves. They are Free, where their Magistrates are confined within certain Bounds set them by the People, and act by Rules prescribed them by the People: And they are Slaves, where their magistrates choose their own Rules, and follow their Lust and Humours. (In Reid 1988: 48)

II. Resources of regulation: sanctions and screens

What devices are available to us as we consider how to reinforce republican institutions so as to make them proof against the corruptibility of those in power? Broadly speaking, there are two sorts of control that we can deploy as we design institutions so as to promote some overall effect like making them corruptibility-proof. I describe the first controls as sanctions, the second as screens (Brennan and Pettit 1993; Pettit 1996*b*).

The most obvious instruments of control are sanctions. Sanctions operate on the set of options before an agent, making some options more attractive or less attractive than they would have been had the sanctions not been in place; they affect the relevant incentives. Sanctions come in negative and positive forms, as penalties or rewards. The negative sanction will penalize the agent for the failure to choose appropriately; the positive sanction will reward the agent for the appropriate choice. It is almost invariably assumed, of course, that sanctions are based on self-interest, so that it is the person themselves and not someone else—even someone they care for—who is penalized or rewarded. I go along with this assumption, as any other sort of sanctioning would be anathema to the cause of non-domination.

When we impose or increase a sanction for a certain form of behaviour, one or both of two things may be involved. We may increase the actual penalty or reward for that behaviour. Or we may take steps to increase the likelihood that any instances of the behaviour will be detected and the appropriate penalty or reward delivered. In each of these initiatives we increase the expected penalty or reward for the behaviour. In the one case the expected penalty or reward goes up via an increase in the actual sanction and without any increase in the probability of detection. In the other case the expected penalty or reward goes up via an increase in the probability of detection and without any increase in the actual sanction.

Sanctions in our sense will usually be recognized by the parties whom they affect, and may be internalized in their deliberations: the parties may reason that the option supported by the sanctions is the one to choose, given the reward it brings with it or the penalty it avoids. But sanctions may also operate without featuring as reasons in this way, and without even entering into the consciousness of the agents they affect. Suppose that, as things stand in a certain situation, agents already have reasons enough—perhaps reasons of virtue—to choose a particular option but that sanctions are introduced, by whatever instrumentality, to support that option. Even if the agents in question do not become aware of the sanctions, still the sanctions may operate to make the choice of that option more secure than it would otherwise have been. They may mean that, were the agents' actual reasons to shift away from the option, so that agents began to choose otherwise, then the agents would generally become aware of the reward forgone or the penalty suffered and would be returned to their original choice. Thus sanctions may operate to make the choice of a certain option more secure without figuring explicitly in the agent's deliberations. They may serve to reinforce a certain form of behaviour even though they do not help to produce it.

The notion of the sanction is familiar to all of us in social life. But there is a second sort of control available in institutional design that is not so commonly recognized. This is the filter, or screen. Sanctions take agents and options as given, and try to influence choice by changing the relative desirability of the options for those agents: by affecting their incentives. Screens operate, by contrast, on the set of agents or options. They are meant to ensure that some agents and not others will get to make certain choices, or that in certain choices some options and not others will be available; in other words, they are designed to affect opportunities rather than incentives.

As sanctions may be negative or positive, serving as penalties or rewards, so screens may also be negative or positive. They may screen out certain agents or options or, perhaps more surprisingly, they may screen in new agents or options: they may empower individuals who were previously not involved, giving them an opportunity to act that they didn't have before, or they may empower the individuals already involved in the relevant situation, putting a new option on the list of alternatives before them.

The screens which operate on individuals will have the effect, under the ideal institutional design, of recruiting to certain tasks those individuals who are more likely—perhaps inherently more likely, perhaps more likely in the context of certain sanctions—to behave in the manner that is socially valued. Appointment and vetting and search procedures, as well as constraints and desiderata on eligibility for office, exemplify screens of the kind available. Consider, for example, the procedure whereby members of a committee are vetted to ensure that they do not have a personal interest—the interest of a friend or foe—in the outcome to be determined by the committee. Or consider the requirement that members of the committee include representatives of certain groups, or that the membership be approved by some independent authority or be subject to appeal by interested parties. All these measures represent obvious screening devices.

But screens can be used to operate on options as well as agents, putting some options on or some options off the list of available alternatives. We put an option on the list of relevant alternatives when we make it possible for a member of the public to voice a complaint or make a claim; for an official to lodge a case for investigating the behaviour of their superiors; or for a house of parliament to refer an issue to a cross-party committee or to an official inquiry. We take an option off the list of relevant alternatives when we take legal or institutional or physical steps that make it effectively hard to access.

Taking an option off the list of available alternatives is not going to be distinguishable, in practice, from sanctioning. It will usually mean introducing a penalty on the attempt to choose the option, or increasing surveillance so that the likelihood of penalization is increased. And, either way, it is going to mean increasing the expected penalty for the choice in question. In the exceptional case, it is true, an option may be screened out by means of a physical or institutional obstacle. But few obstacles are absolute—most just raise the costs, and therefore the penalty, attaching to an attempt to act in the manner prohibited—and so here too screening an option out is going to be indistinguishable from sanctioning it. For our purposes, therefore, I shall assimilate measures of screening out options to the category of sanctions, and when I refer to option-screens in what follows I shall only have in mind measures for screening in options.

III. Against deviant-centred regulation

Given that sanctions and screens represent the tools available in institutional design, the question is how we should deploy them in the cause of guarding against the corruptibility of authorities and promoting freedom as non-domination. There are two broad strategies of regulation and stabilization. One focuses primarily on those who will immediately deviate in the absence of controls, the other on those who will tend in the first instance to comply: they may be corruptible but they do not start out as corrupt. I call the strategies respectively the deviant-centred and the complier-centred strategies of institutional design (Pettit 1996*b*). I argue here, at a fairly abstract level, against the first strategy and then in the next section I offer grounds for supporting the second. In the last section of the chapter I try to indicate what relying on the complier-centred strategy would amount to in the life of a republic.

The deviant-centred strategy begins from the thought that if selfish or factional interest leads people—some people, at any rate—away from compliance, then we should make institutional interventions which ensure that, on the contrary, compliance becomes the self-interested option for such deviants. We should increase people's motivation to comply by rigging the pay-offs in favour of compliance. If the expected self-interest score for deviating is X and the expected self-interest score for complying is something less, then we should introduce sanctions which ensure that the balance is redressed, at least in some measure. Institutional design should be guided by the aim of putting such motivators in place as will keep more and more potential deviants on the desired track.

The ideal way to implement the deviant-centred strategy would be to identify the motivator, if any, that is required for each individual and to make sure that it is in place. But, of course, that custom-built approach is not going to be feasible in our world; we cannot have different sanctions for different individuals. So how then should we proceed with the strategy? The obvious reply is that we should consider the perfectly self-interested individual and put in place sanctions which ensure, at the least, that if such an individual is convicted of deviation, then the sanction will be of a kind and level to cause them to regret doing what they did. I say that we should ensure this 'at the least', because the aim of deterring such individuals—deterring them under uncertainty as to whether deviators will be apprehended and convicted—may require even heavier sanctions.

The general idea with the deviant-centred strategy, then, will be to provide more motivation than is necessary for most in order to make sure that the motivation is sufficient for all. The approach amounts to treating all of those it constrains, not just as corruptible, but as actively corrupt. Perhaps they are not actively corrupt as a matter of fact; perhaps the republican tradition, as I have interpreted it, is right on that question. No matter. It is still good policy, so it is argued, to guard against that worst-case eventuality (Brennan and Buchanan 1981). Defenders of the strategy naturally associate themselves with Mandeville (1731: 332), for whom the best sort of constitution is the one which 'remains unshaken though most men should prove knaves'.

The deviant-centred strategy is unattractive inasmuch as it flies on one wing: it relies entirely on sanctions and sees no important place for screens. It is also unattractive inasmuch as it requires that those who run the system have significant sanctioning powers and inevitably represent a threat in their own right. *Quis custodiet custodes?* Who will guard against the guardians? But those features apart, the strategy raises a variety of worries of a kind that have come into prominence with recent observations on how regulation can often be counterproductive.

Those observations start from the assumption that, as some defenders concede, people are not as deviant or knavish as the strategy takes them to be. Look at the sorts of considerations that weigh with us, or seem to weigh with us, in a range of common-or-garden situations. We are apparently moved in our dealings with others by considerations that bear on their merits and their attractions, that highlight what is expected of us and what fair play or friendship requires, that direct attention to the good we can achieve together or the past that we share in common, and so on through a complex variety of deliberative themes. And not only are we apparently moved in this more or less public-spirited way. We clearly believe of one another—and take it, indeed, to be a matter of common belief—that we are generally and reliably responsive to claims that transcend and occasionally confound the calls of self-regard. That is why we feel free to ask each other for favours, to ground our projects in the expectation that others will be faithful to their past commitments, and to seek counsel from others in confidence that they will present us with a more or less impartial rendering of how things stand.

It would be a miracle if this image that we sustain in relation to ourselves and one another were deeply misleading. In various contexts we no doubt indulge more self-seeking considerations; the market is the obvious example. And in some of those contexts we no doubt try to hide that self-seeking in more flattering stories about ourselves. But it would be a miracle if we were not moved in good part by the more or less public-spirited considerations that figure in the common image of ourselves and our fellows.

It would be a miracle, in particular, if those considerations had no hold whatsoever in the realms of the public authorities. For there is no reason to think that as people go to the polls, enter the legislature or the administration, or serve in the courts or bureaucracy, their sensitivity to culturally framed, more or less public-spirited considerations suddenly evaporates. On the contrary, the existence of a salient ethos of public behaviour should ensure that even if corruption occurs, it will never be the first and natural recourse.

One defender of the knaves strategy, David Hume, suggests that politics is different, and that actually people are generally corrupt in this realm. He admits that people are not inevitably knavish in their personal dealings, suggesting that the fear of being thought dishonourable keeps them honest. But he claims that in politics they can always make common cause with a faction that shares their interest, and can satisfy their desire for honour within the group. 'Honour is a great check upon mankind: But where a considerable body of men act together, this check is, in a great measure, removed; since a man is sure to be approved of by his own party, for what promotes the common interest; and he soon learns to despise the clamours of his adversaries' (Hume 1994: 24). But if this is his only argument, even Hume ought to admit that people may be public-spirited in many public roles. For it is only in some roles—for example, in legislative roles—that people can make common cause with those of a self-serving faction and ignore the dishonour that they may attract outside that group.

Let us assume, then, that, however corruptible they are, people in power are not always actively corrupt; they have a natural, culturally supported tendency to think in public-spirited terms and to make their decisions on a public-spirited basis. This assumption invites us to consider the likely effects of deviant-centred sanctions, not on actively corrupt deviants, but rather on those who have an independent disposition to comply with whatever are the public norms governing their behaviour. It turns out that there are a variety of negative effects, and that these give us reason to wonder whether a deviant-centred strategy can do much or indeed any good; they point us towards ways in which the strategy may be counterproductive. However successful it is with the natural deviants, it may cause natural compliers to do worse than we might otherwise have expected.

The problem with deviant-centred sanctions that are designed with knaves in mind is that they communicate an unflattering image of the motivation and commitment of all the agents to whom they apply; to the naturally compliant they may even seem to be downright insulting. They will be penalties or rewards whose only possible rationale is the assumption that those to whom they apply are, precisely, knaves; they will be of a kind or a level that makes them, as we may say, knave-apt. The imposition of such knave-apt sanctions will tend to alienate and demoralize the naturally compliant, to get their backs up and to encourage a hostile, defensive mentality among them. Whatever use they have in controlling the knaves, that good effect is likely to be off-set by bad effects on the compliance of those who are not knavish by disposition. Clocking workers in and out of the office may get the work-shy to appear for the hours required but it can also undermine the commitment of the naturally industrious.

This problem may be avoided in certain cases, of course. Consider the penalty that attaches, under a rule of law, to legislators who pass severe legislation: the sanction is that the legislators will have to suffer the harsh effects of the laws themselves. This sanction does not communicate a knavish image of legislators—it is not knave-apt—because it is neutrally motivated, being a side-product of other requirements on legislation. Or consider the increase of sanction involved in screening everyone who enters parliamentary quarters for possession of dangerous weapons; this increases the expected penalty, though not the actual penalty, for carrying such a weapon. The sanction is not a knave-apt penalty—it does not represent a knave-apt increase of penalty—because it is necessary to guard against an extreme eventuality and it does not discriminate between legislators and others; as in the other case, it is motivated independently of a knavish assumption about the legislators. But it is unlikely that the sanctions devised under a deviant-centred strategy will generally escape knave-aptness on these grounds. Willy-nilly, many of the sanctions supported by the strategy are going to hold out an image of the people regulated that will be very unappealing to the naturally compliant.

When sanctions are knave-apt, when they are unflattering or insulting to those who are regulated, then they are likely to have a negative impact on the compliance of those we may think of (if the expression is not too sexist) as the knights (Le Grand 1996). Such a negative impact is not only intuitively plausible; it is also substantiated in the empirical literature on regulation (see Ayres and Braithwaite 1992; Bardach and Kagan 1982; Brehm and Brehm 1981; Sunstein 1990*a*: ch. 3; Sunstein 1990*b*; Grabosky 1995; Brennan 1996). Without going into the details of that literature, it may be useful to list some of the well-documented patterns.

There are six particularly salient effects which are worth mentioning; they need no annotation, since they are so intuitively plausible.

1. *Hiding of virtue*. Many compliers are likely to be motivated by the regard and trust that their compliance earns: more on this later; but that motivation is undermined if rewards or penalties are so knave-apt that people can only expect their compliance to be seen as knavishly prudent, not as virtuous.

2. *Labelling*. Labelling, at least when it stigmatizes people, is effective in leading them to act according to label, and introducing knave-apt sanctions in an undiscriminating way can have the effect of labelling all relevant parties, including the naturally compliant, as potential deviants.

3. *Sanction-dependency*. Even if compliers continue to comply in the presence of knave-apt sanctions, their compliance may become sanction-dependent—it may become conditional on identifying suitable rewards or penalties—and they may be more likely to deviate when a suitable temptation arises.

4. *Defiance*. Compliers may feel themselves alienated, undervalued, resentful, even defiant, in face of sanctions that represent them as parties who need watching; and such feelings are quite likely to reduce their motivation to comply.

5. *Closing of ranks*. The introduction of knave-apt sanctions, in particular penalties, may cause those whom they affect to develop solidarity, so that they are unwilling to blow the whistle on one another, they close ranks around anyone under threat, and they develop the habit of shifting the blame onto other individuals or groups.

6. *Adverse selection*. The salience of knave-apt sanctions, be they rewards or penalties, may mean that spontaneous compliers are no longer attracted to public office; the people attracted may be those whose motivation would not be undermined by the presence of such sanctions (Brennan 1996).

IV. For complier-centred regulation

The deviant-centred strategy is driven by the need to deal with the knave: that is, with the most actively corrupt person around. The complier-centred strategy is driven by the need to deal with the more ordinary sort of individual who mostly deliberates, where it is appropriate, in a public-spirited way. The idea is that institutional design should look in the first place to building on the positive dispositions of this sort of person and only consider in the second place how to cope with those who are actively corrupt. It should build to strength, looking for the means to stabilize compliant dispositions, and only look later at how to compensate for weakness: how to guard against the problems to which the not so naturally compliant give rise.

I will present the complier-centred strategy in three principles (following Pettit 1996b). The first says that possibilities of screening should be explored prior to considering the options for sanctioning; the second that the sanctioning devices introduced should be, as far as possible, supportive of public-spirited deliberation; and the third that the sanctioning devices should also be motivationally effective.

First principle: screen before sanctioning

The first principle is that in institutional design we should look at possibilities of screening before we investigate sanctioning prospects. If the population of agents relevant in a given piece of institutional design can be screened so that those who appear there are generally not explicitly and more or less exclusively moved by self-interest—they are inclined to deliberate about their choices in the more or less public-spirited currency that is contextually appropriate to the choice at hand—then it may be possible to ensure the desired degree of compliance without resort to knave-apt sanctions. Again, if suitable, novel options can be put on the list of available alternatives, it may be possible to induce people to act appropriately without such sanctioning interventions. Of course opportunities for screening will not always be available and, even when they are, they may be too costly to be really feasible. But if they are available, and if they are really feasible, then the first principle says that institutional designers should try to exploit them.

The more commonly recognized screening device is the agent-centred one that tries to screen out some of the individuals relevant in a given setting. A good example is the procedure whereby the members of a jury are vetted, so as to ensure that no friends or enemies of the accused, and no one prejudiced for or against them, is included in the group. If we are dealing with such a screened group of people, then we can be fairly optimistic that they will conform to the norm of trying conscientiously to determine whether the evidence establishes guilt beyond reasonable doubt. If we are not, then all sorts of dangers present themselves, and it may seem that only a draconian form of sanctioning—with all the attendant difficulties discussed earlier—can offer any hope of keeping the jurors in line.

But the possibilities of screening include screening people in, as well as screening them out. Suppose we hope that jurors will generally be moved by the value of conscientious deliberation, with the voice of self-interest quietened, and that if they are not, then they will be sanctioned by the disapproval that is likely to be aroused in others by a more cavalier approach (Pettit 1993*a*: ch. 5; Brennan and Pettit 1993). In this case, we will not just screen for the elimination of anyone with a special interest in the outcome. We will also try to ensure that there is a mixed group of jurors, so that it is really a cavalier attitude that attracts disapproval and really conscientiousness that wins approbation; we will try to screen in appropriate jurors as well as screening out inappropriate ones. If the group of jurors is of a similar background, and if a certain judgement in respect of the accused would generally be expected from someone of that background, then there may be more approval to be won by conforming to that expectation than there is by being conscientious.

Apart from trying to screen agents out or screen agents in, we may try to impose a screen on options; in particular, we may try to screen certain options in, for, as we have seen, screening options out is more or less tantamount to imposing a form of sanctioning. Consider arrangements whereby people become entitled to make complaints along certain channels, or officials in certain circumstances are given the opportunity to blow the whistle on superiors, or juries are enabled to seek legal advice on questions that arise in their deliberations, or a parliament establishes the possibility of referring certain issues to committee. These represent devices for screening in options on the part of the agents in question, and they can obviously have important effects on how people in official positions are led to behave. Like agent-screening, option-screening may well allow us to avoid recourse to knave-apt sanctions. It would seem to be the merest common sense, given the line of argument pursued against the deviant-centred strategy, to explore all such measures of screening before looking to what sanctions are necessary.

The screen-first principle is not only attractive in its own right. It also fits nicely with the general presumption in the republican tradition that a constitution should design things so that the virtuous—'the choicest persons of the nation' (Sydney 1990: 558)—come to the top. Madison articulates the spirit of the principle in Federalist 57:

The aim of every political constitution is, or ought to be, first to obtain for rulers men who possess most wisdom to discern, and most virtue to pursue, the common good of the society; and in the next place, to take the most effectual precautions for keeping them virtuous whilst they continue to hold their public trust. (Madison *et al.* 1987: 343)

The first principle implements what Morton White sees as Madison's guiding idea in institutional design: that we should take the different motivation of different individuals and groups as given, and then try to allocate opportunity to motivation in the manner that best promotes the common good (White 1987).

Second principle: sanction in a complier-supportive way

So much, then, for the proposition that in institutional design we should look to screening initiatives before making any sanctioning interventions. The second principle that I associate with the complier-centred strategy is that we should look for sanctioning as well as screening devices but, in particular, for sanctioning devices that are supportive of the naturally compliant whom we have put in government: for devices, in Madison's words, that would constitute 'the most effectual precautions for keeping them virtuous whilst they continue to hold their public trust'.

Given the effectiveness of screening, might it not enable us to avoid sanctions completely in our design of institutions? No, for at least two reasons. First, we are assuming that no one in power is incorruptible, however uncorrupt they may actually be; thus the absence of all sanctions, like the impunity given by the ring of Gyges, might well cause them to become corrupt. And second, the absence of sanctions might undermine the assurance of the public at large and the assurance of uncorrupt officials—with bad effects on the compliance of those individuals—that officials generally are uncorrupt.

But if sanctioning devices of some kind are necessary, the second proposition insists that they should be complier-supportive in character. We saw in the last section that knave-apt sanctions can activate self-interested deliberation on the part of agents who would otherwise be guided by more or less public-spirited considerations—considerations, we may assume, that would support compliance—and that, in doing this, it can lead agents towards non-compliance. The lesson of that argument is that institutional design should try to avoid the knave-apt rewards and penalties that are likely to have such a disruptive effect. It should seek out sanctions that tend to retain and even reinforce spontaneous compliance.

One way of ensuring that penalties or rewards do reinforce spontaneous compliance is, as I have mentioned, to devise things so that the sanctions are neutrally motivated. Neutrally motivated sanctions make sense without any knavish assumptions about the agents to whom they apply, and their imposition is not insulting or unflattering to those agents. Thus there is no reason why the presence of such penalties and rewards should have a negative impact on the spontaneous compliance of more virtuous individuals or groups.

This observation points us towards one class of sanctions for which we should look in developing a complier-centred strategy of regulation. But there is also a second and more important class of sanctions for which we can look in pursuing that strategy. These are sanctions that not only fail to be insulting or unflattering to those on whom they are imposed; their successful deployment positively flatters the agents in question. They are rewards and penalities that project an assumption, at least when they are effective in securing compliance, that the agents are knightly rather than knavish, virtuous rather than corrupt. The sanctions are not just neutrally motivated, they are motivated on a basis of confidence and admiration; if you like, they are optimistically motivated.

The best way of introducing these sanctions may be to go to an example. Take again the jury—or indeed any committee—where the compliant, public-spirited pattern of behaviour is conscientious voting, and where members are aware of what this requires (Abramson 1994). Suppose that we have screened the body in question, so that no one has a special interest in the outcome and the committee is representative of a wide spread of opinion. And suppose that we have established sanctions against intrusion and intimidation which ensure that the doings of the committee can remain confidential and that jurors need not fear for their safety. These moves make it likely that most members of the committee will spontaneously apply themselves to the brief before them and seek to make a conscientious decision: they suggest that, with the voice of self-interest damped, people will display the public-spirited deliberation that ensures conscientious voting.

What sorts of sanction might be supportive of this pattern of deliberation? It is the custom with any jury, and with most committees, that the chair will call on members to declare their voting intentions and to defend them to others. When the members defend themselves, they must do so in terms that do not depend for their appeal on holding a particular, sectional perspective, because we have screened the committee so that it is not stacked in favour of any such perspective. Unless members can give a good justification of how they are inclined to vote, then—a justification that is persuasive across different perspectives—they will lose face with the others; they will look silly or prejudiced. Thus we can see that in the situation described there are sanctions at work that may help to keep in line anyone who is inclined to stray: for example, anyone who is impatient of the time taken up by the meeting and who announces their views in a peremptory fashion (Pettit 1993*a*; Brennan and Pettit 1993). Anyone who strays in this way will lose the regard of others on the committee.

The regard-based rewards and penalties that operate in such a context exemplify what I describe as optimistically motivated, as distinct from just neutrally motivated, sanctions. The existence of those rewards and penalties does not imply that the agents are knavish: it does not imply, for example, that they have no real interest in being conscientious. Nor does the existence of that set of sanctions remain neutral on the question of whether they are knavish or not. On the contrary, so far as it is effective in securing compliance, so far as it delivers the reward of a good opinion, or fails to deliver the penalty of a bad opinion, the system projects an image of the agents as conscientious in character.

No one gains such a reward in full and no one fully avoids such a penalty—no one is given regard for being virtuous and conscientious—if they are taken to be acting as if they were virtuous while not actually being virtuous: if they are taken, for example, to be acting as if they were virtuous in order just to win regard. To the extent that the behaviour is ascribed to something other than virtuous motivation—to the extent, for example, that it is ascribed to the desire for regard—it earns less regard. As Jon Elster (1983: 66) observes, perhaps with some overstatement, 'The general axiom in this domain is that nothing is so unimpressive as behaviour designed to impress.' Thus, to the extent that the regard-based sanctions work, to the extent that they fail to deliver a bad opinion, or actually deliver a good one, they present a flattering image of the agents constrained. The sanctioning system operates on the basis of an optimistic picture of the sorts of person in question.

The regard sanctions that we have illustrated in the jury case are of a kind that can in principle be mobilized in any committee or in any forum where there is a debate to be conducted and a collective decision to be made. But sanctions related to regard can also operate outside the context of a committee or a forum of any kind. Clearly, the public figure can derive a great reward from being well considered, or suffer a great penalty in being ill considered, particularly when this is a matter of common knowledge. And clearly the public servant is exposed to similar sanctions, so far as there are means—credible and reliable means—of giving or withholding recognition, as in awards, promotions, honours, and the like.

There is an interesting analogy between regard-based sanctioning and sanctioning by means of the invisible hand: say, the sanctioning that allegedly persuades the sellers in a free market to sell at the competitive price. The invisible hand involves people in non-intentionally rewarding or punishing others for doing certain things. Buyers intentionally take their custom away from the seller who charges more than others, for example, but it is non-intentional on their part that this punishes such a seller and pushes the seller towards charging only the competitive price. When positive or negative sanctions of regard are deployed in response to what an agent does, the rewarding or punishing is not just non-intentional in that sense. Because the response is one of thinking well or badly of the agent, it is inherently unintentional: it is not intentional under any description, being an attitude that the respondent cannot help forming. Where we speak of the invisible hand in the first case we may mark the difference between the cases—and emphasize the gentle, sustained sort of pressure exercised under the desire of regard—by speaking here of the intangible hand (Pettit 1993*a*: ch. 5; Brennan and Pettit 1993).

The second principle in the complier-centred strategy of regulation tells us that sanctioning is necessary as well as screening but that sanctioning should be supportive of spontaneous or virtuous compliance. We saw in the last section how deviant-centred sanctions, whether penalties or rewards, may disrupt those who are spontaneously disposed to be compliant, and the idea here is that the sanctions with which we support our screens should not be like that. We have seen in this section that they will not be like that insofar as they are motivated independently of a knavish assumption about the agents in question. They may be motivated neutrally, as when there is a reason for having them other than the acceptance of a knavish assumption. Or, even better, they may be motivated optimistically, as when the reason they materialize is that the agents are taken to be virtuous. Such optimistically motivated sanctions are exemplified, perhaps exemplified exclusively, by the regard-based sanctions of the intangible hand.

As we noticed that the screen-first principle is well supported in the republican tradition, we should also mention that the tradition is intimately associated, and associated as far back as Cicero, with a reliance on incentives of shame and glory. John Locke (1975: 353–4) offers one of the most striking statements of the point of view shared in the tradition generally:

For though Men uniting into Politick Societies, have resigned up to the public the disposing of all their Force, so that they cannot employ it against any Fellow-Citizen, any farther than the Law of the Country directs: yet they retain still the power of Thinking well or ill; approving or disapproving of the actions of those whom they live amongst, and converse with: And by this approbation and dislike they establish amongst themselves, what they will call Virtue and Vice.

The incentives of shame and glory are invoked throughout the later republican tradition. Montesquieu is famous, for example, for having argued that in moderate, monarchical regimes—including the sort of monarchy that conceals a republic (Montesquieu 1989: 70)—the spring of all action is honour. 'In monarchical and moderate states, power is limited by that which is its spring; I mean honour, which reigns like a monarch over the prince and the people' (Montesquieu 1989: 30). Again, the incentives of shame and glory appear in the *Federalist Papers* as one of the two great securities, alongside the possibility of discovery and impeachment, against the abuse of power (Madison, *et al.* 1987: 406). Joseph Priestley (1993: 33) offers a restrained gloss on the idea in question.

Magistrates, being men, cannot but have, in some measure, the feelings of other men. They could not, therefore, be happy themselves, if they were conscious that their conduct exposed them to universal hatred and contempt. Neither can they be altogether indifferent to the light in which their characters and conduct will appear to posterity.

As the demise of republicanism coincided with the rise of the notion of the invisible hand, so it coincided with a loss of confidence in the possibility of using the intangible hand in order to support public virtue. While David Hume (1994: 24) was prepared to concede that 'honour is a great check upon mankind', for example, he himself had come to think that it was a debased currency, associated with aristocratic 'debauchees' and 'spendthrifts' (p. 294). He was followed in this opinion by others, in particular by the influential figure of William Paley, who appeared in our story of the decline of the republican conception of liberty. 'The Law of Honour is a system of rules constructed by people of fashion, and calculated to facilitate their intercourse with one another; and for no other purpose' (Paley 1825: 2).

Apart from the association with aristocracy, the rise of the invisible-hand way of thinking may have helped to cause a retreat from reliance on honour. The invisible-hand paradigm of institutional design involves letting people pursue—shamelessly pursue—their interests, and rigging things so that a public benefit still results. Under that paradigm, the idea of relying on forces of approval and disapproval in order to get people to conform to some pattern may seem no less quaint than that of relying on their native virtue (see Hirschman 1977). Those who followed Mandeville and Smith in their enthusiasm for the invisible hand may have been led, by that very fact, to lose interest in the possibility of invoking the complementary, intangible hand.

There is no need to reject the possibility of deploying the intangible hand, however, just on account of believing in the invisible hand. Adam Smith himself acknowledged the power of both:

Nature, when she formed man for society endowed him with an original desire to please, and an original aversion to offend his brethren. She taught him to feel pleasure in their favourable, and pain in their unfavourable regard. She rendered their approbation most flattering and most agreeable to him for its own sake; and their disapprobation most mortifying and most offensive (Smith 1982: 116)

Smith seems to have held that the reason why people seek more and more of the material goods that economists ordinarily discuss is that such goods confer distinction, standing, and, ultimately, regard. We do not have to follow him in this, but it is certainly reasonable to follow him in thinking that people care both about more or less material benefits and about the benefits of being well regarded. Those desires each have a place in human life, and even if the fulfilment of one raises the chances of fulfilling the other there is no reason to think that either is a purely derived, instrumental concern.

Despite psychological evidence to the contrary (see Baumeister and Leary 1995), there are two arguments that are often presented nowadays for why we cannot rely on forces of regard. One is associated with sociology, the other with economics, and it may be useful to comment on them in concluding this discussion.

The sociological argument is that forces of approval and disapproval work effectively only in small-scale societies and have little or no power in the modern, anonymous world (Toennies 1887). It is easy to see what motivates this thought. You are generally going to be known to others in a small-scale society; and so it is certainly true that the benefit associated with someone's noticing you do something good, or the loss associated with their seeing you do something bad, is multiplied by their capacity to remember that it was you, someone recognizable by face or name, who did it, and by their related capacity to report on your action to others.

But this is not to say that the forces of approval and disapproval have no place in modern, more or less anonymous society (Braithwaite 1993). Two points are relevant. The first is that we appear to cherish approval, and worry about disapproval, even when we are not known to others or, if we are known, even when we are not going to have further dealings with the others in question. Consider how we flinch at being seen doing something embarrassing, even when total strangers are involved: think of being seen picking your nose by another driver, for example, as you sit in a traffic jam. Or consider how we shrink from looking silly in a context like that of the jury room, where we may never again see the people who witness our embarrassment.

But that consideration apart, the anonymity of modern society is easily exaggerated. While we may each lack a name on the street of a big city, that namelessness is quite consistent with being well known in a range of the interlocking circles that fill the space of the modern world. Some of these circles will be small of radius, like the circles of friendship and workplace and sports associations; others will be of much larger compass, like the circles of the extended family, the professional association, even the email network. There may not be the same concentration of recognition and identity in the modern world that there was in small-scale, premodern society. But having a name in many different, partial communities may facilitate the forces of approval and disapproval just as powerfully as having a name in the one community that exhausts every aspect of your life.

Another reason for doubting the power of approval and disapproval can be found in a recent tradition of economic thinking. Various thinkers have argued against the feasibility of the idea that people might police one another approbatively into a certain pattern of behaviour and might thereby overcome a collective action predicament: might thereby get one another to display a certain sort of virtue. The problem raised is sometimes described as the enforcement dilemma.

Either people are spontaneously virtuous, it is said, in which case there is no need for the enforcement of virtue; or they are not spontaneously virtuous, in which case there is no possibility of getting them to enforce virtue. The problem derives from the alleged fact that if compliance involves costs sufficient to inhibit suitable behaviour, there are costs associated with enforcement which ought equally to be sufficient to inhibit suitable enforcement. James Buchanan (1975: 132–3) puts the crucial premise succinctly. 'Enforcement has two components. First, violations must be discovered and violators identified. Second, punishment must be imposed on violators. Both components involve costs' (see too Taylor 1987: 30).

But the enforcement dilemma does not raise a great problem for the possibility that people should police one another, via sanctions of negative and positive regard, into certain patterns of behaviour (Pettit 1990). Visibility and access can be so assured that people do not have to do any work to discover violations and identify violators. And, more strikingly, people do not have to do any work in order to form, and be assumed to form, a high or a low opinion of someone else; the intangible hand operates without any intentional effort. The mistake made by those who think that there really is an enforcement dilemma is to imagine that approving and disapproving always means going out of your way to express approval and disapproval. It need not mean this. People clearly want to be thought well of, and not to be thought badly of, regardless of whether those thoughts issue in personal praise or censure. And so we can reward or punish people for what they do without lifting a finger or uttering a word.

Third principle: structure sanctions to cope with possible knavery

We have seen that, under the complier-centred strategy of institutional design, screening options should be investigated before possibilities of sanctioning, and that, as far as possible, sanctioning interventions should be supportive of those who tend to comply. Since there are liable to be explicitly self-interested agents present in any area of social life, however, and since we all have our moments of purely self-interested motivation, it is important in the institutional design of that area that we put in place sanctions that are motivationally effective for the knavish: sanctions that are sufficient to motivate the knaves on whom the deviant-centred strategy focuses. That is what our third principle counsels. We must find sanctions that are capable of coping, not just with the compliant, but also with those who are permanently or temporarily of a more callous disposition.

This principle will be satisfiable to the extent that we can identify independently motivated sanctions that may serve to keep even the knavish in line. But it is not always easy to come by neutrally motivated sanctions that can do this job. And, while optimistically motivated sanctions may be more generally available, they will often be insufficient to cope with knaves: the desire for regard may have little or no hold upon such individuals. So what are we to do in such a case? How are we to ensure that even knaves can be motivated? No system is going to be wholly satisfactory, to be sure; knaves will never be contained completely. But any system of sanctioning that is worthy of consideration must put some restraints on those who are inclined to be non-compliant. It must be able to reduce the potential damage that non-compliers can do, and it must be able to reassure compliers that their efforts are not exploited or derided by those of a different cast.

The way out of the problem is to ensure that sanctions, in particular penalties, are devised in an escalating hierarchy (Ayres and

Braithwaite 1992; Brien forthcoming). At the lowest level, there can be sanctions that apply to all public authorities and that are ideally supportive of compliance: say, sanctions of persuasion and regard. But if the sanctions at that level prove incapable of keeping someone in line—if the person is found to breach the relevant regulation and proves to be something of a knave—then sanctions can be invoked at a higher, more severe level. The process can go on for a number of stages, advancing up a hierarchy towards what Ayres and Braithwaite describe as the big gun. The big gun will be a knave-apt sanction, of course, projecting an unflattering assumption about the agents to whom it applies. But that need not be a problem, for the big gun will not be pointed at agents generally, only at those agents who have proved themseves not to be compliant under neutrally or optimistically motivated sanctions.

The system envisaged in the first two principles would seem to be fatally vulnerable to the damage that a knave could do. It could scarcely recommend itself in the absence of something like the escalation possibility, whatever the demerits of the alternative, deviant-centred strategy. But given the possibility of escalating penalties to deal with knaves, I think that we can be reasonably sanguine about the complier-centred strategy. We can keep our focus on ordinary, compliant individuals, as that strategy recommends, while having a clear conscience about the provisions for dealing with knavish outliers. This completes the exposition of the compliant-centred strategy that I recommend for trying to stabilize the ideal republic. It remains now to illustrate the sorts of measure to which the strategy would point.

V. The strategy in practice

Constitutionalism and democracy

The constitutionalist, democratic republic described in the last chapter offers an image of the form that a state has to take if it is to reduce the presence of arbitrary will—whether that be a good will or a bad will—in the coercive apparatus of the state. But the constitutionalist and democratic measures recommended for the reduction of arbitrary will have little chance of proving resistant to the determined efforts of sectionally motivated officials; they are bound to leave loopholes for such enemies of the public good to exploit. That is why we have needed to explore the resources available for stabilizing the ideal republic, rendering it proof against the vagaries of human nature.

Before we consider how the regulatory resources identified might be used to stabilize the ideal republic, however, it is important to recognize that the constitutionalist and democratic measures for which I argued in articulating republican forms do already introduce important regulatory controls. The constitutionalist, democratic republic which I described involves a variety of screening and sanctioning devices—and, in the nature of the case, independently motivated devices—for the promotion of its own stability. I did not mention this in raising the problem of how to stabilize the ideal republic at the beginning of this chapter. But in the light of our discussion of screens and sanctions, and of the different strategies of stabilization, we can readily recognize the presence of such stabilizers in the regime described.

The empire-of-law condition involves the requirement that government act via law, not on a case-by-case basis, in particular that it act via laws that are general, non-retrospective, adequately promulgated, precise, and the like. That is bound to mean that those in government are more constrained than they would otherwise be in respect of things they might want to do in furthering sectional aims. The condition puts out of effective reach—it subjects to prohibitive sanctions—courses of action that might otherwise be attractive from the point of view of their private interests. And the condition also has the effect of putting various incidental sanctions into place for the disciplining of those in government. Consider the requirement that the law is to apply to those who make it as well as to others. This means that if those in government make bad laws, say, laws that are excessively severe or taxing, they will have to suffer the bad effects of those laws in common with others. 'They may make prejudicial wars, ignominious treaties, and unjust laws,' as Algernon Sydney (1990: 571) put it. 'Yet when the session is ended, they must bear the burden as much as others.'

The dispersion-of-power constraint requires that legislative, executive, and judicial decisions should generally be put in separate hands, that legislative decisions should be placed in the hands of different houses, and the like. This constraint is essential, as we argued, if the authorities are not to have the status of arbitrary powers; like the empire-of-law condition, it is independently motivated. But the constraint serves also to make it more probable that the authorities, corruptible though they may be, will cleave to the path of virtue: that is, will discharge their offices with due consideration for just the public good. The constraint effectively removes certain options from the list of alternatives within the control of any of the relevant authorities; thus, whether they like it or not, the legislators cannot determine how the laws they frame will be applied in individual cases. And the constraint means that the authorities are accountable in various ways to one another and subject, therefore, to mutual sanctioning; thus, the legislature can censure the executive for failing to execute its laws properly, and the judiciary can expose the legislature to criticism by finding the laws it makes out of keeping with certain constitutional provisions (see Pasquino 1994: 114).

The last constitutionalist condition that I mentioned was the counter-majoritarian principle, according to which it should always be more rather than less difficult for those in power to change certain important areas of law. This condition serves, like the first two, to guard in an important measure against the influence of those sectional interests, in particular those majority interests, that may happen to be represented in government. It means that easy majoritarian options are effectively ruled out of court, and that those in government have to follow more difficult and testing tracks if they are to succeed in getting relevant laws changed. The condition is not only going to serve as a protection against arbitrary will; it is also going to serve as a source of stability in an environment where majority coalitions might otherwise succeed in bending things to their own purpose.

But not only does constitutionalism necessarily involve the presence of devices for stabilizing the republic; the democratic process that we described is bound to have a similar effect. The fact that those in power are required, and required as a matter of common knowledge, to base their decisions on considerations of the public good means that there is a standard in relation to which they are bound to be judged in the opinion of the public. It means that they can clearly win a good opinion for themselves by conforming, and manifestly conforming, to the demands on their office. And it means that they will have to confront the possibility of shame and ignominy if they try to use their office for the pursuit of their own private ends. Under a contestatory regime, after all, no public authority is safe from challenge and exposure.

One singularly important element in the contestatory image of democracy is a legislative body that is deliberative, not just in the sense of basing decisions on considerations of common interest, but in the sense of representing an inclusive and interactive debating chamber. And here in particular we can see a source of important, regard-based sanctions. For such a chamber is going to work, at its best, in the manner of the jury discussed in the last section; it is going to be a forum where members are rewarded for arguing faithfully to what are perceived as shared interests and are punished for arguing in a sectional or careless manner. Cass Sunstein (1993*b*: 244) puts the point persuasively.

The requirement of justification in public-regarding terms—the civilizing force of hypocrisy—might well contribute to public-regarding outcomes. It may 'launder' preferences by foreclosing certain arguments in the public domain, including, for example, those involving racial or sexual, prejudice. It might even bring about a transformation in preferences and values, simply by making venal or self-regarding justifications seem off-limits.

This comment on the disciplinary power of debate connects with a familiar theme in the work of Juergen Habermas (1989; 1990). Habermas imagines that, as different parties come to present reasons for and against different options, they will be obliged to argue in non-sectional terms of the kind that can appeal to anyone; and that as they do this, they will tend to internalize the habit and become truly detached, senatorial discussants (Elster 1986*b*; Pettit 1982; Goodin 1992*a*: ch. 7). One reason that people may be obliged to argue in these terms—even if they are not spontaneously inclined to do so—is that otherwise they cannot enjoy the acceptance and approval of their colleagues in the forum.

The project of designing stabilizers for our ideal republic, then, need not involve a radical break with the project of identifying the forms—the constitutionalist and democratic forms—that a republican state has to assume if it is to reduce the presence of arbitrary will. Articulating the shape that a republic has to assume if it is not to be a dominating presence means articulating a shape under which there are plentiful devices available for policing public officials. In particular, of course, it means putting many independently motivated devices in place—usually independently motivated sanctions—so that there is no problem of the sort that arises with deviant-centred regulation. The rewards and penalties deployed may be neutrally motivated, as with the sanctions imposed by various constitutionalist constraints, or they may be optmistically motivated, as with the regard-based sanctions introduced under a deliberative democracy.

Within the republican tradition itself, the enterprise of identifying ideal republican forms went hand in hand with that of finding the best means of republican regulation (Philp 1996). Thus when writers like James Harrington (1992) described the outlines of their utopian vision they were as much concerned with the means of rendering their utopia stable as they were with the articulation of their vision. John Rawls (1971) has popularized a distinction between ideal political theory which looks at the ideal of the just society in abstraction from the problem of non-compliance and the more realistic sort of theory that would consider what is needed under only partial compliance (Pettit 1994*a*). The distinction would not have made much sense for the republican tradition. In that tradition, the ideal of the republic where power is not dominating—the ideal of the republic where arbitrary will is at a minimum—is scarcely distinguishable from the ideal of the republic where the authorities are effectively checked and balanced: effectively channelled into the paths of virtue.

But though the ideal republic already involves various regulatory, self-stabilizing measures, it is equally clear that there are many other means available for pursuing its stabilization. The key to devising such means of control and stability lies in exploring the different principles supported by the complier-centred strategy of regulation. Some brief remarks on each principle will indicate the sort of research that needs to be pursued here; as before, the precise measures that should be put in place cannot be identified in advance of empirical investigation.

The first complier-centred principle

The screen-first principle counsels us to look at screening possibilities before we look elsewhere, as we wonder how best to ensure the resilience or stability of the ideal republic. And those possibilities teem. We may hope that those who stand for legislative office are reasonably worthy of office, so far as parties play a role in the selection of candidates: say, so far as the local party organization appoints a committee to determine who is the most attractive candidate. We may hope that those who are candidates for offices in government are of reasonable calibre to the extent that parties again play a role or, if not parties in general, at least the members of the party that have been elected to the legislature. And we may hope that those appointed to bureaucratic positions in the administration, as well as those appointed to the bench, will be suitably qualified so far as there are various vetting procedures, and procedures of confirmation, to weed out the unworthy.

There are possibilities of screening in suitable candidates for public office as well as screening out unsuitable ones. The committee that exercises a negative screening effect may also serve as a search committee that goes out in pursuit of the sorts of candidate that should prove most attractive to the party, to the government, to the public, or whatever. Or the candidates from whom a selection is made may have to have been nominated in a manner designed to pick out those particularly suitable for office. It is clear, as with negative screens, that such devices may be misused: say, that they may be biased towards those with visibility rather than towards those with virtue. But it is equally clear, I think, that some imaginative institutional design ought to reveal ways of reliably screening in the good, and screening out the bad.

Possibilities of screening arise with actions and initiatives as well as with individuals. Thus we may screen in procedures that enable people to make claims and complaints, or to refer matters to independent committees, or to call in expert advice, or to blow the whistle on a superior. It is obvious that we can use such screening devices, before we ever consider sanctioning initiatives, to make a certain result more probable. Suppose, for example, that it is difficult to get politicians to make reasoned decisions on certain issues—say, on issues of conscience or crime or monetary policy—because of the pressures to which constituents will subject them. If we screen in the possibility that those politicians can refer such a matter to a committee of experts who are not going to be subject to similar pressures, then we may easily make the desired result attainable. The politicians may be happy to pass the buck and the experts may be more than willing to do their impartial best; after all, they will be independently motivated to establish themselves as informed and impartial judges.

The second complier-centred principle

Having put suitable screens in place, the complier-centred strategy requires us to look for sanctions that can operate in the discretionary spaces left by those screens, and that can do so without undermining naturally compliant dispositions. The sanctions we explore, however, must be motivated independently of an assumption that the officials are knaves; otherwise they may have the various perverse effects mentioned earlier in this chapter. Some of these sanctions will be capable of being neutrally motivated; they will be sanctions that can be defended on other, institutional grounds, say on grounds related to the republican need to reduce the presence of arbitrary will. But the sanctions most worth exploring are likely to be those optimistically motivated rewards and penalties that depend on people's love of regard.

These sanctions are going to be available under three conditions. One, it is a matter of common knowledge in the community that certain standards apply to relevant public offices. Two, anyone who offends against those standards will be seen to offend, and anyone who scores well will be seen to score well. And three, there is an ethos of free and honest expression established in the community—an ethos of forthrightness—sufficient to ensure that people's attitudes of approval and disapproval can be readily divined from what they say and, indeed, from what they do not say (Pettit 1994*b*). There is no possibility of getting sanctions of regard into place unless there is a shared conception of what deserves regard, positive or negative, unless the performance of agents in relation to the standards is visible, and unless people's attitudes in response to the perception of that performance are reliably decipherable.

These observations argue for the importance of establishing forums for the discussion of the ethics of public life, and perhaps for seeking agreement on appropriate standards of behaviour: on the standards appropriate for politicians and ministers, for example, for members of the bureaucracy and members of public bodies, for players in the criminal-justice system, ranging from judges to attorneys to police officers and prison wardens, and for those in the media who play a crucial monitoring role in public life. The observations argue equally for the importance of putting reliable channels of publicity and information in place, so that the performance of the relevant parties is systematically brought to attention. And the observations argue, finally, for the importance of ensuring, so far as this can be ensured, that there is an established ethos of people's speaking their mind, so that what they say and do not say in criticism or praise of officials is effectively communicative of their attitudes.

It may seem naïve of me to put faith in the power of the intangible hand, and I should stress that it may not be able to achieve much unless its operation is supported by radical screening procedures. Take the case of the police. I do not suppose that an emerging emphasis on police ethics, a growing requirement of transparency, and an ethos of forthright expression would do much to improve police behaviour, short of steps being taken to ensure that police are not exposed, as they often currently are, to the sorts of temptation that the suppliers of illegal drugs can put their way. Nor do I think that the moves would achieve much in this area without some screening against the emergence of the them-and-us mentality that police officers are often alleged to have towards the public. I say nothing here on the sorts of screen that might guard against such possibilities; but I do want to emphasize that, as the first principle has it, such screening is certainly necessary, and that intangible-hand sanctioning is unlikely to make much of a mark in its absence.

The idea of a legislative assembly, and the idea of making those in government responsible to such an assembly, points us towards a set of arrangements that ought to boost a suitable economy of regard. For where there is such an assembly there will usually be a well-established sense of relevant standards, there will be systematic channels of information and publicity, and there will be a culture of forthrightness in criticism and commendation of members. The general assembly and various cross-party subcommittees, then, are forums where members may expect to suffer or flourish in the regard stakes, as it is made clear both what is expected and what has been achieved. And these arrangements for mobilizing regard should be reinforced in a culture where the doings of parliament quickly come to public attention, and quickly attract commendation or censure, through media coverage and commentary.

We all know that these arrangements can get to be perverted as political parties close ranks, as the media are influenced by sectional interests, and various other corruptions of republican process take hold. But in principle there ought to be ways of ensuring the proper operation of the system. There ought to be ways of exploiting regard-related incentives so that parties are shamed if they do close ranks excessively, or a media organization is shamed—say, thanks to a watchdog commission—if it is judged not to have offered a fair account of the facts. If a party is not to be held up to ridicule in national and international forums—say, in the media, or among various social movements—then it had better make some show of being more than a shamelessly sectional faction. And if it is to make such a show of being more than a faction, then it has to espouse a public-spirited profile. It has to be able to present itself, more or less credibly, as a group that is concerned with the common good, and which differs from other public-spirited groups only in taking a different view about how that good is best promoted.

What of sanctioning devices that bear on non-parliamentary figures: bureaucrats and judges and the like? The most important thing to notice here is that appointment and promotion are the main means whereby people gain positive regard in these areas, as non-appointment and non-promotion are the main means of suffering the negative. Thus, so far as well-structured committees can be made responsible for appointments and promotions, there is every reason for expecting incentives of regard to work well. But it is also worth noting that the judge, or indeed the bureaucrat, gains positive regard in relevant circles through having their decisions upheld on appeal, and are exposed to negative regard through having those decisions overturned. A regime of professional recognition governs the lives of those on the bench and in the bureaucracy, and it offers considerable hope of deploying effectively the controls of the regard mechanism.

The third complier-centred principle

It remains finally to mention in this overview that there is a third measure to which the complier-centred strategy would direct us, as we look for ways whereby we may hope to check and control those in power, and thereby stabilize the ideal republic. Not only should we investigate all that can be done in screening for agents and actions, and in putting complier-supportive sanctions in place; we should also consider how to arrange for the escalation of sanctions that may prove necessary in order to cope with the true knave: the person who manages to get into a position of power and who, once there, is determinedly bent on pursuing their own personal or sectional ends.

I have been assuming throughout this discussion that those in power are subject like everyone else to the ordinary sanctions of law. Certain privileges may be required for the proper exercise of parliamentary or judicial functions; if debate is to be open and robust, for example, it may be necessary to give parliamentary contributors protection against certain charges of libel. But I assume that the ordinary sanctions of the law will cover many serious offences by people in power, such as offences of financial impropriety, theft, physical violence, or anything of that kind.

I also assume that those in power are going to be subject to some special and very severe sanctions that are motivated neutrally by the requirements of constitutionalism and democracy. One example here might be the sanction of parliamentary impeachment for certain offences in public office. When significant discretion is given to public officials, the only way of guarding against the presence of arbitrary will may be to establish rigorous modes of parliamentary scrutiny, and to hold out the prospect of impeachment in the event of abuses coming to light.

The ordinary sanctions of the law, and special sanctions of these kinds, should serve to guard in significant measure against the knaves who may find their way into government. But even with offences that do not attract such sanctions, there ought to be a way of increasing the penalties for repeat offenders, and of targeting knaves. The minister who is rebuked for a first offence, for example, should expect to be stood down for a second, banned from holding office for a third, and so on. Unless there is escalation of this kind, there may be little hope of deterring real villains and, worse still, little hope of getting rid of them from public life.

Conclusion

The cause of republican liberty, by the argument of the last chapter, is the cause of constitutionalism and democracy. But words like 'constitutionalism' and 'democracy', and words also like 'liberty' and 'republic', have a tendency to get capitalized. And, with that capitalization the corresponding ideas have a tendency to attract breathless, often witless, devotion. I hope that one effect of this chapter may be to demystify the ideal which I have been trying to articulate, revealing it as a goal that relies for its promotion on arrangements that are essentially pedestrian and humdrum.

It was customary earlier in the century to refer disparagingly to the Fabians and other such practical-minded reformers as 'gas-and-water-works socialists'. But it is no longer so clear what there was to disparage in the achievement of these figures; they have left us a rather more solid and attractive legacy than anything that can be traced to their more romantic, high-flying comrades. What I want to argue for in this book is a sort of gas-and-water-works republicanism. Certainly the goal is a dispensation under which the high ideal of freedom as non-domination flourishes. And certainly that dispensation requires a regime under which constitutionalism and democracy rule. But constitutionalism and democracy come to be stabilized only via arrangements that are no more intellectually beguiling than the infrastructure of gas and water supply.

There is hardly a more humdrum reality in political life, for example, than that of the committee. Yet if the argument of this chapter is on the right lines, then our republican faith may have to depend crucially on getting this most pedestrian of institutions to work reliably. The committee consists of a body of individuals selected for a particular time or for a particular task: to hear appeals and make recommendations; to search out candidates and make appointments; to promote or dismiss those in current employment; or to investigate charges and review performance. It may assume a very formal status, as in a judicial body like the jury, or an executive body like the cabinet, or it may have a status that is more or less informal. The committee is the enzyme of the body politic, at least in the republican conception of that body.

There is a tendency in many contemporary circles to denounce committees as unrepresentative. Committees may well be unrepresentative in the sense of not being appointed by democratic election. But consistently with not being elected, they may be representative in the further sense of embodying the main points of view that are present in the community. And consistently with not being elected, they may often hold out the best prospect available of having decisions made on a non-arbitrary basis: on a basis that effectively rules out control by sectional interests or sectional ideas.

Of course committees, as we may know, may often fail. The

committee may be stacked, despite the best vetting procedures, with those who have a special interest in the outcome; or the effect of the desire for regard may be neutralized despite efforts at ensuring confidentiality, by outside intimidation. Again, the committee may be vitiated by an unwillingness among members to pursue mutual interrogation as to the reasons for any judgement made. Or, more basically still, the arrangement may be undermined by the appearance of divisions in the society that make some members willing to present themselves as 'shameless' to others. A society can become so divided that committee members care only for the regard of those in their own particular subculture, whether the basis of the division relates to colour or creed, for example, class or gender.

If we embrace the republican vision of politics, then it should be clear that the pressing questions for investigation bear on pedestrian matters such as how to ensure the high-level performance of committees. These are the sorts of issue that concerned Machiavelli, Harrington, and Montesquieu, as well as the authors of *Cato's Letters* and the *Federalist Papers*. They are questions about the shaping and reshaping of institutions; in particular, they are questions about how best to make institutions serve the cause of people's freedom as non-domination.

Political theorists have long neglected such questions in favour of more metaphysical or foundational matters. They have preferred to spend more of their time reflecting on the meaning of consent, or the nature of justice, or the basis of political obligation, than they have on mundane issues of institutional design. They have chosen to do ideal theory, in John Rawls's phrase, rather than the sort of theory that would tell us how best to advance our goals in the actual, imperfect world. Such a detachment from institutional analysis may be consistent with certain political philosophies but it would mean the death of any serious concern for freedom as non-domination.

CHAPTER 8

─────

Civilizing the Republic

I believe that the institutions characterized in the previous three chapters are indispensable for furthering the rich republican conception of freedom described earlier. And I also believe that they fit well with the republican tradition of institutional thinking and design. But these institutions cannot walk on their own. They are dead, mechanical devices, and will gain life and momentum only if they win a place in the habits of people's hearts.

Suppose that people did not generally identify with those institutions. Suppose that they regarded them as alien impositions, for example, and viewed with disdain or distrust those who argued for their legitimacy and those who worked for their implementation. Is there any chance that the institutions would remain long in place? Surely not. No purely legal institutions have a chance of surviving a substantial level of popular alienation or scepticism. No system of law has a hope of being effective if the law does not command a considerable measure of belief and respect. As Dr Johnson said: 'A country is in a bad state which is governed only by law because a thousand things occur for which the laws cannot provide' (Boswell 1970: 274).

What is going to be necessary, over and beyond the design of suitable republican laws, for the success of the sort of regime at which we have been aiming? We may assume that the laws we have designed really do serve the cause of non-domination well; we may assume that they prescribe suitable aims and forms for the republic, and that they introduce a potentially effective apparatus for regulating the officials of the republic. What are such laws going to require by way of supplementation if freedom as non-domination really is going to be advanced?

The answer is, in a word, norms. The laws must be embedded in a network of norms that reign effectively, independently of state coercion, in the realm of civil society. Civil society is society under the aspect of an extrafamilial, infrapolitical association; it is that form of society that extends beyond the narrow confines of family loyalty but that does not strictly require the existence of a coercive state (Taylor 1995: essay 11; Gellner 1994; Kumar 1993). If the state is to be able to find a place in the hearts of the people, and if the laws of the state are to be truly effective, those laws will have to work in synergy with norms that are established, or that come to be established, in the realm of civil society. The laws must give support to the norms and the norms must give support to the laws.

The point is not original. The importance of having civil norms that mesh with political laws has been recognized from the earliest days in the republican tradition. Machiavelli is quite clear, for example, that there is no hope of enforcing a republic of laws in a society that is not already characterized by *buoni costumi*: by good customs or morals (Rubenstein 1991: 51). He says that 'just as good morals, if they are to be maintained, have need of the laws, so the laws, if they are to be observed, have need of good morals' (Machiavelli 1965: 241).

Some of the norms required by a republican regime may be society-wide, bearing on how anyone in the society should behave. Others may be specific to those in certain roles or groups. They may bear on how someone in public office should behave, for example, or on how someone should behave if they are a member of a disadvantaged minority. And in either case the norms may require a variety of law-supportive responses. Perhaps the response required is the kind of behaviour that also happens to be prescribed by the law, as when norms condemn the very actions that are identified as criminal offences; perhaps it is whatever behaviour the law enjoins, as when norms require conformity to legally established conventions such as driving on the right or the left; perhaps it is the sort of behaviour that helps to enforce the law, as when norms require people to report offences; or perhaps it is behaviour designed to make law responsive to certain hitherto neglected problems, as when norms enjoin people to be critical and demonstrative about inadequate laws.

We know what it means to have certain institutional forms established by the laws. But what does it mean to say that there are norms in existence that work in harmony with those laws? Suppose, for example, that there is a civil norm to the effect that you ought to contribute to any collective effort that achieves a benefit in which you share. What is involved in saying that such a norm—such a society-wide norm—is established (Pettit 1990)?

One thing involved in any such case is the claim that relevant parties—in the case of a society-wide norm, people in the society as a whole—generally abide by the regularity in question: in this case, they tend to contribute to collective efforts that benefit them. Were that not true, the norm would not be established in the society: it would represent nothing more than an unfulfilled wish or prescription. But it is not going to be enough for a norm to be established that it is a matter of behavioural regularity in the society. Were that enough, then it would be a norm that people sleep at night or that they keep themselves warm or that they cook their meat: and those regularities are not norms in any intuitive sense, only matters of common taste. So what else is necessary for a norm to be established, beyond the fact that it is a matter of behavioural regularity?

When there is a norm rather than just a matter of common taste in place, then a salient difference is that relevant parties generally approve of the behaviour in question and/or disapprove of the absence of such behaviour. If we say that it is a norm across a certain society that you should contribute to any collective enterprise that benefits you, then we mean to imply, not just that people tend to make such contributions, but that people also tend to approve of anyone who makes them or to disapprove of anyone who fails to do so. They may be surprised to discover that someone prefers to sleep during the day, or not to keep warm, or to eat their meat uncooked; but, other things being equal, they will be more or less indifferent to the discovery. People will not just be surprised, however, to discover that someone fails to contribute to a collective effort from which that person benefits: not, at any rate, if that offends against an established, society-wide norm. They will tend to disapprove of the failure to contribute; they will tend to think ill of the person in question.

If it is a norm in a society, therefore, that someone should behave in a certain way, then first, relevant parties will generally behave in that way; and second, relevant parties will generally approve of anyone's behaving in that way and/or disapprove of anyone's failing to do so. To approve and disapprove in the relevant sense will be to have a disposition to praise or blame the person—to their face or, more likely, behind their backs—if a suitable occasion presents itself. Sometimes we approve or disapprove in this sense, on the grounds that the behaviour in question does or does not suit our own purposes. But when there is a civil norm in question, in particular a norm that is shared with others, then it is natural to suppose that the required approval or disapproval will materialize on more neutral grounds: on the grounds that it does or does not suit the purposes of others besides the agent, or that it does or does not promote the interests of society as a whole or of some other relevant group.

For something to be established as a norm, however, a third important condition also has to be fulfilled. Not only should the behaviour
be a matter of general compliance and a matter of general approval
among relevant parties. The approval in question should help to
ensure the compliance. The fact that people approve of anyone's con-
tributing to a general cause, or disapprove of anyone's failing to contribute, should make it more likely or more secure that people will
indeed contribute on that pattern. This condition is quite weak, since
it says nothing about how effective the approval should be in ensuring
the compliance, but it is none the less important. It serves to mark off
genuine norms from patterns of behaviour that generally attract
approval but that are in no way affected by that approval. It may be a
regularity that people eat every day, and it may even be a pattern of
which people generally approve. But given that the reason people eat
every day is unlikely to connect with the fact of such approval, we are
hardly going to describe that regularity as a norm.

In order for a regularity to be a norm, then, the elements of compliance and approval that I have identified must actively engage with one
another; they cannot remain in inert apposition. They may engage
with one another, for example, to the extent that parents encourage
their children to adopt the norms by showing that that is necessary for
parental approval. Or they may engage in virtue of the fact that while
virtuous people conform to the norms spontaneously, few are wholly
or permanently virtuous, and their motivation may benefit from reinforcement by the pattern of approval and disapproval on offer (Pettit
1995*b*).

Three conditions, then, are needed for the existence of a norm: first,
that relevant parties generally display the pattern of behaviour in question; second, that they generally approve of someone's doing so
and/or disapprove of someone's not doing so; and third, that this habit
of approval makes the behaviour more likely or secure than it would
otherwise be. Where those three conditions are fulfilled, of course, it
is likely to be a matter of common belief that they are fulfilled—or at
least of common belief in the relevant group—and we may wish to add
that as a fourth condition. Everyone is going to want to know what the
norms in their society are, and equally everyone is going to be in a
position to tell what they are. Moreover, those facts are salient to
everyone, at least in the relevant group, so that everyone is in a position to recognize, not just that it is a norm that something or other
should be done, but also that everyone relevant recognizes that this is
a norm. Thus we are directed to the familiar hierarchy of common
knowledge, at least in the form in which it continues: and no one dis-

believes in that common recognition, no one disbelieves in that disbelief, and so on (Lewis 1969: 56).

We can return, at last, to the claim with which we began. That claim
is that the laws introduced under the regime described in the previous
three chapters need to mesh with norms of civil society if the regime is
to have any hope of being reliably established. Let the laws conflict
with such norms, let the laws fail to be actively supported by such
norms, and the chances of realizing the ideal republic that we are after
must be radically diminished.

Suppose that there are norms established across a society, and in relevant groups within the society, that support a republican pattern of
laws. In that case the norms, like the laws, will have a republican character: they will be consistent with, and indeed supportive of, a dispensation in which everyone enjoys freedom as non-domination. The
norms will not be essentially sectional or factional, for example, as in
norms that prescribe the welfare of a particular group, at whatever
general cost, or norms that dictate taking revenge on outsiders for various offences against members of that group. Those who are party to
the required norms—those who embody such norms in their habits of
action and approval—will not be hostile to the common good; on the
contrary, they will display what we naturally describe as a public-
spirited character.

When I said that republican laws must be embedded in a network of
civil norms, therefore, I could as well have said that republican laws
must be supported by habits of civic virtue or good citizenship—by
habits, as we may say, of civility (Selznick 1992: 389–90)—if they are
to have any chance of prospering. In putting the requirement in this
manner, of course, the connection between my claim and the republican tradition generally should become even more salient. In many
minds that tradition is primarily distinguished, not by its distinctive
conception of liberty, and not by its image of the form that constitutionalism and democracy and regulation should take, but by its insistence on the need for civic virtue: on the need, in my preferred phrase,
for civility (Burtt 1993). One of the recurrent themes in the tradition
is that the republic requires a basis in widespread civility; it cannot live
by law alone.

This chapter is devoted to that theme. In the next section, I look at
some different grounds on which civility is required to support a
republic; these are not meant to be exhaustive but only illustrative. In
the section after that I consider how far a republic can expect or ensure
that such civility will come to be established. And then in the final section I show that the civil republic envisaged here is likely to be a

society where people establish linkages of trust and where ordinary, infrapolitical life thrives.

I. The need for civility

The first and most important reason why a republic is going to need to have its laws embedded in a network of norms is that people enjoy a higher degree of non-domination under a regime where there are norms to support republican laws. Where the laws reign in isolation from civil norms, perhaps even in conflict with such norms—if indeed such a regime is feasible—people will tend to respect those laws and to desist from arbitrary interference with others only when the legal and other costs of interfering happen to outweigh the benefits. They will respect those laws reluctantly and perhaps resentfully, not out of a sense of what civility requires. But that means that compliance by others with the law is going to be so contingent on circumstances, and so unwilling, that it cannot do much in the way of establishing a person's undominated status. Each person will be undominated, each person will be proof against arbitrary interference by others, only insofar as they manage to stay in the legal limelight, away from the darker corners where interference can go unresisted and unpunished.

The reliable enjoyment of non-domination, therefore, requires more than the existence of laws that stake out the areas in which you are to be proof against interference; it requires that there are also socially established norms that give an added salience and security and lustre to those areas. If there are such norms in place, then it will be a matter of reliable, perhaps unthinking inclination that leads others to respect you in those areas. You will not have to depend just on the effectiveness of the law for your freedom as non-domination; you will also be able to put your trust in the power of established norm. The field of social force in virtue of which others are led to show restraint and respect and you are enabled to live in non-domination will have a two-dimensional aspect. Others will be moved to acknowledge your place and your standing, not just by a susceptibility to legal sanction, but also by a spontaneous, culturally reinforced civility (Spitz 1995*a*).

It is a common observation among those who study compliance that the reasons most people obey the law in law-abiding communities derive, not from fear of legal sanctions, but from a sense that the law is fair (Braithwaite 1989; Tyler 1990). More specifically, so the studies tend to show, most people's reasons for obedience derive from a sense that the law is procedurally fair, being shaped and applied on an informed, principled basis and without undue influence from any sectional perspective (Tyler and Mitchell 1994; see also Lind and Tyler 1988). People do not weigh up the legal sanctions and come to be deterred by them. They see the law as legitimate and that leads them, at least within certain limits, they give it their unquestioned compliance.

This observation gives support to our first argument for the necessity of civility. For people will presumably see a republican pattern of law as legitimate, and will give it more or less unquestioned compliance, precisely when the law is supported by republican norms: precisely when it does not enjoin anything that runs counter to such norms and it is formed and applied in a way that is consistent with such norms. Republican laws will reliably attract compliance, then, and people will reliably enjoy the freedom as non-domination which such laws hold out as a prospect, only when the laws are buttressed by suitable norms, only when legal compliance is occasioned or reinforced by widespread civility.

A second reason for thinking that widespread civility is necessary relates, not to the need for supporting obedience to the law, but to the need to have the law keep track of people's changing and clarifying interests and ideas: to the need to have the law satisfy the constraints associated with democratic contestability. Suppose that there is some type of offence against people's freedom as non-domination which is not generally recognized as an offence. Suppose, for example, that while some form of government activity does not track the interests or ideas of a particular group in the society, this is not established as a fact within the culture. In such a case it will be possible to get the offence recognized only if there are people in that group, or at least people identified with the group, who are prepared to act in the group's name. They do not just complain on their own behalf. They display a form of civility which leads them to work at organizing the group and at articulating shared grievances; in their disposition to approval and action, they embody norms of fidelity and attachment to that group.

Think of the revolution in attitudes which many societies have recently experienced on questions to do with the role of women or the place of ethnic minorities. It is not very long since activities and utterances which now have an offensive and a shameful profile would have passed without remark in those societies: would have been taken as routine and unobjectionable. If things have changed for the better so that truly objectionable utterances and activities have become subject to formal or informal sanction, then that is the effect of civility in a more creative role than that which is associated with obedience to the law. Suppose that those who worked for the changes achieved had not internalized norms related to the good of the groups in question. Suppose they had each been focused only on themselves and their families and had not extended their concern to such larger objects of attachment. In that case it is very doubtful whether the changes in question would ever have been realized.

The fact is that different groupings often represent quite different perspectives, and that it is hard for outsiders to remain alert to the interests and ideas of those involved. This may be hard for reasons of inadequate motivation: not being themelves at risk under threats to those groupings, outsiders may fail to pay due attention to what is happening. Or it may be hard for reasons of perception and insight: not being party to the practices and sensibilities of those who belong to the groupings, outsiders may not be able to see or articulate the problems in question (Pettit 1994a). This lesson has been eloquently taught by the practice of governments, even relatively benevolent governments, in the traditional, unrepresentative politics of race and gender. A republic in which there are different groupings and different interests needs a politics of difference (Young 1990); and a politics of difference is possible only where there is widespread, group-centred civility.

I have illustrated the second ground for requiring widespread civility by reference to the civility that can emerge in association with ethnic and gender groupings. But it is important to recognize that the civility required is needed across a much broader range than these examples may suggest. Think of the politics that has been waged in many societies, to a lesser or greater effect, on behalf of consumers or prisoners or war-widows, on behalf of those with various handicaps, those in deprived geographical areas, or those who identify themselves as homosexuals. Such forms of politics are often essential for the articulation of important interests, and they are all going to require the group-centred forms of civility that I have been discussing.

But not only is the second ground for requiring widespread civility relevant with a large range of groups, it is also sometimes relevant with the largest group of all: the society, even the world, as a whole. The most striking example here is the sort of civility manifested by those who have articulated, often in the teeth of sectional opposition, the need for environmental awareness and protection. It is extremely doubtful that governments would have been forced to take account of environmental considerations, even in the inadequate measure to which they currently do so, if people were not generally responsive to a norm requiring concern for the common good: a norm requiring efforts on behalf of that good even when free-riding looks like the rational, self-interested response (Pettit 1986). If the law is to be kept on track, if it is to remain conscious of and responsive to people's interests and ideas, then there has to be a form of civility available that will drive, not just a politics of difference, but a politics of common concern.

This point should be obvious, of course, even without going to the issues of common concern that the environmental movement represents. While the ideal of republican law presupposes that there is a high level of group-centred civility available, it must also presuppose that such partial forms of civility do not drive out the civility that goes with a concern for the society as a whole. It is now commonplace to recognize that people can have different identities, as they act in one context out of this allegiance, in that context out of another. What should also be obvious is that people can display different forms of civility, as they simultaneously acknowledge the hold of norms that relate, here to the welfare of one group, there to the welfare of another (Fraser 1992). The point to recognize with the politics of difference is that, while it requires partial forms of civility in order to be effective, it also requires a disposition on the part of people, even people of quite different perspectives, to display a civility that relates to the society as a whole. Let people cease to countenance society-wide norms in their enthusiasm for more local affiliations, and the republic will degenerate into a battlefield of rival interest groups. It will cease to be a forum where democracy works in the deliberative, inclusive, and responsive pattern that we described earlier.

So much for the first two ways in which widespread civility is needed in order to provide a grounding for the institutional republic. A third reason for requiring such civility relates not to compliance and obedience, and not to the articulation of new legal causes, but to the effective implementation of legal and related sanctioning. Let us suppose that the ideal republic has been designed to identify and hold up for sanction a suitable range of activities: these may be criminal activities, for example, or the sorts of activity that we want to discourage among officials. In order for sanctions to work as deterrents, the offences must be reliably detected and the offenders reliably identified. And the only hope of ensuring such a pattern of effective sanctioning is to have norms that lead people not just to approve of compliance with the laws, and to disapprove of non-compliance, but to make clear what their attitudes are—to be forthright in their commendation and censure (Pettit 1994*b*)—and if necessary to identify and report offenders in relevant forums.

The necessity of civility in this respect is obvious from the fact that there is a severe limit on how far the police can identify offenders or even detect offences. That is true with political corruption, where ordinary citizens need to be ready to blow the whistle on bribery or simony or whatever, and with environmental pollution, where green movements represent the only effective watchdogs available. It is true also with domestic violence, where women often depend on their friends to report offences, or to put the offender to shame, or to provide the support necessary for them to be willing to report the offences themselves. But it is true in more humdrum areas too. It is only if ordinary members of a community are prepared to complain about petty theft, or littering, or vandalism, that there is any hope of legal sanctioning being effective (Karstedt-Henke 1991). Ordinary people must be willing to support such sanctioning by making personal and communal disapproval manifest and, if that becomes necessary, by calling in the legal authorities.

The need for widespread civility on this third front is well marked in the traditional republican principle according to which the price of liberty is eternal vigilance. What civility achieves here is the mounting of a level of vigilance, and therefore a level of exposure to sanction, which would be quite impossible in its absence. What it achieves in particular, under traditional assumptions, is the mounting of exacting vigilance in relation to those who hold power within the state. The established wisdom was that power particularly needs to be watched, because power is essentially corrupting. The tenet of the eighteenth-century commonwealthman gives typical expression to the idea. 'As he never saw much Power possessed without some Abuse, he takes upon him to watch those that have it; and to acquit or expose them according as they apply it to the good of their country, or their own crooked Purposes' (quoted in Robbins 1959: 120).

The emphasis on the need for vigilance, whether with public officials or with other citizens, fits with contemporary insights on social control. Theorists of regulation distinguish between the police-patrol and the fire-alarm mode of oversight (McCubbins and Schwartz 1984). In the first we rely on active police surveillance for the detection of problems; in the second we rely on someone's blowing the whistle and calling in the fire brigade. The fire-alarm mode is much cheaper, it raises fewer dangers of corruption, and it is liable to be much more effective: after all, no police officer can cover very much ground. But fire-alarm oversight corresponds precisely with the traditional notion of virtuous vigilance. It is a form of oversight that goes naturally with the widespread acceptance of corresponding norms: that is, with widespread civility.

Before leaving this point, I might mention that, while traditional republicans almost all recognize the need for virtue in the sense of vigilance, there is an interesting divergence between those who think that vigilance can be more or less routinized and those who believe that it requires an active, ever restless citizenry. Montesquieu (1989) represents someone who holds that things can be organized so that without any tumult, without any hue and cry, we can ensure the smooth functioning of the republic: the smooth functioning of the moderate society, as he would put it, in which liberty and tranquillity is assured for all. Adam Ferguson (1767), on the other hand, rails against this vision, arguing that there is no hope for liberty unless complacency is kept continually at bay and the ordinary people remain alert to the worst that the powerful can do. The rule of law that Montesquieu found and praised in Britain is fine, so Ferguson (1767: 167) says. 'But it requires a fabric no less than the whole political constitution of Great Britain, a spirit no less than the refractory and turbulent zeal of this fortunate people, to secure it.'

The issue between these two sides is essentially empirical, and we should leave it for investigation elsewhere. But there is one salient fact about advanced societies which suggests that it is Ferguson's lead, not Montesquieu's, that we should follow. This is that, at least in some areas, say areas of environmental pollution, the power of offenders to reassure ordinary people—in effect, to tranquillize them—is so great that it may require an active opposition, even an opposition of enthusiasts and crusaders, in order to ensure that offences are effectively identified and offenders made to answer for what they have done.

II. The supply of civility

I have been documenting the ways in which republican laws need the support of republican norms: the support, in other words, of republican forms of virtue or good citizenship or civility. But the question now is what the republican state can do in order to facilitate the appearance and operation of the required civility. Is it possible for laws to be so designed and so arranged that they nurture the fulfilment of the very civil conditions on which their success—their success as guarantors of non-domination—depends? Can the state do anything to make it likely that the laws which enshrine the aims and forms of the republic will be securely based in civil norms?

Ensuring the legitimacy of law

The one salient thing that the state must do is to ensure that the laws in question are established in common perception as legitimate interventions in civil life. It can expect only laws of this manifestly legitimate character to be supported by civil norms. And if it fails to deliver such laws then, plausibly, it must expect to diminish the fund of republican civility. What are people going to do if they find a system of laws that does not answer to the sorts of concern highlighted in their civil responses? Assuming that the laws are firmly and fixedly in place, it is all too likely that they will retreat into an attitude of indifference or hostility towards the state. But if people do retreat in this way, then there will be less and less scope for the exercise of civility and less and less reason to expect civility to spread and prosper.

But granted that the republican state has to establish the salient legitimacy of its laws, how is it to go about accomplishing that task? A first, ideological requirement is that it should be able to represent freedom as non-domination both as a commanding good and as a good that its laws are designed to further; this connects with my discussion of publicity in the Chapter 5. And a second, institutional requirement is that the republican state should manifest itself as a forum in which contestatory democracy is a palpable, stable reality and no one is subject to domination by those in power: both the things pursued by the authorities, and the ways in which they pursue them, are required to pass general muster.

The fulfilment of this institutional condition is necessary for—and likely to facilitate—the fulfilment of the ideological one. If every group in the society is manifestly in a position to contest any of the aims or forms or activities adopted by the state, as under the institutional requirement, then it is hard to see how the laws enshrined and applied in that state could fail to present themselves, however implicitly, as effective means of ensuring against domination; it is hard to see how the ideological requirement could fail to be satisfied as well. And it is only if every group is in this position, as under the institutional requirement, that we can expect the laws to present themselves as effective means of ensuring against domination; no amount of ideology is going to compensate for such a manifest, institutional failure.

The line that we are defending here has connections with the republicanism of Jean Jacques Rousseau (Spitz 1995*a*: 341–427). The main component in freedom, according to Rousseau, is the enjoyment of non-vulnerability to the will of others; the enjoyment, as he tends to put it, of non-dependency. But non-vulnerability can only be guaranteed for each under a law that is internalized by others as a legitimate and welcome form of constraint, not as a forceful imposition that will be systematically resisted and strategically avoided. How to ensure that the law will be internalized in this way and will not present itself as an alien restraint? Rousseau's solution is to require that the law satisfy his version of the democratic constraint: that it be identified, under conditions of full participation, as a matter of the general will.

The solution suggested here requires also that the law satisfy the democratic constraint, but a constraint of contestatory, not majoritarian, democracy. The laws must be fit to survive the challenges that they confront under conditions of deliberative, inclusive, and responsive democracy. In particular, they must be fit to survive those challenges in a regime that is bolstered against corruption by the presence of stabilizing factors like those that I discussed in the previous chapter. If the laws have proved themselves fit to be selected in such a democratic, contestatory environment, then that is the best sort of proof available that they are legitimate interventions in civil life. The laws will present themselves, not just as sanctioning devices, but as instruments that signal what civility requires.

If the laws serve for most people as signals of what suitable civil norms require, not just as sanctioning measures, then that is bound to increase the chances that the laws will enjoy civil acceptance and support. It is bound to facilitate those habits of civility on the presence of which the very success of law depends. The main aim of a republican state, therefore, must be to present itself as a legal regime that enjoys civil legitimation, and that demands compliance on the part of those who are civilly minded.

But is there anything else that a republican state can do to foster and promote the sort of civility on which its success depends? There are obvious steps that it can take to ensure that the education system holds out the required civility as something to be admired, not dismissed out of ignorance or cynicism. But it is painfully obvious in most societies that those measures easily deteriorate into the sort of propaganda that bores or alienates. So is there anything else that the state can do on this front?

Fostering the intangible hand

We know little or nothing about how to generate widespread civility where it has more or less ceased to exist. Who is to say what the state can do in a society where civility and the expectation of civility are at a minimum—where there is little of what James Coleman (1990:

300–21) calls social capital—and where people only put their trust in friends and family (Gambetta 1988)? But is there anything that we can say about what the state should not do in circumstances where there is already a good fund of civility available? If we accept the points made in the previous chapter about the intangible hand, then one observation is hard to resist. This is that the state must be very careful not to introduce heavy-handed patterns of control that are likely to undermine the influence of this more or less autonomous mode of regulation.

The intangible hand helps to nurture a pattern of behaviour by holding out the prospect that its manifestation will earn the good opinion of others and/or the failure to manifest it will earn the bad. If we assume that people care about the regard of others, seeking their high regard and fleeing their low regard, then it is natural to think that the intangible hand can be an important way of establishing and securing certain patterns of behaviour. I argued in the previous chapter that it can be an important influence on those who serve in official positions, and that if things are well designed, it can be an important influence for good. We should now recognize that it can be an important and positive influence in encouraging fidelity to civil norms more generally and that the state must be careful not to do anything to diminish this influence.

Under our definition of what it is for a norm to exist, the pattern of behaviour required is going to attract approval and/or the failure of the behaviour is going to attract disapproval. But this means that civility carries an inbuilt reward, and the lack of civility an inbuilt penalty (Pettit 1990). Being honourable is likely to go with being honoured, being dishonourable likely to go with being dishonoured. Other things being equal, then, we may expect that if a pattern of civility is established in a society, then that pattern will tend to be self-reinforcing. So long as nothing is done to disturb the pattern of sanctions on offer, we may expect those sanctions to stabilize people's civility.

In the general run, of course, people will be civil out of the sheer habit of civility. That is as well, indeed, since we saw that regard is only going to be available in full measure when civility is assumed to materialize on a spontaneous basis, not out of a strategic wish for some other end: not even out of a wish for the regard itself. But when people experience temptation and weakness of will, for example, and when spontaneous virtue fails, we may expect them to be generally kept in line by recognizing the sanctions of regard to which they are subject. The presence of those sanctions ought to guard civility against the dangers of such occasional lapses (Pettit 1995*b*).

If civility is widespread in a society, then the state ought to be very careful not to undermine it by doing anything to disturb these motors of regard. It is part of established wisdom that the state ought not to get in the way of the wonders which the invisible hand can bring about in the provision of market goods. It ought to be part of established wisdom that equally the state ought not to get in the way of the marvels which the intangible hand can facilitate in the supply of civic virtue.

How might the state get in the way of the intangible hand and do itself a disservice by reducing the civility available? I will mention one possibility, which was already signalled in my discussion of how a deviant-centred strategy of regulation—a form of regulation designed primarily to cope with knaves—can project a very unflattering image of the agents regulated and can thereby have negative effects on their behaviour. If those who put in extra, unpaid hours at their work are required to clock in and clock out, under a pattern of intrusive management, then it is obvious that that may cause them to work less than before. The lesson of my earlier discussion was that this sort of counterproductivity is a permanent possibility when agents are treated like knaves. We mentioned various counterproductive effects that can materialize including, for example, that agents can be negatively labelled, can become dependent on sanctions, can assume an attitude of defiance, and can close ranks against outsiders.

One of the dangers that the state must avoid is recourse to a pattern of regulation and legislation which has effects of this kind, and which tends to counter the influence of the intangible hand in sustaining civility. And the danger in question, it turns out, is not a purely abstract possibility. For the reigning ideology about how the state should seek to discipline citizens, in particular those citizens that it employs for various tasks, sees no role whatsoever for the intangible hand. It suggests that there are only two modes of control available, each of them inimical to this sort of mechanism.

The first control acknowledged is the discipline of the invisible hand that is associated with the free market in goods and services and with the market-like structures that are more or less consciously introduced in political and related spheres. The other is the discipline, as we might call it, of the iron hand: the discipline associated with the deployment of centralized state sanctions and with the monitoring required for the application of those sanctions. One of the most striking things about contemporary democracies is the strengthening assumption that in institutional planning we are faced with a stark choice between the invisible hand and the iron hand: between a strategy of marketing and a strategy of management. The idea is that this choice corresponds with the established dichotomy between spontaneous and imposed order, decentralized and centralized control (Hayek 1988).

This dichotomous view of regulatory possibilities has had a very bad effect on the behaviour of states in a number of areas. It has particularly affected the attitude taken to the various autonomous and quasi-autonomous bodies that belong to civil society but that states are generally expected to support or subsidize. I am thinking of hospitals, schools, universities, research institutes, broadcasting stations, public utilities, women's refuges, consumer bodies, indigenous people's commissions, and the like. Confident that they are themselves subject to the allegedly market-like discipline of popular election—this, under the interest-group pluralism discussed in the previous chapter—politicians have come to argue that it is essential to introduce similar market-like mechanisms into these areas or, failing the availability of those mechanisms, to impose a tough and uncompromising pattern of management. How can we throw public money at such bodies, so it is asked, unless we assure ourselves that the public is getting value for its dollar?

But the strategy of tough management often communicates an image of agents as uncivil and knavish and often generates the bad effects of deviant-centred sanctioning. And so, when such a strategy is put in place, civility in the relevant areas can be quickly undermined. Think of the likely effects on teachers, for example, if they are required to record and account for how they spend every hour, if they are under constant pressure to establish a satisfactory performance relative to abstract indicators, if they are given little or no discretion on curricular, disciplinary, or other fronts, and if they generally have to live under the presumption of being lazy unless proven productive. Where teachers will usually take pride in their effort and achievement, and enjoy the rewards of a corresponding status in the local school and community—where teachers will usually be susceptible to the influence of the intangible hand—the tough-management regime is likely to diminish the prospect or importance of these rewards and to diminish spontaneous civility. I do not say that management is not important. But an appreciation of the role of the intangible hand makes it clear that tough management can often be bad management.

We had been discussing the question whether the state can do much, apart from ensuring the salient legitimacy of its interventions, to foster the sort of civility on which its own success depends. While the considerations just mentioned have a certain anecdotal character, I hope they make clear that the state must be careful to try to legislate and regulate in a way that leaves scope for the intangible hand to sustain patterns of civility. It must avoid falling into the trap of focusing on deviants and treating everyone in the areas it controls as if they were knaves. It must try, on the contrary, to create a regulatory environment within which the intangible hand flourishes. Whatever controls are adopted, it should ensure that the standards expected in different areas of performance are clear to all concerned; that there is also an expectation in place that agents will voluntarily meet those standards, not just meet them under duress; and that there is sufficient visibility to enable relevant parties to see who is satisfying those standards and who is not.

Internalization and identification

In concluding this discussion of the supply of civility, there is one further matter that I would like to mention. We naturally think of civility, and of virtue in general, as a matter of internalizing values that stretch people's desires beyond the compass of narrow, selfish concerns. But that image may make civility seem less natural and more demanding than it actually is. It misses out on the fact that civility involves, not just internalizing values, but also identifying with the groups whose interests are associated with those values (Kelman 1958). And so it fails to register the fact that without civility a person may be deprived of dimensions of identity that are attractive and even compelling. It marks the efforts of self-denial that are required for the achievement of civility, but it does not mark the costs to the identity of the self that are involved in failing to achieve it.

To be a personal self, conscious of your identity over time, is to own a certain heritage of experiences and feelings, beliefs and judgements, plans and commitments, achievements and failures. It is to treat those experiences as conscious sources of memory, those beliefs as bases for reasoning, those plans as constraints on deliberation, and those achievements and failures as sources of pride and shame. It is not to be alienated from this heritage but to acknowledge that this is where you are coming from: this is what you are.

But while each of us is a personal self in this sense—in this sense of owning a personal heritage—it is also true of each of us that we often suspend the hold that that self has and allow ourselves to be recruited to other identities. We find ourselves responding in a way that owns, not a personal heritage, but a heritage that is shared with others. Consider the nationalist who takes the experiences of their nation as a starting-point and tries to make a judgement on what their country has to learn. Consider the theologian who takes the doctrines of his or her church as given and worries about what they imply in this or that contemporary context. Consider the business executive who takes part in decision-making routines on the unquestioned assumption that certain corporate plans are already fixed in place. Or consider the member of a political party who feels pride or shame in what the party has done in the past. In each of these cases, the agent is letting their personal self go offline, as it were, and is allowing a different identity—a national or religious or corporate or political identity—to take over in its place.

Identification is the process whereby an agent takes on such a larger identity. One way of describing it might be to say that the personal self remains always in place and that identification is an instrumentally motivated choice, adopted because the personal self sees it as useful to its own ends or values (Blau 1964; Homans 1961). That mode of description overlooks the fact, however, that identification is not an intentional initiative but something that comes to people as naturally as breathing (Turner 1987). No doubt it is true that, were a certain identification to work against the interests of the personal self, then the agent might rethink it and might take steps to inhibit the process (Pettit 1995*b*). And no doubt it is true that, should that identification raise a problem for the agent's evaluative commitments—perhaps a problem for other identifications—then again the agent might rethink and revise (Pettit 1997). But these facts are quite consistent with identification being an unmotivated, unchosen feature of how we naturally conduct our lives (see V. Braithwaite, forthcoming).

One reason for emphasizing the unchosen nature of identification in general, and of this or that identification in particular, is that that emphasis answers to our phenomenology. But another is that it fits with the fact that as we change identification then, in the old ocular metaphor, we also change point of view. We do not maintain the unchanging perspective of the personal self when we move from one communal identity to another. Rather we change perspectives, now seeing things from this point of view and now from that. If you like, we change selves: we come to feel and think and plan as if we were not an insulated person but a person in whom socially more extended entities have assumed life.

The internalization image of civility, to return to our main theme, represents fidelity to civil norms as an exercise in overcoming the self, whether the norms internalized be those of the society as a whole or just those of particular subgroups. But civility is as much a matter of identification as it is of internalization, for when I internalize civil norms I can be described, at one and the same time, as identifying with the group whose norms they are.

This is true, at any rate, when the norms in question promote a common good of that group: a good which no one can achieve for themselves except in the measure that it is achieved for some or all others. If the norms prescribe a form of compromise among competing members of a group, in order that each should be able to realize essentially conflicting ends, then fidelity to such norms may not involve identification with the group as a whole. But we saw in the first part of the book that freedom as non-domination is not of this kind. It is a common good to the extent that no member of a vulnerable group— no woman or black and, ultimately, no member of the society as a whole—can hope to achieve it fully for themselves without its being achieved for all members: no member can hope to achieve it fully for themselves except so far as membership of the group ceases to be a badge of vulnerability. With norms that are related to the promotion of this good—with norms of republican civility—it is inconceivable that someone could internalize those norms without at the same time identifying with the group whose welfare the norms promote.

Communitarians complain that liberal philosophies of the state shut down possibilities of identification, as we saw earlier. If they have a good argument for this conclusion, it may be that liberals do not countenance essentially common goods as ends for the state to promote. They typically see the state as designed to ensure a decent compromise between people's conflicting ends, people's conflicting conceptions of the good. Fidelity to the norms required for the state's success in ensuring such a compromise will not necessarily involve any identification with the polity as a whole, or even with other groups; on the contrary, the rationale assigned to the state will tend to emphasize people's separateness and people's competition with one another. But no such argument is going to work against republicanism. For the norms of civility that are required for fostering freedom as non-domination are norms of solidarity with others, not norms of compromise, and they are intimately tied to adopting group-level points of view.

It is important to recognize the linkage between the internalization of republican norms and identification, because it reveals that civility is not just a matter of denying the personal self. It is also a matter of letting other identities take over in your person. It is a matter of owning heritages of experience and belief and intention that transcend your personal concerns, whether those be the heritages that bind you, say, to other women, or other members of your ethnic group, or, ultimately, other citizens.

Identification is a natural phenomenon, and the fact that civility is a matter of identification augurs well for its accessibility and robustness. When someone devotes a day to clearing up litter on a public beach, when a woman spends one night each week helping in a refuge for battered wives, when an individual takes up a cause like that of prisoners' rights, or when a teacher lets their work invade the weekend, there is no need to picture the achievement as a triumph of will over instinct. What the person does in any such case can be described, equally faithfully, in terms of their honouring an identity that may be as intimate and important to them as their most personal concerns. We all like identifying with others in the enactment and assertion of collective identities; indeed, we can hardly help getting caught up in such communal concerns. And so there need be no miracle of self-denial involved in the manifestation of widespread civility within a community. Such civility need only testify to the irrepressibly social nature of our species.

The theme that I have been emphasizing in this last discussion resonates with a recurrent strand in the republican way of thinking about civic virtue. This is the strand of thought that tends to associate such virtue with love of country (see Taylor 1989; Viroli 1995; Miller 1995). For once we see that civility involves identification as well as internalization, we recognize that civility is bound to mean identifying in good part with the society or polity considered as a whole. And such identification is just what we mean by patriotism. In Charles Taylor's (1989: 166) expression of the theme, 'I feel the bond of solidarity with my compatriots in our common enterprise.' Patriotism can degenerate into a thoughtless nationalism of 'my country for good or ill', of course, but if it goes with a proper republican form of civility it is bound to represent the attitude, rather, of 'my country for the values it realizes': 'my country for the freedom with which it provides us'.

We may not be able to identify with the liberal state, then, for the fact that it gives each of us our private portions of satisfaction; the things that satisfy me may compete with the things that satisfy you, and our competition for what the polity provides may reinforce us in our distinct, personal identities. But we can surely identify with the republican polity for the fact that it gives each of us, and each of us to the extent that it gives all, the measure of non-domination that goes with being a fully incorporated member: a fully authorized and a fully recognized citizen. If we cherish our own citizenship and our own freedom, we have to cherish at the same time the social body in the membership of which that status consists.

III. Civility and trust

I have discussed some reasons why the institutional republic characterized in previous chapters needs a grounding in widespread civility. And I have looked at how far we may expect such civility to be forthcoming and at what the state can do to nurture it. In this final section I turn to the connection between widespread civility and widespread trust. I want to show that the civil society that the institutional republic presupposes is a society in which we may expect trust to materialize and prosper.

A person might be virtuous without anyone else presuming on that virtue: without anyone else acting on the presumption that the person is virtuous, say by putting themselves in his or her hands. A person might be trustworthy, in other words, without anyone else actually trusting them. Others might not be predisposed to believe in the trustworthiness; not believing in it, they might never put it to the test; and not putting it to the test, they might never find reason to revise their view (Hardin 1992).

In making my case for the need of widespread civility, I ruled out the possibility of such virtue coming apart from others' presuming on it. I took widespread civility to imply that there were suitable republican norms established in relevant groups, and that these were established as a matter of common knowledge among the parties involved. If there is widespread civility in that sense, then the people in question know of one another's civility and may be expected to presume upon it: they may be expected to take group initiatives, for example, that make sense only if others in the group are not going to let them down. Thus in itemizing the need for widespread civility, and in indicating what the state can do to promote such civility, I was arguing in effect for a civil society where suitable forms of trust are exercised and rewarded.

I was arguing in particular, I should say, for a society where suitable forms of personal trust are exercised and rewarded. When we rely confidently on someone to behave in a certain way because there are independent sanctions available that support that form of behaviour, then we trust that person in an impersonal fashion. When we rely confidently on someone to behave in that way because we think that the perception of our reliance will activate a cooperative disposition—say, will trigger civic virtue—and will make the behaviour that much more attractive to them, then we trust the agent in a personal way (see Baier 1986). To believe in a dispensation of widespread civility is to believe in a dispensation where there is a good deal of that personal trust.

This observation makes for a connection between my argument and one of the recurrent themes in recent social science. A decent legal and political order is only possible, according to this line of thought, in a society where there is a lot of active, successful trusting and a relatively intense level of civil life (Putnam 1993; Gellner 1994). Such a civil life is associated with the making of relationships, and the pursuing of common ends, beyond the motivating confines of the family but not yet under the auspices of a coercive state. It manifests itself in the pursuit of market activities, in the formation of clubs and associations, and above all in the appearance of social movements that are orientated to this or that aspect of what is perceived as the public good. If there is not a healthy level of civil life in a society, if there is not a sustained pattern of mutual trust, so the argument goes, then people do not develop a natural identification with others and a spontaneous commitment to what will advance the interests they share. They restrict their effective commitments to the circle of family and friends, and they lose a capacity for the more general forms of identification associated, in our sense, with civility.

The other side of the virtue for which we have been arguing, then, is trust, in particular personal trust. Not only are people reliably committed to republican norms of behaviour, but they each regularly rely on one another to display such commitments. They confidently put themselves in the hands of public officials, be they police or politicians or bureaucrats, even when that reliance is not supported by the existence of effective constraints on those officials. They treat other citizens with the same confident reliance, being prepared to accept reliance even when they are exposed and vulnerable: even when they have to trust the testimony or advice of relative strangers. And they treat fellow members of smaller groups, say groups that have a common political purpose, with a more or less ubiquitous attitude of confident reliance; they act on the presumption that they will never be left out on a limb, making efforts that are not supported by their fellows.

Since the best reason for trusting someone is that they are trustworthy, it is hardly suprising that the other side of widespread civility should be a high degree of trust in this sense of confident reliance (Pettit 1996a). The result is particularly unsurprising, given that republicanism is associated, not just with a dispensation of widespread civility, but also with a world in which being free is associated with the experience of tranquillity and standing. But there are some reasons why republicanism may not seem to go well with the endorsement of personal trust—or just trust, as I shall often say—and it will be useful, in conclusion, if we see why they are not compelling.[1]

Trust and vigilance

The first reason why republicanism may seem to fit uncomfortably with a dispensation of trust is that republican civility, as I have mentioned, is closely associated with the virtue of vigilance: the virtue of remaining alert, especially in dealing with powerful authorities, to the possibility that others may be behaving in a corrupt, sectional fashion. The price of liberty in the republican tradition is represented as eternal vigilance. But doesn't vigilance mean distrust (Ely 1981)? And doesn't eternal vigilance require the eternal refusal of trust—the refusal of personal trust—at least in relations with authorities?

Suppose republicans were to espouse eternal vigilance in the sense presumed in this challenge. Suppose that they were to refuse to feel confidence in any public official on whom they rely or are forced to rely. In that case, they would be denying that the very tranquillity and boldness that are traditionally associated with republican liberty is ever properly available. They would be saying that the price on which republican liberty is available, eternal vigilance, is a price which ensures that that very liberty loses much of its value. It ceases to have any legitimate connection to a sense of security, for example, a sense of not having to use strategy with others, and a sense of intersubjective status. Or at least this is so in respect of relations with the powerful.

This line of thought shows either that there is a deep inconsistency in the various things that I have been arguing in the name of republicanism or that the sense in which vigilance is traditionally required is not inconsistent with an attitude of confident reliance on the powerful. I argue that vigilance does not necessarily require a refusal of reliance, or an attitude of diffidence in reliance, and so that the second possibility is the one that obtains.

The key to my argument is a distinction between having trust in someone—in particular personal trust—and expressing trust in someone. To trust someone in the sense of having trust in them involves confidently assuming reliance upon them. But whether or not I have such trust, I may or may not choose to express trust. Whether or not I feel an attitude of confidence in the reliance assumed, for example, I may or may not choose to express trust in the way that leads me to say: 'I have decided to trust you in this and I can only hope that you will

---

[1] I am grateful to Geoffrey Brennan and Richard Arneson for raising them.

not let me down.' To trust someone in that expressive sense is not to rely with confidence upon them, or at least not necessarily, but to go through the expressive motions of relying with confidence upon them.[2]

What goes for trust goes, naturally, for distrust: in particular, for personal distrust. I will distrust someone in the ordinary sense of feeling and instantiating distrust to the extent that I feel no confidence that they will prove reliable, and do not actually rely upon them—do not build my plans around their proving reliable—or at least not for personal reasons. I will distrust them in the expressive sense just to the extent that I go through the expressive motions of not relying with confidence upon them. If I have no choice but to rely upon them, for example, I will express personal distrust to the extent that I insist on external checks or constraints and try to ensure on an independent basis that they do not let me down.

I see no tension between the republican belief in a dispensation of widespread civility and personal trust and the emphasis on maintaining eternal vigilance. For vigilance clearly involves only expressive distrust. The republican recommendation is that, whatever confidence people feel in the authorities, they will have all the more reason to feel such confidence—to enjoy such personal trust—if they always insist on the authorities going through the required hoops in order to prove themselves virtuous. To be vigilant in this sense will not be to feel an attitude of distrust towards the authorities—or at least not necessarily—but to maintain a demanding pattern of expectations in their regard: to insist that they should abide by certain procedures, for example, that they should accept challenges to their actions in parliament or in the press, that they should allow access to information on relevant aspect of their personal lives, and so on.

It should be clear from earlier discussions why it might make sense to maintain expressive distrust—to maintain the body language of distrust—while actually feeling no distrust: while actually being of a trustful mentality. People may feel an attitude of trust because they believe that the authorities are uncorrupt, and that they will reliably behave in the proper manner. But there are good reasons, none the less, why they may go through the expressive motions of distrust, insisting on the necessity of various checks and constraints. It may be that in the absence of such checks and constraints, there is room for arbitrary will on the part of the authorities. And it may be that, however uncorrupt the authorities actually are, human corruptibility means that, in the absence

---

[2] My thanks to Simon Blackburn for a helpful conversation about this.

of the checks and constraints implemented by expressive distrust, they would begin to develop habits of corruption. The absence of such checks and constraints could be as corrupting as the ring of Gyges.

Not only is there no inconsistency in having personal trust in the authorities while expressing personal distrust, it is even possible for people to make it clear to the authorities that they are espousing this dual posture. They can quite easily present the routines of distrust as constraints that are required in general, and that help to keep the best of us honest, while communicating the sense that they personally, or they as a group, are actually quite confident of the virtue and goodwill of the authorities in question. They can go through the established routines of expressive distrust and show in other less established ways that actually they feel considerable personal trust in the authorities. In this way, people might insist on the received expressive distrust while avoiding any negative effects of the kind associated with representing the authorities as knaves.

The upshot, I hope, is clear. The republican emphasis on vigilance stems from a belief that those in authority must be subjected to quite demanding checks and constraints: that this may be the only way of guarding against arbitrary will and coping with corruptibility. But that emphasis is quite consistent with enjoying, and with displaying in other ways, an attitude of confident reliance on the authorities. There is no incoherence at the heart of republican tenets. On the contrary, the allegedly conflicting views fit quite naturally together.

Trust and non-domination

A second reason why republicanism may be thought to fit uncomfortably with endorsing a dispensation in which people systematically trust one another is that the reliance involved in trust is tantamount to dependence or vulnerability, and that any complacency about such reliance is inconsistent with believing in the value of freedom as non-domination. Non-domination involves 'an independency upon the will of another', in Algernon Sydney's (1990: 17) phrase, and it seems to be downright inconsistent to hail this value while hymning the merits of a dispensation in which people confidently embrace forms of mutual reliance or dependence. If republicans attach themselves to the value of independency and non-domination, are they not required in consistency to disavow any relationships, voluntarily assumed or not, in which reliance is imposed upon people? Are they not required to espouse an image of human society in which everyone does their utmost not to be beholden or indebted or vulnerable in any way to another?

Absolutely not. The regime of mutual reliance and trust to which republicans look in seeking a pattern of widespread civility is a dispensation which, from their point of view, maximizes the prospects for freedom as non-domination. It is built on an institutional infrastructure of republican law and regulation, which is designed to do everything possible at that level of planning to guard against domination. While it invokes reinforcing structures of civility, and structures of trust in such civility, that is only because it sees there the best hope of showing people beyond patterns of domination. The guiding idea is that there is only so much that institutional safeguards can effect in combating domination. Ultimately the republic has to rely on safeguards that are less tangible in nature, and perhaps less satisfying to the imagination.

The imagery of non-domination is easily reduced to the picture of a life lived under secure guard, and under sure guidance, in a land of dangers and pitfalls: a land, in Locke's (1965: 348) phrase, of 'bogs and precipices'. But the lesson of our reflections in this and the previous chapter is, precisely, that this imagery is inadequate. Non-domination is not maximized in the society where each person cowers behind the heaviest, highest walls that they can build or that the state can provide. To rely on such walls and on such walls only would be to cast other people in the role of enemies and to call down war upon yourself. The lesson of our discussion is that the best hope of furthering the republican ideal is certainly to do whatever can be done in the heavy materials of institutional protection, but also to build with other, less cumbersome fabrics. In particular, the lesson is that we must also build with materials of civic virtue and trust, even though they offer less satisfying images of solidity and security.

There is a sort of paradox on offer here. Unless the seed is buried, it shall not bring forth life. And unless people are willing to accept various forms of reliance and to trust themselves personally to one another, in particular to the security offered by the civility of others, they shall not be able to enjoy the best that is available in the way of non-domination. People must be willing to accept an inevitable degree of reliance on the public authorities, trusting ultimately in the virtue of those officials. People must be willing to accept the fact of often having to be vulnerable to others, and often having to trust themselves to the civility of those others not to do them harm. And people must be willing to go along with one another in associations and movements that are essential for republican success but that inevitably require patterns of mutual reliance and personal trust.

But perhaps I should not overdo the aspect of paradox. Even when people are protected against arbitrary interference by independent checks and constraints, we have to speak of trust. The trust involved here is impersonal in character, since the source of the confidence that others will not let you down is that they are independently constrained not to do so. In the case that gives rise to the challenge we are considering, things are more or less parallel. People are still protected against arbitrary interference by checks and constraints but the ultimate protection hailed is given by the civility of the agents in question. People are now invited to trust those agents, not just on the impersonal basis that there are independent controls in place, but also on the personal basis that they are suitably virtuous. They are possessed of such civility that the attraction of acting in the manner on which others rely on them to act is increased by the recognition of that reliance.

Acts of personal trust

If there is anything substantial in the challenge that we have just been considering, it is not that we give up on the central republican value when we invoke an institutional and civil dispensation that requires a lot of reliance and a lot of trust, in particular personal trust. But does the objection have another message? Does it suggest, perhaps, that someone who espouses the value of freeom as non-domination cannot think in a positive light about unforced overtures of personal trust in other people? The charge would be that while we may be justified in embracing the dispensation described as the best way of ensuring overall freedom as non-domination—while we may be justified in personally trusting the authorities that have to be established under any republic—there is still a tension between espousing the value of freedom as non-domination and thinking well of acts of personal trust: thinking well of acts in which we voluntarily and manifestly place ourselves at the mercy of another.

This charge would not be damaging to the overall architecture of our argument—unlike the other challenges it would not reveal any deep inconsistency in our position—but it might make the value of republican freedom look less attractive than we suggested. Much of what is best in life comes from overtures of personal trust, as when we initiate relationships of love and friendship by risking ourselves in such acts: by showing that we confidently put ourselves at the mercy of the other person. Republican liberty is going to seem rather less grand than we may have been assuming if an attachment to that liberty would inhibit the taking of such overtures.

There are three points that I want to make in response to this criticism. The first is that the creative acts of personal trust envisaged in the objection are only going to be possible within a context, and more generally within a society, where each of the parties involved enjoys more or less equal levels of non-domination and enjoys the status that goes with this. For if they do not each enjoy such freedom and standing, if one of them is in a dominating position relative to the other, then the acts in question are not going to be effective in the same way. If the dominating person goes through the motions of putting themselves at the mercy of the dominated, that is going to look like a condescending charade. And if the dominated person goes through such motions, that is going to look like a fawning or toadying posture. It is only if the parties can look one another in the eye, confident in the shared enjoyment of freedom as non-domination, that an overture of personal trust can have the communicative and creative potential described.

The second point that I want to make is that when acts of personal trust are potentially communicative and creative in this way, then they are going to appeal to someone who cherishes freedom as non-domination. I am never so safe as when I am in the hands of a lover or friend. If it takes an act of personal trust, an act of putting myself at the mercy of another, in order to usher such a relationship into place, then so be it. Even in terms of the value of non-domination—and we never suggested that this is the only value in human life—such an act of personal trust will look like a bold but sensible overture.

The third point I want to add takes us back to the intangible hand that has figured so prominently in these discussions. Not only do overtures of personal trust presuppose the enjoyment of freedom as non-domination among the parties involved. And not only can they serve to promote the further enjoyment of that good. They can also look like particularly rational means of pursuing that goal from within the republican perspective defended here, in particular from within a perspective that gives an important place to the intangible hand.

We saw in the previous chapter that the intangible hand represents a means of regulating those in power, and we have seen in this that it is an important way of supporting civic virtue more generally; it is a way of encouraging fidelity to norms of civility, both among the powerful and also in the society at large. Once we recognize the place of the intangible hand in social life, we can see a role for it to play, not just in supporting civility—and thereby in supporting personal trust—but also in supporting overtures of personal trust more directly. Acts of trust, as I have put it elsewhere, can display a certain cunning. They can put the intangible hand into action and thereby help to ensure their own rationality (Pettit 1996*a*).

The idea very briefly is this. Acts of personal trust can serve in certain contexts—particularly in contexts where the trustee is not entirely constrained by independent sanctions—to express either the message that the trustee is possessed of suitable virtue, or the message that if the trustee does not let down the trustor then they will be taken to have proved themselves suitably virtuous. Those acts, as we may say, can express a belief in the virtue of the trustee or a presumption on that virtue. But in either case it is clear that if the trustee is going to enjoy the good opinion of the trustor—or of others who are witnesses to the act of trust—then they had better not let the trustor down. And that means that as a trustor contemplates an overture of trust in one of the relevant contexts, in relative ignorance of whether the trustee is actually possessed of virtue or not, they can reassure themselves that the very act of trust is bound to be supportive of compliance by the trustee. The act of trust means that the trustee has something to win by proving reliable, something to lose by proving unreliable; it recruits the intangible hand in its own support.

To make an overture of trust in such circumstances, then, is to provide the trustee with an incentive to do the very thing which the trustor is relying on them to do. It is a sort of bootstraps operation, wherein the trustor takes a risk and, by the very fact of taking that risk, shifts the odds in their own favour. As Hegel spoke of the cunning of reason, so we can speak here of the cunning of trust. The act of personal trust is an investment by the trustor which will pay dividends only in the event that the trustee behaves appropriately, and like any investment it will have a risky side. But it is not as risky as it may at first seem. In the very act whereby the trustor is put at risk, the trustee is given a motive not to let that risk materialize. The trustor can bank on the fact that, if the trustee does let the risk materialize, there will be a loss on both sides. The trustor will suffer the cost of the reliance, it is true. But equally the trustee will suffer the loss of the trustor's good opinion, and the cost of gaining a bad reputation among those who know of what has happened.

Not only is republican vigilance consistent, then, with endorsing a regime of civility and personal trust. And not only is the republican goal of promoting non-domination consistent with relying on such a regime for the advancement of that ideal. It also turns out that, consistently with endorsing the republican theory of freedom and government, we can see sense and value in people's relying on overtures of personal trust to build up a world of supportive relationships around them. There is nothing mean or narrow about republican ends or republican means. The project culminates quite naturally in the vision of a society where civility and trust are widespread.

REPUBLICANISM:
A PROPOSITIONAL SUMMARY

Part I. Republican Freedom

Chapter 1. Before Negative and Positive Liberty

1. The negative conception of freedom as non-interference and the positive conception of freedom as self-mastery are not the only available ideals of liberty; a third alternative is the conception of freedom as non-domination which requires that no one is able to interfere on an arbitrary basis—at their pleasure—in the choices of the free person.

2. Contrary to established assumptions, the conception of freedom which was espoused in the long republican tradition was not the positive notion; in particular, it was not the notion of freedom as democratic self-mastery that Constant described as the liberty of the ancients.

3. Among the other two alternatives the republican conception endorsed the ideal of freedom as non-domination, not the ideal of freedom as non-interference. This is evident in the fact that it regarded all those who are subject to another's arbitrary will as unfree, even if the other does not actually interfere with them; there is no interference in such a case but there is a loss of liberty. The non-interfering master remains still a master and a source of domination.

4. That republicans saw freedom in this way is evident also in the fact that they did not think that a non-mastering and non-dominating interferer would compromise people's freedom; there is interference in such a case but there is no loss of liberty. They believed that it is possible for the law to be non-arbitrary and to represent a non-mastering interferer of this type.

5. As the conception of freedom as non-interference was introduced by Hobbes to defend Leviathan against republicans, so it was used to defend British rule in the North American colonies against the republican criticism that Parliament had arbitrary power over the colonists. The argument was that since all law is a form of interference all law reduces people's liberty and no legal system—not that of Leviathan, not that in the American colonies—can be dismissed as singularly inimical to freedom.

6. This new conception became respectable through the work of people like Bentham and Paley, who saw in it a way of conceiving of freedom that would allow even dominated agents like women and servants—so far as they did not suffer actual interference—to count as free.

7. Unlike traditional republicans, Bentham and Paley did not feel able to limit the constituency of citizens to mainstream, propertied males, and their inclusivism in this respect, which neo-republicans must also share, may explain why they regarded the republican ideal of freedom as too demanding.

Chapter 2. Liberty as Non-domination

1. Interference involves an intentional or quasi-intentional worsening of someone's choice situation: it may reduce the range of options available, or—in a lesser or greater measure—alter the expected pay-offs assigned to those options or determine which outcomes will result from which options and what actual pay-offs, therefore, will materialize.

2. Interference will occur on an arbitrary basis to the extent that it is controlled by the *arbitrium*—the will or judgement—of the interferer: to the extent, in particular, that it is not forced to track the interests and ideas of those who suffer the interference.

3. One party dominates another just so far as they have the capacity to interfere on an arbitrary basis in some of the other's choices; this domination may be more or less intense, depending on the severity and ease and arbitrariness of the interference available, and it may be more or less extensive, depending on the range of choices affected.

4. Where such domination occurs, it will tend to be a matter of common knowledge among relevant parties: each will know that the person is dominated, each will know that each knows this, and so on; the main exception is when the domination involves hidden manipulation.

5. Domination in the sense defined may occur without actual interference: it requires only the capacity for interference; and interference may occur without any domination: if the interference is not arbitrary then it will not dominate.

6. Non-domination involves the absence of domination in the presence of other people: it is a social ideal which requires that, though there are other people who might have been able to interfere with the person on an arbitrary basis, they are blocked from doing so.

7. Such non-domination may be advanced in a society either

through people coming to have equal powers or through a legal regime stopping people from dominating one another without itself dominating anyone in turn.

8. When someone enjoys non-domination that will usually be a matter of common knowledge among relevant parties, so that non-domination has a subjective and intersubjective aspect: it is associated with tranquillity, in Montesquieu's phrase, and with the ability to look others in the eye.

9. The considerations that led Paley and the new liberal tradition to prefer the idea of freedom as non-interference are not decisive. Notwithstanding those allegations, there is no confusion of ends and means involved in the idea of freedom as security against arbitrary interference.

10. Notwithstanding those allegations, furthermore, freedom as non-domination comes in degrees both of intensity and extent. It can increase in intensity so far as compromising factors—the dominating presences that make people unfree—are reduced; it can increase in extent so far as conditioning influences—the natural, cultural or legal limitations that make people non-free but not unfree—are diminished.

11. Nothwithtanding those allegations, finally, freedom as non-domination is not an impossibly radical ideal; the substantial demands that it would make on the state look capable of being satisfied in our world, even if they were not capable of satisfaction in Paley's.

12. While freedom is defined as the antonym of domination, it should be noticed that domination does not exhaust the varieties of power; under other conceptions, indeed, non-domination is itself a form of power. Dominating power exists in virtue of an agent's capacity—exercised or not—for a certain influence over another person: specifically, in virtue of a capacity for an intentional and negative form of influence on what that other agent chooses.

Chapter 3. Non-domination as a Political Ideal

1. The superior value of non-domination needs to be established in a comparison with freedom as non-interference; we need not discuss the value of freedom as self-mastery or autonomy, since a state which is orientated to non-domination—assuming that it is enough to orientate the state in that way—will also facilitate the achievement of autonomy.

2. The superior attraction of freedom as non-domination comes out in the fact that its maximization would require the promotion of three benefits that the maximization of non-interference could ignore:

the absence of uncertainty, the absence of a need to defer strategically to the powerful, and the absence of a social subordination to others.

3. The connection between freedom as non-domination and these benefits is such that that freedom is a primary good, in John Rawls's sense; it is something that people have reason to want for themselves, no matter what else they want.

4. But freedom as non-domination is not the sort of good that can be left to people to pursue for themselves in a decentralized way; all the signs are that it is best pursued for each under the centralized, political action of all: it is best pursued via the state.

5. The political pursuit of freedom as non-domination should be attractive, not just for small homogeneous polities, but in the modern, pluralistic state; the admonitions of theory-weary, world-weary critics look like counsels of premature despair.

6. The natural way to cast freedom as non-domination is in the role of a value that the state should try to promote, not in the role of a constraint that it has to honour; this, moreover, is the way in which it is generally cast in the republican tradition: the tradition is consequentialist in character.

7. Two dimensions need to be taken into account in the promotion of freedom as non-domination—the intensity of non-domination and the extent of undominated choice—but some plausible assumptions mean that we should look to intensity first and extent only in the second place.

8. When non-domination is promoted by certain political and other institutions—when people are guarded against possibilities of arbitrary interference in their lives—that effect is not causally distinct from the institutions; like the immunity produced by antibodies in the blood, the non-domination is constituted by such institutional arrangements: it has an inherently institutional existence.

Chapter 4. Liberty, Equality, Community

1. An egalitarian good is one such that its maximum realization tends to occur at a point where it is more or less equally distributed across the relevant constituency; most established political values, including freedom as non-interference, are not egalitarian in this sense.

2. Freedom as non-domination is a significantly egalitarian good. Maximizing the non-domination that people enjoy requires that they enjoy that non-domination with equal intensity, even if it does not require in the same way—require independently of most empirical contingencies—that they enjoy it over exactly the same extent. The

project is closely tied to the ideal of structural equality under which people are equally proof against domination, even if it is not similarly linked to equality in regard to resources and opportunities: that is, to material equality.

3. While the republican project of maximizing non-domination will allow that children and certain dependent adults have to be denied the standard range of undominated choice—that is necessary for their development or preservation—it should not tolerate any domination of such people; in this respect, it remains egalitarian.

4. A communitarian good is one that has both a social and a common character. It is social insofar as its realization requires that people are involved in mutual, intentional interaction; it is common insofar as it can be realized for one only if it is realized for some or all others.

5. Freedom as non-domination is a communitarian good. It can be realized only under an arrangement involving people in communal interaction. And it can be realized for one person only so far as it is realized for others in the vulnerability classes to which that person belongs: thus, a woman can be fully free in this sense only insofar as womanhood is not a badge of vulnerability, only insofar as all women are free.

6. The communitarian character of freedom as non-domination means that the freedom of a community is as basic a notion as the freedom of individuals, and that there is every reason, as communitarians require, why people should be able to identify with a state that promotes such freedom.

Part II. Republican Government

Chapter 5. Republican Aims: Causes and Policies

1. The republican philosophy of government, according to which the role of the state is to promote freedom as non-domination, has to be judged on John Rawls's method of reflective equilibrium, by reference to whether it gives us a picture of what the state should do and be which we can reflectively endorse.

2. Looking at what the republican state should do, the first thing to notice is that republicanism offers the state a pluralistic language in which to formulate the grievances it should seek to rectify: a language of freedom in which it is possible to make sense of a variety of claims that are made on the state.

3. The pluralism of the language shows up in the variety of causes of which it can offer a plausible articulation; these include, not just the familiar, conservative demand for order and predictability—and indeed private property—but also causes as various as environmentalism, feminism, socialism, and multiculturalism.

4. The republican language can achieve this degree of pluralism because the ideal of freedom as non-domination is inherently dynamic: it requires people's interests and ideas to be systematically tracked by the state, and so it leaves room for newly emerging or newly clarifying interests and ideas to force a reinterpretation of what such freedom requires.

5. When it comes to the specific policies that the ideal of freedom as non-domination would support—particularly, the policies it would support in combating the sort of domination associated with private *dominium* or resources—two things stand out: one, that the ideal is politically less sceptical than the ideal of freedom as non-intereference, since it recognizes the possibility of non-dominating government; and two, that it is socially more radical, since it requires not just the absence of arbitrary interference but the absence of capacities for arbitrary interference.

6. There are five large areas of policy-making—they bear, respectively on external defence, internal protection, personal independence, economic prosperity, and public life—and in all of these areas it is possible to discern the broad and often distinctive outlines of what a republican philosophy of government would require; but the requirements can only be detailed in the light of empirical information: republicanism is a research programme for policy-making, not a once-for-always blueprint.

Chapter 6. Republican Forms: Constitutionalism and Democracy

1. The republican state must not only seek to combat the effects of *dominium* in giving rise to domination; it must also guard against the domination that can be associated with the *imperium* of government; it must be concerned with what the state is as well as with what it does: with the forms as well as with the aims of the state.

2. If the way in which government operates is not to be subject to manipulation on an arbitrary basis, then there are a number of constitutionalist conditions which it must plausibly fulfil, and these have also been identified as important in the republican tradition.

3. A first is the empire-of-law condition, according to which government should operate by law, not case by case, and in particular by

a sort of law that satisfies established constraints: by a sort of law that is general, non-retrospective, well-promulgated, precise, and so on.

4. A second is the dispersion-of-power constraint, according to which governmental power should be divided out among many hands; this supports the division of legislative, executive, and judicial functions but also other forms of dispersing power, as in bicameral and federal arrangements.

5. A third is the counter-majoritarian condition, according to which it should be made more rather than less difficult for majority will to change at least certain fundamental areas of law; this condition can be implemented in any of a number of ways, ranging from presumptions in favour of common law to constitutionally guaranteed constraints.

6. No matter how constrained a constitutionalist system is, there is always discretion in government: there has to be discretion among the legislators, of course, since they are the ones who make the laws; but there is also going to be discretion among those in the executive and judicial areas, since the interpretation of law is never fully constrained by legislation.

7. The only way for a republican regime to guarantee that this exercise of discretion is not hostile to the interests and ideas of people at large, or of some section of the community, is to introduce systematic possibilities for ordinary people to contest the doings of government.

8. This points us towards the ideal of a democracy based, not on the alleged consent of the people, but rather on the contestability by the people of everything that government does: the important thing to ensure is that governmental doings are fit to survive popular contestation, not that they are the product of popular will.

9. A contestatory democracy will have to be deliberative, requiring that decisions are based on considerations of allegedly common concern, if there is to be a systematically available basis for people to challenge what government does; the challenge may be that the considerations invoked are not appropriate, or that the initiative taken is not supported by them.

10. A contestatory democracy will also have to be inclusive, making room for people from every quarter to be able to press challenges against legislative or executive or judicial decisions; this requirement means that government will have to be representative of different sections of the population, that channels of contestation will have to be well established in the community, and that government will have to be guarded against the influence of business organizations and other powerful interests.

11. A contestatory democracy, finally, will have to be responsive to

the contestations that are brought against government decisions. There will have to be arrangements for giving a proper hearing—a proper hearing, not necessarily a popular hearing—to the complaints made in different areas; there will have to be decision-making procedures in place that enjoy general credibility; and in the event of that credibility failing, there will have to be possibilities of secession or ways of giving dissidents the special sort of status accorded traditionally to conscientious objectors.

12. This contestatory conception of democracy has priority over the accounts given of likely republican aims, and likely constitutionalist constraints, in the sense that those accounts should be seen as outlines of what is likely to pass muster in a contestatory democracy.

13. The emerging conception of democracy insists that the point is to create a testing environment of selection for the laws, rather than to have laws that are consensually designed. It connects with the emphasis in premodern republicanism on the virtue of having laws that have stood the test of time and that are part of an ancient constitution. And it connects also with the traditional view that the people have the right to challenge and resist laws that are arbitrary in character: that this indeed is what constitutes the people as sovereign.

14. The conception represents a stark alternative to the picture of interest-group pluralism that is so often invoked in the characterization of how democracy does or should work; it argues for a foregrounding of reason where that conception would rather see reason backgrounded.

Chapter 7. Checking the Republic

1. The constitutionalist and democratic institutions that have been described are designed to reduce the room for arbitrary decision-making in government—thus they would be necessary even if people were as public-spirited as angels—but we need also to consider what steps can be taken to place checks on those who run the republic, given the imperfections of human nature.

2. There is no particular difficulty for republicanism in guarding against problems of zealotry among government officials, since the pursuit of non-domination, unlike the pursuit of other values, would not give zealots much reason to take the law into their own hands.

3. But there is a need to guard against the corruptibility of human beings: even if most people are not actively corrupt, and are quite disposed to acknowledge and pursue what virtue requires, they are capable of being corrupted if they are exposed to powerful temptations.

4. The institutional resources available for guarding against corruptibility boil down to possibilities of sanctioning and screening: possibilities of punishing or rewarding what people do and possibilities of screening for the presence of suitable agents and options.

5. One strategy in institutional design is to start from the need to cope with the worst agents around—the so-called knaves—and to introduce sanctions that will serve even to control such antisocial types.

6. This deviant-centred strategy is subject to well-known difficulties, however, all of which derive from the fact that most people are not knaves—most are naturally responsive to legitimate demands—and that a pattern of sanctioning designed for knaves is liable to alienate such agents and reduce their degree of compliance.

7. An alternative strategy starts from the assumption that many people are not knaves and tries to build on that strength; it would support a screening for suitable agents; then a form of sanctioning designed to work with such non-knavish agents; and, finally, a structure of fall-back sanctioning that can cope with occasional knaves.

8. The most important element required under this complier-centred strategy is a form of sanctioning that will not alienate agents. One way of sanctioning agents without alienating them will be to have sanctions that are motivated independently of an assumption that the parties involved are knaves: to have sanctions that are needed on a neutral basis.

9. But the most striking possibility for a non-alienating form of sanctioning is asssociated with the reward of people's good opinion, and with the penalty of their bad opinion; such a regard-based form of sanctioning, which operates in an essentially non-intentional way—as if by an intangible hand—can discipline agents while communicating a positive image of their virtue.

10. When we consider the constitutionalist and democratic institutions that were introduced to reduce the scope for arbitrary will, it turns out that they often put in place independently motivated devices, even regard-based sanctions, that can serve an important regulatory role.

11. But over and beyond endorsing such devices, there is scope for considering how the complier-centred strategy might be systematically deployed in the design of regulatory controls on public officials; this would lead us to look for suitable screening devices in the first place, then for non-alienating sanctions to control the agents selected, and finally for sanctions suitable for those repeat offenders who fit the profile of knaves.

12. Political philosophy often goes for abstract and romantic themes, neglecting humdrum issues of the sort discussed here: neglecting, for example, issues to do with how best to organize committees. The ideal of freedom as non-domination suggests that pedestrian matters of institutional design are of the first importance; it argues for a gas-and-water works version of republicanism.

Chapter 8. Civilizing the Republic

1. The laws that advance the aims of the republic, institutionalize its forms, and establish regulatory controls need to be supported by republican civil norms—need to be supported by widespread civic virtue, by widespread civility—if they are to have any chance of being effective; the legal republic needs to become a civil reality.

2. That a pattern of behaviour is a civil norm in a certain group means that nearly every relevant party conforms to it, nearly every party approves of conformity and or disapproves of deviation, and this approval-cum-disapproval helps to promote or secure the behaviour; moreover, it usually means that those conditions are a matter of common knowledge in the group.

3. One reason that widespread civility is needed is that people can be assured of their non-domination only so far as others recognize normative reasons for respecting them, not just reasons connected to fear of legal sanctions.

4. Another is that if the republic is to be systematically sensitive to the interests and ideas of people—often newly emergent, newly articulated interests and ideas—then there have to be people who are virtuous enough to press appropriate claims; this applies both in the politics of difference and in the politics of common concerns.

5. A last reason why widespread civility is needed is that the public authorities cannot hope to identify and sanction all offences against republican laws and norms; ordinary people also have to be committed enough to perform in that role or to support the efforts of the authorities: ordinary people have to maintain the eternal vigilance that constitutes the price of republican liberty.

6. The most important thing for the state to do by way of encouraging the widespread civility that it needs for its own success is to establish the republican legitimacy of its laws in the public mind; and this it can best do by being an effective, contestatory democracy.

7. Widespread civility is likely to be supported by the intangible hand of regard-based sanctioning, since the honourable are destined in most circumstances to be the honoured, and the state must be careful

not to impose forms of sanctioning which might get in the way of that process.

8. There is a real danger that the state can do this, given the common neglect of the intangible hand: given the common assumption that the only controls available to government are the invisible hand of effective marketing and the iron hand of tough management.

9. Civility or civic virtue may not be so difficult of achievement as it often seems. It involves not just the internalization of public values and the disciplining of personal desires; given the communitarian nature of freedom as non-domination, it also involves identification with larger groups, even with the polity as a whole, and access to new and satisfying identities.

10. The achievement of widespread civility is equivalent to the achievement of a pattern of widespread personal trust—a pattern, supported by a belief in civility, of confident mutual reliance—and it means the establishment of a flourishing civil society.

11. The belief in the need for civility and trust is consistent with the republican emphasis on the necessity of vigilance. Republican vigilance involves going through the motions of personal distrust, with a view to keeping the authorities on their toes, and is consistent with maintaining a high level of trust.

12. Believing in the need for civility and trust is also consistent with valuing the independency associated with freedom as non-domination; the argument of this chapter is, paradoxically, that it is only when people behave in a manner that goes with widespread personal trust that freedom as non-domination can be achieved on a large scale.

13. Finally, there is no inconsistency in embracing the republican ideas presented here and believing that overtures of personal trust, even overtures that put the trustor at risk, can be positive and desirable initiatives; such acts presuppose the relative non-domination of the parties involved, they often serve further to promote a person's freedom as non-domination, and they can be particularly sensible means to that end, given a recognition of the power of the intangible hand.

BIBLIOGRAPHY

ABRAMSON, JEFFREY (1994), *We, the Jury: The Jury System and the Ideal of Democracy* (New York: Basic Books).

ACKERMAN, BRUCE (1991), *We the People, i: Foundations* (Cambridge, Mass.: Harvard University Press).

ARENDT, HANNAH (1958), *The Human Condition* (Chicago: University of Chicago Press).

—— (1973), *On Revolution* (Harmondsworth: Pelican).

ARROW, KENNETH (1963), *Social Choice and Individual Values*, 2nd edn. New York: Wiley).

ATIYAH, P. S. (1979), *The Rise and Fall of Freedom of Contract* (Oxford: Oxford University Press).

AYRES, IAN, and BRAITHWAITE, JOHN (1992), *Responsive Regulation* (New York: Oxford University Press).

BAIER, ANNETTE (1986), 'Trust and Antitrust', *Ethics*, 96: 231–60.

BAILYN, BERNARD (1965), *The Ideological Origins of the American Revolution* (Cambridge, Mass.: Harvard University Press).

BALDWIN, TOM (1984), 'MacCallum and the Two Concepts of Freedom', *Ratio*, 26: 125–42.

BALL, TERENCE (1993), 'Power', in Goodin and Pettit (1993).

BARDACH, EUGENE, and KAGAN, ROBERT A. (1982), *Going by the Book: The Problem of Regulatory Unreasonableness* (Philadelphia: Temple University Press).

BARON, HANS (1966), *The Crisis of the Early Italian Renaissance*, 2nd edn. (Princeton, NJ: Princeton University Press).

BARRY, BRIAN (1965), *Political Argument* (London: Routledge).

—— (1995), *Justice as Impartiality* (Oxford: Oxford University Press).

BAUMEISTER, ROY F., and LEARY, MARK R. (1995), 'The Need to Belong: Desire for Interpersonal Attachments as a Fundamental Human Motivation', *Psychological Bulletin*, 117: 497–529.

BENTHAM, JEREMY (1843), 'Anarchical Fallacies', in *The Works of Jeremy Bentham*, ii, ed. J. Bowring (Edinburgh: W. Tait).

—— (1871), *Theory of Legislation*, 2nd edn. (London: Truebner).

BERLIN, ISAIAH (1958), *Two Concepts of Liberty* (Oxford: Oxford University Press).

BERMAN, HAROLD J. (1983), *Law and Revolution* (Cambridge, Mass.: Harvard University Press).

—— (1994), 'The Origins of Historical Jurisprudence: Coke, Selden, Hale', *Yale Law Journal*, 103: 1651–738.

BLACKSTONE, WILLIAM (1978), *Commentaries on the Laws of England*, 9th edn. (New York: Garland, facsimile of 1783 edn.).

BLAU, PETER (1964), *Exchange and Power in Social Life* (New York: Wiley).

BLOM, HANS W. (1995), *Causality and Morality in Politics: The Rise of Naturalism in Dutch Seventeenth-Century Political Thought* (The Hague: CIP-Gegevens Koninklijke Bibliotheek).

BOCK, G., SKINNER, Q., and VIROLI, M. (eds.) (1990), *Machiavelli and Republicanism* (Cambridge: Cambridge University Press).

BOSWELL, JAMES (1970), *Journal of a Trip to the Hebrides with Samuel Johnson*, (ed.) R. W. Chapman (Oxford: Oxford University Press).

BRADSHAW, BRENDAN (1991), 'Transalpine humanism' in J. H. Burns and M. Goldie (eds.), *The Cambridge History of Political Thought* (Cambridge: Cambridge University Press).

BRAITHWAITE, JOHN (1989), *Crime, Shame and Reintegration* (Cambridge: Cambridge University Press).

—— (1993), 'Shame and Modernity', *British Journal of Criminology*, 33: 1–18.

—— and PETTIT, PHILIP (1990), *Not Just Deserts: A Republican Theory of Criminal Justice* (Oxford: Oxford University Press).

BRAITHWAITE, VALERIE (forthcoming). 'Games of Engagement: Postures within the Regulatory Committee', *Law and Policy*.

BRATMAN, MICHAEL E. (1987), *Intentions and Plans, and Practical Reason* (Cambridge, Mass.: Harvard University Press).

BREHM, SHARON S., and BREHM, JACK W. (1981), *Psychological Reactance: A Theory of Freedom and Control* (New York: Academic Press).

BRENNAN, GEOFFREY (1996), 'Selection and the Currency of Reward', in R. E. Goodin (ed.), *The Theory of Institutional Design* (Cambridge: Cambridge University Press).

—— and BUCHANAN, JAMES (1981), 'The Normative Purpose of Economic "Science": Rediscovery of an Eighteenth Century Method', *International Review of Law and Economics*, 1: 155–66.

—— and LOMASKY, LOREN (1993), *Democracy and Decision: The Pure Theory of Electoral Preference* (Oxford: Oxford University Press).

—— and PETTIT, PHILIP (1990), 'Unveiling the Vote', *British Journal of Political Science*, 20: 311–33.

—— —— (1993), 'Hands Invisible and Intangible', *Synthèse*, 94: 191–225.

BRIEN, ANDREW (forthcoming), 'Regulating Virtue', *Business and Professional Ethics Journal*, 16.

BUCHANAN, JAMES (1975), *The Limits of Liberty* (Chicago: Chicago University Press).

BURNS, J. H., with GOLDIE, MARK (eds.) (1991), *The Cambridge History of Political Thought 1450-1700* (Cambridge: Cambridge University Press).

BURTT, SHELLEY (1993), 'The Politics of Virtue Today: A Critique and a Proposal', *American Political Science Review*, 87: 360–8.

CAMPBELL, T. D. (1996), *The Legal Theory of Ethical Positivism* (Brookfields, Vt.: Dartmouth).

CAPLOW, THEODORE (1994), *Perverse Incentives: The Neglect of Social Technology in the Public Sector* (Westport, Conn.: Praeger).

CLEGG, STEWART (1989), *Frameworks of Power* (London: Sage).

COADY, C. A. (1993), 'Dirty Hands,' in Goodin and Pettit (1993).

COHEN, G. A. (1993), 'Equality of What? On Welfare, Goods, and Capabilities', in Nussbaum and Sen (1993).

COHEN, JOSHUA (1986), 'An Epistemic Conception of Democracy', *Ethics*, 97: 26–38.

—— (1989), 'Deliberation and Democratic Legitimacy', in Hamlin and Pettit (1989).

COHEN, MORRIS (1933), 'The Basis of Contract', *Harvard Law Review*, 4: 553–92.

COLEMAN, JAMES (1974), *Power and the Structure of Society* (New York: Norton).

—— (1990), *The Foundations of Social Theory* (Cambridge, Mass.: Harvard University Press).

COLEMAN, JULES, and FEREJOHN, JOHN (1986), 'Democracy and Social Choice', *Ethics*, 97: 6–25.

COLISH, MARCIA L. (1971), 'The Idea of Liberty in Machiavelli', *Journal of the History of Ideas*, 32: 323–50.

CONNOLLY, WILLIAM (1983), *The Terms of Political Discourse*, 2nd edn. (Princeton, NJ: Princeton University Press).

CONSTANT, BENJAMIN (1988), *Political Writings*, (ed.) B. Fontana, (Cambridge: Cambridge University Press).

CORNISH, W. R., and CLARK, G. DE N. (1989), *Law and Society in England 1750–1950* (London: Sweet and Maxwell).

CRAWFORD, MICHAEL (1993), *The Roman Republic*, 2nd edn. (Cambridge, Mass.: Harvard University Press).

D'AGOSTINO, FRED (1996), *Free Public Reason: Making it Up As We Go* (New York: Oxford University Press).

DAHL, ROBERT (1956), *A Preface to Democratic Theory* (Chicago: University of Chicago Press).

DICEY, A. V. (1960), *An Introduction to the Law of the Constitution*, (ed.) E. C. S. Wade, 10th edn. (London: Macmillan).

DWORKIN, GERALD (1988), *The Theory and Practice of Autonomy* (Cambridge: Cambridge University Press).

DWORKIN, RONALD (1978), *Taking Rights Seriously* (London: Duckworth).

ELKIN, STEPHEN L. (1987), *City and Regime in the American Republic* (Chicago: Chicago University Press).

ELSTER, JON (1983), *Sour Grapes* (Cambridge: Cambridge University Press).

—— (1986), 'The Market and the Forum: Three Varieties of Political Theory', in J. Elster and A. Hilland (eds.), *Foundations of Social Choice Theory* (Cambridge: Cambridge University Press).

ELY, J. H. (1981), *Democracy and Distrust: A Theory of Judicial Review* (Cambridge, Mass.: Harvard University Press).

EVANS, CALEB (1775), *British Constitutional Liberty. A Sermon Preached in Broad-mead, Bristol, Nov 5 1775* (Bristol).

FEINBERG, JOEL (1972), *Social Philosophy* (Englewood Cliffs, NJ: Prentice-Hall).
—— (1986), *Harm to Others*, i (Oxford: Oxford University Press).
FERGUSON, ADAM (1767), *An Essay on the History of Civil Society* (Edinburgh: Millar and Caddel; repr. New York: Garland, 1971).
FERRY, LUC, and RENAUT, ALAIN (1985), *Philosophie politique: des droits de l'homme a l'idee republicaine* (Paris: Presses Universitaires Françaises).
FILMER, SIR ROBERT (1991), *Patriarcha and Other Writings*, (ed.) J. P. Sommerville (Cambridge: Cambridge University Press).
FINK, Z. S. (1962), *The Classical Republicans: An Essay in the Recovery of a Pattern of Thought in Seventeenth Century England*, 2nd edn. (Evanston, Ill.: Northwestern University Press).
FINLEY, MOSES (1973), 'The Freedom of the Citizen in the Greek World', in M. Finley (ed.), *Democracy: Ancient and Modern* (London: Chatto and Windus).
FINN, PAUL (1993), *Abuse of Official Trust: Conflict of Interest and Related Matters*, Second Report on Integrity in Government (Research School of Social Sciences, Australian National University).
FISHKIN, JAMES (1991), *Democracy and Deliberation: New Directions for Democratic Reform* (New Haven, Conn.: Yale University Press).
—— (1995), 'Bringing Deliberation to Democracy: The British Experiment', *The Good Society*, 5/3: 45–9.
FONER, ERIC (1970), *Free Soil, Free Labor, Free Men: The Ideology of the Republican Party Before the Civil War* (Oxford: Oxford University Press).
FONTANA, BIANCAMARIA (ed.) (1994), *The Invention of the Modern Republic* (Cambridge: Cambridge University Press).
FRASER, NANCY (1992), 'Rethinking the Public Sphere', in Craig Calhoun (ed.), *Habermas and the Public Sphere* (Cambridge, Mass.: MIT Press).
—— and GORDON, LINDA (1994), 'A Genealogy of *Dependency*: Tracing a Keyword of the U.S. Welfare State', *Journal of Women in Culture and Society*, 19: 309–36.
FULLER, L. L. (1971), *The Morality of Law* (New Haven, Conn.: Yale University Press).
FUSTEL DE COULANGES, N. D. (1920), *La Cité antique: étude sur le culte, le droit, les institutions de la Grèce et de Rome* (Paris: Hachette).
GAMBETTA, DIEGO (1988), 'Mafia: the Price of Distrust', in Gambetta (ed.), *Trust: Making and Breaking Cooperative Relations* (Oxford: Blackwell).
GAUS, G. F. (1983), *The Modern Liberal Theory of Man* (London: Croom Helm).
—— (1990), *Value and Justification: The Foundations of Liberal Theory* (New York: Cambridge University Press).
GAUTHIER, DAVID (1986), *Morals by Agreement* (Oxford: Oxford University Press).
GELLNER, ERNEST (1994), *Conditions of Liberty: Civil Society and Its Rivals* (London: Hamish Hamilton).

GEUSS, RAYMOND (1981), *The Idea of Critical Theory* (Cambridge: Cambridge University Press).

GOODIN, ROBERT (1984), *Protecting the Vulnerable* (Chicago: University of Chicago Press).

GOODIN, R. E. (1992*a*), *Motivating Political Morality* (Cambridge, Mass.: Blackwell).

—— (1992*b*), *Green Political Theory* (Oxford: Polity).

—— and PETTIT, P. (eds.) (1993), *A Companion to Contemporary Political Philosophy* (Oxford: Blackwell).

GRABOSKY, PETER N. (1995), 'Counterproductive Regulation', *International Journal of the Sociology of Law*, 23: 347–69.

GRAY, JOHN (1986), *Hayek on Liberty*, 2nd edn. (Oxford: Oxford University Press).

GUARINI, E. F. (1990), 'Machiavelli and the Crisis of the Italian Republics', in Bock *et al.* (1990).

GWYN, WILLIAM B. (1965), *The Meaning of the Separation of Powers* (The Hague: Nijhoff).

HAAKONSSEN, KNUD (1991), 'From Natural Law to the Rights of Man: A European Perspective on American Debates', in Lacey and Haakonssen (1991).

—— (1994), 'Introduction', in Hume (1994).

—— (1995), *Moral Philosophy and Natural Law: From Hugo Grotious to the Scottish Enlightenment* (Cambridge: Cambridge University Press).

HABERMAS, JUERGEN (1989), *Habermas on Society and Politics: A Reader*, (ed.) S. Seidman (Boston: Beacon Press).

—— (1990), *Moral Consciousness and Communicative Action*, tr. C. Lenhardt and S. W. Nicolsen (Cambridge: Polity).

—— (1994), 'Three Normative Models of Democracy', *Constellations*, 1: 1–10.

—— (1995), *Between Facts and Norms: Contributions to a Discourse Theory of Law and Democracy*, tr. W. Rehg (Cambridge, Mass.: MIT Press).

HAMLIN, ALAN, and PETTIT, PHILIP (eds.) (1989), *The Good Polity* (Oxford: Blackwell).

HARDIN, RUSSELL (1992), 'The Street-Level Epistemology of Trust', *Politics and Society*, 21: 505–29

HARRINGTON, JAMES (1992), *The Commonwealth of Oceana and A System of Politics*, (ed.) J. G. A. Pocock (Cambridge: Cambridge University Press).

HART, H. L. A. (1982), *Essays on Bentham* (Oxford: Oxford University Press).

HAYEK, F. A. (1978), *New Studies in Philosophy, Politics, Economics and the History of Ideas* (London: Routledge).

—— (1988), *The Fatal Conceit: The Errors of Socialism*, (ed.) W. W. Bartley III (Chicago: University of Chicago Press).

HEY, RICHARD (1776), *Observations on the Nature of Civil Liberty and the Principles of Government* (London).

HILL, BRIDGET (1986), *The First English Feminist: Reflections upon Marriage and other writings by Mary Astell* (Aldershot: Gower).

HINDESS, BARRY (1996), *Discourses of Power* (Oxford: Blackwell).

HIRSCHMAN, ALBERT O. (1977), *The Passions and the Interests: Political Arguments for Capitalism before Its Triumph* (Princeton, NJ: Princeton University Press).

—— (1984), 'Against Parsimony: Three Ways of Complicating Some Categories of Economic Discourse', *American Economic Review Proceedings*, 74: 88–96.

HOBBES, THOMAS (1968), *Leviathan*, (ed.) C. B. MacPherson (Harmondsworth: Penguin).

HOLMES, STEPHEN (1988), 'Gag Rules or the Politics of Omission', in J. Elster and R. Slagstad (eds.), *Constitutionalism and Democracy* (Cambridge: Cambridge University Press).

—— (1989), 'The Permanent Structure of Antiliberal Thought', in Rosenblum (1989).

—— (1995), *Passions and Constraint: On the Theory of Liberal Democracy* (Chicago: University of Chicago Press).

HOMANS, GEORGE (1961), *Social Behavior: Its Elementary Forms* (New York: Harcourt, Brace, & World).

HOROWITZ, MORTON J. (1977), *The Transformation of American Law 1780-1860* (Cambridge, Mass.: Harvard University Press).

HUME, DAVID (1994), *Political Essays*, (ed.) K. Haakonssen (Cambridge: Cambridge University Press).

HUTTON, WILL (1995), *The State We're In* (London: Cape).

INGRAM, ATTRACTA (1994), *A Political Theory of Rights* (Oxford: Oxford University Press).

JACKSON, FRANK, and PETTIT, PHILIP (1995), 'Moral Functionalism and Moral Motivation', *Philosophical Quarterly*, 45: 20–40.

JAMES, SUSAN (1992), 'The Good-enough citizen: Citizenship and Independence', in Gisela Bock and Susan James (eds.), *Beyond Equality and Difference: Citizenship, Feminist Politics and Female Subjectivity* (London: Routledge).

KARSTEDT-HENKE, SUSANNE (1991), 'Risks of Being Detected, Chances of Getting Away', in J. Junger-Tas, L. Boedermaker, and P. van der Laan (eds.), *The Future of the Juvenile Justice System* (Leuven: Acco).

KELLY, DONALD R. (1991), 'Law', in Burns and Goldie (1991).

KELMAN, H. C. (1958), 'Compliance, Identification and Internalization: Three Processes of Attitude Change', *Journal of Conflict Resolution*, 2: 51–60.

KELMAN, MARK (1987), *A Guide to Critical Legal Studies* (Cambridge, Mass.: Harvard University Press).

KINDER, D. R., and KIEWIET, D. R. (1979), 'Economic Discontent and Political Behavior: The Role of Personal Grievances and Collective Economic Judgements in Congressional Voting', *American Journal of Political Science*, 23: 495–527.

—— —— (1981), 'Sociotropic Politics: The American Case', *British Journal of Political Science*, 11: 129–61.

KORSGAARD, CHRISTINE (1993), 'Commentary on Cohen and Sen', in Nussbaum and Sen (1993).

KRIEGEL, BLANDINE (1995), *The State and the Rule of Law*, tr. M. A. LePain and J. C. Cohen (Princeton, NJ: Princeton University Press).

KRYGIER, MARTIN (1990), 'Marxism and the Rule of Law: Reflections After the Collapse of Communism', *Law and Social Inquiry*, 15: 633–63.

KUKATHAS, CHANDRAN (1989), *Hayek and Modern Liberalism* (Oxford: Oxford University Press).

KUMAR, KRISHAN (1993), 'Civil Society: An Inquiry into the Usefulness of an Historical Term', *British Journal of Sociology*, 44: 375–95.

KYMLICKA, WILL (1995), *Multicultural Citizenship* (Oxford: Oxford University Press).

LACEY, M. J., and HAAKONSSEN, KNUD (eds.) (1991), *A Culture of Rights: The Bill of Rights in Philosophy, Politics and Law, 1791 and 1991* (Cambridge: Cambridge University Press).

LARMORE, CHARLES (1987), *Patterns of Moral Complexity* (New York: Cambridge University Press).

—— (1993), *Modernité et morale* (Paris: Presses Universitaires de France).

LE GRAND, JULIAN (1996), 'Knights, Knaves or Pawns? Human Behaviour and Social Policy', *Journal of Social Policy*, 26.

LEVIN, MICHAEL (1984), 'Negative Liberty', *Social Philosophy and Policy*, 2: 84–100.

LEWIS, DAVID (1969), *Convention* (Cambridge, Mass: Harvard University Press).

—— (1983), *Philosophical Papers*, i (Oxford: Oxford University Press).

LIND, E. ALLEN, and TYLER TOM R. (1988), *The Social Psychology of Procedural Justice* (New York: Plenum).

LIND, JOHN (1776), *Three Letters to Dr Price* (London: T. Payne).

LOCKE, JOHN (1965), *Two Treatises of Government*, (ed.) Peter Laslett (New York: Mentor).

—— (1975), *An Essay Concerning Human Understanding*, (ed.) P. H. Nidditch (Oxford: Oxford University Press).

LONG, DOUGLAS C. (1977), *Bentham on Liberty* (Toronto: University of Toronto Press).

LUKES, STEVEN (1974), *Power: A Radical View* (London: Macmillan).

—— (1992), 'Power' in L. C. Becker and C. B. Becker (eds.), *Encyclopedia of Ethics* (New York: Garland).

LYONS, DAVID (1982), 'Utility and Rights', *Nomos*, 24: 107–38.

MACCALLUM, GERALD C. (1967), 'Negative and Positive Freedom', *Philosophical Review*, 74: 312–34.

MCCLOSKEY, H. J. (1963), 'A Note on Utilitarian Punishment', *Mind*, 72: 599.

MCCUBBINS, M. D., and SCHWARTZ, T. (1984), 'Congressional Oversight Overlooked: Police Patrols vs Fire Alarms', *American Journal of Political Science*, 28: 165–79.

MACDONAGH, OLIVER (1958), 'The 19th Century Revolution in Government: A Reappraisal', *Historical Journal*, 1: 52–67.

—— (1980), 'Pre-transformations: Victorian Britain', in E. Kamenka and A. Erh-Soon Tay (eds.), *Law and Social Control* (London: Edward Arnold).

MACHAN, TIBOR R., and RASMUSSEN, DOUGLAS R. (1995), *Liberty for the 21st Century: Contemporary Libertarian Thought* (Lanham, Md.: Rowman and Littlefield).

MACHIAVELLI, NICCOLÒ 1965), *The Complete Works and Others*, tr. Allan Gilbert (3 vols., Durham, NC: Duke University Press).

MACINTYRE, ALASDAIR (1987), *After Virtue*, 2nd edn. (London: Duckworth).

—— (1994), 'A Partial Response to My Critics', in John Horton and Susan Mendus (eds.), *After MacIntyre* (Cambridge: Polity).

MCLEAN, IAIN (1987), *Public Choice: An Introduction* (Oxford: Blackwell).

MADISON, JAMES, HAMILTON, ALEXANDER, and JAY, JOHN (1987), *The Federalist Papers*, (ed.) Isaac Kramnik (Harmondsworth: Penguin).

MAITLAND, F. W. (1981), 'A Historical Sketch of Liberty and Equality', in *Collected Papers*, i, (ed.) H. A. L. Fisher (Buffalo, NY: W. S. Hein).

MAJONE, GIANDOMENICO (1996), 'Regulatory Legitimacy', in Majone (ed.), *Regulating Europe* (London: Routledge).

MANDEVILLE, BERNARD (1731), *Free Thoughts on Religion, the Church and National Happiness*, 3rd edn. (London).

—— (1924), *The Fable of the Bees, or Private Vices, Public Benefits*, (ed.) F. B. Kaye (Oxford: Oxford University Press).

MANENT, PIERRE (1987), *Histoire intellectuelle du libéralisme: dix leçons* (Paris: Calmann-Lévy).

MANIN, BERNARD (1994), 'Checks, Balances and Boundaries: The Separation of Powers in the Constitutional Debate of 1787', in Fontana (1994).

MANSBRIDGE, JANE, and OKIN, SUSAN MOLLER (1993), 'Feminism', in Goodin and Pettit (1993).

MARX, KARL (1970), *Capital: A Critique of Political Economy*, i, tr. from the 3rd German edn. (London: Lawrence and Wishart).

MEYERSON, DENISE (1991), *False Consciousness* (Oxford: Oxford University Press).

MICHELMAN, FRANK (1986) 'The Supreme Court 1985 Term', *Harvard Law Review*, 100: 4–77.

MILL, J. S (1969), *Essays on Ethics, Religion and Society*, vol. x of *Collected Works* (London: Routledge).

—— (1970), 'The Subjection of Women', in A. S. Rossi (ed.), *Essays on Sex Equality* (Chicago: University of Chicago Press).

—— (1977), *Essays on Politics and Society*, vol. xviii of *Collected Works*, (London: Routledge).

MILLER, DAVID (1990), *Market, State and Community* (Oxford: Oxford University Press).

—— (1995), *On Nationality* (Oxford: Oxford University Press).

MONTESQUIEU, CHARLES DE SECONDAT (1989), *The Spirit of the Laws*, tr. and (ed.) A. M. Cohler, B. C. Miller, and H. S. Stone (Cambridge: Cambridge University Press).

MORANGE, JEAN (1979), *Les Libertés politiques* (Paris: Presses Universitaires de France).

NICOLET, CLAUDE (1982), *L'Idée républicaine en France (1789–1924)* (Paris: Gallimard).

NIPPEL, WILFRIED (1994), 'Ancient and Modern Republicanism', in Fontana (1994).

NOZICK, ROBERT (1974), *Anarchy, State, and Utopia* (New York: Basic Books).

NUSSBAUM, MARTHA C., and SEN, AMARTYA (eds.) (1993), *The Quality of Life* (Oxford: Oxford University Press).

OLDFIELD, ADRIAN (1990), *Citizenship and Community: Civic Republicanism and the Modern World* (London: Routledge).

O'LEARY-HAWTHORNE, JOHN, and PETTIT PHILIP (1996), 'Strategies for Free-Will Compatibilists', *Analysis*, 56: 191–201.

PAGDEN, ANTHONY (ed.) (1987), *The Languages of Political Theory in Early Modern Europe* (Cambridge: Cambridge University Press).

PAINE, TOM (1989), *Political Writings*, (ed.) Bruce Kuklick (Cambridge: Cambridge University Press).

PALEY, WILLIAM (1825), *The Principles of Moral and Political Philosophy*, vol. iv of *Collected Works* (London: C. and J. Rivington).

PARFIT, DEREK (1984), *Reasons and Persons* (Oxford: Oxford University Press).

PASQUINO, PASQUALE (1994), 'The Constitutional Republicanism of Emmanuel Sieyes', in Fontana (1994).

—— (1996). 'Popular Sovereignty: What Does It Mean?', mimeo, CREA, École Polytechnique, Paris.

—— (forthcoming), 'Political Theory, Order and Threat', *Nomos*.

PASSMORE, JOHN (1993), 'Environmentalism', in Goodin and Pettit (1993).

PATEMAN, CAROLE (1988), *The Sexual Contract* (Oxford: Polity Press).

PATTEN, ALAN (1996), 'The Republican Critique of Liberalism', *British Journal of Political Science*, 26: 25–44.

PATERSON, A. B. (1921), *The Collected Verse of A. B. Paterson* (Sydney: Angus and Robertson).

PATTERSON, ORLANDO (1991), *Freedom in the Making of Western Culture* (New York: Basic Books).

PATTON, PAUL (1994), 'Metamorpho-logic: Bodies and Powers in *A Thousand Plateaus*', *Journal of the British Society for Phenomenology*, 25: 157–69.

PETTIT, PHILIP (1982), 'Habermas on Truth and Justice', in G. H. R. Parkinson (ed.), *Marx and Marxisms* (Cambridge: Cambridge University Press).

—— (1986), 'Free Riding and Foul Dealing', *Journal of Philosophy*, 83: 361–79.

—— (1989*a*), 'The Freedom of the City: A Republican Ideal', in Hamlin and Pettit (1989).

—— (1989*b*), 'A Definition of Negative Liberty', *Ratio*, n.s. 2: 153–68.

—— (1990), '*Virtus Normativa*: A Rational Choice Perspective', *Ethics*, 100: 725–55.

—— (1991), 'Consequentialism', in P. Singer (ed.), *A Companion to Ethics* (Oxford: Blackwell).

—— (1992), 'Instituting a Research Ethic: Chilling and Cautionary Tales', *Bioethics*, 6: 89–112.

—— (1993*a*), *The Common Mind: An Essay on Psychology, Society and Politics* (New York: Oxford University Press).

—— (1993*b*), 'Negative Liberty, Liberal and Republican', *European Journal of Philosophy*, 1: 15–38.

—— (1993*c*), 'Liberalism and Republicanism', *Australasian Journal of Political Science*, 28 (special issue on Australia's Republican Question): 162–89.

—— (1994*a*), Review of John Rawls, *Political Liberalism*, *Journal of Philosophy*, 91: 215–20.

—— (1994*b*), 'The Enfranchisement of Silence: An Argument for Freedom of Speech', in Tom Campbell and Wojciech Sadurksi (eds.), *Freedom of Communication* (Aldershot: Dartmouth).

—— (1994*c*), 'Liberal/Communitarian: MacIntyre's Mesmeric Dichotomy', in John Horton and Susan Mendus (eds.), *After MacIntyre: Critical Perspectives on the Work of Alasdair MacIntyre* (Cambridge: Polity Press).

—— (1995*a*), 'The Cunning of Trust', *Philosophy and Public Affairs*, 24: 202–25.

—— (1995*b*), 'The Economic Mind: *Homo Economicus* as Virtual Reality', *Monist*, 78: 308–29.

—— (1996*a*), 'Freedom as Antipower', *Ethics*, 106: 576–604.

—— (1996*b*), 'Institutional Design and Rational Choice', in R. E. Goodin (ed.), *The Theory of Institutional Design* (Cambridge: Cambridge University Press).

—— (1996*c*). 'Our Republican Heritage', *Eureka Street*, 6/6.

—— (1997), 'The Consequentialist Perspective on Ethics', in Marcia Baron, Philip Pettit, and Michael Slote, *Consequentialism, Kantianism, Virtue Ethics* (Oxford: Blackwell).

—— (forthcoming), 'Republican Theory and Criminal Punishment', *Utilitas*.

—— and SMITH, MICHAEL (1990), 'Backgrounding Desire', *Philosophical Review*, 99: 565–92.

—— —— (1996), 'Freedom in Thought and Action', *Journal of Philosophy*, 93.

—— with BRAITHWAITE, JOHN (1993), 'Not Just Deserts, Even in Sentencing', *Current Issues in Criminal Justice*, 4: 225–39.

—— —— (1994), 'The Three Rs of Republican Sentencing', *Current Issues in Criminal Justice*, 5: 318–25.

PHILLIPS, ANNE (1995), *The Politics of Presence* (Oxford: Oxford University Press).

PHILP, MARK (1985), 'Power', in A. Kuper and J. Kuper (eds.), *Encyclopedia of the Social Sciences* (London: Routledge).

—— (1996), 'Republicanism and Liberalism: On Leadership and Political Order', *Democratization*, 3.

PITKIN, HANNA (1988), 'Are Freedom and Liberty Twins?' *Political Theory*, 16: 523–52.

POCOCK, J. G. A. (1975), *The Machiavellian Moment: Florentine Political Theory and the Atlantic Republican Tradition* (Princeton, NJ: Princeton University Press).

—— (ed.), (1977) *The Political Works of James Harrington* (Cambridge: Cambridge University Press).

—— (1987), *The Ancient Constitution and the Feudal Law: A Reissue* (Cambridge: Cambridge University Press).

POSTEMA, GERALD (1995), 'Public Practical Reason: An Archaeology', *Social Philosophy and Policy*, 12: 43–86.

PRICE, RICHARD (1991), *Political Writings*, (ed.) D. O. Thomas (Cambridge: Cambridge University Press).

PRIESTLEY, JOSEPH (1993), *Political Writings*, (ed.) P. N. Miller (Cambridge: Cambridge University Press).

PUTNAM, ROBERT D. (1993), *Making Democracy Work: Civic Traditions in Modern Italy* (Princeton, NJ: Princeton University Press).

RAAB, FELIX (1965), *The English Face of Machiavelli: A Changing Interpretation 1500-1700* (London: Routledge).

RAHE, PAUL ANTHONY (1992), *Republics, Ancient and Modern: Classical Republicanism and the American Revolution* (Chicago: University of Chicago Press).

RANSOM, R. L., and SUTCH, RICHARD (1977), *One Kind of Freedom* (Cambridge: Cambridge University Press).

RAZ, JOSEPH (1986), *The Morality of Freedom* (Oxford: Oxford University Press).

RAWLS, JOHN (1971), *A Theory of Justice* (Oxford: Oxford University Press).

—— (1993), *Political Liberalism* (New York: Columbia University Press).

REID, JOHN PHILLIP (1988), *The Concept of Liberty in the Age of the American Revolution* (Chicago: Chicago University Press).

RIALS, STEPHANE (1983), *Textes politiques français* (Paris: Presses Universitaires de France).

RIKER, WILLIAM (1982), *Liberalism Against Populism* (San Francisco: W. H. Freeman).

ROBBINS, CAROLINE (1959), *The Eighteenth Century Commonwealthman* (Cambridge, Mass.: Harvard University Press).

ROSENBLUM, NANCY L. (ed.) (1989), *Liberalism and the Moral Life* (Cambridge, Mass.: Harvard University Press).

RUBENSTEIN, NICOLAI (1991), 'Italian Political Thought 1450–1530', in Burns and Goldie (1991).

RYAN, ALAN (1993), 'Liberalism', in Goodin and Pettit (1993).

SANDEL, MICHAEL (1984), *Liberalism and Its Critics* (Oxford: Blackwell).

SCANLON, T. M. (1982), 'Contractualism and Utilitarianism', in A. Sen and B. Williams (eds.), *Utilitarianism and Beyond* (Cambridge: Cambridge University Press).

SCHAUER, FREDERICK (1991), *Playing by the Rules* (Oxford: Oxford University Press).

SELZNICK, PHILIP (1992), *The Moral Commonwealth: Social Theory and the Promise of Community* (Berkeley, Calif.: University of California Press).

SEN, AMARTYA (1983), 'Poor, Relatively Speaking', *Oxford Economic Papers*, 35: 153–68.

—— (1985), *Commodities and Capabilities* (Amsterdam: North-Holland).

SHAPIRO, IAN (1990), *Political Criticism* (Berkeley, Calif.: University of California Press).

SHKLAR, JUDITH (1989), 'The Liberalism of Fear', in Rosenblum (1989).

SKINNER, QUENTIN (1974), 'The Principles and Practice of Opposition: The Case of Bolingbroke versus Walpole', in Neil McKendrick (ed.), *Historical Perspectives: Studies in English Thought and Society in Honour of J. H. Plumb* (London: Europa).

—— (1978), *The Foundations of Modern Political Thought* (2 vols., Cambridge: Cambridge University Press).

—— (1983), 'Machiavelli on the Maintenance of Liberty', *Politics*, 18: 3–15.

—— (1984), 'The Idea of Negative Liberty', in R. Rorty, J. B. Schneewind, and Q. Skinner (eds.), *Philosophy in History* (Cambridge: Cambridge University Press (1984).

—— (1990*a*), 'Thomas Hobbes on the Proper Signification of Liberty', *Transactions of the Royal Historical Society*, 40: 121–51.

—— (1990*b*), 'Pre-Humanist Origins of Republican Ideas', Bock *et al.* (1990).

—— (1996), *Reason and Rhetoric in the Philosophy of Hobbes* (Cambridge: Cambridge University Press).

SMITH, ADAM (1976), *An Inquiry into the Nature and Causes of the Wealth of Nations*, (ed.) R. H. Campbell, A. S. Skinner, and W. B. Todd (Oxford: Oxford University Press).

—— (1982), *The Theory of the Moral Sentiments*, (ed.) D. D. Raphael and A. L. McFie (Indianapolis: Liberty Classics).

SPINOZA, BENEDICT DE (1951), *A Theologico-Political Treatise and A Political Treatise*, tr. R. H. M. Elwes (New York: Dover).

SPITZ, JEAN-FABIEN (1994), 'The Concept of Liberty in "A Theory of Justice" and Its Republican Version', *Ratio Juris*, 7: 331–47.

—— (1995*a*), *La Liberté politique* (Paris: Presses Universitaires de France).

—— (1995*b*), 'Le Républicainisme, une troisième voie entre libéralisme et communautarianisme', *Le Banquet*, 7/2: 215–38.

SPRINGBORG, PATRICIA (1995), 'Mary Astell (1666-1731), Critic of Locke', *American Political Science Review*, 89: 621–33.

STIGLER, GEORGE (1971), 'The Theory of Economic Regulation', *Bell Journal of Economics and Management Science*, 2: 3–21.

STOLJAR, S. J. (1975), *A History of Contract at Common Law* (Canberra: Australian National University Press).

SUGDEN, ROBERT (1996), 'The Metric of Opportunity', mimeo, Faculty of Social Sciences, University of East Anglia, Norwich.

SUNSTEIN, CASS R. (1990*a*), *After the Rights Revolution: Reconceiving the Regulatory State* (Cambridge, Mass.: Harvard University Press).

—— (1990*b*), 'Paradoxes of the Regulatory State', *University of Chicago Law Review*, 57: 407–41.

—— (1993*a*), *The Partial Constitution* (Cambridge, Mass.: Harvard University Press).

—— (1993*b*), *Democracy and the Problem of Free Speech* (New York: Free Press).

—— (1993*c*), 'The Enduring Legacy of Republicanism', in S. E. Elkin and K. E. Soltan (eds.), *A New Constitutionalism: Designing Political Institutions for a Good Society* (Chicago: University of Chicago Press).

SWANTON, CHRISTINE (1992), *Freedom: A Coherence Theory* (Indianapolis: Hackett).

SYDNEY, ALGERNON (1990), *Discourses Concerning Government*, (ed.) T. G. West (Indianapolis: Liberty Classics).

—— (1996), *Court Maxims*, (ed.) H. W. Blom, E. H. Muller, and Ronald Janse (Cambridge: Cambridge University Press).

SYLVAN, RICHARD (1984–5), 'A Critique of Deep Ecology', *Radical Philosophy*, 40: 2–12; 41: 10–22.

TAYLOR, CHARLES (1985), *Philosophy and the Human Sciences* (Cambridge: Cambridge University Press).

—— (1989), 'Cross-Purposes: The Liberal–Communitarian Debate', in Rosenblum (1989).

—— (1995), *Philosophical Arguments* (Cambridge, Mass.: Harvard University Press).

TAYLOR, MICHAEL (1987), *The Possibility of Cooperation* (Cambridge: Cambridge University Press).

TEN, C. L. (1993), 'Constitutionalism and the Rule of Law', in Goodin and Pettit (1993).

THOMPSON, E. P. (1975), *Whigs and Hunters: The Origin of the Black Act* (London: Allen Lane).

THOMPSON, WILLIAM (1970), *Appeal of One Half of the Human Race, Women, Against the Pretensions of the Other Half, Men, to Retain Them in Political, and Thence in Civil and Domestic, Slavery* (New York: Source Book Press).

TOENNIES, F. (1887), *Community and Society* (New York: Harper and Row).

TRENCHARD, JOHN, and GORDON, THOMAS (1971), *Cato's Letters*, 6th edn. (1755) (New York: Da Capo).

TRUMAN, D. (1951), *The Governmental Process* (New York: Knopf).

TUCK, RICHARD (1979), *Natural Rights Theories: Their Origin and Development* (Cambridge: Cambridge University Press).

—— (1989), *Hobbes* (Oxford: Oxford University Press).

—— (1993), *Philosophy and Government 1572–1651* (Oxford: Oxford University Press).

TUCKER, ABRAHAM (1834), *The Light of Nature Pursued*, (ed.) John Mildman (2 vols., London: T. Tegg and Son).

TULLY, JAMES (1993), 'Placing the Two Treatises', in Nicholas Phillipson and Quentin Skinner (eds.), *Political Discourse in Early Modern Britain* (Cambridge: Cambridge University Press).

TURNER, J. C. (1987), *Rediscovering the Social Group: A Self-categorization Theory* (Oxford: Blackwell).

TYLER, TOM R. (1990), *Why People Obey the Law* (New Haven, Conn.: Yale University Press).

—— (1992), 'A Relational Model of Authority in Groups', *Advances in Experimental Social Psychology*, 25: 115–91.

—— and MITCHELL, G. (1994), 'Legitimacy and the Empowerment of Discretionary Legal Authority: The United States Supreme Court and Abortion Rights', *Duke Law Journal*, 43: 703–815.

VAN PARIJS, PHILIPPE (1995), *Real Freedom for All* (Oxford: Oxford University Press).

VILE, M. J. C. (1967), *Constitutionalism and the Separation of Powers* (Oxford: Oxford University Press).

VIROLI, MAURIZIO (1990), 'Machiavelli and the Republican Idea of Politics', Bock *et al.* (1990).

—— (1992), *From Politics to Reason of State: The Acquisition and Transformation of the Language of Politics 1250–1600* (Cambridge: Cambridge University Press).

—— (1995), *For Love of Country* (Oxford: Oxford University Press).

WALDRON, JEREMY (1989), 'The Rule of Law in Contemporary Liberal Theory', *Ratio Juris*, 2: 79–96.

—— (1993), *Liberal Rights: Collected Papers 1981–91* (Cambridge: Cambridge University Press).

WARTENBERG, THOMAS E. (1990), *The Forms of Power: From Domination to Transformation* (Philadelphia: Temple University Press).

WEBER, MAX (1978), *Economy and Society*, (ed.) G. Roth and C. Wittich (Berkeley, Calif.: University of California Press).

WEINSTEIN, W. L. (1965), 'The Concept of Liberty in Nineteenth-Century Political Thought', *Political Studies*, 13: 156–7.

WEINTRAUB, JEFF (1988), *Freedom and Community: The Republican Virtue Tradition and the Sociology of Liberty* (MS).

WEST, DAVID (1990), *Authenticity and Empowerment* (Brighton: Harvester).

WHITE, MORTON (1987), *Philosophy, The Federalist, and the Constitution* (New York: Oxford University Press).

WINCH, DONALD (1978), *Adam Smith's Politics: An Essay in Historiographic Revision* (Cambridge: Cambridge University Press).

WIRSZUBSKI, C. (1968), *Libertas as a Political Idea at Rome* (Oxford: Oxford University Press).

WOLLSTONECRAFT, MARY (1982), *A Vindication of the Rights of Women*, (ed.) Ulrich H. Hardt (New York: Whitston).

WORDEN, BLAIR (1991), 'English Republicanism', in Burns and Goldie (1991).

YOUNG, I. M. (1990), *Justice and the Politics of Difference* (Princeton, NJ: Princeton University Press).

ZUCKERT, MICHAEL P. (1994), *Natural Rights and the New Republicanism* (Princeton, NJ: Princeton University Press).

INDEX

Abramson, J. 223
Ackerman, B. 9, 181
Administrative arm of government 192, 193
Agencies of the state 171, 173
American Revolution 20, 29, 33–5, 39, 42–4, 129, 133, 175
Anonymity 228
Anthropocentrism 137, 138
Anxiety 85, 89
Approval 227–9, 244
Arbitrariness 55, 57, 63, 173, 174, 184, 230, 233
Arbitrary power 10, 25, 26, 31, 36, 52, 56
  and will 230, 233, 265, 272, 279
Arendt, H. 8, 19
Arenson, R. 263
Arrow, K. 204
Astell, M. 48, 139, 176
Atiyah, P. S. 62, 164
Autonomy, personal 81, 82, 185–6, 257–9
Ayres, I. 7, 169, 218, 229

Baier, A. 261
Bailyn, B. 34
Baldwin, T. 18
Ball, T. 61
Bardach, E. 218
Baron, H. 19
Barry, B. 103, 169, 187
Baumeister, R. F. 227
Behaviour, standards of 236
Belief 165–7
Bentham, J. 44–6, 49, 50, 66, 96
  conception of liberty 18, 43, 47, 272
Berlin, I. 17, 18, 21, 22, 27, 50, 72
Berman, H. 20, 182
Bicameralism 178, 191
Blackburn, S. 264
Blackstone, W. 20, 41, 43, 101
Blau, P. 258
Blom, H. W. 7, 21
Bock, G. 7, 19
Bolingbroke, Lord 33
Boswell, J. 241
Bradshaw, B. 210

Braithwaite, J. 51, 107, 150, 207
  criminal justice 153–7
  regulatory theory 7, 169, 196, 218, 227, 230, 246
Braithwaite, V. 258
Brehm, S. S. 218
Brehm, J. W. 218
Brennan, G. 204, 224, 225, 263
  opinion polling 168, 192
  sanctions 212, 216, 218–19, 221
Brien, A. 230
Buchanan, J. 216, 228
Burke, E. 100
Burtt, S. 245

Campbell, T. D. 176
Capabilities, basic 158, 161
Capital, social 254
Capitalism 141
Caplow, T. 155
Cato's Letters 29, 33
Chartist movement 143
Checks and balances 212, 265
Children, status of 119, 120
Choice 24, 25, 53, 58, 76, 77, 89, 93, 118, 119
Cicero 5, 19
Citizenship 27, 36, 37, 39, 251
Civil liberty 43, 45, 46, 66
Civil society 80, 148, 241, 243, 245
Civility 246–51, 254, 255, 258–68, 280, 281
  group-centred 248
  supply of 251–3, 257
Civitas 27, 36, 66
  see also Citizenship
Clark, G. de N. 62, 142
Clegg, S. 79
Coady, C. A. 207
Coercion 24, 37, 41–3, 45, 54, 148
Cohen, G. A. 158
Cohen, J. 189, 192
Cohen, M. R. 165
Coke, Sir Edward 182
Coleman, James 164, 253
Coleman, Jules 192
Colish, M. L. 28, 32

Collective action 142
Committees 239, 240
Common concern 249
Common interest 198, 232, 249
Common knowledge 58–61, 70–2,
    165–7, 235
Commonwealthman tradition 6, 9, 43,
    133, 202, 212, 250
  development of 20–21, 101, 129
  and slavery 33, 39, 164
Communitarianism 8, 96, 120–5, 144,
    259, 275
Community 274
Compliance 207, 244, 246, 247
Complier-centred regulation 215,
    219–30, 234–9, 279
Connolly, W. 52
Consent 61–3, 184–6, 202
Consequentialism 81, 97–102, 147, 207
Constant, B. 18, 27, 50, 271
Constitution 6, 108
Constitution, US 180
Constitutional provision 65, 67–9, 93,
    94, 95
  strategy of 151, 152
Constitutionalism 172–87, 189–205,
    230–5, 238, 276, 278
Contestability 61–3, 183–95, 198,
    200–3, 205
  procedures for 196, 197, 199
Contestation 232, 252, 253, 277, 278, 280
  channels of 193
Contract 62, 142, 164, 165, 202
Control, social 250
Cooperation, multinational 152, 153
Cornish, W. R. 62, 142
Corruption 210–11, 216–18, 222, 237,
    250, 265, 278, 279
Counter-majoritarian condition 180–3,
    277, 232
Crawford, M. 27, 36
Criminal justice system 153–7, 196
Crosthwaite, J. 48
Culture, indigenous 145, 146

D'Agostino, F. 169
Dahl, R. 204
de Tocqueville, A. *see* Tocqueville
Decision-making:
  bargain-based 187
  debate-based 3, 4, 187–9
  public 184–8, 190, 200, 203, 278

Defence, external 150–3, 276
Defiance 219
Deliberation 130, 131, 189, 190, 200,
    253, 277
Democracy 2, 174–6, 183–205, 230–5,
    238, 252, 253, 276, 278, 280
  contestatory 277
  deliberative 277
  ideal of 277
  inclusive 232, 277
  responsive 277
Democratic participation 8, 27–30, 50,
    81, 109, 140
Deviant-centred regulation 215–19, 279
Dicey, A. V. 179
Disapproval 227–9
Discipline 255
Discretion 175, 176, 277
Dispersion-of-power condition 177,
    178, 179, 180, 183, 231, 277
Dissent 200
Distrust 264, 265
Domestic violence 250
Domination 9, 22–6, 35, 51, 59–66, 76,
    78, 79, 208, 272
  as opposite of freedom 110
  definition of 52–8
  extent of 58, 75
  intensity of 58, 75
  reduction of 104
  relationship of 52
Dominium 13, 112, 130, 150, 166, 171
Due process 175
Dworkin, R. 111
Dworkin, G. 76

Economic policy 164, 165
  prosperity 150, 163–5, 276
Economic theory 1, 6
Egalitarianism, material 113, 117–19,
    120, 161
  structural 113–17
Elections 192, 203
Elitism 48, 96, 117
Elkin, S. L. 7
Elster, J. 224, 233
Ely, J. H, 263
Empire-of-law condition 173–7, 180,
    183, 231, 276
Employment 163
English Civil War 20
Environmentalism 134–8, 146, 249, 250

Equality 12, 49, 110–13, 117, 119–21, 125, 274, 275
Equilibrium, reflective 11, 102, 106, 130, 275
Ethics 106, 236
Ethnic minorities 144–6, 247
Evans, C. 40
Executive functions 177–80
Extent of domination 58, 75
  of freedom 103–6
  of non-domination 76, 113, 118, 119, 159, 160, 274
External defence 150–3, 276

Fabians 239
Fairness 1, 121, 246
Feasibility:
  moral 207, 209
  psychological 207, 209
Federal system 179
Federalist Papers 20, 30, 100, 101, 180, 221, 222, 226, 240
Feinberg, J. 50
Feminism 134, 138–40, 144, 146
Ferguson, A. 251
Ferry, L. 7
Fichte, J. G. 18
Filmer, Sir Robert 38, 40, 41, 45
Filters 213
  see also Screens
Financial system, stability of 163
Fink, Z. S. 19, 20
Finley, M. 19
Finn, P. 202
Fishkin, J. 168, 169
Foner, E. 143
Fontana, B. 7, 19
Forums for discussion 236
Fraser, N. 149, 249
Fraternity 125
Free labour movement 143
Free will 25
Freedom:
  as absence of interference 9, 10, 12, 21–3, 31–47, 49, 50, 76, 83–5, 98, 111, 117, 121, 123, 271, 273, 276
  as non-domination 4, 6, 12, 21–3, 25, 31–44, 48, 51, 73–8, 83, 266–8, 271–275, 280
  extent of 103–6
  ideal of 25, 47, 78, 98–102, 111, 112
  intensity of 103–6

  negative conception of 9
  republican conception of 241, 272
  see also Liberty, Non-interference, and Non-domination
Freedom of the city, freedom of the heath 67
French Revolution 20, 125, 133
Frerejohn, J. 87, 192
Friendship 92
Fuller, L. L. 174
Funding of political candidates 194
Fustel de Coulanges, N. D. 19

Gambetta, D. 254
Gaus, G. 10, 169
Gauthier, D. 187
Gellner, E. 148, 242, 262
Geuss, R. 60
Good:
  common 121, 122, 124, 125, 259
  communitarian 275
  instrumental 83–7, 90
  personal 82
  primary 90–2, 274
  social 121, 122
Goodin, R. 136, 160, 233
Gordon, L. 149
Gordon, T. 20, 29, 33
Government:
  authoritarian 38
  form of 150
  philosophy of 127
Grabosky, P. N. 218
Gray, J. 50, 89
Green political theory 135–8
Grotius, H. 101
Guarini, E. F. 28
Gwyn, W. B. 38, 80, 178, 179
Gyges, ring of 211, 222, 265

Haakonssen, K. 100, 101, 183
Habermas, J. 189, 233
Hale, Sir Matthew 182
Hamilton, A. 100
Happiness 49, 121, 207
Hardin, R. 261
Harrington, J. 5, 32, 33, 163, 240
  concept of liberty 28–9, 125, 233
  freedom and citizenship 36, 39, 48, 66, 173
  and republican tradition 5, 19
  and slavery 32–33

Hart, H. L. A. 44
Hayek, F. A. 50, 89, 204
Hegel, G. W. F. 18
Herder, J. G. 18
Hey, R. 43
Hierarchy of sanctions 230, 238
Hill, B. 48, 139
Hindess, B. 79
Hirschman, A. O. 226
Hobbes, T. 18, 37, 38, 39, 41–5, 50, 66,
    94, 125, 271
Holmes, S. 9, 46, 72, 97, 196
Homans, G. 258
Honour 226
Horowitz, M. J. 62
Humanism 189
Hume, D. 47, 100, 217, 226
Hutton, W. 7

Ideal, non-domination as 80–97
Identification 259, 260
Imperium 13, 112, 150, 166, 171
Inclusiveness 110, 190–4, 232, 253, 277
Independence, personal 150, 158–63,
    265, 276
Indeterminacy 104, 105
Indigenous culture 145, 191
Information, public 167–9
Ingram, A. 21, 101, 162
Institutions 1, 12, 100, 107, 108, 130
    design of 211, 215, 220, 222, 229, 240,
    241, 266, 274, 279, 280
    republican 129, 206–9
Instutitionalization 152, 153
Intangible hand 225, 227, 236, 253–7,
    268, 269, 281
Intensity of domination 58, 75
    of freedom 103–6
    of non-domination 76, 113–18, 159,
    160, 274
Interest, common 198, 232, 249
Interest group 202–5, 256
Interference 23–5, 35, 52–7, 63–6, 89,
    94, 208, 271, 272
    absence of 17
    arbitrary 69, 73, 84–7, 89, 112, 113,
    146, 149, 160, 171, 267, 276
    evils of 27–30
Internal protection 150, 153–7, 276
Intersubjectivity of freedom 71, 72
Invisible hand 203, 204, 224–7, 255,
    256

James, S. 140
Jefferson, T. 18
Johnson, S. 241
Judicial arm of government 177–80,
    192, 193
Jurisprudence 101, 182
Justice 121

Kagan, R. A. 218
Kant, I. 18
Karstedt-Henke, S. 250
Kelly, D. R. 182
Kelman, H. C. 176, 257
Kiewiet, D. R. 192
Kinder, D. R. 192
Knavery 216–19, 229, 230, 238, 279
Knowledge, common 58–61, 70–2,
    165–7, 235
Korsgaard, C. 96
Kriegel, B. 13, 130, 177
Krygier, M. 176
Kukathas, C. 50, 89
Kumar, K. 242
Kymlicka, W. 146

Lacey, M. J. 101
Language:
    of politics 130–5
    republican 275, 276
Larmore, C. 9, 136
Law 46, 50, 84, 174–7, 182, 201, 251–3
    and liberty 35–41, 66, 271
    common 89
    design of 241–242, 245–7, 266, 277,
    278, 280
    legitimacy of 252
    powers of 120
    system of 104
Le Grand, J. 218
Leary, M. L. 227
Legislative functions 177–80, 191, 192,
    236
Legitimation, political 2, 6, 199
Levin, M. 142
Lewis, D. 59, 166, 245
Liberalism 8, 9, 10, 12, 18, 50, 72, 96,
    110, 117, 120, 132, 141, 273
    deontological version of 99
Libertarians 9, 10
Libertas 27, 66
Liberty:
    of the ancients and moderns 18, 50

civil 43, 45, 46, 66
ideal of vii, 26
natural 43, 66
negative 14, 18, 19, 21–3, 25, 27–34, 50, 51, 271
as non-interference 41
personal 46
positive 17–19, 21–3, 27, 50, 51, 270
see also Freedom
Lind, E. A. 199, 247
Lind, J. 17, 42–4, 48, 49
Locke, J. 40, 43, 62, 100, 101, 164, 202, 225, 266
Lomasky, L. 168, 204
Long, D. 44, 45, 47
Lukes, S. 53, 60
Lyons, D. 207

MacCallum, G. C. 25
MacDonagh, O. 62, 197
Machan, T. R. 9
Machiavelli, N. 5, 19, 28, 32, 71, 100, 148, 182, 210, 240, 242
MacIntyre, A. 19, 97, 129
Madison, J. 10, 20, 30, 46, 101, 177, 178, 211, 212, 221, 222, 226
Maitland, F. W. 28–31, 173, 174
Majone, G. 179
Majority rule 62, 181–3, 232, 277
Mandeville, B. 204, 216, 226
Manent, P. 10
Manin, B. 180
Mansbridge, J. 139
Market, free 203, 205, 225, 255, 256
Marx, K. 18, 141
Marxism 176
McCloskey, H. J. 207
McCubbins, M. D. 250
McLean, I. 204
Media 167, 168, 169
Meyerson, D. 60
Michelman, F. 7, 10
Mill, J. S. 18, 47, 49, 139
Miller, D. 52, 121, 260
Milton, J. 29, 61, 71
Minority cultures 144–6, 247
Mitchell, G. 199, 247
Montesquieu, C. 10, 18–20, 41, 71, 100, 108, 153, 154, 157, 177, 226, 240, 251, 273
Morange, J. 50
Movements, social 262

Multiculturalism 134, 143–6
Murphy, L. 87
Natural liberty 43, 66
Nedham, M. 178
Negative liberty 50, 51
Nicolet, C. 7
Nippel, W. 27, 29
Non-arbitrariness 184, 185
Non-consequentialism 97–102
Non-domination 23–6, 47, 66, 67, 70–2, 75, 96, 265, 273
distribution of 92–5, 112
extent of 76, 113, 118, 119, 159, 160, 274
as a form of power 69
freedom as 4, 6, 12, 51, 266–268, 271–275, 280
as a goal 97–109
intensity of 76, 113–18, 159, 160, 274
as a personal good 82–93
as a political ideal 49, 80–97, 134, 135
and the state 107–9
strategies for achieving 67, 68
Non-interference 23–7, 50, 81, 99, 107, 132, 149
freedom as 10, 12, 45–7, 98, 121, 123, 271, 273, 276
Non-manipulability 172–83, 186
Normative ideas 1, 2
Norms 241–7, 249, 251–4, 258, 259, 268, 280
Nozick, R. 99

Okin, S. 139
Oldfield, A. 7, 19, 36, 100, 117
Opinion, public 168, 169
Orthonomy 81
O'Leary-Hawthorne, J. 25

Pacificism 98
Pagden, A. 7, 19, 33
Paine, T. 18, 29, 35, 56, 100, 101, 202
Paley, William 27, 45–7, 49, 67, 96, 272, 273
influences on 44, 226
objections to freedom as non-domination 73–8
Parfit, D. 95
Parsimony in criminalization 154, 157
Participation, democratic 8, 27–30, 50, 81, 109, 140
Pasquino, P. 10, 28, 202, 232

Passmore, J. 136
Pateman, C. 48, 139
Paterson, A. B. 143
Patten, A. 27
Patterson, O. 32
Patton, P. 79
Penalties 218
    regard-based 224
Personal independence 46, 150, 158–63
Personal trust 262, 264, 265, 267–9
Pettit, P. 7, 81, 121, 186, 187, 191, 192,
    235, 242, 254, 258, 262
    criminal justice 154–7, 197
    non-domination 51, 66, 76, 91, 97–8,
    150, 207, 209
    non-interference 24–6, 53, 77, 88
    regulation 212, 215, 220–1, 224–5,
    228, 233, 244, 248, 249, 269
Phillips, A. 191
Philosophy, political 2–5, 11, 12, 19,
    102, 106, 130, 131, 240
    Green 135–8
Philp, M. 60, 122, 170, 233
Pitkin, H. 27, 28
Pluralism 136, 146, 147, 202–5, 275, 276,
    278
    interest-group 256
Pocock, J. 7, 19, 20, 29, 210
Policies, republican 147–70, 276
    see also Republicanism
Policy:
    economic 164, 165
    institutional 1
    legal 164
    social 149
Populism 8–10, 19, 179, 180
Positive liberty 50, 51
Postema, G. 91
Poverty 121
Power 9, 59, 63–5, 78, 79, 250, 273
    arbitrary 112, 147, 173, 174, 183
    decision-making 172, 183
    reciprocal 67, 68, 94, 95, 151
Power-ratio 114–16, 118
Powers, separation of 177–80, 231, 277
Pragmatism 136
Preference satisfaction 204, 205
Price, R. 7, 29, 34, 40, 42, 43, 48, 49, 64,
    71, 73, 74, 210
Priestley, J. 27, 29, 34, 35, 71, 86, 175,
    226
Productivity 163

Property, private 135
Prosperity, economic 150, 163–5, 276
Protection, internal 150, 153–7, 276
Public information 168, 169
Public life 150, 165–70, 276
Public opinion 168, 169
Public space 167, 168
Publicity 252
    as an ideal 169, 170
Pufendorf, S. 101
Punishment 155–7, 197
Putnam, R. D. 262

Raab, F. 19, 20
Rahe, P. A. 7, 20
Ransom, R. L. 61
Rasmussen, D. R. 9
Rawls, J. 11, 50, 90, 102, 111, 117, 130,
    136, 169, 233, 240, 274, 275
Raz, J. 10, 81
Reciprocal power, strategy of 94, 95, 151
Reflective equilibrium 11, 102, 106, 130,
    275
Regard 224, 227–9, 235, 237, 254, 255,
    279
Regulation 210–30, 250, 256, 257, 266,
    279
    complier-centred 234–9
    of the media 169
Reid, J. P. 34, 43, 201
Renaissance, Italian 133
Renaut, A. 7
Representation 192–4, 239
Republic:
    civil 245
    ideal of 233, 234
    reasons of 188
    stability of 210, 211, 231, 234
    traditional 129
Republican concept of freedom 27, 78,
    92, 241
Republican ideal 7, 240
    theory 11–13, 105, 275, 276
    tradition 4–9, 20–2, 29–44, 48, 51, 71,
    73, 80, 95, 96, 110, 117, 172, 179,
    189, 233, 271, 272, 274, 278
Republicanism 11, 81, 82, 99–101, 113,
    120, 126, 129–34, 139–47, 263, 267,
    269
    feasibility of 206–9
Resources 13, 36, 59, 60, 67–9, 94
Responsiveness 195, 200, 253, 277

Rewards, regard-based 224
Rials, S. 189
Rights, natural 101
Riker, W. 18
Robbins, C. 20, 33, 40, 250
Robinson, D. 54
Roman republic 20, 27, 28, 32, 36, 133
Rousseau, J.-J. 18, 19, 30, 125, 252, 253
Rubenstein, N. 100, 182, 242
Rule-of-law constraints 174–6
Russell, B. 98
Ryan, A. 9

Sanctions 212–15, 217–30, 235–8, 246,
    249, 279
Sandel, M. 96
Scanlon, T. M. 169, 187
Schauer, F. 176
Schwartz, T. 250
Screens 212–15, 220–30, 234–6, 238, 279
Secession 199
Security 73
Selection, adverse 219
Self, personal 257–9
Self-mastery 22, 25–7, 81, 82, 271
Selznick, P. 177, 245
Sen, A. 158, 161
Sentencing 156–7
Separation of powers 177–80, 231, 277
Shame 226
Shapiro, I. 185
Sherman, R. 189
Shklar, J. 72
Sieyes, Abbé 189
Skinner, Q. 7, 19, 27, 28, 33, 37, 50, 87, 189
Slavery 31–5, 39
Smith, A. 158, 186, 226, 227
Smith, M. 81, 88, 91, 204
Social capital 254
Social control 250
Social movements 193, 249, 262
Social policy 149
Socialism 134, 140–4, 146
Society, civil 148
Socioeconomic independence 158–63
Space, public 167, 168
Spinoza, B. 71
Spitz, J. F. 7, 18, 19, 27, 30, 50, 51, 53,
    62, 107, 126, 170, 246, 252
Springborg, P. 48, 139
State 6, 8, 9, 63, 78, 82, 105, 118, 148,
    150, 242, 276

agencies of 171, 173
aim of 106, 111
minimal 99
pluralistic 95, 96
Stigler, G. 204
Stigmatization 219
Stoljar, S. J. 62, 164
Strategies for achieving non-domination
    67, 68
Strategy of reciprocal power 94, 95
Strategy, need for 87–92
Subjectivity 71, 72
Subordination 88–91
Sugden, R. 76
Sunstein, C. 7, 187, 188–9, 194, 202, 205,
    218, 232, 233
Sutch, R. 61
Swanton, C. 102
Sydney, A. 29, 33, 34, 39, 48, 56, 61, 176,
    183, 202, 221, 231, 265
Sylvan, R. 135–8

Taxation 148, 149, 175
Taylor, C. 7, 18, 58, 77, 103, 148, 242,
    260
Taylor, H. 139
Taylor, M. 228
Ten, C. L. 174
Thompson, E. P. 176, 177
Thompson, W. 139
Tocqueville, A. 18, 19
Toennies, F. 227
Tort, law of 157
Trade linkages 163
Trenchard, J. 20, 29, 33, 212
Truman, D. 204
Trust 202, 261–4, 266, 267
    having and expressing 263–5, 268
    personal 262, 264, 265, 267–9, 281
Tuck, R. 37, 94, 100, 101
Tucker, A. 44
Tully, J. 21, 40, 101
Turner, J. F. 258
Tyler, T. R. 153, 199, 246, 247

Uncertainty 85, 86, 88–90, 92
United Nations 152
Utilitarianism 111, 121, 207

Van Parijs, P. 76
Vigilance 250, 251, 263–7, 269, 281
Vile, M. J. C. 178, 179

Violence, domestic 250
Viroli, M. 7, 8, 19, 260
Virtue 212, 219, 228, 251, 260, 261, 268,
    269, 281
Vulnerability 5, 122, 124, 125, 145, 252

Wage slavery 141, 142
Waldron, J. 76, 176
Walpole, Sir Robert 33
War 151
Wartenberg, T. E. 60, 79
Weber, M. 52
Weinstein, W. L. 72
Weintraub, T. 7
Welfare 1, 6, 149, 161–3
West, D. 60

Whig tradition 33, 39
White, M. 222
Will:
    arbitrary 230, 233, 265, 272, 279
    general 253
Winch, D. 204
Wirszubski, C. 27, 32, 36, 71, 117
Wollstonecraft, M. 61, 139
Women, status of 48, 49, 123, 191, 247
Worden, B. 29, 61, 71, 101

Young, I. M. 56, 63, 124, 139, 169, 191,
    248

Zealotry 208
Zuckert, M. P. 101